Developmental Cognitive Neuroscience

09

To my parents, Krystyna Dobraczynska and James Johnson, who provided both my nature and my nurture

Developmental Cognitive Neuroscience

An Introduction

Third Edition

Mark H. Johnson

with Michelle de Haan

⊛WILEY-BLACKWELL

A John Wiley & Sons, Ltd., Publication

This third edition first published 2011
© 2011 Mark H. Johnson

Edition history: Blackwell Publishers Ltd (1e, 1997); Blackwell Publishing Ltd (2e, 2005)

Blackwell Publishing was acquired by John Wiley & Sons in February 2007. Blackwells publishing program has been merged with Wiley's global Scientific, Technical, and Medical business to form Wiley-Blackwell.

Registered Office
John Wiley & Sons Ltd, The Atrium, Southern Gate, Chichester, West Sussex, PO19 8SQ, United Kingdom

Editorial Offices
350 Main Street, Malden, MA 02148-5020, USA
9600 Garsington Road, Oxford, OX4 2DQ, UK
The Atrium, Southern Gate, Chichester, West Sussex, PO19 8SQ, UK

For details of our global editorial offices, for customer services, and for information about how to apply for permission to reuse the copyright material in this book please see our website at www.wiley.com/wiley-blackwell.

The right of Mark H. Johnson to be identified as the author of this work has been asserted in accordance with the UK Copyright, Designs and Patents Act 1988.

Library of Congress Cataloging-in-Publication Data

Johnson, Mark H. (Mark Henry), 1960–
  Developmental cognitive neuroscience : an introduction / Mark H. Johnson ; with Michelle de Haan. – 3rd ed.
    p. ; cm.
  Includes bibliographical references and index.
    ISBN 978-1-4443-3085-4 (hb : alk. paper) – ISBN 978-1-4443-3086-1 (pb : alk. paper)
  1. Cognitive neuroscience. 2. Developmental neurobiology. I. De Haan, Michelle, 1969– II. Title.
    [DNLM: 1. Neuropsychology. 2. Brain–physiology. 3. Cognition. 4. Human Development. WL 103.5 J68d 2011]
    QP360.5.J64 2011
    612.8'233–dc22

                                                                            2010011925

A catalogue record for this book is available from the British Library.

Set in 10.5/13pt, Minion-Regular by Thomson Digital, Noida, India
Printed in Singapore by Markono Print Media Pte Ltd

1 2011

100621130 5

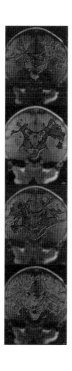

Contents

List of Figures

Figures listed below without a page number appear in the color plate section. The color plate section appears between pages 138 and 139.

List of Tables

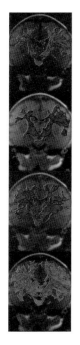

Preface to the Third Edition

In the 13 years since publication of the first edition of this book, the field of developmental cognitive neuroscience has expanded enormously, and the number of researchers active in the field, and the papers they produce, has increased by at least an order of magnitude. Accompanying this growth has been a plethora of conferences, edited volumes and monographs. This dramatic expansion has made the challenge of selecting what new material to include in this third edition somewhat daunting. As in previous editions, the selection of material reflects my own biases, but with a focus on domains in which there are clear examples of the developmental cognitive neuroscience approach. This inevitably means that there are topics in cognitive development or developmental neuroscience that are not addressed. The quantity of new work in the field also makes it increasingly difficult for one person to cover all areas. Therefore, I am very grateful that Michelle de Haan agreed to update and revise Chapters 8, 9 and 10 (previously 6, 7 and 8).

Like any introduction to a new interdisciplinary field, students and researchers come from different parent disciplines and, therefore, will bring different background expertise with them to reading this book. Thus, in order to improve the progression of build-up of knowledge for the reader, this edition includes two new background foundation chapters (2 and 3). The first of these introduces the established and new methods and paradigms that are critical for advances in the field, and also gives an overview of the different populations and developmental disorders that have been studied. The second new chapter reflects a major new trend in the field for the integration of molecular and population genetics with studies of brain development and function. Anticipating the increasing importance of this approach, the new Chapter 3 introduces the reader to the basics of genetics as relevant to developmental psychology and neuroscience.

Other significant revisions to several chapters of the book includes a greater focus on mid-childhood and adolescence, on practical applications of basic research, and on the emergence of functional networks of brain regions. In line with changes in the field, there is also increased discussion of data from different structural and functional imaging methods. Additionally, to assist the teacher there are now "key discussion points" provided at the end of each chapter, which can be used along with the website associated with the book (www.wiley.com/go/johnson/dcn) that has essay, short answer, and multiple choice test questions as well as downloadable figures. As with previous editions, this basic introduction serves as a "feeder" into more detailed and comprehensive edited volumes. Specifically, this third edition recommends many further readings from Nelson and Luciana's excellent 2008 *Handbook of Developmental Cognitive Neuroscience* (2nd edn), and some readers may wish to use the two volumes together.

As with the previous editions, I am indebted to colleagues and collaborators for educating and informing me on a variety of topics in the field. My colleagues at the Centre for Brain and Cognitive Development, and our distinguished visitors to London, continue to keep me abreast of current developments in a variety of topics. I also continue to be indebted to those who have commented on chapters in this and previous editions of the book including Rick Gilmore, Michelle de Haan, Annette Karmiloff-Smith, Denis Mareschal, Gaia Scerif and Gert Westermann. Sarah Lloyd-Fox, Kim Davies, Amy Proferes, Helena Ribeiro, and Leslie Tucker all contributed invaluably to the production of this edition.

Preface to the Second Edition

In the eight years since publication of the first edition of this book, developmental cognitive neuroscience has grown from newborn to toddler: still uncertain on its feet, but just beginning to put together fragments of knowledge. While the first edition was described by one leading figure as "a clarion call for a new way of doing both developmental psychology and cognitive neuroscience," the present edition puts more emphasis on making sense of the data already in hand.

Since the last edition a number of trends have become apparent in the field. First, the field has actually settled on the phrase "developmental cognitive neuroscience" as the name that best describes it. While it could be said that the first edition was the book that gave the field its name, it is my hope that its most important contribution was in attracting new researchers to the topic. Another trend of note is that some of the more heated debates about both behavioral and neuroscience evidence are becoming resolved as more evidence from different sources and methods becomes available. A surprising amount of agreement is breaking out in the field, with many issues turning out to be not black or white, but a subtle and interesting shade of grey. A third trend in the field is the recent flurry of books and review chapters. This made me question whether or not there was still a need for this book. On reflection, however, I have convinced myself that a basic introduction that serves as a "feeder" into more detailed and comprehensive edited volumes is still valuable. In fact, teachers should note that this second edition is specifically designed to be used with one or more of three current edited volumes (Nelson & Luciana, 2001; Johnson, Munakata, & Gilmore, 2002; de Haan & Johnson, 2003), and specific recommendations for further reading from these volumes are highlighted throughout the text. Since our young field can often feel somewhat fragmented to the student, I continue to believe that the single voice and unified perspective presented in this book are important.

Because this book is intended as an introduction, its coverage is necessarily selective. While this was challenging for the first edition, the massive increase in data over the past years made the prospect of choosing what to exclude even more daunting. As in the first edition, my choices were guided by focusing on areas where the developmental cognitive neuroscience approach has been most avidly pursued, rather than topics dominated by a developmental psychology or an adult cognitive neuroscience approach. Needless to say, my own particular interests and biases are evident throughout.

As with the first edition, I am indebted to colleagues and collaborators for educating and informing me on a variety of topics. I was privileged to chair a panel to review the current state of our knowledge on the development of Perception, Attention, and Memory (funded by the McDonnell and Sackler foundations). The discussions and presentations at these meetings brought me up to date, and particularly helped with the new chapter on Objects and Number. My colleagues at the Centre for Brain and Cognitive Development, particularly Gergely Csibra and Denis Mareschal, kept me abreast of current developments in a variety of fields. Rick Gilmore, Gaia Scerif, and Gert Westermann kindly provided their comments on a draft of the revisions to the book. Michelle de Haan, Brian Hopkins, and Annette Karmiloff-Smith gave me comments on specific chapters. From Blackwell, Sarah Bird persuaded me to undertake the second edition, and Jennie Brown, Justin Dyer, Roberta Herrick, Katie Menssen, Leslie Tucker, and Agnes Volein all contributed invaluably to the production.

Teachers may wish to note that a website accompanies this book with teaching aids: www. wiley.com/go/johnson/dcn

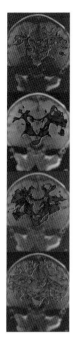

Preface to the First Edition

In the first chapter of this book I describe some of the factors responsible for the recent emergence of a subdiscipline at the interface between developmental psychology and cognitive neuroscience. I have chosen to refer to this new field as "developmental cognitive neuroscience," though it has been known under a number of other terms such as "developmental neurocognition" (de Boysson-Bardies, de Schonen, Jusczyck, McNeilage, & Morton, 1993). Though a series of edited volumes on the topic has recently appeared, like most newly emerging disciplines there is a time lag before the first books suitable for teaching appear. This book and the Reader which I edited in 1993 (Johnson, 1993) are initial attempts to fill the gap. While some may believe these efforts to be premature, my own view is that the lifeblood of any new discipline is in the students and postdocs recruited to the cause. And the sooner they are recruited, the better.

Is developmental cognitive neuroscience really significantly different from other fields that have a more extended history, such as developmental neuropsychology or cognitive development? Clearly, it would be unwise to rigidly demarcate developmental cognitive neuroscience from related, and mutually informative, fields. However, it is my belief that the emerging field has a number of characteristics that makes it distinctive. First, while there is some disagreement about exact definitions, the fields of developmental neuropsychology and developmental psychopathology focus on atypical development, while commonly comparing them to normal developmental trajectories. In contrast, cognitive neuroscience (including the developmental variant outlined in this book) focuses on normal cognitive functioning, but uses information from deviant functioning and development as "nature's experiments" which can shed light on the neural basis of normal cognition. This book is therefore not intended as an introduction to the neuropsychology of developmental disorders. For such information the reader is referred to the excellent introductions by Cicchetti and Cohen (1995) and Spreen, Risser, and Edgell (1995).

Second, unlike many in cognitive development, this book adopts the premise that information from brain development is more than just a useful additional source of evidence for supporting particular cognitive theories. Rather, information about brain development is viewed as both changing and originating theories at the cognitive level. Third, developmental cognitive neuroscience restricts itself to issues at the neural, cognitive, and immediate environmental levels. In my view it is a hazard of some interdisciplinary fields that the focus of interest is diffused across many different levels of explanation. This is not to deny the importance of these other levels, but a mechanistic interdisciplinary science needs to restrict both the domains (in this case aspects of cognitive processing) and levels of explanation with which it is concerned. Finally, developmental cognitive neuroscience is specifically concerned with understanding the relation between neural and cognitive phenomena. For this reason, I have not discussed evidence from the related field of developmental behavior genetics. In general, developmental behavior genetics tends to be concerned with correlations between the molecular level (genetics) and gross behavioral measures such as IQ. With some notable exceptions, little effort is made to specifically relate these two levels of explanation via the intermediate neural and cognitive levels. Having pointed out the different focus of developmental cognitive neuroscience, my hope is that this book is written to be both accessible and informative to those in related and overlapping disciplines.

The above comments go some way to explaining the choice of material that I have presented in the book. However, I have no doubt that there is a substantive amount of excellent experimentation and theorizing that could have been included but was not. Since this is intended as a brief introduction to the field, I have chosen to focus on a few particular issues in some detail. Of course, the choice of material also reflects my own biases and knowledge since the book is intended as an introductory survey of the field as viewed from my own perspective. I apologize in advance for the inevitable omissions and errors.

The book is aimed at the advanced-level student and assumes some introductory knowledge of both neuroscience and cognitive development. Students without this background will probably need to refer to more introductory textbooks in the appropriate areas. I also hope that the book will attract developmentalists with an interest in learning more about the brain, and cognitive neuroscientists curious as to how developmental data can help constrain their theories about adult functioning. But most of all I hope that the book inspires readers to find out more about the field, and to consider a developmental cognitive neuroscience approach to their own topic.

Acknowledgments

The author and publishers gratefully acknowledge the following for permission to reproduce copyright material:

Figure 2.1 from S. Lloyd-Fox, A. Blasi and C.E. Elwell (2010) Illuminating the developing brain: The past, present and future of functional near infrared spectroscopy. *Neuroscience and Biobehavioural Reviews*. Reprinted with permission from Elsevier.

Figure 2.2 reprinted by permission of Michael Crabtree.

Figure 2.3 reprinted by permission of Sarah Lloyd-Fox.

Figure 2.4 images courtesy of Dr Sean Deoni, King's College London and Brown University.

Figure 3.1 from J. Stiles (2008) *The fundamentals of brain development: Integrating nature and nurture*. Cambridge, MA: Harvard University Press. Copyright © 2008 by the President and Fellows of Harvard College. Reprinted by permission of the publisher.

Figure 3.2 from K.M. Cornish, J. Turk, J. Wilding, V. Sudhalter, F. Munir, F. Kooy, and R. Hagerman (2004) Annotation: Deconstructing the attention in fragile X syndrome: A developmental neuropsychological approach. *Journal of Child Psychology and Psychiatry, 45*, 1042–1053. Reprinted by permission of Wiley-Blackwell.

Figure 4.4 images courtesy of the Centre for NeuroImaging Sciences, King's College London and the Birkbeck-UCL Centre for NeuroImaging.

Figure 4.5 from J. LeRoy Conel (1939–1967) *The postnatal development of the human cerebral cortex*, vols. I–VIII. Cambridge, MA: Harvard University Press, Copyright © 1939, 1941, 1947, 1951, 1955, 1959, 1963, 1967 by the President and Fellows of Harvard College. Reprinted by permission of the publisher.

Figure 4.6 from J. Stiles (2008) *The fundamentals of brain development: Integrating nature and nurture*. Cambridge, MA: Harvard University Press. Copyright © 2008 by the President and Fellows of Harvard College. Reprinted by permission of the publisher.

Figure 4.7 from P. Fransson, B. Skiöld, S. Horsch, A. Nordell, M. Blennow, H. Lagercrantz, and U. Aden (2007) Resting-state networks in the infant brain. *Proceedings of the National Academy of Sciences, USA, 104*, 15531–15536. Copyright © 2007 National Academy of Sciences, USA. Reprinted by permission of the publisher.

Figure 4.8 from B. J. Casey, N. Tottenham, C. Liston, and S. Durston (2005) Imaging the developing brain: What have we learned about cognitive development? *Trends in Cognitive Sciences, 9*, 104–110. Which is a modified version of a figure from R. A. Thompson and C. A. Nelson (2001) Developmental science and the media: Early brain development. *American*

Psychologist, 56, 5–15. Copyright © 2005 Elsevier Ltd. Reprinted by permission of the publisher.

Figure 4.10 from A. W. Toga, P. M. Thompson, and E. R. Sowell (2006) Mapping brain maturation. *Trends in Neuroscience, 29*, 148–158. Reprinted by permission of Dr Arthur W. Toga and Dr Paul M. Thompson, Laboratory of Neuro Imaging at UCLA.

Figure 4.11 from P. Shaw, D. Greenstein, J. Lerch, L. Clasen, R. Lenroot, N. Gogtay, A. Evans, J. Rapaport, and J. Giedd (2006) Intellectual ability and cortical development in children and adolescents. *Nature, 440*, 676–679. Reprinted by permission of Nature Publishing Group.

Figure 7.5 from M. H. Johnson (2005) Sub-cortical face processing. *Nature Reviews Neuroscience, 6*, 766–774. Reprinted by permission of Nature Publishing Group.

Figure 7.6 from K. S. Scherf, M. Behrmann, K. Humphreys, and B. Luna (2007) Visual category-selectivity for faces, places and objects emerges along different developmental trajectories. *Developmental Science, 10*, F15–F30. Reprinted by permission of Wiley-Blackwell.

Figure 8.1 from F. Bloom, C. A. Nelson, and A. Lazerson (2001) *Brain, mind, and behavior* (3rd ed.), New York: Worth Publishers. Reprinted by permission of Worth Publishers.

Figure 8.2 from P. J. Bauer (2006) Constructing a past in infancy: A neuro-developmental account. *Trends in Cognitive Sciences, 10*, 175–181. Reprinted by permission of Elsevier Ltd.

Figure 8.3 from F. Vargha-Khadem, D. G. Gadian, K. E. Watkins, A. Connelly, W. van Paesschen and M. Mishkin (1997) Differential effects of early hippocampal pathology on episodic and semantic memory. *Science, 277*, 376–380. Reprinted by permission of AAAS.

Figure 10.1 from T. Klingberg (2006) Development of a superior frontal-intraparietal network for visuo-spatial working memory. *Neuropsychologia, 44*, 2171–2177. Copyright © 2006 with permission from Elsevier.

Figure 12.2 adapted from a figure by M. K. Belmonte, G. Allen, A. Beckel-Mitchener, L. M. Boulanger, R. A. Carper and S. J. Webb (2004) Autism and abnormal development of brain connectivity. *The Journal of Neuroscience, 24*, 9228–9231.

Figure 12.3 from K. Supekar, M. Musen, and V. Menon (2009) Development of large-scale functional brain networks in children. *PLoS Biology, 7*, e1000157. Reprinted by permission of the authors and of Public Library of Science, Biology.

Abbreviations

ADHD	attention deficit/hyperactivity disorder
ASL	American Sign Language
CANTAB	Cambridge Neuropsychological Testing Automated Battery
DLPFC	dorsolateral prefrontal cortex
DNMS	delayed non-match to sample
EEG	electroencephalography
ERP	event-related potential
FEF	frontal eye fields
FFA	fusiform face area
fMRI	functional magnetic resonance imaging
GABA	Gamma-aminobutyric acid
HD-ERPs	high-density event-related potentials
IMHV	intermediate and medial part of the hyperstriatum ventrale
IS	interactive specialization
ISI	inter-stimulus interval
LGN	lateral geniculate nucleus
MGN	medial geniculate nucleus
MRI	magnetic resonance imaging
Nc	negative component
NIRS	near infra-red spectroscopy
PET	positron emission tomography
PFC	prefrontal cortex
PKU	phenylkctonuria
PN	projection neuron
SLI	specific language impairment
SOA	stimulus onset asynchrony
SP	spike potential
STS	superior temporal sulcus
WS	Williams syndrome

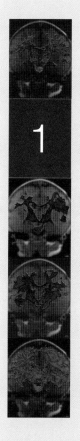

1

The Biology of Change

In this introductory chapter I discuss a number of background issues for developmental cognitive neuroscience, beginning with historical approaches to the nature–nurture debate. Constructivism, in which biological forms are an emergent product of complex dynamic interactions between genes and environment, is presented as an approach to development that is superior to accounts that seek to identify pre-existing information in the genes or external environment. However, if we are to abandon existing ways of analyzing development in terms of "innate" and "acquired" components, this raises the question of how we should best understand developmental processes. One scheme is proposed for taking account of the various levels of interaction between genes and environment. In addition, a dissociation is introduced between innate representations and architectural constraints on the emergence of representations within neural networks. Following this, a number of factors are discussed that demonstrate the importance of the cognitive neuroscience approach to development, including the increasing availability of brain imaging and molecular approaches. Conversely, the importance of development for analyzing the relation between brain structure and cognition is reviewed. In examining the ways in which development and cognitive neuroscience can be combined, three different perspectives on human functional brain development are discussed: a maturational view, a skill learning view, and an "interactive specialization" framework. Finally, the contents of the rest of the book are outlined.

Developmental Cognitive Neuroscience (Third Edition) Mark H. Johnson with Michelle de Haan
© 2011 Mark H. Johnson

1.1   Viewpoints on Development

As every parent knows, the changes involved in the growth of children from birth to adolescence are truly amazing. Perhaps the most remarkable aspects of this growth involve the brain and mind. Accompanying the four-fold increase in the volume of the brain during this time are numerous and sometimes surprising changes in behavior, thought, and emotion. An understanding of how the developments in brain and mind relate to each other could potentially revolutionize our thinking about education, social policy, and disorders of mental development. It is no surprise, therefore, that there is increasing interest in this new branch of science from grant funding agencies, medical charities, and even Presidential summits. Since the publication of the first edition of this book in 1997, this field has become known as *developmental cognitive neuroscience*.

Developmental cognitive neuroscience has emerged at the interface between two of the most fundamental questions that challenge humankind. The first of these questions concerns the relation between mind and body, and specifically between the physical substance of the brain and the mental processes it supports. This issue is fundamental to the scientific discipline of cognitive neuroscience. The second question concerns the origin of organized biological structures, such as the highly complex structure of the adult human brain. This issue is fundamental to the study of development. In this book I will show that light can be shed on these two fundamental questions by tackling them both simultaneously, and specifically by focusing on the relation between the postnatal development of the human brain and the cognitive processes it supports.

The second of the two questions above, that of the origins of organized biological structure, can be posed in terms of *phylogeny* or *ontogeny*. The phylogenetic (evolutionary) version of this question concerns the origin of species, and has been addressed by Charles Darwin and many others since. The ontogenetic version of this question concerns individual development within a life span. The ontogenetic question has been somewhat neglected relative to phylogeny, since some influential scientists have held the view that once a particular set of genes have been selected by evolution, ontogeny is simply a process of executing the "instructions" coded for by those genes. By this view, the ontogenetic question essentially reduces to phylogeny. In contrast to this view, in this book I argue that ontogenetic development is an active process through which biological structure is constructed afresh in each individual by means of complex and variable interactions between genes and their environments. The information is not in the genes, but emerges from the constructive interaction between genes and their environment (see also Oyama, 2000). However, since both ontogeny and phylogeny concern the emergence of biological structure, some of the same mechanisms of change have been invoked in the two cases.

FURTHER READING Oyama (2000).

The debate about the extent to which the ontogenetic question (individual development) is subsidiary to the phylogenetic question (evolution) is otherwise known as the nature–nurture issue, and has been central in developmental psychology, philosophy, and neuroscience. Broadly speaking, at one extreme the belief is that most of the information necessary to build a human brain, and the mind it supports, is latent within the genes of the individual. While most of this information is common to the species, each individual has some specific information that will make them differ from others. By this view, development is a process of unfolding or triggering the expression of information within the genes.

At the opposing extreme, others believe that most of the information that shapes the human mind comes from the structure of the external world. Some facets of the environment, such as gravity, patterned light, and so on, will be common throughout the species, while other aspects of the environment will be specific to the individual. It will become clear in this book that both of these extreme views are ill conceived, since they assume that the information for the structure of an organism exists (either in the genes or in the external world) prior to its construction. In contrast to this, it appears that biological structure emerges anew within each individual's development from constrained dynamic interactions between genes and various levels of environment, and is not easily reducible to simple genetic and experiential components.

It is more commonly accepted these days that the mental abilities of adults are the result of complex interactions between genes and environment. However, the nature of this interaction remains controversial and poorly understood, although, as we shall see, light may be shed on it by simultaneously considering brain and psychological development. Before going further, however, it is useful to review briefly some historical perspectives on the nature–nurture debate. This journey into history may help us avoid slipping back into ways of thinking that are deeply embedded in the Western intellectual tradition.

Throughout the 17th century there was an ongoing debate in biology between the so-called "vitalists," on the one hand, and the "preformationists," on the other. The vitalists believed that ontogenetic change was driven by "vital" life forces. Belief in this somewhat mystical and ill-defined force was widespread and actively encouraged by some members of the clergy. Following the invention of the microscope, however, some of those who viewed themselves as being of a more rigorous scientific mind championed the preformationist viewpoint. This view argued that a complete human being was contained in either the male sperm ("spermists") or the female egg ("ovists"). In order to support their claim, spermists produced drawings of a tiny, but perfect, human form enclosed within the head of sperm (see Figure 1.1). They argued that there was a simple and direct mapping between the seed of the organism and its end state: simultaneous growth of all the body parts. Indeed, preformationists of a religious conviction argued that God, on the sixth day of his work, placed about two hundred thousand million fully formed human miniatures into the ovaries of Eve or sperm of Adam (Gottlieb, 1992)!

Of course, we now know that such drawings were the result of overactive imagination, and that no such perfectly formed miniature human forms exist in

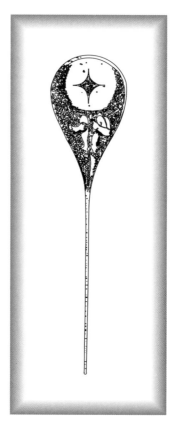

Figure 1.1 Drawings such as this influenced a seventeenth-century school of thought, the "spermists," who believed that there was a complete preformed person in each male sperm and that development merely consisted in increasing size.

the sperm or ovaries. However, as we shall see, the general idea behind preformationism, that there is a pre-existing blueprint or plan of the final state, remained a pervasive one for many decades in biological and psychological development. In fact, Oyama (2000) suggests that the same notion of a "plan" or "blueprint" that exists prior to the development process has persisted to the present day, with genes replacing the little man inside the sperm. As it became clear that genes do not contain a simple "code" for body parts, in more recent years, "regulator" and "switching" genes have been invoked to orchestrate the expression of the other genes. Common to all of these versions of the nativist viewpoint is the belief that there is a fixed mapping between a pre-existing set of coded instructions and the final form. We will see in Chapter 3 that the relationship between the genotype and its resulting phenotype is much more dynamic and flexible than previously supposed.

On the other side of the nature–nurture dichotomy, those who believe in the structuring role of experience also view the information as existing prior to the end state, only the source of that information is different. This argument has been applied to psychological development, since it is obviously less plausible for physical growth.

An example of this approach came from some of the more extreme members of the behaviorist school of psychology who believed that a child's psychological abilities could be entirely shaped by its early environment. More recently some developmental psychologists who work with computer models of the brain have suggested that the infant's mind is shaped largely by the statistical regularities latent in the external environment (so-called "statistical learning"). While such efforts can reveal hitherto unrecognized contributions from the environment, it will become evident in this book that these computer models can also be an excellent method for exploring types of interaction between intrinsic and extrinsic structure.

FURTHER READING Mareschal et al. (2007); Munakata, Stedron, Chatham, and Kharitonova (2008).

The viewpoints discussed above share the common assumption that the information necessary for constructing the final state (in this case, the adult mind) is present prior to the developmental process. While vitalists' beliefs were sometimes more dynamic in character than preformationists', the forces that guided development were still assumed to originate with an external creator. Preformationism in historical or modern guises involves the execution of plans or codes (from genes) or the incorporation of information from the structure of the environment. Oyama (2000) argues that these views on ontogenetic development resemble pre-Darwinian theories of evolution in which a creator was deemed to have planned all the species in existence. In both the ontogenetic and phylogenetic theories of this kind a plan for the final form of the species or individual exists prior to its emergence.

A more recent trend in thinking about ontogenetic development is constructivism. Constructivism differs from preformationist views in that biological structures are viewed as an emergent property of complex interactions between genes and environment. Perhaps the most famous proponent of such a view with regard to cognitive development was the Swiss psychologist Jean Piaget. The essence of constructivism is that the relationship between the initial state and the final product can only be understood by considering the progressive construction of information. This construction is a dynamic process to which multiple factors contribute. There is no simple sense in which information either exclusively in the genes or in the environment can specify the end product. Rather, these two factors combine in a constructive manner such that each developmental step will be greater than the sum of the factors that contributed to it. The upshot of this viewpoint is not that we can never understand the mapping between genetic (or environmental) information and the final product, but rather that this mapping can only be understood once we have unravelled some of the key interactions that occur between genetic and environmental factors during ontogeny. Unfortunately, this means that there are unlikely to be quick breakthroughs in understanding the functions of regions of the human genome for psychological development.

FURTHER READING   Piaget (2002); Mareschal et al. (2007).

Until recently the constructivist view suffered from the same problem as vitalism, in that the mechanisms of change were poorly specified and the emergence of new structures from old resembled the conjuror's trick of making a rabbit appear from a hat. Even the "mechanisms" proposed by Piaget appeared somewhat elusive on closer inspection. Another problem with the constructivist approach was that, despite its emphasis on interaction, it was unclear how to analyze development in the absence of the traditional dichotomy between innate and environmental factors. By taking a cognitive neuroscience approach to psychological development, in conjunction with a number of new theoretical approaches, we will see that it is now possible to flesh out the constructivist approach to development and to provide new ways to analyze cognitive and brain development.

1.2   Analyzing Development

Viewpoints on cognitive development that involve reducing behavior to information derived from genes, on the one hand, and/or information derived from the external environment, on the other, have commonly used the distinction between "innate" and "acquired" components. The term "innate" has rarely been explicitly defined, and has a somewhat chequered history in developmental science. Indeed, it has been dropped from use, and even actively banned, in many areas of developmental biology. The main reason for the term having been dropped from use in fields of biology such as ethology and genetics is because it is simply no longer useful since it has become evident that genes interact with their environment at many levels, including the molecular. One compelling example of this point, discussed by Gottlieb (1992), concerns the formation of the beak in the chick embryo.

The production of the (toothless) beak in the chick embryo results from the coaction of two types of tissue. However, if, in an experimental situation, one of these types of tissue (mesenchyme) is replaced with the same tissue from a mouse, then teeth will form instead of a beak! Thus, as Gottlieb (1992) points out, the genetic component that is necessary for the chick to produce teeth has been retained from the reptilian ancestry of birds. More generally, the phenotype that emerges from these chick genes can vary dramatically according to the molecular and cellular context in which they are located.

FURTHER READING Gottlieb (2007).

Thus, there is no aspect of development that can be said to be strictly "genetic," that is, exclusively a product of information contained within particular genes. If the term "innate" is taken to refer to structure that is specified exclusively by genetic information, it refers to nothing that exists in the natural world, except for genes themselves. In cognitive science, however, use of the term "innate" has persisted despite repeated calls for it to be dropped from use (e.g., Gottlieb, 1992; Hinde, 1974; Johnston, 1988; Oyama, 2000). Presumably its persistent usage reflects the need for a term to describe the interaction between factors intrinsic to the developing child and features of the external environment. In considering this issue, Johnson and Morton (1991) suggested that it is useful to distinguish between the various levels of interaction between genes and their environment. Some of these are shown in Table 1.1. Within this analysis, the term "innate" refers only to changes that arise as a result of interactions that occur within the organism, and does not equate with "genetic." That is, it refers to the *level of the interaction between genes and environment, and not to the source of the information.* I will adopt this working definition of the term in this book. Interactions between the organism and aspects of the external environment that are common to all members of the species, the species-typical environment (such as patterned light, gravity, etc.), were referred to as "primal" by Johnson and Morton. Interactions between the organism and aspects of the environment unique to an individual, or subset of member of a species, were referred to as "learning."

Based on a series of experiments on the effects on brain structure of rearing rats in impoverished or comparatively enriched early environments, Greenough, Black, and Wallace (2002) proposed a similar distinction between two types of information storage induced by the environment. Changes induced by aspects of the environment that are common to all members of a species were classified as "experience-expectant" information storage (= "species-typical"), and are associated with

Table 1.1   Levels of interaction between genes and their environment

Levels of Interaction	Term
Molecular	Internal environment
Cellular	Internal environment (innate)
Organism–external environment	Species-typical environment (primal)
	Individual-specific environment (learning)

selective synaptic loss. The second type of information incorporated by the brain through interaction with the environment was referred to as "experience-dependent" (= "individual-specific"). This referred to interactions with the environment that are, or can be, specific to an individual and are associated with the generation of new synaptic connections. Clearly, the boundary between these types of experience is often difficult to ascertain, and there have been many instances from ethological studies where behaviors thought to be innate turn out to be primal on closer study.

FURTHER READING Greenough et al. (2002).

Using this framework it is possible to analyze aspects of development into underlying components. Normally in developmental psychology this is done in terms of components of cognition or behavior. In a cognitive neuroscience approach, by contrast, we can use evidence from different components of brain structure to constrain our thinking about cognitive development. Specifically, we can inquire into the extent to which aspects of a given neural circuit are innate (defined above as the product of interactions within the organism, and not sensitive to experience). Different aspects of brain structure and function are probably differentially sensitive to the effects of postnatal experience. The following analysis, which for simplicity I apply to the example of a simple abstract neural network, will assist in the later discussion of brain development and plasticity. A similar, but more detailed, analysis is presented in Elman et al. (1996).

The human brain is composed of very complex neural circuits bathed in a variety of chemicals that can regulate and modulate function. Therefore, when considering ways to analyze plasticity in such circuits it is useful to start with a simpler system that shares the same general properties. Connectionist neural network models involve nodes (simplified neurons) and links that can vary in strength (simplified synapses and dendrites). Learning in such networks takes place by varying the strength or extent of connections between nodes according to learning rules, some of which approximate those thought to be used in real brains (such as "Hebbian" learning rules).

FURTHER READING Munakata et al. (2008); Mareschal et al. (2007).

Figure 1.2 shows a simple connectionist neural network. There are a number of ways it could be sensitive to training. First, the basic architecture of the network could alter as a result of experience. This could involve a change in the number of nodes, the learning rule, or the extent to which the nodes are interconnected. There

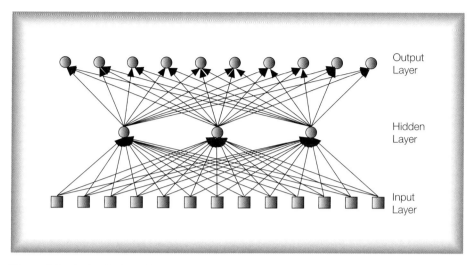

Figure 1.2   A simple three-layered connectionist neural network in which groups of nodes are joined by links. Changes in the strength of links as a result of training are determined by a learning rule.

are, in fact, a few neural network models that change in this way. Another possibility is that while the basic architecture of the network is fixed, the strength of the connections between the nodes varies according to a weight-adjustment learning rule. This is the way that most connectionist neural networks encode information. Since representations in artificial connectionist networks are dependent on the particular pattern of link strengths between nodes, allowing these to vary with the input means that different representations may emerge as a result of experience. In terms of the brain, we can think of these changes as residing in the details of microcircuits and synaptic efficacy. When the basic architecture of the network is fixed but the link strengths vary, we may say that the network shows an *innate architecture. More specifically, the representations that emerge as a result of training are constrained by the architecture of the network.* In Chapter 4 we will review evidence consistent with the view that the primate cerebral cortex imposes architectural constraints on the development of representations.

   Within this framework, there are, however, also two other possibilities. The first of these is that both the basic architecture of the network and the patterns and strengths of links between nodes are innate (as defined in Table 1.1), and thus insensitive to external input. I will refer to this as the network possessing *innate representations.* In later chapters we will see that there is little evidence that the human neocortex possesses innate representations. The second alternative possibility is that both the architecture and the detailed pattern and strength of links are malleable as a result of training. In Chapter 4 we will see that only under extremely atypical environmental conditions, or in cases of genetic atypicality, do we see changes in the basic architecture of the primate brain.

1.3   Why Take a Cognitive Neuroscience Approach to Development?

Until the past decade, the majority of theories of perceptual and cognitive development were generated without recourse to evidence from the brain. Indeed, some authors argued strongly for the independence of cognitive-level theorizing from considerations of the neural substrate (e.g., Morton, Mehler, & Jusczyk, 1984). Evidence from the brain was thought to be either distracting, irrelevant, or hopelessly complex. However, our understanding of brain function has improved significantly over the past twenty years or so. Accordingly, many believe that the time is now ripe for exploring the interface between cognitive development and brain development, and a spate of books on the topic have appeared (e.g., de Haan, Johnson & Halit, 2003; Johnson, Munakata, & Gilmore, 2002; Nelson, de Haan, & Thomas, 2006; Nelson & Luciana, 2008; Stiles, 2008). Further, the integration of information from biology and cognitive development sets the stage for a more comprehensive psychology and biology of change than was previously thought possible: a *developmental cognitive neuroscience*. By the term "cognitive neuroscience" I include not only evidence about brain development, such as that from neuroanatomy, brain imaging, and the behavioral or cognitive effects of brain lesions, but also evidence from ethology. Ethology, a science pioneered by Tinbergen, Lorenz, and others in the 1940s and 1950s, concerns the study of a whole organism within its natural environment (see Hinde, 1974; Lorenz, 1965; Tinbergen, 1951). We shall see that ethology is a powerful complement to neuroscience, and that the two fields combined can change the way we think about critical issues in perceptual and cognitive development.

In general, insights from biology have begun to play a more central role in informing thinking about perceptual and cognitive development, for a number of reasons. First, a range of powerful new methods and tools have become available to cognitive neuroscientists. These techniques permit questions to be asked more directly than before about the biological basis of cognitive and perceptual development. These methods are discussed in Chapter 2.

Importantly, theories which incorporate and reveal relationships between brain structures and cognitive functions will be useful in understanding the effects of early brain injury or genetic disorder on cognitive development. Some of the different clinical groups that have been studied are discussed in Chapter 2. In addition, evidence derived from infants with congenital and acquired brain damage will be discussed throughout later chapters. Beyond its clinical utility, this approach can also contribute to the development of theories about functional specification, critical periods, and plasticity in the brain. Thus, there is a two-way interaction between clinical evidence and basic research in developmental cognitive neuroscience.

1.4   Why Take a Developmental Approach to Cognitive Neuroscience?

Ontogenetic development is the constructive process by which genes interact with their environment at various levels to yield complex organic structures such as the brain and the cognitive processes it supports. The study of development is necessarily multidisciplinary since new levels of structure that emerge as a result of this process (such as particular neural systems) often require different levels and methods of analysis from those that preceded them. The flip side of this is that development can be used as a tool for unraveling the interaction between seemingly disparate levels of organization, such as that between the molecular biology of gene expression and the development of cognitive abilities such as object recognition. Further, the human adult brain, and the mind it sustains, is composed of a complex series of hierarchical and parallel systems which has proven very difficult to analyze in an exclusively "top-down" manner. Brain damage induced by surgical lesions, or by accident or stroke, is unlikely to cleanly dissociate different levels of hierarchical organization. The developmental approach may allow different levels of hierarchical control to be observed independently. Specifically, it presents the opportunity to observe how various neurocognitive systems emerge and become integrated during development. For example, in Chapter 5 we will see how different brain pathways underlying eye movement control emerge and become integrated during development.

1.5   The Cause of Developmental Change

Those inclined to see development as the unfolding of pre-existing information in the genes tend to adopt a maturational view of developmental psychology in which infants have reduced versions of the adult mind which increase by steps as particular brain pathways or structures mature. In contrast, taking a constructivist view of development involves attempting to unravel the dynamic relations between intrinsic and extrinsic structure which progressively restrict the phenotypes that can emerge. The distinction between these two approaches has also been noted by Gottlieb (1992), who refers to them as "predetermined epigenesis" and "probabilistic epigenesis." Predetermined epigenesis assumes that there is a unidirectional causal path from genes to structural brain changes to brain function and experience. In contrast, probabilistic epigenesis views the interactions between genes, structural brain changes, and function as bidirectional:

Predetermined epigenesis:

(Unidirectional structure–functional development)

genes → brain structure → brain function → experience

Probablistic epigenesis:

(Bidirectional structure–functional development)

genes ↔ brain structure ↔ brain function ↔ experience

(*Source*: Gottlieb, 1992)

Thus, by the predetermined epigenesis view the infant mind is viewed as being comparable to adults with focal brain injury. That is, specific cognitive mechanisms are either present or absent at a given age. For example, parallels have been drawn between infants and patients with frontal lobe deficits. Circuits that support components of the adult system are assumed to come "on-line" at various ages. However, while this approach is likely to provide a reasonable first approximation for normal developmental events, it is unlikely to provide a full account in the long run.

An alternative approach to investigating the relation between the developing brain and cognition is associated with a probabilistic epigenesis approach to biological development. This viewpoint assumes that development involves the progressive restriction of fate. Early in development a system, such as the brain/mind, has a range of possible developmental paths and end states. The developmental path and end state that result are dependent on the particular sets of constraints that operate. This type of analysis of ontogenetic development derives from work on the development of body structure by D'Arcy Thompson (1917) and C.H. Waddington (1975), among others.

Waddington (whose work greatly influenced Piaget) proposed that there are developmental pathways, or necessary epigenetic routes, which he termed "chreods." Chreods can be conceptualized as valleys in an epigenetic landscape such as that shown in Figure 1.3. Self-regulatory processes (which Waddington called

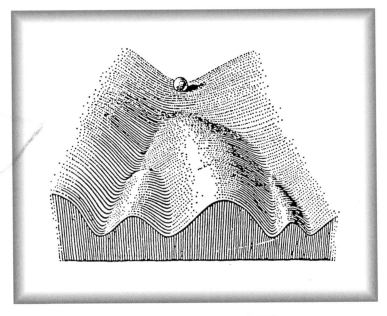

Figure 1.3   The epigenetic landscape of Waddington (1975).

"homeorhesis") ensure that the organism (conceptualized as a ball rolling down the landscape) returns to its channel following small perturbations. Large perturbations, such as being reared in darkness, can result in a quite different valley route being taken, especially when these occur near a decision point. These decision points are regions of the epigenetic landscape where a small perturbation can lead to a different route being taken. Thus, while for the typically developing child the same end point will be reached despite the small perturbations that arise from slightly different rearing environments, a deviation from the normal path early in development (high up the hill), at a decision point, or a major perturbation later in development, may cause the child to take a different developmental path and reach one of a discrete set of possible alternative end states (phenotypes).

Aside from Waddington's informal conceptualization, the constructivist (probablistic epigenesis) approach to development is currently more difficult to work with since we have few theoretical tools for understanding emergent phenomena in complex dynamic systems. By this view, developmental disorders are possible developmental trajectories that are responses to different sets of constraints. This implies that from the moment when the developmental trajectory deviates from the normal one, a variety of new factors and adaptations will come into play, making it likely that some reorganization of brain functioning will take place. In contrast to the maturational approach (causal epigenesis), therefore, applying the mapping between brain regions and functions found in typical adults to such cases may be only partially informative. It should be stressed that the constructivist view just outlined does not seek to downplay the role of genetic factors. Rather, it seeks to understand the emergence of new structures and functions through the complex interactions between genes and their different environments.

1.6 Three Viewpoints on Human Functional Brain Development

Relating the neuroanatomical changes that occur during the development of the brain to the remarkable changes in motor, perceptual, and cognitive abilities during the first decade or so of human life presents a considerable challenge. Throughout this book, I will discuss evidence inspired by three distinct, but not necessarily incompatible, viewpoints on human functional brain development. These are: (1) a maturational perspective, (2) interactive specialization, and (3) a skill learning viewpoint.

As mentioned earlier, much of the research to date attempting to relate brain to behavioral development in humans has been from a maturational viewpoint in which the goal is to relate the "maturation" of particular regions of the brain, usually regions of the cerebral cortex, to newly emerging sensory, motor, and cognitive functions. Evidence concerning the differential neuroanatomical development of brain regions is used to determine an age when a particular region is likely to become functional. Success in a new behavioral task at this age may then be attributed to the maturation of this "new" brain region. By this view, functional brain development is the reverse of adult neuropsychology, with the difference that specific brain regions are added-in instead of being damaged.

Despite the intuitive appeal and attractive simplicity of the maturational approach, we will see during the course of this book that it does not successfully explain some major aspects of human functional brain development. Further, associations between neural and cognitive changes based on age of onset can be theoretically weak due to the great variety of neuroanatomical and neurochemical measures that change at different times in different regions of the brain.

In contrast to the above approach a specific constructivist viewpoint, "interactive specialization," assumes that postnatal functional brain development, at least within the cerebral cortex, involves a process of organizing patterns of inter-regional interactions (Johnson, 2001, 2002). According to this view, the response properties of a specific region are partly determined by its patterns of connectivity to other regions, and their patterns of activity. During postnatal development, changes in the response properties of cortical regions occur as they interact and compete with each other to acquire their role in new computational abilities. From this perspective, some cortical regions may begin with poorly defined functions, and consequently are partially activated in a wide range of different contexts and tasks. During development, activity-dependent interactions between regions hone the functions of regions such that their activity becomes restricted to a narrower set of circumstances (e.g., a region originally activated by a wide variety of visual objects may come to confine its response to upright human faces). The onset of new behavioral competencies during infancy will therefore be associated with changes in activity over several regions, and not just with the onset of activity in one or more additional region(s). I will expand further on this theory in Chapter 12.

A third perspective on human functional brain development, skill learning, involves the proposal that the brain regions active in infants during the onset of new perceptual or motor abilities are similar, or identical, to those involved in complex skill acquisition in adults. For example, with regard to perceptual expertise, Isabel Gauthier and colleagues have shown that extensive training of adults with artificial objects (called "greebles") eventually results in activation of a cortical region previously associated with face processing, the "fusiform face area" (Gauthier, Tarr, Anderson, Skudlarksi, & Gore, 1999). This suggests that the region is normally activated by faces in adults, not because it is prespecified for faces, but due to our extensive expertise with that class of stimulus. Further, it encourages parallels with the development of face processing skills in infants (see Gauthier & Nelson, 2001). While it remains unclear how far parallels can be drawn between adult expertise and infant development, to the extent that the skill learning hypothesis is correct, it presents a clear view of a continuity of mechanisms throughout the life span. Finally, skill learning is not necessarily incompatible with interactive specialization, and sometimes the two viewpoints make similar predictions.

1.7   Looking Forward

The next chapter reviews some of the different methods currently used to study emerging brain structures and functions. Although atypical development is not the primary focus of this book, throughout the review of typical development evidence from atypical development is discussed where relevant. Focusing in particular on three developmental disorders (dyslexia, autism, and Williams syndrome), we see that specific neurocognitive deficits can result from diffuse damage to multiple brain systems. Brain damage in prenatal development can divert the child from one developmental path to another. However, it is possible that different types of brain damage can result in the same adult end state (phenotype), somewhat like the discrete number of valleys in Waddington's epigenetic landscape. In contrast to this, brain damage in later life (perinatal and early postnatal) is commonly compensated for by other parts of the brain. Thus, at this later stage a focal brain lesion may have only mild diffuse cognitive consequences, resembling Waddington's self-organizing adaptation keeping the organism within a certain chreod and resulting in the same general phenotype.

In Chapter 3 we introduce some basic facts about genes and discuss what is known about their expression during human development, while in Chapter 4 we present the current state of knowledge about the pre- and postnatal development of the human brain. While the general sequence of developmental events is very similar for all mammals, the timing of human development, and especially human postnatal development, is protracted. This extended period of postnatal development is associated with a greater extent of area of the cerebral cortex, in particular the prefrontal regions. The more extended postnatal development observed in humans reveals differential rates of development in aspects of brain structure (e.g., different cortical areas and layers). The more differentiated picture of postnatal brain development in humans has also been used to make predictions about the emergence of function.

Focusing on the cerebral cortex, neurobiological and brain imaging studies indicate that the cortex probably does not possess innate representations (in the sense discussed earlier). Rather, early in life large-scale regions of the cortex have approximate biases that make them best suited to supporting particular types of computations. The fairly consistent structure–function relations observed in the cortex of typical human adults appear to be the consequence of multiple constraints both intrinsic and extrinsic to the organism, rather than of detailed intrinsic genetic specification. In the following chapters a number of domains of perceptual, cognitive, and motor development that have been associated with neural development are reviewed. In each of these domains I attempt to reveal some of the sources of constraint on the representations that emerge within cortical circuits. Examples of combinations of constraints from the correlational structure of the external environment, the basic architecture of the cortex, and the influence of subcortical circuits are discussed.

In Chapter 12, mechanisms and types of changes in representations during human postnatal development are discussed, and the interactive specialization viewpoint on human functional brain development is expanded further. The emergence of specific functions in cortical areas is seen as a product of interactions within the brain, and between the brain and its external environment. Just as the child develops within a social and physical environment, and the brain within a body ("embodiment"), each cortical area develops its functionality within the context of the whole brain ("embrainment"). In the final chapter a number of conclusions and recommendations for future research are made.

Key Issues for Discussion

- To what extent do researchers investigating issues in cognitive neuroscience in adults need to consider evidence from development?
- What aspects of the typical developing child's environment are likely to be "experience-expectant" and "species-typical"?
- To what extent can Waddington's "epigenetic landscape" satisfactorily account for the recovery of some cognitive functions following early brain damage?

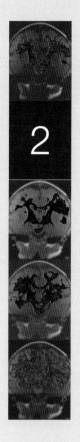

2 Methods and Populations

This chapter provides background on the different methods used, and populations studied, in developmental cognitive neuroscience. Behavioral techniques for studying infants and children have been available for several decades, but recent advances in eye tracking have opened new possibilities for finer grained analyses. A relatively new set of tools relate to the generation of structural and functional maps of brain activity based on changes in either cerebral metabolism, blood flow, or electrical activity. For some questions these new neuroimaging methods have replaced research on animals, while for other important scientific questions, such as genetic manipulation or gene expression, there remains no substitute to animal research. In addition to typically developing infants and children, researchers in developmental cognitive neuroscience have also turned their attention to studying children with developmental disorders of genetic origin such as autism and Williams syndrome, and cases of early deprivation due to sensory limitations or poor social context. By employing different methods and studying various different populations we will gain powerful leverage on key questions in the field.

Developmental Cognitive Neuroscience   (Third Edition)   Mark H. Johnson with Michelle de Haan
© 2011 Mark H. Johnson

2.1   Introduction

Progress in a field of science critically depends on three things; empirical discoveries, the development of theories to account for the available evidence and to make predictions for future work, and methods. The importance of the latter is often underestimated in the history of science. However, at least for developmental cognitive neuroscience, a strong case can be made that progress could have been much more rapid in the past had current technology been available. Over the past decades, however, new technology has arisen, and we have learned how to apply existing technology to the special constraints imposed by studying infants and children. Behavioral methods for studying infants and children have been available for several decades, but are incrementally being improved and extended. A relatively new set of tools relate to neuroimaging—the generation of "functional" maps of brain activity based on changes in either cerebral metabolism, blood flow, or electrical activity. We will see that for some issues the new neuroimaging methods have replaced research on animals, while for other important scientific questions there remains no substitute to animal research. In addition to typically developing infants and children, researchers in developmental cognitive neuroscience have also turned their attention to studying children with developmental disorders of genetic origin such as autism and Williams syndrome. Comparisons of these syndromes to each other, and to the typical trajectory of development, gives us powerful leverage to understand some of the basic principles underlying neurocognitive development. In addition, cases of early deprivation due to sensory limitations or poor social context are not just important to study for clinical or societal reasons, but they can also shed light on the importance of specific kinds of early experience for later development.

2.2   Behavioral and Cognitive Tasks

Since the 1950s behavioral and cognitive analyses of child development have moved from an important early stage of "natural history" where Piaget and others described some of the striking phenomena associated with development, such as the apparent lack of object permanence (see Chapter 6), to a variety of ingenious experimental ways to gather information about psychological change in infants, toddlers, and children. One of the major challenges to studying infants and toddlers that had to be overcome was the need for behavioral tasks that do not involve verbal instruction or require sophisticated responses like pressing specific keys or buttons. Further, young infants only have a short attention span in terms of the length of time they are prepared to cooperate with the experimenter. Thus, studies involving extensive training periods are not feasible either. Fortunately, however, a number of methods have been developed for testing infants that build on their natural tendencies to look at conspicuous and novel visual stimuli. One of these procedures, called "preferential looking," involves presenting paired visual stimuli, and recording the time that the infants choose to look at each. Another procedure, called "habituation," involves showing the same stimulus repeatedly until the infant shows a clear decrease in the time she spends looking at it. When a certain criterion for the looking decrement is reached, a novel stimulus is presented and the increase or recovery in looking time is recorded. If there is significant recovery of looking time, we may infer that the infant can discriminate between the two stimuli. If there is little or no recovery, we may infer that the infant is unable to discriminate between them. Other techniques for eliciting discriminative responses from young infants include using rate of sucking to measure habituation, the use of an eye-tracker to determine exact patterns of looking, and the use of heart rate measures.

FURTHER READING Aslin (2007); Karatekin (2008).

Another useful way of linking brain development to behavior across different age groups is the "marker task." This method involves the use of specific behavioral tasks which have been related to one or more brain regions in adult humans and non-human primates by neurophysiological and/or brain imaging studies. By studying the development of performance on the task at different ages and in different contexts, the researcher can gather evidence about how the observed behavioral change is accounted for by known patterns of brain development. In this book, we will see that the marker task approach has been taken in several different domains of cognition. There are also weaknesses of the marker task approach, such as that findings from one specific task sometimes do not generalize to others that seem closely related, and it can be difficult to directly compare results from groups of participants that differ significantly. Another challenge of the marker task approach stems from the design of a task that is sufficiently limited in its demands as to give interpretable results with infants or young children, and yet sufficiently demanding to call upon "interesting" cognitive capacities. Finally, we will see in several chapters that different brain regions may be critical for the same task at different ages. Thus, the interpretation of marker task results is made more complex. Nevertheless, the marker task approach is a useful methodology that can provide initial insights into the development of neurocognitive systems.

2.3   Assessing Brain Function in Development

With the exception of one very new method, the techniques available for observing the functioning of the young human brain are those already well developed in research on adults (see Figure 2.1 in the color plate section). High-density event-related potentials (HD-ERP) is a method of recording the electrical activity of the brain by means of sensitive electrodes that gently rest on the surface of the scalp (see Figure 2.2 in the color plate section). These sensors detect tiny changes in electrical voltage at the scalp surface caused by groups of neurons within the brain firing together. These recordings can either be of the spontaneous natural electrical rhythms of the brain (electroencephalography [EEG]), or the electrical activity evoked by a stimulus presentation or action (event-related potentials [ERPs]). When studying ERPs the data from many trials is averaged so that the spontaneous EEG unrelated to the stimulus presentation averages out to zero. In recent years, there has also been recent interest in rapid bursts of high-frequency EEG (such as the gamma or 40 Hz frequency) that appear to be related to stages of information processing in the brain (event-related oscillations [EROs]; Csibra, Davis, Spratling, & Johnson, 2000).

FURTHER READING Csibra, Kushnerenko, & Grossmann (2008); Csibra & Johnson (2007).

With a high density of sensors placed on the scalp, algorithms can be employed which infer the position and orientation of the brain sources of electrical activity (dipoles) for the particular pattern of scalp surface electrical activity. Some of the assumptions necessary for the successful use of these algorithms are actually more likely to be true of infants than adults. For example, lower levels of skull conductance and fewer cortical convolutions may improve the accuracy and interpretability of HD-ERP results in infants relative to adult subjects (but see Johnson et al., 2001, and Nelson, 1994, for discussion of this methodology as applied to infants).

HD-ERP and related methods are an excellent way to study brain functions even in very young babies. However, while they offer excellent time resolution (of the order of milliseconds) it is difficult to obtain anything other than coarse spatial resolution (e.g., frontal versus temporal lobes). A method that has far greater spatial resolution, albeit at the expense of temporal resolution, is functional MRI. As different regions of the brain are activated, the cells in that area require oxygen delivered through networks of tiny blood vessels. Oxygen is transported in the blood by a molecule called hemoglobin, and when a brain region is active it calls for more oxygen resulting in a localized increase in oxygenated hemoglobin and a decrease in deoxygenated hemoglobin. The change in the blood oxygen level dependent (BOLD) response is detected by MRI, thus allowing the non-invasive measurement of cerebral blood oxygen levels in the different parts of the brain with a spatial resolution on the order of millimeters and a time resolution of several seconds.

This technique for studying brain function is now routinely being applied to children from 6 or 7 years old in several laboratories. However, for a variety of reasons it remains technically challenging to use this method with children younger than this age. However, studying infants is possible, particularly if they are sleeping or drowsy while passively listening to auditory stimuli such as speech or music. There are a variety of complex issues about the analysis of fMRI data from children and its comparison to that collected in adults (see Thomas & Tseng, 2008). In addition to conventional fMRI analysis focused on specific regions of interest, recently developed analysis methods allow the researcher to assess the degree of functional connectivity between different brain regions. As we will see later (Chapter 12), this approach allows us to test hypotheses about the emergence of coordinated functional brain networks during development.

FURTHER READING Thomas & Tseng (2008).

A new method that also measures brain activity through the levels of oxygen in the blood, including the BOLD signal, is Near Infra-Red Spectroscopy (NIRS). This is a form of optical imaging, meaning that it depends on measuring minute changes in the absorption and scatter or bending of weak light beams as they pass through the skull and brain (see Lloyd-Fox, Blasi, & Elwell, 2010; Meek, 2002). Tiny light emitters and detectors are embedded within a cap and carefully placed on the child's head (see Figure 2.3 in the color plate section). Like fMRI, changes in blood oxygenation due to brain activity can be detected with this method, but NIRS is less sensitive to motion artifacts and does not require confinement in a scanner. Therefore, NIRS potentially provides an excellent alternative to fMRI for use with infants and toddlers. Indeed, the relatively thin skull of very young children means that light passes through more easily, and thus better optical signals are usually obtained. While the technique is still being developed in several laboratories, there are now more than thirty papers published that use this method to study brain functions in babies.

FURTHER READING Lloyd-Fox, Blasi, & Elwell (2010); Mehler, Nespor, Gervain, Endress, & Shukla (2008).

2.4   Observing Brain Structure in Development

Part of the goal of developmental cognitive neuroscience is to relate changes in brain function and cognition to changes in the underlying brain structure. For decades, the study of postnatal human brain structural development depended on traditional neuroanatomical methods applied to postmortem human or animal tissue. These methods involve staining neurons and their processes with substances that make them more clearly visible under the microscope. One of these stains (the Golgi stain) was invented by a founding father of neuroscience and Nobel prize winner, Camillo Golgi (1843–1926). For human postmortem tissue, such analyses are painstakingly slow and difficult, and tend to be based on relatively small numbers of children due to the difficulties associated in gaining such tissue. Furthermore, those children who unfortunately come to autopsy have often suffered from trauma or diseases that complicate generalizations to normal brain development. Perhaps the most notable series of studies conducted with this approach came from Conel, who between 1939 and 1967 published several volumes of detailed drawings of the postnatal development of human cortex (see Figure 4.5 in Chapter 4). More recently, the advent of the electron microscope has allowed scientists to study changes at even smaller scales, such as the formation or loss of synapses on dendrites (Chapter 4).

In addition to studies of brain activation, MRI allows the opportunity for us to study the development of brain structure in healthy living babies and children. While this is an enormous methodological advance on traditional postmortem neuroanatomy, until recently such MRI methods only allowed a dissociation between the brain's grey matter (clusters of neurons and their local processes and connections) and white matter (bundles of connecting fibers) at an order of magnitude less detailed than microscope images. Nevertheless, as we will see in Chapter 4, there is a recent explosion of knowledge about the trajectories of postnatal anatomical brain development. In recent years, new analytic methods are emerging that allow us to go beyond the simple assessment of the shape and quantity of white and grey matter and begin to trace the pathways of major structural connections between regions in the brain. One such method, Diffusion Tensor Imaging (DTI), uses measures of the motion of water molecules to give detailed pictures of fiber tracts and their development. Other methods of tracing fiber tracts during development are currently being investigated (Figure 2.4 in the color plate section). Such methods will be important for testing predictions about the precise relation between structural connectivity and function in brain development.

FURTHER READING   O'Hare & Sowell (2008); Wozniak, Mueller, & Lim (2008).

2.5   Animal Studies and Genetics

As we will see in Chapter 4, the vast majority of what we currently know about brain development comes from research on other species. While there are obviously some differences between species, the overwhelming majority of basic phenomena are common to most or all species studied. Additionally, in behavioral development a number of animal models have reached a stage where some of the principles discovered are applicable to aspects of human development (see Blass, 1992). One example discussed later in this book (Chapter 7) is visual imprinting in the newly hatched chick. The advantage of an animal model, such as the chick, is that further research can reveal the particular regions of the chick brain involved, and then identify electrophysiological, neuroanatomical, and molecular correlates of this process. Finally, an anatomically informed computer model of the neural network supporting the behavioral change has been developed and tested. Understanding a simple case of behavioral development such as this can inform basic issues such as the neural basis of sensitive periods for learning (O'Reilly & Johnson, 2002). Further, the dissociation of neural systems underlying components of imprinting in the chick has been used to argue for a similar dissociation in the development of face recognition in human infants (see Chapter 7). Thus, studying simple animal models can both directly and indirectly inform our understanding of how brain development relates to the more complex cognitive and behavioral changes observed in humans. In another example of the application of animal models to human development, comparisons between the behavioral development of humans and other primates can illuminate the importance of language to changes in other domains of cognition (see Chapter 9). Consequently, while homologies between species must be made with great care, well-studied animal models increasingly provide useful theoretical and empirical insights into cognitive development in humans.

FURTHER READING   Bachevalier (2008); Matsuzawa (2007).

In the next chapter we will discuss genetic methods in more detail. However, at this point it is useful to note that techniques exist in molecular genetics which allow the lesioning of particular genes from the genome of an animal. An example of this is the deletion of the alpha-calcium calmodulin kinase II gene which results in so-called "knockout" mice being unable to perform certain learning tasks when adults (Silva, Paylor, Wehner, & Tonegawa, 1992; Silva, Stevens, Tonegawa, & Wang, 1992). This method opens new vistas in the analysis of genetic contributions to cognitive and perceptual change in animals, and may be particularly fruitful when applied to well-studied animal models of development such as visual imprinting in chicks and song learning in passerine birds. These animal models may also be useful when investigating the role of genetic deletions/atypicalities for neurocognitive development in disorders of known genetic origin.

2.6   Developmental Disorders

In addition to needing a variety of different methods to study typically developing infants and children, developmental cognitive neuroscience also involves the study of differences in development caused by genetics, early brain damage or trauma, or abnormal early experiences. While the study of atypical developmental pathways (more traditionally called "developmental neuropsychology" or "developmental psychopathology") is clearly important for clinical and societal reasons, it can also inform us about the causal factors and basic processes important in typical development.

While this book has focused primarily on the typical trajectory of development of the human brain, we will allude to a number of different developmental disorders of assumed genetic origin. As we will discuss further in the next chapter, genetic deviations can involve mutations of single genes (such as Fragile-X and phenylke-tonuria), abnormalities in chromosomal structure (such as Down's syndrome), and microdeletions that involve several genes from one part of a chromosome (such as Prader-Willi and Williams syndrome). There are also several developmental disorders that are believed to have complex genetic bases involving multiple genes of small effect (e.g., autism). Two of the disorders mentioned most frequently in this book are autism and Williams syndrome.

Autism is a relatively common developmental disorder (with an incidence including the spectrum of related disorders of around 1% of the population). Genetic studies of autism have revealed a complex and evolving story with more than twenty different genes currently being implicated. Recent reviews lead to the conclusion that the genetic contribution to the disorder involves many genes of small effect, and that there are probably multiple different combinations of genetic factors that can give rise to autism (Happé, Ronald, & Plomin, 2006). There is also evidence for an interaction with environmental factors (see Frith, 2003, for review). Many of the core deficits of the developmental disorder autism lie in the domain of social relations with others, though there are many non-social cognitive deficits as well. Major behavioral symptoms include atypical eye contact, an apparent unawareness of the existence of thoughts of others, a reluctance to be held or touched by others, repetitive behaviors such as rocking or hand flapping, and commonly a fascination for certain objects or other inanimate aspects of their environment. Alongside these deviant behaviors are often deficits in other cognitive and language skills, such as echolalia (repeating words and sentences heard previously). Autism includes a spectrum of related disorders that share many of the same symptoms. For example, individuals with Asperger's syndrome have some similar social difficulties, but alongside a normal verbal IQ (Happé, 1994; Pennington & Welsh, 1995).

FURTHER READING   Frith (2003); South, Ozonoff, & Schultz (2008).

In contrast to the specific social deficit seen in autism, Williams syndrome participants appear at first sight to have good social skills. Williams syndrome (WS; also known as infantile hypercalcemia) is a relatively rare disorder of genetic origin effecting approximately 1 in 20,000 to 50,000 births (Greenberg, 1990). The disorder can now be diagnosed in early infancy through genetic or metabolic markers, and is typified by a number of physical and cognitive characteristics.

Evidence from structural neuroimaging indicates that WS brains are only about 80–85% of the overall volume of typical brains, but there are no obvious gross atypicalities or lesions (Jernigan & Bellugi, 1994). Currently, the only evidence for a specific focus of damage is that they show a relative increase in volume in particular lobules on the cerebellum. This cerebellar atypicality contrasts with autism, in which the same lobules are relatively smaller than normal (Jernigan & Bellugi, 1994). At the cytoarchitectonic level, a preliminary analysis by Galaburda, Wang, Bellugi, and Rosen (1994) found disturbances within cortical layers and decreased myelination. Given the lack of evidence for any discrete focal lesions, the specificity of the neurocognitive profile that WS participants present is striking.

FURTHER READING   Karmiloff-Smith (2008).

It is often suggested that the pattern of spared abilities in WS suggests approximately the opposite of deficits described for autism, and this raised the initial hypothesis that people with WS have intact a functional brain system corresponding to a "social module" (see Chapter 7). Specifically, one hypothesis advanced is that the social brain network remains intact in WS, while being specifically damaged in autism. However, this hypothesis is now regarded as an over-simplification following further research (see Chapter 7). Nevertheless, it does illustrate the potential value of comparing and contrasting different developmental disorders in similar experimental paradigms.

2.7   Atypically Developing Brains

When considering the brain correlates of developmental disorders of genetic origin, there are at least four levels at which they can be described; (1) gross brain anatomy, (2) individual "deficit" areas, (3) functional neural systems and pathways, and (4) neurochemistry and microcircuitry (see Table 2.1). Over the past decades there have been many specific hypotheses advanced about the neural deficits that cause, or correlate with, different disorders. Initially, these claims often involved a search for discrete localized cortical or subcortical "lesions" resulting from the atypical genetics. However, it has become clear that, at least when studied in later childhood or as adults, many developmental disorders involve widespread systemic subtle differences in brain structure and function. To take the case of autism, Rumsey and Ernst (2000) summarize their review of functional imaging of autistic disorders as "...studies of brain metabolism and blood flow thus far have yet to yield consistent findings, but suggest considerable variability in regional patterns of cerebral synaptic activity" (p. 171). Other authors reviewing work on

Table 2.1 A thumbnail sketch of some of the major developmental disorders. For the sake of comparison, the table focuses on contrastive aspects of different disorders

Disorder	Genetic Basis	Illustrative Brain Atypicality	Behavioral Phenotype
Phenylketonuria	Single gene (mutated PAH)	Low dopamine levels in prefrontal cortex	Deficits in executive function, working memory
Fragile-X	Single gene (silenced FMRI gene)	Relative decrease in volume of cerebellum; atypical dendritic spine morphology throughout neocortex	Retardation, hyperactivity, attention problems, autistic symptoms, visuospatial and numeracy problems
Down's syndrome	Chromosomal (extra chromosome 21, translocation or mosaic)	Microcephaly	General retardation, but relative strengths in visuospatial cognition and weak verbal abilities
Turner syndrome	Chromosomal (absence of X in females)		Visuospatial and numeracy deficits, but verbal IQ in normal range
Prader-Willi syndrome	Microdeletion/duplication (SNRPN, NDN)	Hypothalamus	Moderate retardation, but sociable; poor in most cognitive domains, and especially verbal skills
Williams syndrome	Microdeletion (chromosome 7, 24–30 genes)	Microcephaly (due to white matter reduction) but with increased proportional volume of cerebellum; cerebellar abnormalities;	Relatively poor at spatial and number tasks, but behaviourally proficient at face processing and language
Autism	Polygenic	Macrocephaly due to increased white matter in many cortical regions	Impaired social function, impaired language, restricted repertoire of interests
Dyslexia/SLI	Polygenic	Increased cerebral white matter throughout cortex in SLI	Deficits in language and/or reading
ADHD	Polygenic	Atypical functioning of widespread cortical areas including frontostriatal and limbic circuitry	Deficits in attention; particularly response inhibition and delay avoidance

autism concur with this conclusion. Deb and Thompson (1998) state that "Various abnormalities of brain structure and function have been proposed, but no focal defect has been reliably demonstrated" (p. 299), and Chugani (2000) concludes that "data from the various imaging modalities have not yet converged to provide a unifying hypothesis of brain mechanisms" with a range of cortical (frontal, medial prefrontal, temporal, anterior cingulate) and subcortical (basal ganglia, thalamus, cerebellum) structures implicated in different studies. According to Filipek (1999) a similar situation obtains with respect to Attention Deficit Hyperactivity Disorder. She concludes that neuroimaging studies "have, in fact, confirmed the lack of consistent gross neuroanatomical lesions or other abnormalities in Attention Deficit" (p. 117). For attention deficit/hyperactivity disorder (ADHD), there are abnormalities in widespread cortical areas including, at a minimum, the frontos-triatal, cingulate, and parietal regions. In sum, for at least these two disorders there is little support for the notion that discrete lesions to functional cortical areas can be observed in developmental disorders. Rather, we tend to see widespread effects in a brain that has actually developed atypically. It is worth noting that the vast majority of cognitive neuroscience studies conducted to date have been done on older children or adults, and it remains possible that more specific effects will be observed in infants or toddlers.

Another important point to note is that the majority of brain abnormalities associated with developmental disorders are not specific to one disorder. For example, an atypical cerebellum has been reported for autism, Fragile-X, Williams syndrome and dyslexia. In my view, these atypicalities that are shared across several developmental disorders are no less interesting, but they do raise the importance of studying general profiles of differences across several brain regions and disorders, rather than focusing heavily on specific phenomena within individual areas or regions in a single developmental disorder. In general, claims about specific neural deficits underlying a developmental disorder need to be treated with caution until other brain areas, and other developmental disorders, are examined in equal depth.

With regard to gross measures of brain structure, overall brain volume can be reduced (microcephaly) or increased (macrocephaly) relative to typical develop-ment. Differences in overall volume can be due to changes in the gray (neurones and their local connectivity) or white (fiber bundles and long-range connectivity) matter. An interesting consequence of several major developmental disorders is that microcephaly or macrocephaly are principally due to deviations in the extent of white matter. For example, a consistent finding from structural imaging of autism is larger cerebral volumes (see Filipek, 1999, for review), particularly in temporal, parietal, and occipital regions. Interestingly, however, this increased volume is due to white matter rather than gray matter (Filipek, Kennedy, & Caviness, 1992). In other words, the fiber bundles connecting regions and mediating inter-regional interaction were affected more than the regions themselves. Preliminary MRI studies of Williams syndrome have shown that, unlike autism, overall brain and cerebral volume is smaller than aged-matched controls (Reiss et al., 2000). Assessment of tissue composition indicates that, compared to controls, individuals with WS have relative preservation of cerebral gray matter volume and disproportionate reduction in cerebral white matter volume. This pattern is restricted to the cerebral hemispheres, and is not found in the cerebellum (Galaburda & Bellugi, 2000; Reiss et al., 2000). Thus, in at least two major developmental disorders of genetic origin, differences in overall cerebral volume appear to be related to the extent of connectivity (white matter) between regions.

The most micro level of neuroanatomy considered for developmental disorders concerns microcircuitry, dendrites, and synapses. As it becomes evident that at least for some syndromes atypicalities are widespread across several regions or systems of the brain, more recent hypotheses have focused on putative differences in synaptic structure (Perisco & Bourgeron, 2006) or connectivity patterns (Just, Cherkassky, Keller, Kana, & Minshew, 2007; Minshew & Williams, 2007). These differences in microstructure are assumed to have compounding effects during postnatal development, that then differentially affect some domains of cognition or types of computation more than others. In later chapters we will review in more detail data from different disorders where these have been specifically associated with deficits in a particular domain (e.g., Chapter 5, ADHD; Chapter 7, autism and Williams syndrome).

2.8   Sensory and Environmental Perturbations

Several populations have been studied by developmental cognitive neuroscientists because they involve sensory or environmental deprivation for at least part of the individual's development. Thus, the scientist can potentially study the effects of experience resulting from sensory or environmental input on human brain and cognitive development. In later chapters of this book we will see examples of how studies on the congenitally deaf have illuminated the study of language acquisition and its brain basis (Chapter 9). Another example of this general approach comes from the work of Maurer and colleagues who have studied individuals who suffered visual deprivation for varying periods of time following birth due to uni- or bilateral dense cataracts. These dense cataracts prevent structured visual input until they are reversed by surgery, usually within the first year. By studying aspects of face processing in this clinical population, this research group has shown that even after years of normal experience of faces some deficits remained (Le Grand, Mondloch, Maurer, & Brent, 2001). In other words, visual deprivation over the first months has detectable life-long effects on face processing. Further, by examining cases of unilateral deprivation it has recently been shown that these effects are more due to right hemisphere (left eye) deprivation. Data such as these present a severe challenge for the "skill learning" approach to human functional brain development, and suggest propensity of the right hemisphere for face processing from the first months.

While the cataract and deaf populations can inform us about effects of sensory deprivation, other populations have been studied that suffered from social deprivation. For example, samples of children raised in orphanages (e.g., during the Romanian communist regime) can subsequently have multiple social, cognitive, and sensorimotor problems (for a review see Gunnar, 2001). While orphanage rearing can be variable in general care quality, at a minimum, stable long-term relationships with caregivers are missing (Rutter, 1998). The outcome from "good" orphanages can include problems with executive functions (see Chapter 10) and social cognition, while other aspects of sensorimotor, cognitive, and linguistic development can recover well. At the other extreme, in a sample of children raised in Romanian orphanages for at least the first 12 months, 12% exhibited features of autism, although even here these symptoms tended to diminish over time (Rutter et al., 1999).

FURTHER READING   Maurer, Lewis, & Mondloch (2008); Shackman, Wismer Fries, & Pollak (2008).

Another population that has recently come under study are children who have been raised in low social economic status homes. Children raised in poor environments, even in otherwise wealthy countries, have a raised risk for a variety of adverse outcomes. The factors that contribute to the low quality rearing environments of these children are varied and may include parental drug abuse, poor diet, and low quality social interactions. A challenge for developmental cognitive neuroscientists in the future will be to devise theory-driven targeted interventions to help alleviate the effects of such poor quality rearing environments (Chapter 13).

Key Issues for Discussion

- What would be an ideal method or technique for studying the development of human brain functions that is not currently available?
- Choose an example of a clear behavioral change during childhood, and discuss what two methods would be most appropriate for revealing the underlying causes and mechanisms of that change.
- Why are populations with particular developmental disorders or with impoverished early environments important for our understanding of the *typical* development of human brain functions?

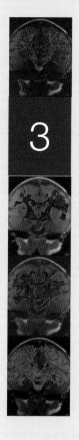

3 From Gene to Brain

This chapter introduces developmental genetics, and outlines contemporary views on the role and structure of genes in building brains and the cognitive processes that they support. The popular twentieth-century view of the gene as a direct blueprint for constructing the brain has been superseded by the contemporary view that genes are expressed differently according to their specific temporal and spatial context, and that even the simplest chemical building blocks of the brain (proteins) originate from multiple and variable gene interactions. These considerations make the view that specific genes "code for" particular facets of cognition implausible. Instead, the path from gene to brain to behavior (epigenesis) is both complex and variable. While this complexity may seem daunting, there are several ways to begin to unravel the genetic contribution to developing brain functions. One strategy is to study the role in the brain of relatively simple molecules that are close to being direct products of gene expression. A second strategy is to study variability between typical individuals in genes, brain functions, and cognition. Correlating differences on multiple measures may reveal associations between particular gene variants, aspects of brain function, and behavioral capabilities. A third approach is to study syndromes in which there are known genetic differences to the general population (see also Chapter 2), or specific individuals with rare mutations. By comparing neurocognitive development in these syndromes to the typical trajectory of development we can gain insights into the functional effects and consequences of some genes. A fourth approach involves animal studies to examine particular classes of genes that are expressed very rapidly as a result of learning or developmental plasticity. Finally, we review work on a particular gene, FOX-P2, that illustrates some of the general points made earlier in the chapter.

Developmental Cognitive Neuroscience (Third Edition) Mark H. Johnson with Michelle de Haan
© 2011 Mark H. Johnson

3.1   The History of the Gene

In Chapter 1 we discussed different viewpoints on development, including the 17th-century debate between the "vitalists" and the "preformationists." During the 19th and 20th centuries this debate continued, centered on efforts to understand the nature of inheritance. While it was clear that some physical traits of mammals, insects, and plants are passed from one generation to the next, the mechanisms and substance involved in this inheritance process remained obscure. We will see that the concept of a gene as first hypothesized by Johannsen in 1911 is not the same as the gene described by Crick and Watson in 1953, and the Crick and Watson notion of a gene is different from that understood by developmental geneticists today.

The first significant step to localizing the material of inheritance was to identify it as being carried within cells, something that was already recognized by embryologists by the latter half of the 19th century. The next question was whether it was the nucleus of the cell, or the surrounding cytoplasm, that controlled the material responsible for inheritance. In a flurry of exciting research around 1900, several scientists rediscovered the earlier work of Gregor Mendel in which he proposed certain "rules of inheritance" based on his work breeding plants, and they identified the nucleus of the cell as the site of the heritable material. Shortly after, Wilhelm Johannsen (1911) coined the terms *gene*, *genotype* (the sum total of all genes), and *phenotype* (the end product or result of gene expression). Over the next forty years these ideas were developed by scientists such as T.H. Morgan who pioneered the use of the fruit fly, Drosophila, for genetic studies. The short breeding cycle of this fly meant that many new experiments could be conducted in a short period of time, resulting in a dramatic increase in our understanding of genetics.

FURTHER READING   Fox Keller (2002); Stiles (2008).

In the early 1950s the search was on to discover which chemical found in the nucleus was responsible for inheritance. Two scientists in London, Rosalind Franklin and Maurice Wilkins, had been using a technique known as "X-ray defraction" to reveal the structure of a molecule called DNA (deoxyribonucleic acid). In 1953 James Watson and Francis Crick based nearby in Cambridge used these data to propose the basic "double helix" structure of DNA that allows it to encode information and pass it on to the next generation. Once the chemical structure of DNA was revealed it turned out to provide an obvious answer to the question of how information was coded and transmitted. That is, the problem of how to translate information to make the proteins that then go on to form complex biological structures such as the brain.

3.2   Principles of Gene Function

The beautiful structure of DNA, a right-handed spiral double helix, is importantly related to its function of retaining and transmitting information in at least two ways (see Figure 3.1). First, DNA involves two nucleotide (molecular unit) strands that are usually intertwined, but that can be unraveled when the genetic information needs to be copied during the divisions of cells to make bodies and brains. Second, each of the strands contains a "code" instantiated as differing sequences of four nucleotide bases (chemical units composed of a sugar-phosphate group and a base compound attached; they are called adenine, guanine, thymine, and cytosine). These nucleotide bases act like two sides of a zip that can be unzipped and a matching other half copied off with the complementary bonding of adenine and thymine, and of guanine and cytosine (see Figure 3.1). Genes are the sequences of nucleotides within a strand of DNA, with the sequences of base compounds providing the basis for gene expression.

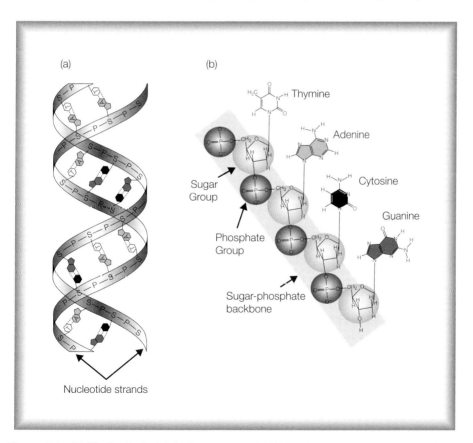

Figure 3.1   (a) The basic double helix structure of DNA in which two nucleotide strands coil around each other. (b) Detail showing how the two strands are linked by chemical bonds between the bases of neucleotides. The four bases are thymine, adenine, cystosine, and guanine.

The next question to be addressed is how strands of DNA make the basic chemical building blocks of biological tissue, proteins. Surprisingly, it was observed that the proteins are constructed relatively far away within the cell from the actual DNA itself. This means that there has to be some intermediary molecule that transfers the information from the DNA to the cellular machinery for making different proteins. The messenger was discovered to be RNA (ribonucleic acid), a closely related molecule to DNA but with a few minor, but critical, differences.

By the early 1960s the identification of DNA and its mechanisms of expression led to the textbook view that all of the genetic information necessary for the development and functioning of an organism was contained in the sequence of nucleotides within the DNA. The view that genes coded directly for the proteins that then compose our bodies (and brains) seemed well established. However, with further research it rapidly became evident that this view was a gross simplification, and that in reality gene expression is a highly dynamic and context-sensitive phenomenon.

The first place where the simple mapping between genes and proteins breaks down is in the complex steps (involving RNA) between the original unraveling and "reading" of a strand of DNA and the actual construction of a protein. Far from the view that one gene codes for one protein, it turns out that the same sequence of DNA can in many cases generate dozens of different specific proteins. A second consideration is that large segments of DNA (as much as 95%) do not appear to code for proteins. For this reason these segments have often been referred to as "junk" DNA, but whether these regions are just evolutionary hangovers or have other currently unknown functions remains unknown. A third caveat to the traditional view is that many genes code for regulatory, rather than structural, proteins. That is, they code for proteins that modulate the expression of other genes, creating complex cascades of interaction that can vary in different locations of the embryo or adult body. These days, genes are also said to be "pleiotropic" that is, one gene can play multiple different roles at different times of development and in different areas of the developing animal or plant. For example, while around 75% of all of the genes in the human genome are expressed in the brain at some point during development, very few, if any, of these genes are expressed only in the brain. Finally, and perhaps most surprisingly, it has recently become evident that in addition to the DNA inherited at conception there are other differences in the cellular machinery that interact with and influence the expression of genes. This machinery is essential to the functioning of the DNA, which is inert without its presence. Thus, inherited cellular factors other than DNA can influence the genes that get expressed during child development. In summary, over recent decades it has become clear that while the complex processes associated with gene expression contribute to the emergence of physical and behavioral traits, the relationship between a specific gene and those traits is often very indirect and complex.

FURTHER READING Plomin, DeFries, McClearn, & McGuffin (2008).

Recently, exciting examples are appearing relating to how the life-long expression of genes in individual animals can be regulated by their early environment. For example, a series of elegant studies by Meaney and colleagues has demonstrated that maternal behavior toward newborn rats regulates the expression of genes involved in the same rats' responses to stress later in life (see Weaver et al., 2004; Zhang & Meaney, 2010). Newborn rats whose mother frequently licks and grooms them during the first week grow up to be less fearful, and show less physiological stress reactions, than newborn rats whose mother is less attentive. Cross-fostering studies (with newborns raised by rats other than their biological mother) show that this lifelong effect on the young rats is induced by the particular mother's behavior and is not directly genetically inherited. In a series of detailed experiments it has been established that the maternal licking and grooming of the newborn sets in motion a series of biochemical reactions that regulates the activity of the mechanisms associated with the expression of particular genes (called the "epigenome"). Thus, early sensory experiences can have life-long effects through permanent changes in the timing and amount of different proteins expressed by the genes. Work such as this has led to the new emerging field of "epigenetics" that will undoubtedly have some exciting implications for developmental cognitive neuroscience in the future.

FURTHER READING Weaver et al. (2004).

3.3   Genetics and Developmental Cognitive Neuroscience

From the perspective of developmental cognitive neuroscience, one of our main challenges for the future is to understand the role of brain function and development in the mapping from genotype to behavioral phenotype (see Pennington 2001, 2002). Broadly speaking, there are at least four different strategies that are currently being taken to understand this mapping.

The first of these directions is to consider cases in which the epigenetic pathway from gene to brain to behavior may be reduced in length and/or complexity. The general strategy here is to study aspects of the brain that are only a few chemical steps away from the direct products of gene expression. Building an organized network of neurons involves a highly complex orchestration of many different genes. However, simple chemicals that modulate neural activity and development, such as neuro-transmitters (see Chapter 4), are much closer to the basic chemical building blocks that genes directly produce (proteins and monoamines). A large variety of simple molecules play important roles in brain development and function and these are the subject of much research in developmental neuroscience (see Stanwood & Levitt, 2008, for a review). However, we now also have a few examples related to human cognitive development.

In Chapter 10 we will discuss a genetic disorder called phenylketonuria (PKU; see Table 2.1 in Chapter 2). PKU is a genetic disorder that leads to low levels of an enzyme (protein molecules that enhance other chemical reactions) that normally helps to convert one amino acid (a building block of proteins) into another one (tyrosine) that is critical for the functioning of an important neurotransmitter in the brain called dopamine (see Chapter 4). Further complications in development then arise from the excess of the first amino acid and a relative lack of the second. These complications include reduced levels of dopamine in the prefrontal cortex (see Chapter 4) that, in turn, has specific effects on cognitive development. While studying cases such as this will inform our understanding of the pathways from gene to brain to behavior, we should note that even the relation between genes and neurotransmitters is complex. For example, it is already known that at least 19 different genes can influence one important brain transmitter system (GABA; Huang, Di Cristo, & Ango, 2007).

A second approach to understanding the epigenetic pathway to emerging brain function is to study the naturally occurring individual differences among individuals in genetic, brain function, and behavioral measures. The genetic contribution to these differences between individuals comes not from a genetic defect, but from slightly different forms of the same gene (called alleles). There are often several different variations in the exact coding sequences of genes. Since humans have two copies of every gene, these variations can either be the same for both copies (homozygous) or different (heterozygous). Alleles can also be found in the non-coding (junk) DNA mentioned earlier. The field of "Behavior(al) Genetics" is partly based on associations between individual differences in alleles and variations in behavior or personality. This approach is now merging with developmental cognitive neuroscience as investigators begin to try to correlate allelic variation with variation in brain functions during development. It is assumed that by directly relating genetic variation to individual brain differences we can avoid the potential complicating factor of the different ways in which brain function relates to cognition, and thence to actual behavior. In this way it is hoped that even stronger correlations will be observed than those between genes and measures of behavior (Fan, Fossella, Sommer, Wu, & Posner, 2003). In later chapters, we will provide an overview of some initial attempts to use this individual differences genetic approach in developmental studies with infants and children.

FURTHER READING Plomin et al. (2008).

The third approach to bringing genetics into developmental cognitive neuroscience involves the study of human syndromes and developmental disorders such as those briefly described in the last chapter. While some syndromes, such as autism, have a complex genetic cause involving many genes each having only a small effect, there are other syndromes in which the genetic basis is better defined. One such syndrome is Fragile-X that involves an allele of the FMR1 gene on the X chromosome (a singular piece of DNA). Simply put, this gene normally involves between 6 and 55 repeats of the genetic coding sequence. However, in affected families the number of repeats can increase between generations until the point where a baby is born with more than 230 repeats in FMR1. At this point the structure becomes unstable and ceases to function, giving Fragile-X syndrome its name. This impairment of the functioning of the gene results in a lack of production of a particular protein (FMR1 protein).

Since males only have one X-chromosome, compared to the two possessed by females, Fragile-X has clearer and more devastating effects in men. In addition to a variety of physical symptoms like an elongated face and flat feet, the syndrome as manifest in males includes some autistic-like symptoms, such as hand flapping and atypical social development, with some Fragile-X individuals meeting the diagnostic criteria for autism. One of the knock-on consequences of the lack of the FMR1 protein is a disturbance in the neurotransmitter called glutamate (see Chapter 4). Current research is attempting to relate the functioning of this neurotransmitter in the brain to some of the cognitive and behavioral differences observed. Although much research still needs to be done, Fragile-X is perhaps currently the best understood example of the complex pathway from genetic abnormality to cognition (see Figure 3.2). Nevertheless, although Fragile-X involves only one gene, the effects of the defect are widespread and the syndrome involves many different aspects of cognition and behavior.

FURTHER READING   Cornish & Wilding (2010).

A variant of this general approach is to start with syndromes known to have uneven cognitive profiles, before working "backwards" to discover their genetic basis. As mentioned earlier, examples of this approach include the search for a genetic basis for autism and for dyslexia. While these approaches have been somewhat successful, it may be that a closer two-way interaction between geneticists and psychologists that focuses on rare cases will be more successful. For example, as we heard in the last chapter Williams syndrome (WS) results from a missing segment of 23 to 28 genes on one chromosome. People with this so-called "microdeletion" normally show the full Williams syndrome physical and cognitive phenotype, including relative strengths in the domains of language and face recognition and serious impairments in visuo-spatial construction abilities and number (Chapters 2, 6 and 7). Recent research has involved the investigation of individual cases in which not all of the Williams syndrome genes are deleted: so-called "partial deletion" patients. Some of these cases have the full Williams syndrome phenotype, some show only a few of the atypicalities, and others show none. By studying in detail the profile of cognitive abilities of such rare cases in detail, a closer understanding of the combinations of genes that contribute to a behavioral phenotype can be reached (Karmiloff-Smith et al., 2003).

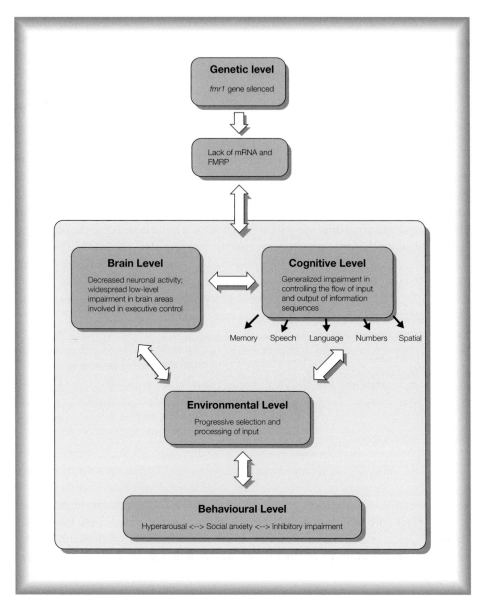

Figure 3.2   An illustration of the complex causal pathway between a genetic level defect and its consequences for behaviour from Fragile-X syndrome.

FURTHER READING   Karmiloff-Smith (2008); Welsh, DeRoche, & Gilliam (2008).

A fourth approach to beginning to understand the complex role of genes in functional brain development is to engineer animal models, most commonly mice, in which particular genes are knocked out. With regard to these "knockout" mouse models (see Chapter 2) it is important to note that it is not sufficient for understanding the role of a gene(s) in a developmental sequence to demonstrate that knocking out the gene in question eliminates a particular behavior in later life. In these experimental cases, and in human developmental disorders with an identifiable genetic abnormality, we may say that the gene defect *causes* the deficit. However, this does not allow us to infer that the gene codes for the aspect of behavior which is disrupted, or that this aspect of behavior is the "function" of the gene, for the reasons discussed above.

Finally, it is possible that the genes that play a role in brain plasticity and transmission in synapses may be most amenable to study of their computational consequences. In these cases we can study changes in the expression of genes that take place even in adult animals. One such example is the so-called "Immediate Early" gene. This special class of genes is involved in rapid plastic changes in the brain that occur during both development and in adult learning. In addition to molecular biological studies of these types of genes, in the future one approach to understanding the contribution of the expression of the genes may be in detailed cellular neural network modeling in which the effects of gene expression can be simulated, and then compared to real neurobiological systems.

3.4 The FOXP2 Gene

One recent example of a gene that has been related to cognition and development is the FOXP2 gene (officially known as Forkhead Box P2). This is perhaps the first "celebrity" gene as it has been the target of many studies, theoretical discussions, and media reports (see also Chapter 9). The story of research on FOXP2 illustrates several of the points made above, and particularly the need to beware of claims that genes "code for" specific aspects of behavior or cognition. The interest of psychologists in the FOXP2 gene began with the discovery of an unfortunate family (the KE family) in which three generations of family history indicated that about half of its members had an inherited language impairment that was initially suggested to be specific to certain aspects of grammar. When the gene associated with this deficit in the family was discovered to be FOXP2 (Lai, Fisher, Hurst, Vargha-Khadem, & Monaco, 2001), popular science writers and some of the media hailed the discovery of "the gene (that codes) for grammar".

As you will read in Chapter 9, research over the past decade has shown these initial claims to be unfounded for several reasons. First, it quickly became evident that the deficits in the affected family members are much broader than grammar alone, and includes coordinating complex mouth movements, timing of rhythmic motor movements, various aspects of language outside grammar, and low general intelligence (Vargha-Khadem, Watkins, Alcock, Fletcher, & Passingham, 1995). A second reason for questioning the specificity of FOXP2 is that it is also found in many other species that obviously do not possess human language skills, such as mice and birds. Nevertheless, knockout mice lacking the FOXP2 function do have significantly reduced vocalizations, and expression of the gene is closely associated with vocal learning in song birds. When this evidence is taken together with functional imaging studies of affected members of the KE family that show underactivation of language areas of the brain during verb generation and repetition tasks (Liégeois et al., 2003), the overall findings suggest that FOXP2 is one of the genes important for learning to control rapid movement sequences. A final reason for questioning the specificity of the function of FOXP2 in relation to language is that it is highly conserved in evolution. In addition to being found in mice and birds, the gene can also be found in reptiles. Like all genes, FOXP2 shows minute changes in the amino acids that compose it over evolutionary time. While some of these small changes could potentially affect the functioning of the gene, it seems more likely that any change in the function of the gene arises from it being active at different points in development or in different places in the developing brain (Carroll, 2005).

FURTHER READING   Marcus and Fisher (2003); Karmiloff-Smith (2008).

Given that FOXP2 appears to be involved in the brain plasticity associated with vocal learning, what exactly is its role? While this is the subject of much current research, it is important to note that FOXP2 is one of a family of so-called "transcription factors." In other words, its molecular function is to transcribe other parts of the DNA into the RNA that makes proteins. This makes the gene well placed to potentially orchestrate the action of a number of other genes. As we will discover in Chapter 9 it is very likely that human language involves many different genes, each of which has only a small effect on the overall outcome. Similarly, FOXP2 has multiple roles in different organs that may differ somewhat between species, and also change with developmental time within the same species.

The story of FOXP2 illustrates some of the complexities and challenges that face the researcher interested in integrating genetics into developmental cognitive neuroscience. Since genes are pleiotropic (genes expressed in the brain are nearly always also expressed in other parts of the body) developmental disorders of genetic origin will inevitably be systemic. For example, in Williams syndrome heart defects are most commonly the cause of diagnosis, and in several other syndromes immune system problems have been reported. Thus, while we should not expect to find simple and direct mappings between particular genes and specific aspects of behavior, cognition, or brain function, there is no doubt that the powerful new methods for analyzing segments of the epigenetic pathway from gene to behavior will open new doors of discovery about the emergence of human brain functions.

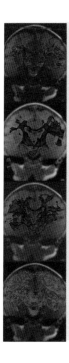

Key Issues for Discussion

- How is the study of the role of genes in functional brain development limited by the methods that we currently have available?
- Compare and contrast different strategies for relating genes to cognition.
- Can genetic evidence be useful for ascertaining the role of experience in a developmental transition in cognition or behavior?
- Is it useful to associate particular genes with the emergence of specific cognitive functions?

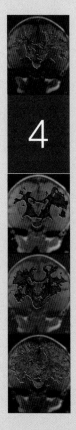

4 Building a Brain

This chapter describes several aspects of the pre- and postnatal development of the brain, with specific reference to humans. We begin with a basic overview of primate brain anatomy, with specific emphasis on perhaps the most important structure of the brain for understanding cognitive development, the cerebral neocortex. We then begin our survey of development by outlining some of the key stages of prenatal brain growth, focusing on the birth, migration, and differentiation of cells that subsequently compose particular brain structures. The most obvious manifestation of postnatal development of the human brain is its four-fold increase in volume between birth and the teenage years. We trace the factors that give rise to this dramatic change. We will discover that the change is mainly due to increases in nerve fiber bundles and myelination, rather than the addition of new neurons. A surprising aspect of brain development is that some measures of structural and neurophysiological brain development, such as the density of synaptic contacts, show a characteristic "rise and fall" during postnatal life. The following section addresses the question of the extent to which the differentiation of the neocortex into areas or regions is prespecified. The "protomap" hypothesis states that the areal differentiation of the cortex is determined by intrinsic molecular markers or prespecification of the proliferative zone. In contrast, the "protocortex" hypothesis suggests that an initially undifferentiated protocortex is divided up largely as a result of input through projections from the thalamus and is activity-dependent. A review of currently available evidence supports a middle-ground view in which large-scale regions are prespecified, while small-scale functional areas require activity-dependent processes. This implies that cortical networks impose architectural constraints on the representations that emerge within them, but there are no innate representations. Further evidence in support of this conclusion comes from a variety of studies on cortical plasticity in newborn rodents. In some of these studies sensory inputs to cortical areas are diverted to other regions, or pieces of cortex are transplanted from one region to another. In both of these cases cortical tissue acquires representations according to the nature of the input, rather than its developmental origins. With some caveats, I suggest that similar conclusions can be drawn about primate cortical development and plasticity. The next section focuses on a clear area of difference between human cortical development and that of other primates: the very extended period of postnatal development. This greatly extended period reveals two differential aspects of cortical development not as clearly evident in other primates: an inside-out pattern of development of layers, and differences in the timing of development across regions. These differential aspects of human cortical development will provide the basis for associations between brain and cognitive development described in later chapters. The chapter concludes with discussion of the postnatal development of some subcortical structures, and with a brief review of our knowledge of the development of neurotransmitters and modulators. The developmental levels of several neurotransmitters mirror aspects of the differential structural development of cortex.

Developmental Cognitive Neuroscience (Third Edition) Mark H. Johnson with Michelle de Haan
© 2011 Mark H. Johnson

4.1   An Overview of Primate Brain Anatomy

This book is written with the assumption that the reader has some basic introductory knowledge of the brain. Nevertheless, in order to ensure sufficient knowledge for the reader to follow this and later chapters we need to recap on some basic facts about the brains of primates, including ourselves. The brains of all mammals follow a basic vertebrate brain plan that is found even in species such as salamanders, frogs, and birds. The major difference between these species and higher primates is in the dramatic expansion of the overlying cerebral cortex, together with associated structures such as the basal ganglia. Human brain development follows closely the sequence of events observed in other primates, albeit on a slower schedule (something we will return to later in this chapter).

The neocortex of all mammals, including humans, is basically a thin (about 3–4 mm) flat sheet. Although complex, its general layered structure is relatively constant throughout its extent (see Figure 4.1). The rapid expansion in the overall size of the cortex during evolution has resulted in it becoming increasingly intricately folded with various indentations (sulci) and lobes (gyri). For example, the area of the cortex in the cat is about 100 cm^2, whereas that of the human is about 2,400 cm^2. This suggests that the extra cortex possessed by primates, and especially humans, is related to the higher cognitive functions they possess. However, the basic relations between principal structures of the brain remain similar from mouse to human.

Most of the sensory inputs to the cortex pass through a structure known as the thalamus. Each type of sensory input has its own particular nuclei within this region. For example, the lateral geniculate nucleus (LGN) carries visual input to the cortex, while the medial geniculate nucleus (MGN) carries information from the auditory modality. Because of the crucial role of the thalamus in mediating inputs to the cortex, some have hypothesized that it also plays a crucial role in cortical development—an idea that will be discussed at greater length later. The flow of information between thalamus and cortex is not unidirectional, however, since most of the projections from lower regions into the cortex are matched by projections from the cortex back down. Some output projections from the cortex pass to regions that are believed to be involved in motor control, such as the basal ganglia and the cerebellum. However, most of the projections from the cortex to other brain regions terminate in roughly the same regions from which projections arrived (such as the thalamus). In other words, the flow of information to and from the cortex is largely bidirectional. For this reason, it is important not to confuse the terms "input" and "output" with "sensory" and "motor." All sensory and motor systems make extensive use of both input and output fibers, with information passing rapidly in both directions along collateral pathways.

The brain has two general types of cells: neurons and glial cells. Glial cells are more common than neurons, but are generally assumed to play no direct role in

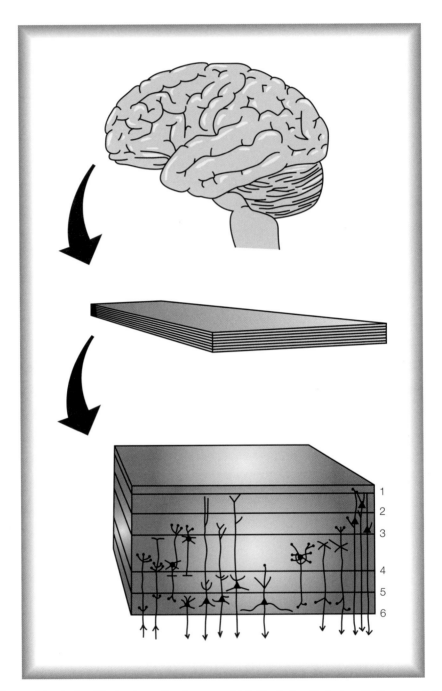

Figure 4.1 A simplified schematic diagram which illustrates that, despite its convoluted surface appearance (top), the cerebral cortex is a thin sheet (middle) composed of six layers (bottom). The convolutions in the cortex arise from a combination of growth patterns and the restricted space inside the skull. In general, differences between mammals involve the total area of the cortical sheet, and not its layered structure. Each of the layers possesses certain neuron types and characteristic input and projection patterns (see text).

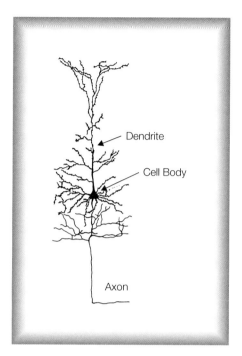

Figure 4.2 A typical cortical pyramidal cell. The apical dendrite is the long process that extends to the upper layers, and may allow the cell to be influenced by other neurons. An axon projects to subcortical regions.

computation. However, as we shall see later they play a very important role in the development of the cortex. The computational unit of the brain has long been thought to be the neuron (Shepherd, 1972). Neurons come in many shapes, sizes, and types, each of which presumably reflects their particular computational function. There appear to be at least 25 different neuronal types within the cortex, although several of these types are relatively rare, and some are restricted to particular layers. About 80% of neurons found in the cortex are *pyramidal cells*, so called because of the distinctive pyramid shape of the cell body produced by the very large apical dendrite (input process), which generally runs tangential to the surface of the cortex (Figure 4.2). These are the neurons whose long axons (output processes) are so often found in the fibers feeding into other cortical and subcortical regions. While pyramidal cells are found in many of the layers of the cortex (generally they are larger in the lower layers and smaller in the upper layers), their apical dendrites often reach into its most superficial layer, layer 1 (see below). This long apical dendrite allows the cell to be influenced by large numbers of cells from other (more superficial) layers and regions. This may be computationally important if the pyramidal cell is a very stable and inflexible class of cell whose output is modulated by groups of more plastic and flexible inhibitory regulatory neurons. Figure 4.1 also shows a schematic section through an area of primate cortex cut at right angles to the surface of the cortex, revealing the layered structure. I will refer to this as the *laminar* structure of the cortex.

As just noted, each of the laminae has particular cell types within it, and each layer has typical patterns of inputs and outputs.

Most areas of the neocortex (in all mammals) are made up of six layers. The basic characteristics that define each layer appear to hold in most regions of the cortical sheet. Layer 1 has few cell bodies. It is made up primarily of long white fibers running along the horizontal surface, linking one area of cortex to others some distance away. Layers 2 and 3 also contain horizontal connections, often projecting forward from small pyramidal cells to neighboring areas of cortex. Layer 4 is the layer where most of the input fibers terminate and it contains a high proportion of spiny stellate (star-shaped) cells on which these projections terminate. Layers 5 and 6 have the major outputs to subcortical regions of the brain. These layers contain a particularly high proportion of large pyramidal cells, with long descending axons. There are also many neurons involved in intrinsic cortical circuits.

Although this basic laminar structure holds throughout most of the neocortex, there are some regional variations. For example, the input layer (layer 4) is particularly thick and well developed in the sensory cortex. Indeed, in the visual system, it is possible to distinguish at least four "sublayers" within layer 4. Conversely, layer 5 (one of the output layers) is particularly well developed in the motor cortex, presumably due to its importance in sending output signals from the cortex. It is also clear that different parts of the cortex have different projection patterns to other parts of the cortex. While there may only be a small number of these characteristic projection patterns from one region of the cortex to another, there is no single pattern that can be said to be characteristic of all cortical regions. Hence this is another dimension of variation that can contribute to regional specialization within the cortex. Further dimensions could include the presence of particular neurotransmitters, and the relative contribution of excitatory versus inhibitory neurotransmitters. Finally, as we will see later, regions may vary in the timing of key developmental events, such as the postnatal reduction in the number of synapses (Huttenlocher, 1990).

4.2   Prenatal Brain Development

The sequence of events during the prenatal development of the human brain closely resembles that of many other vertebrates. Shortly after conception a fertilized cell undergoes a rapid process of cell division, resulting in a cluster of proliferating cells (called the blastocyst) that somewhat resembles a bunch of grapes. Within a few days, the blastocyst differentiates into a three-layered structure (the embryonic disk). Each of these layers will further differentiate into a major organ system. The endoderm (inner layer) turns into the set of internal organs (digestive, respiratory, etc.), the mesoderm (middle layer) turns into the skeletal and muscular structures, and the ectoderm (outer layer) gives rise to the skin surface and the nervous system (including the perceptual organs).

The nervous system itself begins with a process known as *neurulation*. A portion of the ectoderm begins to fold in on itself to form a hollow cylinder called the *neural tube*. The neural tube differentiates along three dimensions: length, circumference, and radius. The length dimension gives rise to the major subdivisions of the central nervous system, with the forebrain and midbrain arising at one end and the spinal cord at the other. The end which will become the spinal cord differentiates into a series of repeated units or segments, while the front end of the neural tube organizes differently with a series of bulges and convolutions forming (see Figure 4.3). By

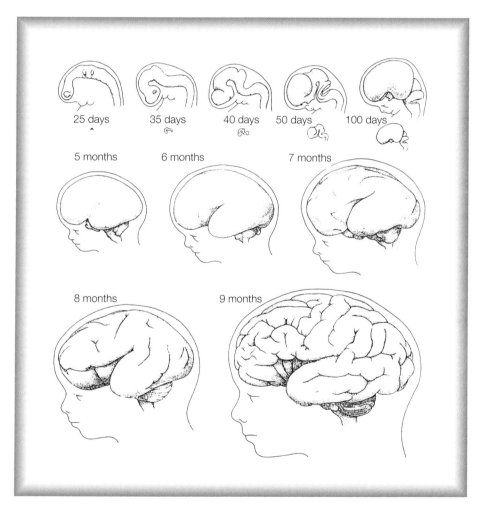

25 days   35 days   40 days   50 days   100 days

5 months   6 months   7 months

8 months   9 months

Figure 4.3 A sequence of drawings of the embryonic and fetal development of the human brain. The drawings of brains beneath 25–100 days are the same images but drawn to the same scale as those in the row below. The forebrain, midbrain, and hindbrain originate as swellings at the head end of the neural tube. In primates, the convoluted cortex grows to cover the midbrain, hindbrain, and parts of the cerebellum. Prior to birth, neurons are generated in the developing brain at a rate of more than 250,000 per minute.

around 5 weeks after conception these bulges can be identified as protoforms for major components of the mammalian brain. Proceeding from front to back: the first bulge gives rise to the cortex (telencephalon), the second gives rise to the thalamus and hypothalamus (diencephalon), the third turns into the midbrain (mesencephalon), and others to the cerebellum (metencephalon), and to the medulla (myelencephalon).

The circumferential dimension (tangential to the surface) in the neural tube is critical, because the distinction between sensory and motor systems develops along this dimension: dorsal (top-side) corresponds roughly to the sensory cortex, ventral (bottom-side) corresponds to the motor cortex, with the various association cortices and "higher" sensory and motor cortices aligned somewhere in between. Within the brain stem and the spinal cord, the corresponding alar (dorsal) and basal (ventral) plates play a major role in the organization of nerve pathways into the rest of the body.

Differentiation along the radial dimension gives rise to the complex layering patterns and cell types found in the adult brain. Across the radial dimension of the neural tube the bulges grow larger and become further differentiated. Within these bulges cells *proliferate* (are born), *migrate* (travel), and *differentiate* (change form) into particular types. The vast majority of the cells that will compose the brain are born in the so-called *proliferative zones*. These zones are close to the hollow portion of the neural tube (which subsequently become the ventricles of the brain). The first of these proliferation sites, the *ventricular zone*, may be phylogenetically older (Nowakowski, 1987). The second, the *subventricular zone*, only contributes significantly to phylogenetically recent brain structures such as the neocortex (i.e. "new" cortex). These two zones yield separate glial (support and supply cells) and neuron cell lines and give rise to different forms of migration. But first we will consider how young neurons are formed within these zones.

FURTHER READING   Nowakowski & Hayes (2002); Sanes, Reh, & Harris (2006); White & Hilgetag (2008).

Neurons and glial cells are produced by division of proliferating cells within the proliferative zones to produce clones (a clone is a group of cells which are produced by division of a single precursor cell—such a precursor cell is said to give rise to a lineage). *Neuroblasts* produce neurons, and *glioblasts* produce glial cells. Each of the neuroblasts gives rise to a definite and limited number of neurons, a point to which I will return later. In at least some cases particular neuroblasts also give rise to particular types of cell. For example, less than a dozen proliferating cells produce all the Purkinje cells of the cerebellar cortex, with each producing about 10,000 cells (Nowakowski, 1987).

After young neurons are born, they have to travel or *migrate* from the proliferative zones to the particular region where they will be employed in the mature brain. There are two forms of migration observed during brain development. The first, and more common, is *passive cell displacement*. This occurs when cells that have been generated are simply pushed further away from the proliferative zones by more recently born cells. This form of migration gives rise to an "outside-in" pattern. That is, the oldest cells are pushed toward the surface of the brain, while the most recently produced cells remain closer to their place of birth. Passive migration gives rise to brain structures such as the thalamus, the dentate gyrus of the hippocampus, and many regions of the brain stem. The second form of migration is more active and involves the young cell moving past previously generated cells to create an "inside-out" pattern. This pattern is found in the cerebral cortex and in some subcortical areas that have a laminar structure (divided into parallel layers).

It is important to emphasize that prenatal brain development is not a passive process involving the unfolding of genetic instructions. Rather, from an early stage interactions between cells are critical, including the transmission of electrical signals between neurons. In one example, patterns of spontaneous firing of cells in the eyes (before they have opened in development) transmit signals that appear to specify the layered structure of the lateral geniculate nucleus (see O'Leary & Nakagawa, 2002; Shatz, 2002). Thus, waves of firing neurons intrinsic to the developing organism may play an important role in specifying aspects of brain structure before sensory inputs from the external world have any effect.

Further Reading   Shatz (2002).

4.3   Postnatal Brain Development

As mentioned earlier, there is a dramatic increase in the total volume of the brain from birth to teenage years (see Figure 4.4). What factors contribute to this developmental change? Using different techniques, this question can be examined at different levels of detail from microscopic (and electron microscope) changes in neurons and synapses, to the larger scale of divisions of the brain into gray (neurons and their local connections) and white matter (myelinated fiber bundles). Beginning at the microscopic scale, a number of measures of brain anatomy and function show a characteristic "rise and fall" developmental pattern during postnatal life. While the progressive and regressive processes should not be viewed as distinct stages, for the purposes of exposition I will discuss them in sequence.

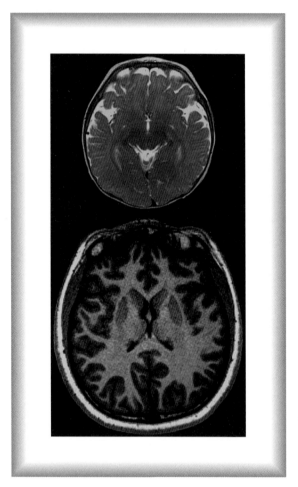

Figure 4.4   MRI structural scans of a 4-month-old infant (top) and a 12-year-old adolescent (below).

At first consideration, people often assume that the postnatal increase in the size of the brain is due to the addition of new neurons. However, this is not the case. The formation of neurons and their migration to appropriate brain regions takes place almost entirely within the period of prenatal development in the human. Although there may be some small-scale addition of neurons in the hippocampus and elsewhere (see later), the vast majority of neurons are present by around the seventh month of gestation (Rakic, 1995). In contrast to the lack of new nerve cell bodies, there is, however, a dramatic postnatal growth of synapses, dendrites, and fiber bundles. Further, nerve fibers become covered in a fatty covering (myelination) that adds further to the bulk of the brain.

Perhaps the most obvious manifestation of postnatal neural development as viewed through the standard microscope is the increase in size and complexity of the dendritic tree of most neurons. An example of the dramatic increase in dendritic tree extent during human postnatal development is shown in Figure 4.5. While the extent and reach of a cell's dendritic arbor may increase dramatically, it also often becomes more specific and specialized. Less apparent through standard microscopes, but more evident with electron microscopy, is a corresponding increase in measures of the density of synaptic contacts between cells.

Huttenlocher and colleagues have reported a steady increase in the density of synapses in several regions of the human cerebral cortex (Huttenlocher, 1990, 1994; Huttenlocher, de Courten, Garey, & Van der Loos, 1982). While an increase in synapses (synaptogenesis) begins around the time of birth in humans for all cortical areas studied to date, the most rapid bursts of increase, and the final peak density, occur at different ages in different areas. In the visual cortex there is a rapid burst at 3 to 4 months, and the maximum density of around 150% of adult level is reached between 4 and 12 months. A similar time course is observed in the primary auditory cortex (Heschl's gyrus). In contrast, while synaptogenesis starts at the same time in a region of the prefrontal cortex, density increases much more slowly and does not reach its peak until after the first year. (It should be noted at this point that there are a variety of possible measures of synaptic density—per cell, per unit dendrite, per unit brain tissue, etc. Careful selection of measures is required so that factors such as increases in dendritic length do not unduly influence the results. Huttenlocher, 1990, discusses some of these issues of appropriate measurement.)

FURTHER READING   Bourgeois (2001); Huttenlocher (2002); Kostović, Judaš, & Petanjek (2008).

Another additive process is myelination. Myelination refers to an increase in the fatty sheath that surrounds neuronal pathways, a process that increases the efficiency of information transmission (see Figure 4.6). In the central nervous system, sensory areas tend to myelinate earlier than motor areas. Cortical association areas are known to myelinate last, and continue the process into the second decade of life (see later). Because myelination continues for many years after birth, there has been a great deal of speculation about its role in behavioral development (Parmelee & Sigman, 1983; Volpe, 1987; Yakovlev & Lecours, 1967). However, while myelination greatly increases the speed of transmission of impulses (by as much as 100 times) it is also important to remember that under-myelinated connections in the young human brain are still capable of transmitting signals and that some connections in the adult brain never myelinate.

FURTHER READING   Klingberg (2008).

Another technique that has been used to study postnatal development is positron emission tomography (PET). A study of human infants with this technique (Chugani,

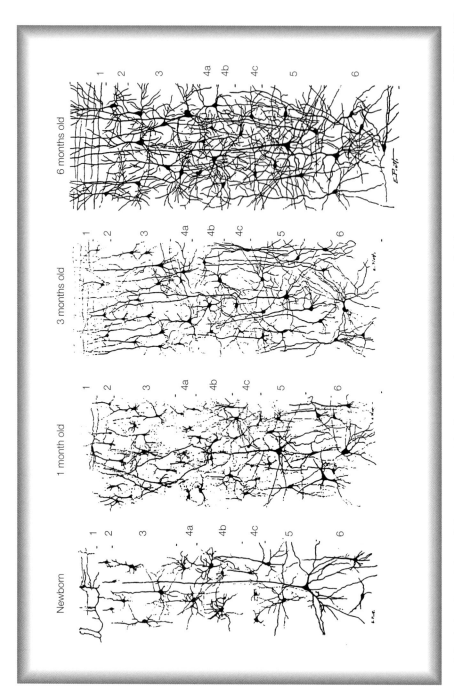

Figure 4.5 A drawing of the cellular structure of the human visual cortex based on Golgi stain preparations from Conel (1939–1967).

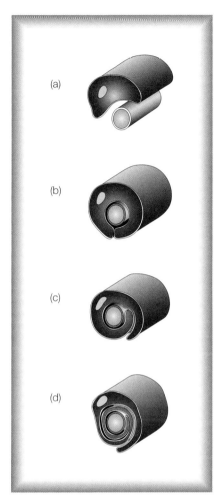

Figure 4.6 The sequence of axon myelination by an oligodendrocyte. A to D shows the sequence of initial contact, then engulfing and surrounding the axon, followed by spiraling around the axon to form the final myelin sheath.

Phelps, & Mazziotta, 2002) reported a sharp rise in overall resting brain metabolism (the uptake of glucose from the blood is essential for cell functioning) after the first year of life, with a peak approximately 150% above adult levels achieved somewhere around 4–5 years of age for some cortical areas. While this peak occurred somewhat later than that in synaptic density, an adult-like *distribution* of resting activity within and across brain regions was observed by the end of the first year. This result has been confirmed more recently in a functional MRI study of brain resting-state networks in infants during sleep (Fransson et al., 2007). Resting-state networks are the spontaneous and intrinsic brain activities that occur in the absence of any overt task, somewhat like the "idle" state of a car engine. Fransson and colleagues observed several resting-state networks that encompassed cortical regions such as the primary visual cortex, bilateral sensory motor areas, bilateral auditory cortex, parietal cortex, and medial and dorsolateral prefrontal cortex (see Figure 4.7 in the color plate section). Although these networks differed from those observed in adults, it suggests that many regions of the infant cortex can be activated in a somewhat coordinated manner.

FURTHER READING   Chugani et al. (2002).

We now turn to regressive events during human postnatal brain development. Such events are commonly observed by those studying the development of nerve cells and their connections in the brains of many animals (for reviews see Sanes et al., 2006). That processes of selective loss have a significant influence on postnatal primate brain development is evident from a number of quantitative measures. For example, in the PET study just mentioned the authors found that the absolute rates of glucose metabolism rise postnatally until they exceed adult levels, before reducing to adult levels after about 9 years of age for most cortical regions.

Consistent with these PET findings, Huttenlocher (1990, 1994) reports quantitative neuroanatomical evidence from several regions of the human cortex that following the increase in density of synapses described above there is then a period of synaptic loss. Like the timing of bursts of synaptogenesis, and the subsequent peaks of density, the timing of the reduction in synaptic density varies between cortical regions. For example, synaptic density in the visual cortex returns to adult levels between 2 and 4 years, while the same point is not reached until between 10 and 20 years of age for regions of the prefrontal cortex. Figure 4.8 in the color plate section illustrates some of these timing differences.

Huttenlocher (1990, 1994) suggests that this initial overproduction of synapses may have an important role in the apparent plasticity of the young brain, a matter that will be discussed in more detail later. There is no strong evidence for this pattern of rise and fall either for the density of dendrites or for the number of neurons themselves in humans or other primates. However, in rodents and other vertebrates cell loss may be more significant.

FURTHER READING   Greenough et al. (2002).

One explanation for the decrease in glucose uptake observed in the PET studies is that it reflects the decrease in synaptic contacts. This hypothesis was investigated in a developmental study conducted with cats (Chugani, Hovda, Villablanca, Phelps, & Xu, 1991). In this study, the peak of glucose uptake in a cat's visual cortex was found to coincide with the peak in overproduction of synapses in this region. However, when similar data from human visual cortex are plotted together (see Figure 4.9), it is apparent that the peak of glucose uptake lags behind synaptic density. An alternative to the hypothesis that reduction of metabolic activity is the result of the elimination

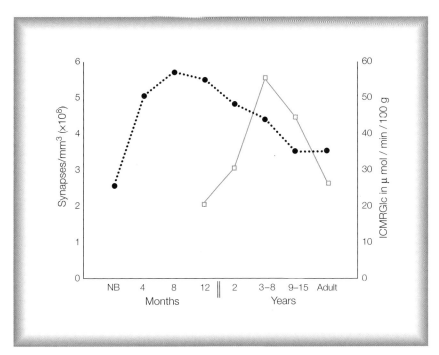

Figure 4.9 Graph showing the development of density of synapses in human primary visual cortex (dotted line: data taken from Huttenlocher, 1990), and resting glucose uptake in the occipital cortex as measured by PET (solid line: data taken from Chugani et al., 1987). ICMRGlc is a measure of the local cerebral metabolic rates for glucose.

of neurons, axons, and synaptic branches is that the same activity may require less "mental effort" once a certain level of skill has been attained.

Most of the developments in the brain discussed so far concern aspects of the structure of the brain. However, there are also developmental changes in what have been known as the "soft soak" aspects of neural function, molecules involved in the transmission and modulation of neural signals. While these will be discussed in more detail in a later section, it is interesting to note at this point that a number of neurotransmitters in rodents and humans also show the rise and fall developmental pattern (see Benes, 1994, for review). Specifically, the excitatory intrinsic transmitter glutamate, the inhibitory intrinsic transmitter GABA (gamma-aminobutyric acid), and the extrinsic transmitter serotonin all show this same developmental trend.

FURTHER READING   Benes (2001); Berenbaum, Moffat, Wisniewski, & Resnick (2003); Cameron (2001).

Thus, the distinctive "rise and fall" developmental sequence is seen in a number of microscopic and metabolic measures of structural and neurophysiological development in the human cortex. Recently, a number of laboratories have developed MRI methods to study the structural development of the brain at a larger scale. As discussed in Chapter 2, MRI reveals brain structure at a more gross scale than neurons and synapses, but sufficient to allow the measurement of gray and white matter in different cortical and subcortical regions. One study described cortical gray matter development in participants from 4 to 21 years (Gogtay et al., 2004). The authors report considerable heterogeneity between different individuals, and between different cortical regions. Nevertheless, they confirmed that cortical gray matter shows the characteristic "rise and fall" pattern described above, and indicative of the pruning or elimination of excess connections between neurons. For some cortical regions most of the rise occurs before puberty, and most of the decline after puberty going into early adulthood. Also broadly consistent with earlier reports based on postmortem neuroanatomical studies, the authors observed that the primary sensory areas of cortex, along with the frontal and occipital poles, show the fastest growth (and decline) curves (see Figure 4.10 in the color plate section). Most of the remainder of the cortex develops in an approximately back-to-front direction, with the prefrontal cortex showing the most delayed curve. The posterior superior temporal cortex, which is a critical part of the social brain network (see Chapter 7) and integrates information from different sensory modalities, develops last according to this measure. The authors suggest that this sequence reflects the evolutionary sequence in which these structures evolved, but this hypothesis is controversial.

Similar MRI data have been collected for the volume of white matter (myelinated fiber bundles), and this shows a general linear increase with age through to early adulthood. The lack of a later decline in this measure may reflect the ongoing life-long myelination of fibers that adds to the overall volume of the brain.

FURTHER READING   O'Hare and Sowell (2008).

Overall, a number of different measures and laboratories have found the rise and fall pattern for neurons and their local connectivity. However, it should be stressed that (a) not all measures show this pattern (e.g., myelination, white matter) and (b) measures such as synaptic density are static snapshots of a dynamic process in which both additive and regressive processes are continually in progress; in other words, there are probably not distinct and separate progressive and regressive phases.

In addition to these caveats, all of the additive and subtractive events just described for normal human brain development must be weighed against a growing literature on individual differences within the normal range. As more sophisticated brain imaging techniques are developed, it becomes increasingly evident that there is considerable variation in structure and function in typical adult subjects. For example, Tramo and his colleagues (1996) reconstructed the cortical areas of two identical twins from MRI scans. Even in the case of genetically identical individuals, the variation in cortical areas was striking, with the occipital lobe occupying 13–17%

of cortical area in one individual, and 20% in the other. These differences between individuals in brain structure may also extend to brain functioning. For example, using functional MRI, Schneider and colleagues studied the areas of activation following upper or lower visual field stimulation. While it had classically been assumed that the upper and lower visual field mapped on to the regions above and below the sulcus, there is in fact a lot of variation, with some typical subjects showing an upper/lower visual field cut that straddles this structure (Schneider, Noll, & Cohen, 1993). This new evidence for variability complements an older literature on individual differences in handedness and hemispheric organization for language (e.g., Hellige, 1993; Kinsbourne & Hiscock, 1983). In view of this variability in typical adults, efforts to construct a timetable for "normal" postnatal brain development in humans must be interpreted with caution.

Building on the evidence for individual variability in the rise and fall in the developmental trajectory of gray matter, Shaw and colleagues (2006) demonstrated from MRI images that it is the trajectory of change in cortical thickness, and not the thickness itself, that best predicts a measure of intelligence (IQ). In this study, more intelligent children (as assessed by IQ) went through a larger and clearer pattern of rise and fall in their cortical thickness between 7 and 19 years of age than did those with more average intelligence scores (see Figure 4.11 in the color plate section). This groundbreaking study suggests that differences in the dynamic changes that occur during development are critical for our understanding of individual differences in intelligence and cognition in adults.

4.4   The Development of Cortical Areas: Protomap or Protocortex?

An ongoing debate among those who study the developmental neurobiology of the cortex concerns the extent to which its structure and function are prespecified, in the sense that they are the result of genetic, molecular, and cellular level interactions and not determined by the pattern of firing of neurons. As we described earlier, the cortex is a layered structure somewhat reminiscent of a cake composed of different layers of sponge, cream, and jam. Orthogonal to the laminar dimension of cortical structure is its differentiation into regions or areas. Returning to our layered cake, we can consider cortical differentiation in regions as being like the slices of a cake some of which may contain thicker jam or cream layers. Figure 4.12 illustrates one of the best-known schemes for dividing the cerebral cortex into areas. In the adult primate most of these cortical areas can be determined by very detailed differences in the laminar structure, such as the precise thickness of certain layers. Often, however, the borderlines between areas are indistinct and controversial. It is commonly assumed that these anatomically defined areas have particular unique functions. While this has proved to be the case for early sensory and motor areas, there are many cases of

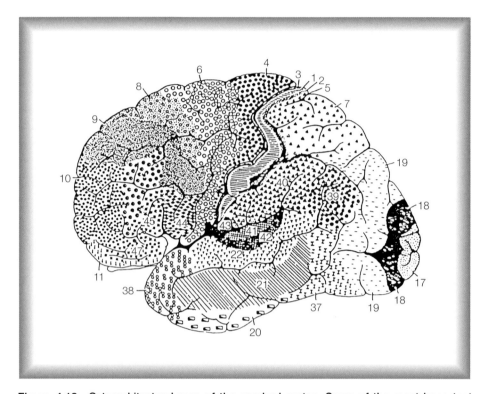

Figure 4.12 Cytoarchitectural map of the cerebral cortex. Some of the most important specific areas are as follows. Motor cortex: motor strip, area 4; pre-motor area, area 6; frontal eye fields, area 8. Somatosensory cortex: areas 3, 1, 2. Visual cortex: areas 17, 18, 19. Auditory cortex: areas 41 and 42. Wernicke's speech area: approximately area 22. Broca's speech area: approximately area 44 (in the left hemisphere) (from Brodmann, in Brodal, 1981).

functional regions or borders that do not neatly correspond to known neuroanatomical divisions. It should be stressed that the division of the cortex into areas with differing functional specializations is not an exact science in that the detailed features of neuroanatomy relevant for supporting different functions are unknown.

Despite these caveats, a century of neuropsychology has taught us that the majority of typical adults tend to have similar functions within approximately the same areas of cortex. This observation has led to a common assumption that the division of the cerebral cortex into structural and functional areas is tightly genetically prespecified. However, as we will see, this assumption is, at best, only partially correct.

The framework outlined in Chapter 1 can be used to ask whether aspects of cortical structure are specified prior to postnatal experience. This question can be asked of both the laminar and the areal structure of cortex. Of course the two dimensions of cortical structure are not entirely independent, since structural areal divisions are partly specified by detailed differences in laminar structure. However, the framework in Chapter 1 allowed for the possibility that while the basic architecture of a network is innate (basic circuitry, learning rules, type and number of cells, etc.), the detailed patterns of (dendritic and synaptic) connectivity are dependent upon experience. In such a case we may say that while the *network imposes architectural constraints on the representations that emerge within it, there are no innate representations.*

In the review that follows I will suggest that several aspects of the structure of the cerebral cortex, including the general laminar structure and large-scale regions, do not require neural activity to be established. Crucially, however, much of the fine-scale division into functional areas involves activity-dependent processes. I begin by returning to the prenatal development of cortex, and probably the most complete theory of the development of cortical structure: the radial unit model proposed by Pasko Rakic (1988).

As mentioned earlier, most cortical neurons in humans are generated outside the cortex itself in a region just underneath what becomes the cortex, the "proliferative zones." This means that these cells must migrate to take up their locations within the cortex. How is this migration accomplished? Rakic has proposed a "radial unit model" of neocortical differentiation that gives an account of how *both* the areal and the layered structure of the mammalian cerebral cortex arise (Rakic, 1988). According to the model, the laminar organization of the cerebral cortex is determined by the fact that each proliferative unit (in the subventricular zone) gives rise to about one hundred neurons. The progeny from each proliferative unit all migrate up the same radial glial fiber, with the latest to be born traveling past their older relatives. A radial glial fiber is a long process that stretches from top to bottom of the cortex and originates from a glial cell. Thus, radial glial fibers act like a climbing rope to ensure that cells produced by one proliferative unit all contribute to one radial column within the cortex. Rakic's proposed method of migration is illustrated in Figure 4.13.

FURTHER READING Rakic (2002).

Rakic's model explains how cortical cells arrange themselves into the thickness of the cortex, but how does the differentiation into specific layers emerge? While we are far from being able to answer this question definitively at this point, one view is that differentiation into particular cell types occurs *before* a neuron reaches its final location. That is, a cell "knows" what type of neuron it will become (pyramidal, spiny stellate, etc.) before it reaches its adult location within the cortex. Some evidence suggests that cells do indeed begin to differentiate before they reach their final vertical location. For example, in genetic mutant "reeler" mice, cells that acquire inappropriate laminar positions within the cortex still differentiate into neuronal types according to their time of origin, rather than the types normally found at their new location. This implies that the information required for differentiation is present at the cell's birth in the proliferative zones; it is not dependent upon their distance from the proliferative zones, or on the characteristics of the neighborhood in which that cell ends up. That is, in the proliferative zones for the neocortex, some cell types may be determined at the stage of division.

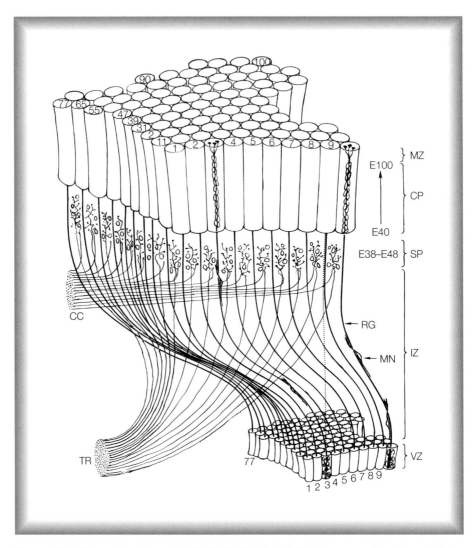

Figure 4.13   The radial unit model of Rakic (1987). Radial glial fibers span from the ventricular zone (VZ) to the cortical plate (CP) via a number of regions: the intermediate zone (IZ) and the subplate zone (SP). RG indicates a radial glial fiber, and MN a migrating neuron. Each MN traverses the IZ and SP zones that contain waiting terminals from the thalamic radiation (TR) and corticocortico afferents (CC). As described in the text, after entering the cortical plate, the neurons migrate past their predecessors to the marginal zone (MZ).

Although in many cases a cell's identity may be determined before it leaves the proliferative zones, some of the properties that distinguish cell types may form later. For example, Marin-Padilla (1990) has proposed that the distinctive apical dendrite of pyramidal cells, which often reaches into layer 1, is a result of the increasing distance between this layer and other layers resulting from the inside-out pattern of growth. Specifically, the increasing separation between layer 1 and the subplate zone which results from young neurons moving into what will become layers 2 to 6 means that cells which have their processes attached to layer 1 will become increasingly "stretched"—that is, their leading dendrite will become stretched tangential to the surface of the cortex, resulting in the elongated apical dendrite so typical of cortical pyramidal cells. As mentioned earlier, this long apical dendrite allows the cell to be influenced by large numbers of cells from other (more superficial) layers.

Another aspect of the laminar structure of cortex that appears to be regulated by intrinsic cellular and molecular interactions concerns the major connections between cells, in particular the inputs from the thalamus. As mentioned earlier, the main input layer in the cortex is layer 4. A series of experiments by Blakemore and colleagues established that the termination of projections from the thalamus in layer 4 is governed by molecular markers. Slices of brain tissue are able to survive and grow in a Petri dish for several days under the appropriate conditions. Indeed, pieces of thalamus of the appropriate age will actually grow connections to other pieces of brain placed nearby. Molnar and Blakemore (1991) investigated if and how a piece of visual thalamus (LGN) would innervate various types of cortical and non-cortical brain tissue.

In initial experiments they established that when a piece of thalamus (LGN) and a piece of visual cortex were placed close together in the dish, projection fibers from the LGN not only invaded a piece of visual cortex of the appropriate age, but also terminated in the appropriate layer 4. Thus, layer 4 appears to contain some molecular stop signal that tells the fibers to stop growing and form connections at that location. Next, they conducted a series of choice experiments in which the visual thalamus had a piece of visual cortex and some other piece of brain placed nearby. The thalamic fibers turned out to dislike cerebellum, rarely penetrating it, but they did grow into hippocampus. However, the growth into hippocampus (a piece of brain that is closely related to neocortex) was not spatially confined in the way it had been for visual cortex, suggesting that it was just a "growth-permitting substrate."

The evidence discussed so far indicates that the laminar structure of cortex probably arises from local cellular and molecular interactions, rather than it being shaped as a result of thalamic and sensory input. That is, the identity and location of neurons are determined before birth. Similarly, incoming fibers "know" in which layer to stop and make synaptic contacts. I now turn to the question of whether the areal structure of the cortex is determined in a similar way.

Traditionally, two opposing possibilities have been put forward to account for the division of cortex into areas:

1. The areal differentiation of cortex is due to a *protomap* (Rakic, 1988). By this view, differentiation into cortical regions occurs early in the formation of the cortex, and is due to intrinsic (to the cortex or its proliferative zones) factors. The activity of neurons is not required. The cortex is viewed as a mosaic from the start such that each cortical area has individually specified features particularly suitable for the input it will receive or the functions it will perform.
2. The different areas of cortex arise out of an undifferentiated *protocortex*. By this view, differentiation occurs later in the development of cortex, and it depends on extrinsic

factors like input from other parts of the brain or sensory systems. The activity of neurons is required (Killackey, 1990; O'Leary, 2002). The division of cortex into areas in the adult brain is influenced by information relayed from the thalamus, and from interactions with other areas of cortex via inter-regional connectivity.

FURTHER READING   O'Leary (2002); Rakic (2002).

There is a large, complicated, and sometimes apparently conflicting literature on the areal differentiation of neocortex (for reviews see Bystron, Blakemore & Rakic, 2008; Kingsbury & Finlay, 2001; Pallas, 2001; Ragsdale & Grove, 2001). Some experiments appear, at first sight, to be compelling evidence for the protomap view. For example, the newborns of a strain of "knockout" rodent (see Chapter 3) that genetically lack connections between the thalamus and the cortex still have normal, well-defined regional gene-expression boundaries within their cortex (Miyashita-Lin, Hevner, Wassarman, Martinez, & Rubinstein, 1999) and some other characteristics of wild-type mice. In another example, *in vitro* studies in which cortical tissue is maintained in culture, and thus isolated from potential extrinsic patterning cues, still show patterns of gene expression consistent with the development of the hippocampus (Tole, Goudreau, Assimacopoulos, & Grove, 2000). Despite these and other studies supporting the idea of genetically specified regionalization of cortex, there are some important caveats, and also an initially surprising amount of evidence in support of the opposing protocortex view.

1. Most of the patterns of gene expression thought to contribute to the differentiation of cortex do not show clearly defined boundaries, but rather show graded expression across large extents of cortex. This suggests that regionalization of cortex could emerge from a combination of different gradients of gene expression. Kingsbury and Finlay (2001) refer to this as a "hyperdimensional plaid" and contrast this with a "mosaic quilt" (protomap) view. Recent evidence indicates that while more than one hundred genes may show graded differential expression between two different cortical areas during development (Leamey et al., 2008), genetic influence over the layered structure of cortex is much more direct. Specifically, evidence indicates that an autonomous and dissociable genetic pathway coordinates the development of the deeper layers of cortex from that which contributes to the mid and upper layers (Casanova & Trippe, 2006).

2. Despite primary sensory regions being the best candidates for genetic prespecification, we will see in the next section of this chapter that even these regions can have their properties significantly changed through experience. Thus, sensory input may be vital at least for the maintenance of cortical divisions.

3. Evidence for cortical differentiation prior to birth does not allow us to conclude that neuronal activity is not important since spontaneous neural activity within the brain is known to be important for differentiation (Shatz, 2002).

FURTHER READING Shatz (2002).

Recent reviews of the evidence converge on views that are mid-way between the protomap and protocortex hypotheses (Bystron et al., 2008; Kingsbury & Finlay, 2001; Pallas, 2001; Ragsdale & Grove, 2001). Most agree that graded patterns of gene expression create large-scale regions with combinations of properties that may better suit certain computations (similar to a very coarse protomap). It is within these large-scale regions that smaller-scale functional areas arise through the activity-dependent mechanisms associated with the protocortex view. A hypothetical example is that one region may receive particular thalamic input projections, overlaid with a certain pattern of neurotransmitter expression, and the presence of specific neuro-modulators. This combination of circumstances, combined with neural activity, may then induce further unique features such as particular patterns of short-range or long-range connectivity. Differentiation into smaller areas within the larger regions may occur through the selective pruning of connections (see Chapter 12). Kingsbury & Finlay (2001) refer to this perspective on cortical differentiation as a "hyperdimen-sional plaid" because the patterning that emerges in a plaid is the result of small changes in many threads. Similarly, O'Leary and colleagues call this general view the "cooperative concentration" model since some different gradients of gene expression may act as opposing forces in shaping cortical regions (Hamasaki, Leingartner, Ringstedt, & O'Leary, 2004).

Research on the combinations of factors that determine cortical differentiation continues to be very active and is a fast-moving field. The most recent findings on developing mice suggest that while patterns of gene expression start off in the graded way described earlier during prenatal development, the patterns become more localized to specific areas even when you prevent thalamic input to the cortex (Hamasaki et al., 2004). However, the role of intrinsic activity within the cortex in this process has yet to be investigated. Another line of recent work investigates a key element of Rakic's protomap hypothesis. According to this, regional differentiation occurs largely through the different numbers of cells generated in different layers in different regions of the cortex. The clearest example of this comes from examination of the primary visual cortex (area 17) in primates that has a larger number of neurons than neighboring regions (such as area 18). As mentioned earlier, this difference results from the number of divisions in the progenitor cells that are assumed to constitute part of the protomap. However, recent research shows that fibers from the thalamus enter the zone with the progenitor cells and have a "mitogenic" effect (Dehay & Kennedy, 2007). A mitogenic effect means that the rate of cell division to create new cells is enhanced. In other words, fibers from the retina that project only to a specific part of the zone containing cortical progenitor cells may influence the rate of production (and therefore number) of new neurons. Thus, intriguingly, the cortical protomap itself may be shaped by input from other regions known to show spontaneous intrinsic waves of neural activity.

Perhaps the biggest challenge for the future is to understand how the emerging structural differentiation of the cortex relates to the emergence of functions, a question that we will return to many times later in this book. In this regard it is important to remember that there are actually only a few examples of clear structural regionalization that map tightly on to functional areas, and there are good reasons to believe that these cases may be exceptions to the general rule. For example, comparisons across a large number of species have led several experts to argue that primary sensory areas that receive direct input from the primary sensory thalamic nuclei are less susceptible to change between species than most of the rest of the cortex (e.g., Krubitzer, 1998). In particular, the primary visual cortex in primates has unique characteristics that have led some to propose that it is the most recently evolved part of cortex. As just mentioned, in the primary visual cortex, inputs from the visual thalamus may regulate the extent of cell proliferation in the ventricular zone (see Dehay & Kennedy, 2007), ensuring that this area of cortex has a rate of neuron production nearly twice that in neighboring areas. The entorhinal cortex, the region of cortex most closely associated with the hippocampus, shows some differentiation from the surrounding cortex as early as 13 weeks after gestation (Kostović, Petanjek, & Judaš, 1993). However, for the majority of cortex in the mouse, and the vast majority in humans, there is currently no evidence for cortical divisions arising through the on/off expression of a single gene rather than gradients of expression across many genes.

To summarize so far, the basic laminar structure of the cerebral cortex in mammals appears to be very general. Cellular and molecular level interactions determine many aspects of the layered structure of cortex and its patterns of connectivity. Cortical neurons are often differentiated into specific computational types before they reach their destination (although some of the characteristic features of cell types are shaped by their journey to that site, e.g., the long apical dendrite that typifies pyramidal cells reflects a literal "stretching" of processes during the migration process). However, this does not mean that cells in a particular area are prespecified for processing certain kinds of information.

A good example of how a region of cortex can become differentiated comes from work on the so-called "barrel fields" that develop in the somatosensory cortex of rodents. Each barrel field is an anatomically definable functional grouping of cells that responds to a particular whisker on the animal's snout (see Figure 4.14). Barrel-fields are an aspect of the areal structure of cortex that emerges postnatally, and are sensitive to whisker-related experience over the first days of life. For example, if a whisker is removed, then the barrel field that normally corresponds to that whisker does not emerge, and neighboring ones may occupy some of the cortical space normally occupied by it (for review see Schlaggar & O'Leary, 1993). Figure 4.14 illustrates how the areal divisions of the cortex arise as a result of similar divisions in structures closer to the sensory surface. In this case, it is almost as if the sensory surface *imposes* itself on to the brain stem, thence to the thalamus, and finally on to the cortex itself. The barrel field compartments emerge in sequence in these areas of the brain, with those closest to the sensory surface forming first, and the cortex patterns emerging last. While there is little evidence that barrel fields are prespecified

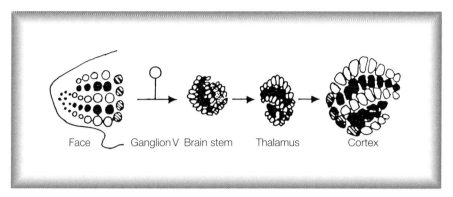

Figure 4.14 Patterning of areal units in the somatosensory cortex. The pattern of "barrels" in the somatosensory cortex of rodents is an isomorphic representation of the geometric arrangement of vibrissae found on the animal's face. Similar patterns are present in the brain stem and thalamic nuclei that relay inputs from the face to the barrel cortex.

in the cortex (but see Cooper & Steindler, 1986), a map of sensory space comes to occupy the somatosensory cortex in a reliable and replicable way.

In this section I have reviewed some of the literature on laminar and areal specification of cortex during typical development, presenting evidence for both the protomap and protocortex accounts. This apparently conflicting evidence can be reconciled by the notion that large-scale regions of cortex have particular combinations of graded gene expression that are then refined into smaller functional areas through activity-dependent processes.

4.5   Cortical Plasticity

While some differentiation of cortex may occur early in development through intrinsic molecular and genetic factors, we have seen that the nature of the information entering a region of cortex is important in ensuring the maintenance and further progression of this differentiation. Further, neural activity driven by inputs may be able to change the function and detailed neuroanatomy of a region. Indeed, a number of experiments have shown that regions of the mammalian cerebral cortex can support a variety of different representations early in development. The evidence for this includes the following:

1. Reducing of the extent of thalamic input to a region of cortex early in life influences the subsequent size of that region (Dehay, Horsburgh, Berland, Killackey, & Kennedy, 1989; O'Leary, 2002; Rakic, 1988). Conversely, changing the quantity of cortex available for thalamic innervation changes the overall pattern of cortical differentiation and not just the affected region.

2. When thalamic inputs are "re-wired" such that they project to a different region of cortex from normal, the new recipient region develops some of the properties of the normal target tissue (e.g., auditory cortex takes on visual representations—Sur, Garraghty, & Roe, 1988; Sur, Pallas, & Roe, 1990).

3. When a piece of cortex is transplanted to a new location, it develops projections characteristic of its new location rather than its developmental origin (e.g., transplanted visual cortex takes on the representations that are appropriate for somatosensory input—O'Leary & Stanfield, 1989).

I will now consider each of these in more detail.

1. The effect on the cortex of manipulating the extent of sensory input (via the thalamus) to an area has been investigated in experiments where the thalamic input to an area of cortex is surgically reduced (Dehay, Kennedy, & Bullier, 1988). Surgical intervention in newborn macaque monkeys can reduce the thalamic projections to the primary visual cortex (area 17) by 50%. This reduction results in a corresponding reduction in the extent of area 17 in relation to area 18. That is, the border between areas 17 and 18 shifts such that area 17 becomes much smaller. Despite this drastic reduction in the radial size of area 17, it is important to note that its laminar structure remains normal. Further, the area which is still area 17 looks identical to its normal structure, and the region which becomes area 18 has characteristics normally associated with that area, and none of those unique to area 17 (Rakic, 1988). Thus, there is (surprisingly) little effect of reducing the extent of sensory projections to area 17 on the subsequent laminar structure of areas 17 and 18. The specific effect of this manipulation is to reduce the *area* of 17 relative to 18, despite the evidence of some prespecification of neuron numbers in this particular region discussed earlier. This indicates that even those cortical areas for which there is some evidence for prespecification can be subsequently modified.

    Even the outputs characteristic of areas 17 and 18 follow the shift in border between them. For example, while area 18 normally has many callosal projections to the other hemisphere, area 17 does not. The region which is normally area 17, but becomes area 18 in the surgically operated animals, has the callosal projection pattern characteristic of normal area 18. A reasonable conclusion reached on the basis of these observations is that the region of cortex that would normally mature into area 17 develops properties that are characteristic of the adjacent area 18 as a result of reducing its thalamic input. Thus, at least some of the area-specific characteristics of cortex appear to be regulated by extrinsic factors, even for regions that show the greatest degree of prespecification.

    In the converse experiment to those just discussed, when the cortical sheet is surgically reduced (in the opossum embryo), it produces a complete, although smaller and distorted, area map (Huffman et al., 1999). Relatedly, in genetically altered strains of mice that lack certain regulatory genes (Emx2 or Pax6), the resulting area map is distorted (Bishop et al., 2000; Mallamaci, Muzio, Chan, Parnavelas, & Boncinelli, 2000). Specifically, regions where these genes are normally expressed at high levels become "compressed" while other regions expand. These experiments illustrate that gradients of gene expression set up scaffolding which then interacts with thalamic input to result in functional areas. However, in atypical situations resulting from surgical or genetic manipulation, thalamic inputs can also shape regions that are not their normal targets.

2. Cross-modal plasticity of cortical areas has now been demonstrated at the neurophysiological level in several mammalian species (for review see Pallas, 2001). For example, in the ferret, projections from the retina can be induced to project to auditory thalamic areas, and thence to auditory cortex. Following a technique initially developed by Frost (1990), this is done by selectively damaging the normal visual cortex and the lateral geniculate (the thalamic target of retinal projections). Lesions are also placed such that auditory inputs do not innervate their normal thalamic target, the medial geniculate. Under these pathological conditions, retinal projections will spontaneously reroute themselves to the medial geniculate nucleus (MGN). Projections from the MGN then project to the auditory cortex as normal. The experimental question concerns whether the normally auditory cortex becomes visually responsive (i.e. in accord with its new input), or whether it retains features characteristic of auditory cortex. The answer is that auditory cortex does become visually responsive. Furthermore, cells in what would have been auditory cortex also become orientation- and direction-selective, and some become binocular.

While these observations are provocative, they do not provide evidence that the auditory cortex as a whole becomes functionally similar to the visual cortex. It is possible, for example, that the visually driven cells in the auditory cortex would fire in isolation from the activity of their colleagues. That is, there may be no organization above the level of the individual neuron. In order to address this issue, evidence that there is a spatial map of the visual world formed across this area of cortex is needed. In order to study this issue, Sur and colleagues recorded from single neurons in a systematic way across the re-wired cortex (Sur et al., 1988; Roe, Pallas, Hahm, & Sur, 1990). These experiments revealed that the previously auditory cortex had developed a two-dimensional retinal map. The authors conclude: "Our results demonstrate that the form of the map is not an intrinsic property of the cortex and that a cortical area can come to support different types of maps" (Roe et al., 1990, p. 818).

Although these neuroanatomical and neurophysiological data support the idea that the auditory cortex can support visual representations, it remains to be established whether these representations can be used to guide the behavior of the animal in the normal way. To investigate this question, Sur and colleagues trained adult ferrets, re-wired in one hemisphere at birth, to discriminate between visual and auditory stimuli presented to the normal hemisphere. After this they probed the functioning of the re-wired hemisphere by presenting visual stimuli that activated only the re-wired pathway. The ferrets reliably interpreted the visual stimulus as visual rather than auditory (von Melchner, Pallas, & Sur, 2000). These results indicate that visual inputs can direct the construction of the appropriate processing circuitry in a region that does not normally handle visual information.

3. Additional evidence for cortical plasticity comes from studies on rodents in which pieces of cortex are transplanted from one region to another early in development. These experiments allow neurobiologists to address the question of whether transplanted areas take on representations appropriate for their *developmental origins*, or the function of the *new location* in which they find themselves.

Pieces of fetal cortex have been successfully transplanted into other regions of newborn rodent cortex. For example, visual cortex neurons can be transplanted into the sensorimotor region and vice versa. Experiments such as these, conducted by O'Leary and Stanfield (1985, 1989), among others, have revealed that the projections and structure of such transplants develop according to their new spatial location rather than their developmental origins. For example, visual cortical neurons transplanted to the sensorimotor region develop projections to the spinal cord, a projection pattern characteristic of the sensorimotor cortex, but not the visual cortex. Similarly, sensorimotor cortical neurons transplanted to the visual cortical region develop projections to the superior colliculus, a subcortical target of the visual cortex, but not characteristic of the sensorimotor region. Thus, the inputs and outputs of a transplanted region take on the characteristics of their new location.

A further question concerns the internal structure of the transplanted region. As discussed earlier, the somatosensory cortex of the rat (and other rodents) possesses characteristic internal structures known as "barrel fields." Barrel fields are an aspect of the areal structure of the cortex, and are clearly visible under the microscope. Each of the barrels corresponds to one whisker on the rat's face. Barrels develop during postnatal growth, and can be prevented from appearing in the normal cortex by cutting the sensory inputs to the region from the face. Furthermore, barrel structure is sensitive to the effects of early experience such as repeated whisker stimulation, or whisker removal (see Schlaggar & O'Leary, 1993, for review). The question then arises whether transplanted slabs of visual cortex take on the barrel field structures that are typical of somatosensory cortex in the rat.

Schlaggar and O'Leary (1991) conducted a study in which pieces of visual cortex were transplanted into the part of the somatosensory cortex that normally forms barrel fields in the rodent. They found that when innervated by thalamic afferents, the transplanted cortex developed barrel fields very similar to those normally observed. Thus, not only can a transplanted piece of cortex develop inputs and outputs appropriate for its new location, but the inputs to that location can organize the internal structure of the cortical region.

At this stage, mention should be made of two caveats to the conclusion that the majority of cortical tissue is largely equipotent early in life. First, most of the transplant and rewiring studies have involved primary sensory cortices. Some authors have argued that primary sensory cortices may share certain common developmental origins that other types of cortex do not (Galaburda & Pandya, 1983; Krubitzer, 1998; Pandya & Yeterian, 1990). It is possible that certain lineages of cortex which differ in detailed ways from other areas of cortex may be more suited for dealing with certain types of information processing. With regard to the transplant experiments discussed earlier, it may be that cortex is only equipotential within a lineage (e.g., primary-to-primary or secondary-to-secondary).

The second caveat to the conclusion that cortex is equipotent is that while transplanted or rewired cortex may look very similar to the original tissue in terms of function and structure, it is rarely absolutely indistinguishable from the original. For example, in the rewired ferret cortex studied by Sur and colleagues (Roe et al., 1990), the mapping of the azimuth (angle right or left) is at a higher resolution (more detailed) than the mapping of the elevation (angle up or down). In contrast, in the normal ferret cortex azimuth and elevation are mapped in equal detail.

4.6   Differential Development of Human Cortex

The main phylogenetic changes in cortical development in primates are in the extent of cortical tissue produced, and the protracted time course of development in humans (see section 4.10). In a later section we overview some of the changes that continue to take place as late as adolescence. In the present section we overview some of the differential development of regions that occurs over the first decade.

With regard to the development of the laminar of the cortex (the layers of the cake), although most cortical neurons are in their appropriate locations by the time of birth in the primate, the "inside-out" pattern of growth observed in prenatal cortical development extends into postnatal life. Extensive descriptive neuroanatomical studies of cortical development in the human infant by Conel over a thirty-year period led him to the conclusion that the postnatal growth of cortex proceeds in an "inside-out" pattern with regard to the extent of dendrites, dendritic trees, and myelination (Conel, 1939–1967). Conel's general conclusions have been validated with more modern neuroanatomical methods (e.g., Becker, Armstrong, Chan, & Wood, 1984; Purpura, 1975; Rabinowicz, 1979), and a modern reanalysis of Conel's original data has deemed it to be highly consistent and reliable (Shankle, Kimball, Landing, & Hara, 1998). In particular, the maturation of layer 5 (deeper) in advance of layers 2 and 3 (superficial) seems to be a very reliably observed sequence for many cortical regions in the human infant (Becker et al., 1984; Rabinowicz, 1979). For example, the dendritic trees of cells in layer 5 of primary visual cortex are already at about 60% of their maximum extent at birth. In contrast, the mean total length for dendrites in layer 3 is only at about 30% of their maximum at birth. Furthermore, higher orders of branching in dendritic trees are observed in layer 5 than in layer 3 at birth (Becker et al., 1984; Huttenlocher, 1990). Interestingly, this inside-out pattern of growth is not evident in the later occurring rise and fall in synaptic density. For this measure, there are no clear differences between cerebral cortical layers.

Differential development in human postnatal cortical growth is also evident in the areal dimension (the slices of the cake), and we will return to this topic in several later chapters. Even in mid-gestation, there is more evidence for differential gene expression in different cortical areas in humans than in other species studied (Dehay & Kennedy, 2009; Johnson et al., 2009). In postnatal development, Huttenlocher (1990, 1994; Huttenlocher & Dabholkar, 1997) reports clear evidence of a difference in the timing of postnatal neuroanatomical events between the primary visual cortex, the primary auditory cortex, and the frontal cortex in human infants, with the latter reaching the same developmental landmarks considerably later in postnatal life than the first two. It is worth noting that this differential development within the cerebral cortex has not been reported in other primate species (Bourgeois, 2001; Rakic, Bourgeois, Eckenhoff, Zecevic, & Goldman-Rakic, 1986). For example, Rakic and colleagues reported that all areas of cortex appear to reach their peak in synaptic density about the same time, around 2–4 months in the rhesus monkey, roughly corresponding to from 7 to 12 months in the human child. Contrary to Huttenlocher's findings, this suggests that there may be a common genetic signal to increase connectivity across all brain regions, simultaneously, regardless of their current maturational state. A sudden event of this kind stands in marked contrast to known region-by-region differences in the time course of cell formation, migration, myelination, and metabolism in the human cortex (Conel, 1939–1967; Yakovlev & Lecours, 1967). The most likely difference between the human results and those from the macaques is that the protracted postnatal development of humans means that regional differences are more evident. In the macaque, however, possible regional differences are compressed into a much shorter time, making them harder to detect (Huttenlocher, 1994). However, Goldman-Rakic (1994) suggests that the differences between the macaque and human results may be due to the neuroanatomical techniques used. Further, the decline in synaptic density in the human brain may not differ between regions, but occur simultaneously at puberty (Bourgeois, 2001).

FURTHER READING Bourgeois (2001); Huttenlocher (2002).

Consistent with the reports from human postmortem tissue, a study in which the functional development of the human brain was investigated by PET has also found differential development between regions of cortex (Chugani & Phelps, 1986; Chugani et al., 2002). In infants under 5 weeks of age glucose uptake was highest in sensorimotor cortex, thalamus, brain stem, and the cerebellar vermis. By 3 months of age there were considerable rises in the parietal, temporal, and occipital cortices, basal ganglia, and cerebellar cortex. Maturational rises were not found in the frontal and dorsolateral occipital cortex until approximately 6–8 months. These develop-ments are shown in Figure 4.15.

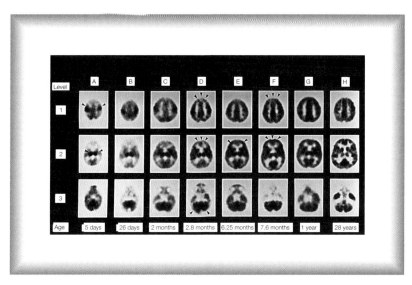

Figure 4.15   PET images illustrating developmental changes in local cerebral metabolic rates for glucose (ICMRGlc) in the normal human infant with increasing age. Level 1 is a superior section, at the level of the cingulate gyrus. Level 2 is more inferior, at the level of caudate, putamen, and thalamus. Level 3 is an inferior section of the brain, at the level of cerebellum and inferior position of the temporal lobes. Gray scale is proportional to ICMRGlc with black being highest. Images from all subjects are not shown on the same absolute gray scale of ICMRGlc; instead, images of each subject are shown with the full gray scale to maximize gray scale display of ICMRGlc at each age. (A) In the 5-day-old, ICMRGlc is highest in sensorimotor cortex, thalamus, cerebellar vermis (arrows), and brain stem (not shown). (B, C, D) ICMRGlc gradually increases in parietal, temporal, and calcarine cortices; basal ganglia; and cerebellar cortex (arrows), particularly during the second and third months. (E) In the frontal cortex, ICMRGlc increases first in the lateral prefrontal regions by approximately 6 months. (F) By approximately 8 months, ICMRGlc also increases in the medial aspects of the frontal cortex (arrows), as well as the dorsolateral occipital cortex. (G) By 1 year, the ICMRGlc pattern resembles that of adults (H).

In addition to the formation of dendritic trees and their associated synapses, most fibers become myelinated during postnatal development. As described earlier, myelin is a membrane wrapping around axons that improves conduction. Owing to the increased fat content of the brain caused by myelination of fibers, structural MRI images can reveal a clear gray–white matter contrast, and this allows quantitative volume measurements to be made during development (see Sampaio & Truwit, 2001). While some controversy remains about the interpretation of images from infants under 6 months (due to a higher than adult water content in both gray and white matter at this age), there is consensus that the appearance of brain structures is similar to that of adults by 2 years of age, and that all major fiber tracts can be observed by 3 years of age (Bourgeois, 2001; Huttenlocher & Dabholkar,

1997). Some reports suggest that after a rapid increase in gray matter volume up to about 4 years of age, there is then a prolonged period of slight decline that extends into adult years (Chugani et al., 2002; but see Huttenlocher & Dabholkar, 1997). Whether this decline in gray matter is due to dendritic and synaptic pruning remains unknown, although in some studies the time course of the rise and fall coincides (Huttenlocher & Dabholkar, 1997). Changes in the extent of white matter are of interest since they presumably reflect inter-regional communication in the developing brain. While increases in white matter extend through adolescence into adulthood, particularly in frontal brain regions (Huttenlocher et al., 1982), the most rapid changes occur during the first 2 years. Myelination appears to begin at birth in the pons and cerebellar peduncles, and by 3 months has extended to the optic radiation and splenium of the corpus callosum. Around 8–12 months the white matter associated with the frontal, parietal, and occipital lobes becomes apparent.

FURTHER READING   Klinberg (2008).

The differential laminar and regional development observed in the human, as described in this section, provides the basis for many of the associations between brain growth and cognitive change to be described in the following chapters. But first we need to review some other aspects of postnatal brain development.

4.7   Postnatal Brain Development: Adolescence

In previous sections we have learned that the trajectory of the development of the brain is not that of a simple linear increase. Rather, it is characterized by more complex patterns involving both rises and falls in different measures. One period of later development that has commonly been associated with "dips" in development is adolescence. While we will discuss changes in adolescence in several of the domain-based chapters that follow, it also worth considering adolescence as a phase of human brain development in its own right.

At the onset of puberty significant changes begin to occur in brain structure and chemistry. These changes involve continuing myelination of connections, and changes in the density of synapses, particularly within the prefrontal region of the cortex. Specifically, a spurt of growth of synapses followed by a period of pruning occurs around the time of puberty. Around the same time, and probably related, is a surge of hormones. One hypothesis is that higher levels of testosterone in boys that occur during puberty may result in reduced synaptic pruning and a consequential greater volume of gray matter in certain frontal regions in men. However, results from studies assessing gender differences in brain development around puberty are somewhat inconsistent and some large-scale longitudinal studies are required (Blakemore & Choudhury, 2006).

In terms of behavior, adolescence is commonly described as a period of increased impulsive and risk-taking behavior, and scientists have investigated the hypothesis that this is related to a lack of inhibitory control, possibly mediated by a "dip" in the functioning of prefrontal cortex (see Chapter 10), or to changes in the brain's "reward" network. Increased activity in the brain's reward network is associated with more risky choices in adults when they are involved in gambling-type tasks. It is known that adolescents show greater activity in their reward network (involving a structure called the nucleus accumbens) than younger children or adults. One recent study investigated whether individual differences in the likelihood of engaging in risky behaviors is associated with activity in the brain circuitry that anticipates a reward in adults, adolescents, and children (Galvan, Hare, Voss, Glover, & Casey, 2006). Results from this and related studies suggest that while both impulsive behavior and risk-taking behavior are prevalent in adolescents, they show different developmental trajectories and have partially different brain bases. Impulsive behavior (lack of inhibition) is related to PFC development and gradually diminishes from childhood to adulthood. In contrast, individuals prone to risky behavior (reward network) are at further risk during adolescence when the brain systems involved in the anticipation of reward are undergoing developmental changes.

During adolescence many other "executive functions" such as selective attention, working memory, problem solving, and multi-tasking improve steadily. While such executive functions are commonly related to the prefrontal cortex, fMRI studies indicate that broad networks of cortical regions are involved in these changes (e.g., Luna, Garver, Urban, Lazar, & Sweeney, 2004).

Some subcortical regions also change their response properties during adolescence, though this may be a reflection of their interactions with the cortex. For example, the amygdala is an important part of the social brain (Chapter 7) that has been consistently related with emotion processing. In adults, the amygdala is activated by the perception of fearful facial expressions. While this structure also responds to fearful faces in children of 11 years, it responds equally to neutral faces at this age, suggesting a less finely tuned function (Thomas et al., 2001). Other studies of amygdala function in development have revealed gender differences over the adolescent period: in females the response of the amygdala to fearful faces decreased during adolescence whereas it did not in males (Killgore, Oki, Yurgelun-Todd, 2001). The opposite pattern was observed for a region of the prefrontal cortex. Killgore and colleagues interpret these findings in terms of the greater increase in the regulation of emotion by females (mediated by prefrontal systems).

Structural MRI studies indicate that there are detectable changes in brain structure, particularly in the prefrontal cortex, during and after adolescence. For example, the loss of gray matter in frontal cortex continues up to the age of 30, and white matter volume continues to increase up to 60 years or beyond (Sowell et al., 2003).

FURTHER READING Olson and Luciana (2008).

4.8   Postnatal Brain Development: The Hippocampus and Subcortical Structures

This chapter has focused primarily on the cerebral neocortex since this is the part of the brain that shows most protracted postnatal development. However, other brain structures such as the hippocampus and cerebellum also show some postnatal development and, as we will see, have been associated with cognitive changes in infancy and childhood. The postnatal development of some subcortical structures (such as the hippocampus, cerebellum, and thalamus) poses something of a paradox: on the one hand, there is much behavioral and neural evidence to indicate that these structures are functioning at birth, while, on the other, they all show some evidence of postnatal development and/or functional reorganization. One explanation for this is that as the neocortex develops postnatally, its interactions with subcortical regions undergo certain changes. Evidence from assessments of functional connectivity during resting states (Chapter 12) suggest that subcortical regions may influence cortical processing more heavily early in development, with cortical networks gradually gaining their independence from subcortical influence during the course of childhood (Supekar, Musen, & Menon, 2009; see Chapter 12).

The limbic system is normally taken to include the amygdala, the hippocampus, and the limbic regions of cortex (cingulate gyrus and parahippocampal gyrus [entorhinal cortex]). While these latter cortical regions follow the same developmental timetable as other regions of the cortex, they are differentiated from the rest of the cortex at an early stage, and are therefore unlikely to show the same degree of plasticity. As discussed earlier, gyral development (folding) does not necessarily indicate architectural specificity. Nevertheless, the gyral folding associated with the cingulate region is discernible as early as 16–19 weeks of gestational age in humans and the parahippocampal gyrus within the temporal lobe at 20–23 weeks gestational age (Gilles, Shankle, & Dooling, 1983). In contrast, other prominent gyri in the cortex do not emerge until 24–31 weeks. The major nuclear components of the limbic system, such as the hippocampus, start to differentiate from the developing temporal lobe around the third and fourth months of fetal development. After this, further differentiation of the hippocampus takes place, resulting in it becoming a rolled structure tucked inside the temporal lobe and surrounded by tissue known as the dentate gyrus (see Seress, 2001, for review). It has been known for some time that in rodents neurogenesis continues into postnatal life in the dentate gyrus region (Wallace, Kaplan, & Werboff, 1977). Recently, it has been confirmed in humans that granule neurones continue to be produced throughout adulthood (for review see Kozorovitskiy & Gould, 2008). This production of new neurons is influenced by hormones, and, at least in rats, some types of learning enhance the number of new neurons produced. The computational importance of adult neurogenesis in this region remains to be determined.

FURTHER READING Kozorovitskiy and Gould (2008); Seress and Abraham (2008).

The cerebellum is a brain structure thought to be involved in motor control, but which probably also plays a role in some aspects of "higher" cognitive functioning. Within 2 months after conception the cerebellum has formed its three primary layers, the ventricular (V), intermediate (I), and marginal (M) layers. However, its development is prolonged and neurogenesis in this region continues postnatally with only about 17% of the final number of granule cells present at birth, and neurogenesis possibly continuing until 18 months (Spreen, Risser & Edgell, 1995). Despite being one of the few regions of the human brain to show postnatal neurogenesis, cerebellar functional development as measured by resting PET shows high glucose metabolic activity as early as 5 days old (postnatal), the same schedule as other sensorimotor regions such as the thalamus, brain stem, and sensorimotor cortex (Chugani, 1994).

4.9   Neurotransmitters and Neuromodulators

The aspects of brain development discussed so far have mainly concerned its neurons and "wiring." However, there are also developmental changes in what has been referred to as "soft soak" aspects of neural function. Soft soak refers specifically to the chemicals involved in the transmission and modulation of neural signals. Neurons and their dendrites can be thought of as lying in a bath composed of various chemicals that modulate their functioning. In addition, other chemicals play a vital role in the transmission of signals from one cell to another. Neurotransmitters in the cerebral cortex may be classified into those that arise within the cortex (intrinsic), and those that arise from outside the cortex (extrinsic; see Benes, 1994). The intrinsic transmitters can be further divided according to whether they have an excitatory effect or inhibitory effect on postsynaptic sites.

The intrinsic excitatory transmitter glutamate is thought to play an important role in the axons of pyramidal cells that project to intrinsic cortical microcircuits, other cortical regions, and subcortical regions (Streit, 1984). In rats, the developmental time course of different glutamatergic pathways varies considerably. In general, however, it is the receptors for the transmitter, rather than the quantity of the transmitter, that increase with postnatal age. This development seems to follow the rise and fall pattern seen in other aspects of neural development. Specifically, in the rat between postnatal days 10 and 15 the amount of glutamate binding in cortical regions increases rapidly and reaches a peak around ten times the levels observed in adults (Schliebs, Kullman, & Bigl, 1986). By day 25 these levels have reduced drastically.

GABA (gamma-aminobutyric acid) is probably the most important intrinsic inhibitory transmitter in the mammalian brain. While there are a variety of ways to measure GABA activity, which sometimes give differing results (see Benes, 1994), in the human the same overall pattern of rise and fall seen for glutamate is also observed for GABA. Specifically, the density of GABA receptors increases rapidly in the perinatal period and doubles over the first few weeks before later declining (Brooksbank, Atkinson, & Balasz, 1981). The extent to which the rise and fall in these intrinsic neurotransmitters mirrors that observed in the structural measures discussed earlier such as glucose uptake and synaptic density is currently unclear and requires further research. It is clear, however, that the levels of GABA can be influenced by the extent of sensory experience (Fosse, Heggelund, & Fonnum, 1989).

Extrinsic neurotransmitters arise from a number of different subcortical locations. One of these transmitters, acetylcholine, originates mainly from the basal forebrain (Johnston, McKinney, & Coyle, 1979). Interestingly, the innervation of cortex by cholinergic fibers follows the "inside-out" pattern of growth described earlier, with the deeper cortical layers being innervated before the more superficial ones. In humans, this cholinergic innervation begins prenatally, though adult levels are not reached until about 10 years old (Diebler, Farkas-Bergeton, & Wehrle, 1979). However, the binding sites within the cortex for this transmitter decrease from birth onwards, possibly due to synaptic pruning (Ravikumar & Sasatry, 1985).

Another neurotransmitter with origins outside the cortex is norepinephrine (or noradrenaline), which originates in a cluster of nuclei called the locus coeruleus. As well as its role as a neurotransmitter, norepinephrine has been associated with cortical plasticity (Kasamatsu & Pettigrew, 1976). In several mammals there is an extensive network of noradrenergic fibers in the cortex at birth which may be more dense than that seen in adults (Coyle & Molliver, 1977). Currently, little developmental information is available on this transmitter in primates (Benes, 1994).

Serotonin originates in the brainstem raphe nuclei, and in both rats and primates the level increases rapidly over the first few weeks of life (Johnston, 1988). In rhesus monkeys the adult pattern of projection of serotonin fibers is reached by the sixth week postnatal, though levels of serotonin continue to rise after this (Goldman-Rakic & Brown, 1982). There is some evidence (from specific binding sites) of a later decrease in serotonin in human cortex and hippocampus (Marcusson, Morgan, Winblad, & Finch, 1984). Like acetylcholine, serotonin is found mainly in the deeper cortical layers at birth, consistent with the structural inside-out gradient of development discussed earlier.

The fourth main extrinsic cortical transmitter, dopamine (which originates in the substantia nigra), likewise shows an inside-out pattern around the time of birth, at least in rats (Kalsbeek, Voorn, Buijs, Pool, & Uylings, 1988). Dopaminergic fibers show the adult pattern of projection into the frontal and cingulate cortex through extended postnatal development in rats (Bruinink, Lichtensteinger, & Schlumpf, 1983).

In summary, it appears that:

- Most intrinsic and extrinsic transmitters are present in the cortex at birth, at least in rats and probably also in humans, but show changes in distribution and overall levels for some time after birth.
- Several transmitters of both intrinsic and extrinsic origins show the characteristic rise and fall evident in some measures of structural neuroanatomical development. Owing to a paucity of human data, it is currently not possible to say to what extent these developmental patterns overlap.
- Several transmitters of extrinsic origin show the same inside-out gradient of cortical development observed in structural measures.
- Neurotransmitters may play multiple roles during development. For example, noradrenaline may also regulate cortical plasticity.
- Some transmitters show a differential distribution throughout the cortex. This differential distribution may play some role in the subsequent specialization of regions of cortex for certain functions.

> FURTHER READING Benes (2001); Cameron (2001); Berenbaum et al. (2003); Richards (2003); Stanwood and Levitt (2008).

.10   What Makes a Brain Human?

An important issue for the work described in this chapter is to what extent human brain development is similar to that of other species. This issue is of the upmost theoretical and practical importance for several reasons. First and foremost, most researchers are ultimately interested in how the human mind arises from its underlying brain development, and several of the topics of later chapters—such as number and language—are assumed to be, to at least some degree, unique to humans. This raises the question of what is unique about the human brain and the developmental processes that give rise to it. A related question is how applicable the studies with other species—such as the studies on cortical plasticity with young rodents reviewed earlier—are to human brain development.

As mentioned earlier, primates generally have a much more prolonged timetable for brain development than other mammals. Even between *Homo sapiens* and other primates there is a wide difference in timing, with our postnatal cortical development being extended by roughly a factor of four longer than other primates. We discussed earlier that this prolonged postnatal development in humans stretches out differential laminar and regional cortical differentiation that are more compressed in time in other species. What is the significance of this stretched-out timetable of brain development? Finlay and Darlington (1995) compared data on the size of brain structures from 131 mammalian species, and concluded that the order of landmarks of brain development is conserved across a wide range of species. Further, they noticed that, controlling for overall brain and body size, the time course of these landmarks was related to the relative size of structures of the brain in a systematic way. Specifically, disproportionately large growth occurs in the late-generated structures such as the neocortex when the overall timetable is slowed. By their analysis, the structure most likely to differ in size in the relatively slowed neurogenesis of primates is the neocortex.

Finlay and Darlington have more recently extended their model of the evolution of the brain to human prenatal development (Clancy, Darlington, & Finlay, 2000). The model predicts that the more delayed the general time course of brain development in a species, the larger the relative volume of the later developing structures (such as the cerebral cortex, and particularly the frontal cortex) will be. In accordance with this general prediction, the slowed rate of development in humans is associated with a relatively larger volume of cortex, and an especially large frontal cortex.

Why would allowing more time for the cortex to develop have the effect of increasing its size? Casting our minds back to the radial unit model proposed by Rakic (1988), a single round of additional symmetric cell division at the proliferative unit formation stage would have the effect of doubling the number of ontogenetic columns, and hence expanding the area of cortex. In contrast, an additional single round of division at a later stage, from the proliferative zones, would only increase the size of a column by one cell (about 1%). There is very little variation between mammalian species in the layered structure of the cortex, while the total surface area of the cortex can vary by a factor of 100 or more between different species of mammal. It seems likely, therefore, that species differences originate (at least in part) in the timing of cell development (i.e. the number of "rounds" of cell division that are allowed to take place within and across regions of the proliferative zones).

Thus, it is likely that the increased extent of cortex in our brains, and particularly prefrontal cortex, is at least in part a happy by-product of slowing down the overall timetable of brain development (but see Dehay & Kennedy, 2009). This suggests that evidence from other mammals will be highly relevant to the study of human brain development since we are looking fundamentally at the same process. One caveat to this conclusion, however, must be that the point on the timetable of brain development at which different animals are born may differ greatly. In this regard, the relatively delayed time course of human brain development also has another very important benefit. It allows a prolonged postnatal period during which interaction with the environment can contribute to the tuning and shaping of circuitry.

Whether it is just the slowed timing of brain development that produces the unique human brain remains controversial. Subtle differences in the steps of cortical development between primates and rodents are already known, and some reports of possibly species-specific progenitor cells or neurons in humans merit further research (Bystron et al., 2008).

11   General Summary and Conclusions

We have reviewed some of the highlights of pre- and postnatal development of the brain. While many of these landmarks of development are similar between humans and other mammals, the timing of human brain development is characterized by being slower and more protracted. According to some theories, this slowed development allows the building of relatively more cortex, and particularly frontal cortex. One major feature of human postnatal development is that brain volume quadruples between birth and adulthood, mainly due to increases in nerve fiber bundles, dendrites, and myelination. Another major feature is that several measures of structure and neurophysiology, such as the density of synaptic contacts, show a characteristic "rise and fall" during postnatal development.

The issue was raised as to whether the differentiation of the neocortex into anatomical and functional areas is prespecified. The "protomap" hypothesis states that the differentiation of the cortex into areas is determined by intrinsic molecular markers or prespecification of the proliferative zones. The "protocortex" hypothesis states that an initially undifferentiated protocortex is divided up largely as a result of input through projections from the thalamus and is activity-dependent. A review of currently available evidence supports a middle-ground view in which large-scale regions are prespecified, while the establishment of small-scale functional areas require activity-dependent processes.

The very extended period of postnatal development seen in the human brain reveals two differential aspects of cortical development not as clearly evident in other primates: an inside-out pattern of development of layers, and differences in the timing of development across regions. These differential aspects of human cortical development will provide the basis for associations between brain and cognitive development described in later chapters.

Key Issues for Discussion

- How essential are animal studies for understanding human brain development?
- What, if any, lines of evidence could definitively decide between the protomap and protocortex accounts of cortical differentiation?
- What might be the functional consequences of the "rise and fall" pattern observed for several measures (like the density of synapses) of postnatal development?
- What clinical conditions in humans allow us to draw conclusions about the plasticity of human cortex in early life?

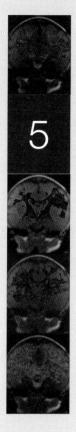

5 Vision, Orienting, and Attention

This chapter reviews selected topics in vision, visual orienting, and visual attention for which attempts have been made to relate brain development to behavioral change. The contribution of peripheral systems (retinal) development in the emergence of basic visual functions is briefly alluded to before discussion of the neural basis of the development of binocular vision. Neuroanatomical and computational modeling evidence highlights the importance of the segregation of inputs to layer 4 cells in the primary visual cortex. A compelling behavioral test of the increased segregation hypothesis is discussed. Moving on from sensory processing to sensorimotor integration, the following section describes an attempt to use the developmental neuroanatomy of the cortex to make predictions about transitions in orienting behavior in infants. A number of behavioral marker tasks for cortical regions involved in oculomotor control are reviewed and discussed in relation to the maturational model. Recent neuroimaging and behavioral studies require modifications to the original model. Finally, experiments concerned with the development of covert (internal) attention shifts in infants and children are described. A number of changes in the flexibility and speed of shifting attention are shown to originate in infancy but continue into childhood.

Developmental Cognitive Neuroscience   (Third Edition)   Mark H. Johnson with Michelle de Haan
© 2011 Mark H. Johnson

5.1   The Development of Vision

Visual pathways, and especially the visual cortex, are among the most studied regions of the brain. More than 25 visual areas of the primate cortex have been identified, and, by means of single-cell recording, neuroimaging, and neuropsychological studies, attempts have been made to understand the functions of these regions. On the behavioral side, much is known about visual psychophysics, and our knowledge about visual cognitive abilities is rapidly expanding. Vision would therefore seem to be a good starting place for studying the functional consequences of the developing brain.

Immediately we begin to consider this issue it becomes obvious that it is hard to determine whether changes in visual abilities during development are due to limitations in the periphery, such as the structure of the eye, lens, or eye muscles, or whether they are due to changes within the brain. It is clear that immaturities in peripheral sensory systems place limits on the perceptual capacities of young infants. For example, it is well known that immaturity of the retina limits spatial acuity. Some have even argued that such limitations are necessary to prevent overwhelming developing visual circuits with too much data too soon (Turkewitz & Kenny, 1982). The issue remains, however, whether peripheral limitations provide the major constraints on the development of perception, or whether development of visual pathways within the brain is the primary limiting factor. While this issue continues to be debated (Iliescu & Dannemiller, 2008), Banks and colleagues (e.g., Banks & Shannon, 1993) conducted an "ideal observer" analysis in which the morphology of neonatal photoreceptors and optics was compared to that of adults. This analysis generated estimates of the contribution of optical and receptor immaturity, as opposed to central immaturities, to deficits in infant spatial and chromatic vision. Observed differences in these aspects of vision between adults and infants turn out to be significantly greater than would be predicted on the basis of peripheral limitations only, indicating that central nervous system pathway development is an important contributing factor in the development of vision. Given that central nervous system factors play an important role even in the development of spatial acuity, we can inquire further into the nature and source of these constraints. Figure 5.1 summarizes some of the steps in visually guided behavior that will be discussed in the next few chapters. Processing related to perceiving and acting on objects is discussed in the next chapter. The processing of social visual stimuli, such as faces, is discussed in Chapter 7. In the present chapter we focus on some aspects of visual processing, orienting, and attention.

FURTHER READING Atkinson and Braddick (2003); Iliescu and Dannemiller (2008); Maurer et al. (2008).

Alongside evidence from behavioral and psychophysiological measures of visual abilities, in recent years investigators have begun to use functional imaging to see which visual pathways and structures can be activated at different ages. Owing to the

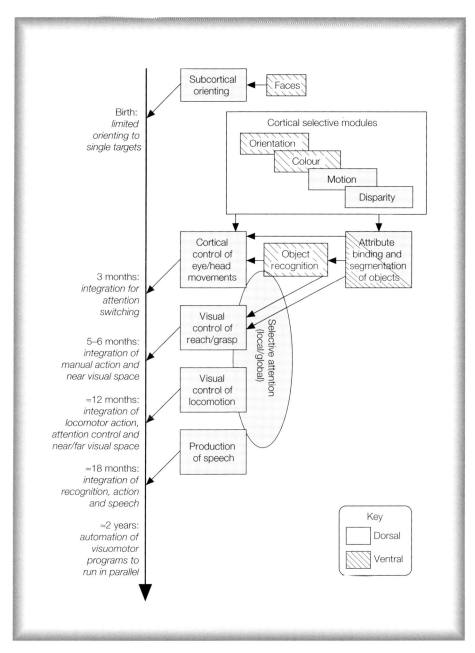

Figure 5.1   Diagram of the developmental sequence of visual behavior (left of vertical line) and ventral- and dorsal-stream neural systems contributing to this (right of vertical line).

difficulties of keeping young infants still for long enough, functional MRI studies with this population typically involve sedated infants being scanned for clinical reasons. Nevertheless, the studies have demonstrated that sedated and sleeping infants respond to visual stimulation in some of the same visual cortical regions as adults (Born, Rostrup, Leth, Peitersen, & Lou, 1996; Born, Rostrup, Miranda, Larsson, & Lou, 2002;

Yamada et al., 1997, 2000). These findings have been confirmed in healthy awake infants using the new technique of optical imaging (NIRS; Chapter 2). Following on from an earlier study with a single site (Meek et al., 1998), Taga and colleagues used a multi-channel optical system to study blood oxygenation in occipital and frontal sites while 2- to 4-month-olds viewed dynamic schematic face-like patterns (Taga, Asakawa, Maki, Konishi, & Koizumi, 2003). The results demonstrated that a localized area of the occipital cortex responded to brief changes in luminance contrasts in the form of event-related changes in blood oxygenation similar to those seen in adults. More importantly, this study has helped establish that this technique can be used in the near future to explore visual function during early infancy.

The central visual field of most primates is binocular, requiring integration of information between the two eyes. This integration is achieved in the primary visual cortex. Functional and anatomical structures observed in layer 4 of the primary visual cortex, so-called "ocular dominance columns," are thought to be important for binocular vision (see Figure 5.2). These columns arise from the segregation of inputs from the two eyes. In other words, neurons in a single ocular dominance column are dominated by input from one eye in adult mammals. Ocular dominance columns are thought to be the stage of processing necessary to achieve binocular vision and, subsequently, detection of disparities between the two retinal images. Owing to the fact that ocular dominance columns are known to have a sensitive period for their formation, and to be sensitive to the differential extent of input from the two eyes, they have become a popular model system for developmental neurobiology (e.g., Bear & Singer, 1986; Kasamatsu & Pettigrew, 1976; Rauschecker & Singer, 1981).

Held (1985) reviewed converging evidence that binocular vision develops at approximately the end of the fourth month of life in human infants. Visually evoked potential measures (short latency ERPs elicited by a conspicuous visual stimulus)

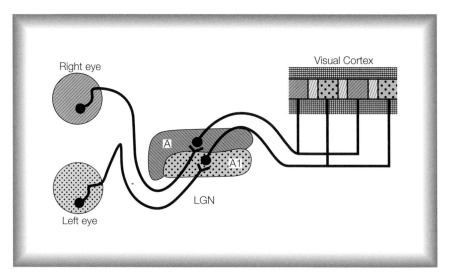

Figure 5.2 Simplified schematic diagram illustrating how projections from the two eyes form ocular dominance columns in the visual cortex.

with dynamic correlograms find evidence for binocularity around 3 months (see Atkinson & Braddick, 2003, for review). One of the abilities associated with binocular vision, stereoacuity, increases very rapidly from the onset of stereopsis, such that it reaches adult levels within a few weeks. This is in contrast to other measures of acuity, such as grating acuity, which increase much more gradually. Held suggested that this very rapid spurt in stereoacuity requires some equally rapid change in the neural substrate supporting it. On the basis of evidence from animal studies, he proposed that this substrate is the development of ocular dominance columns found in layer 4 of the primary visual cortex. While Held's proposal was initially based on a simple causal association between the formation of ocular dominance columns and the onset of binocularity, other research in his laboratory has been concerned with describing a link between the process of change at the two levels.

As mentioned in the previous chapter, processes of selective loss commonly contribute to the sculpting of specific pathways in the cortex. Neurophysiological evidence indicates that the inputs from the two eyes to the cortex are initially mixed so that they synapse on common cortical neurons in layer 4 (see Figure 5.3). These

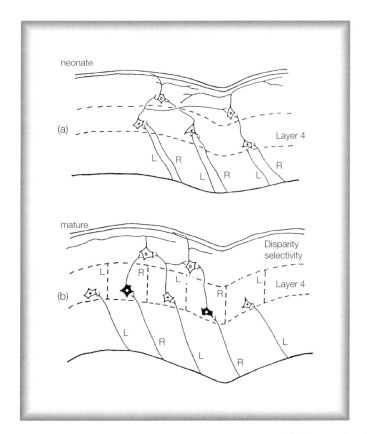

Figure 5.3 (a) Afferents from both eyes synapse on the same cells in layer 4, thereby losing information about the eye of origin. (b) Afferents are segregated on the basis of eye origin (R and L), and consequently recipient cells in layer 4 may send their axons to cells outside of that layer so as to synapse on cells that may be disparity-selective.

layer 4 cells project to disparity-selective cells (possibly in cortical layers 2 and 3). During ontogeny, geniculate axons originating from one eye withdraw from the region, leaving behind axons from the other eye. Held suggested that it is these events at the neural level that give rise to the sudden increase in stereoacuity observed by behavioral measures in the human infant.

This process of selective loss has the information-processing consequence that information from the two eyes which was previously combined in layer 4 of the primary visual cortex becomes segregated (Held, 1993). Specifically, there will be a certain degree of integration between the eyes that will decline once each neuron receives innervation from only one eye. Held and colleagues elegantly demonstrated this increasing segregation of information from the two eyes by showing that infants under 4 months can perform certain types of integration between the two eyes that older infants cannot. In this experiment, Held and his colleagues presented a grating to one eye of an infant, and an orthogonal grating to the other eye (Shimojo, Birch, & Held, 1983). Infants under 4 months perceived a single grid-like representation instead of two sets of gratings that were orthogonal to each other. This is because, presumably, synaptic inputs from the individual eyes have not segregated into ocular dominance columns. As a result, a given cortical layer 4 neuron may have synaptic inputs from each eye and will effectively "see" the image from each eye simultaneously. That is, information from the two eyes would be summed in layer 4, resulting in an averaging of the two signals. Since the inputs from each eye summate, in the case of the orthogonal gratings a grid was perceived. Older infants (older than 4 months of age) do not perceive this grating because neurons in cortical layer 4 of striate cortex only receive inputs from one eye. The inputs to layer 4 have been segregated from one another, and a given layer 4 neuron will receive input from one eye or the other.

The loss of these connections is probably due to the refinement of synapses by selective loss. This refinement most likely occurs through activity-dependent neural mechanisms since it has been shown that the formation of ocular dominance columns can be experimentally blocked by reducing neuronal activity (Stryker & Harris, 1986). However, while these processes may strengthen and maintain ocular dominance columns, some research indicates that the initial formation of the columns can occur without structured visual experience in animals (see Iliescu & Dannemiller, 2008, for review). It is possible that the prenatal intrinsic spontaneous waves of retinal activity discussed in Chapter 4 structure the LGN into eye-specific layers. This would happen because neighboring cells in one retina (left or right) will fire at nearly the same time, but not be correlated with activity in cells from the other retina. Since "cells that fire together wire together" eye-specific layers could form spontaneously. These eye-specific layers in the LGN could then potentially impose their structure on the developing visual cortex.

In several parts of this book we will discuss different streams of visual processing in the brain. Visual processing in the primate brain is initially divided into a subcortical route involving structures such as the superior colliculus, pulvinar and amygdala, and several cortical routes that spread out from the LGN and primary visual cortex. In Chapter 7, we will discuss relations between the subcortical route and activation of cortical circuits in the processing of social stimuli. In Chapter 6, we will examine the differential processing of object and number information in two cortical streams; the dorsal (*where* or *action*) pathway, and the ventral (*what* or *perception*) pathway. In the next section of this chapter we focus on cortical and subcortical routes that are involved in the control of eye movements and actions.

5.2   The Development of Visual Orienting

In the previous section attempts to relate brain development of an aspect of sensory processing were discussed. In this section we move to a domain, visual orienting, which allows the study of the effects of brain development on the integration between sensory input and motor output. Visual orienting involves moving the eyes and head in response to, or in anticipation of, a new sensory stimulus. Most of the tasks to be described involve stimuli that are well within the visual capacities for infants, and involve a form of action (movements of the eyes) which infants can readily accomplish. Thus, while there is continuing development of both sensory and motor processing throughout infancy, through carefully designed experiments we are able to focus more on the integration between sensory input and motor output.

There are also other reasons for studying the development of visual orienting. One of these is that over the first year of life it is the human infant's primary method of gathering information from its environment (Aslin, 2007). These shifts of gaze allow the infant to select particular aspects of the external world for further study and learning. For example, as we will see in Chapter 7, simply by shifting the head and eyes infants can ensure that they are exposed to faces more than to other stimuli. In addition, most of what we have learned about mental processes in infants has come from tasks in which some measure of looking behavior, such as preferential looking or habituation to a repeatedly presented stimulus, is used (see Chapter 2).

Despite the importance of shifts of eye gaze in early infancy, however, until the past decade very little was known about how the development of the brain relates to changes in visual orienting abilities. This was despite a substantial literature on the neural basis of saccades (eye movements) which comes from neuropsychological and neuroimaging studies of human adults, as well as single-cell recording and lesion studies in non-human primates (see Andersen, Batista, Snyder, Buneo, & Cohen, 2000, for review).

In one of the first attempts to relate brain development to behavioral change in the human infant, Gordon Bronson (1974, 1982) argued that the early development of vision and visual orienting could be attributed to a shift from subcortical visual processing to processing in cortical visual pathways over the first 6 months of life. Specifically, Bronson cited evidence from electrophysiological, neuroanatomical, and behavioral studies that the primary (cortical) visual pathway is not fully functioning until around 3 months postnatal. As discussed earlier, it has more recently become evident that there is some, albeit limited, cortical activity in newborns, and that the onset of cortical functioning probably proceeds by a series of graded steps, rather than in an all-or-none manner. Meanwhile, neurophysio-logical research on monkeys and neuropsychological research with human adults has revealed that there are multiple pathways involved in oculomotor (eye movement) control and attention shifts in the primate brain. A number of the structures and pathways involved in oculomotor control in primates are illustrated in Figure 5.4.

FURTHER READING Atkinson and Braddick (2003); Iliescu and Dannemiller (2008); Johnson (2002); Richards (2001, 2003).

Most of the pathways and structures illustrated in Figure 5.4 are known to be involved in particular types of information processing related to the execution and planning of eye movements. When considering the integration between sensory inputs and motor outputs it is important that the pathways discussed can be traced from the source of the input (the eye) to the muscles that shift the eyes. A diagram of such pathways may look different from one that just shows pathways for sensory processing. In Chapter 6 we will discuss the dissociation between visual pathways for action and perception.

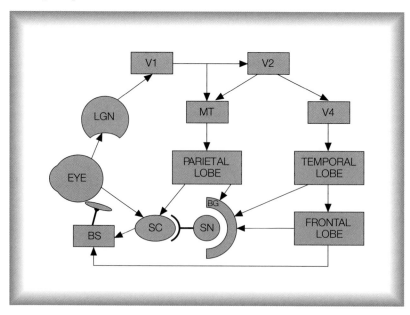

Figure 5.4 Diagram representing some of the main neural pathways and structures involved in visual orienting and attention. BS, brain stem; LGN, lateral geniculate nucleus; V1, V2, and V4, visual cortical areas; MT, middle temporal area; SC, superior colliculus; SN, substantia negra; BG, basal ganglia.

Four brain pathways will be discussed here. The first is the pathway from the eye to the superior colliculus. This subcortical pathway has input mainly from the temporal visual field (the peripheral or outer half of the field of each eye), and is involved in the generation of rapid reflexive eye movements to easily discriminable stimuli. The other three pathways to be discussed here share a projection from the eye to cortical structures via the midbrain (thalamic) visual relay, the lateral geniculate nucleus (LGN), and the primary visual cortex (V1). The first of these goes both directly to the superior colliculus from the primary visual cortex and also via the middle temporal area (MT). Some of the structures on this pathway are thought to play an important role in the detection of motion and the smooth tracking of moving objects. The next pathway proceeds from V1 to other parts of the visual cortex and thence to the frontal eye fields (FEF). As we will see later, this FEF pathway is thought to be involved in more complex aspects of eye movement planning such as anticipatory saccades and learning sequences of scanning patterns. Finally, there is a more complex and less well-understood pathway that involves tonic (continual) inhibition of the superior colliculus (via subcortical structures called the substantia nigra and basal ganglia). Schiller (1985) proposed that this pathway ensures that the activity of the colliculus can be regulated. Others suggest that this oculomotor pathway forms an integrated system with the frontal eye fields and parietal lobes (e.g., Alexander, DeLong, & Strick, 1986) and that it plays some role in the regulation of the subcortical oculomotor pathway by the other cortical pathways.

The challenge has been to relate the development of these various pathways to the visuomotor competence of the infant at different ages. The three perspectives on the development of human brain function offer different views on this. According to the maturational view, we need to relate the sequential development of the different pathways to the onset of new functions as assessed by marker tasks. According to the skill learning view, the infant's brain needs to acquire the sensorimotor skill of generating accurate and informative saccades, and so areas involved in skill acquisition will be important. Finally, according to the interactive specialization view, some of the pathways will initially have poorly defined borders and functions (a lack of specialization) and only with experience will they become dissociable.

Of these three approaches, the maturational view has held sway with regard to visual orienting. To date, this has involved two complementary approaches: predictions about the sequence of development of the pathways from developmental neuroanatomy (Atkinson, 1984; Johnson, 1990), and the administration of marker tasks (see Chapter 2) to ascertain the functional development of particular structures or pathways. An example of the first approach was originally presented over a decade ago (Johnson, 1990). In this analysis I proposed that, first, the characteristics of visually guided behavior of the infant at particular ages are determined by which of the pathways (shown in Figure 5.4) are functional, and, second, which of the cortical pathways are functional is influenced by the developmental state of the primary visual cortex. The basis of this claim at the neuroanatomical level lies in three sets of observations. First, the primary visual cortex is the major (though not exclusive) "gateway" for input to most of the cortical pathways involved in oculomotor control

(Schiller, 1985). Second, the primary visual cortex shows a postnatal continuation of the prenatal "inside-out" pattern of cortical growth described in Chapter 4, with the deeper layers (5 and 6) showing greater dendritic branching, length, and extent of myelination than more superficial layers (2 and 3) around the time of birth. Third, there is a restricted pattern of inputs and outputs from the primary visual cortex (e.g., the projections to V2 depart from the upper layers—see Chapter 4). By combining these observations with information about the developmental neuro-anatomy of the human primary visual cortex, I hypothesized the following sequence of development of cortical pathways underlying oculomotor control: the subcortical pathway from the eye directly to the superior colliculus (probably including cortical projections from the deeper layers of V1 to superior colliculus), followed by the cortical projection which inhibits the superior colliculus pathway, followed by the pathway through cortical structure MT, and finally the pathway involving the frontal eye fields and related structures.

Following these predictions derived from developmental neuroanatomy, we can return to behavioral experiments to see if the transitions here support the predicted sequence of pathway development. Beginning with the newborn infant, evidence from measures of the extent of dendritic arborization and myelination indicate that only the deeper layers of the primary visual cortex are likely to be capable of supporting organized information-processing activity in the human newborn. Since the majority of feed-forward intracortical projections depart from outside the deeper layers (5 and 6), most of the cortical pathways involved in oculomotor control will only be receiving weak or disorganized input at this stage. However, evidence from various sources, such as visually evoked potentials, indicate that information from the eye is entering the primary visual cortex in the newborn. Thus, while some of the newborn's visual behavior can be accounted for in terms of processing in the subcortical pathway, I argued in my 1990 paper that there is also information processing occurring in the deeper cortical layers at birth. At least two characteristics of visually guided behavior in the newborn are consistent with predominantly subcortical control such as saccadic pursuit tracking and preferential orienting to the temporal field. To go through these in more detail:

- The ability of infants to track a moving stimulus in the first few months of life has two characteristics (Aslin, 1981). The first is that the eye movements follow the stimulus in a "saccadic" or step-like manner, as opposed to the smooth pursuit found in adults and older infants. The second characteristic is that the eye movements tend to lag behind the movement of the stimulus, rather than predicting its trajectory. Therefore, when a newborn infant visually tracks a moving stimulus, it could be described as performing a series of saccadic eye movements. Such behavior is consistent with subcortical control of orienting.
- Newborns much more readily orient toward stimuli in the temporal, as opposed to the nasal (the half of the visual field of each eye closer to the nose) visual field (e.g., Lewis, Maurer, & Milewski, 1979). Posner and Rothbart (1981) suggest that midbrain structures such as the colliculus can be driven most readily by temporal

field input. This proposal has been confirmed in studies of adult "blindsight" patients by Rafal, Smith, Krantz, Cohen, and Brennan (1990), who established that distracter stimuli placed in the temporal "blindfield" had an effect on orienting into the good field, whereas distracter stimuli in the nasal blindfield did not. Evidence from studies of infants in which a complete cerebral hemisphere has been removed (to alleviate epilepsy) indicate that the subcortical (collicular) pathway alone is capable of generating saccades toward a peripheral target in the cortically "blind" field (Braddick et al., 1992).

Around 1 month of age infants show "obligatory attention" (also known as "sticky fixation") (Hood, 1995; Johnson, Posner, & Rothbart, 1991; Stechler & Latz, 1966). That is to say, they have great difficulty in disengaging their gaze from a stimulus in order to make a saccade to another location. Sometimes an infant around 1 month of age can spend as long as several minutes fixedly gazing at a seemingly uninteresting aspect of the environment, such as a section of carpet, before bursting into tears! Although this phenomenon is still poorly understood, I suggested that it was due to the development of tonic inhibition of the colliculus via the substantia nigra (see Figure 5.4). Since this pathway projects from the deeper layers of the primary visual cortex to the colliculus, it is hypothesized to be the first strong cortical influence on oculomotor control. This (as yet) unregulated tonic inhibition of the colliculus has the consequence that stimuli impinging on the peripheral visual field no longer elicit an automatic exogenous saccade as readily as in newborns.

By around 2 months of age infants begin to show periods of smooth visual tracking, although their eye movements still lag behind the movement of the stimulus. At this age they also become more sensitive to stimuli placed in the nasal visual field (Aslin, 1981) and also more sensitive to coherent motion (Wattam-Bell, 1990). I proposed that the onset of these behaviors coincides with the functioning of the pathway involving structure MT. The enabling of this route of eye movement control may provide this cortical stream with the ability to regulate activity in the superior colliculus.

Associated with further dendritic growth and myelination within the upper layers of the primary visual cortex strengthening the projections from V1 to other cortical areas, around 3 months of age the pathways involving the frontal eye fields may become functional. This development may greatly increase the infant's ability to make "anticipatory" eye movements and to learn sequences of looking patterns, both functions associated with the frontal eye fields. With regard to the visual tracking of a moving object, now not only do infants show periods of smooth tracking, but their eye movements often predict the movement of the stimulus in an anticipatory manner. A number of experiments by Haith and colleagues have demonstrated that anticipatory eye movements can be readily elicited from infants by this age. For example, Haith, Hazan, and Goodman (1988) exposed 3½-month-old infants to a series of picture slides which appeared either on the right- or on the left-hand side of the infant. These stimuli were either presented in an alternating sequence with fixed inter-stimulus interval (ISI), or with an irregular alternation pattern and ISI. It was observed that the regular alternation pattern produced more stimulus anticipations

Table 5.1   Summary of the relation between developing oculomotor pathways and behavior

Age	Functional Anatomy	Behavior
Newborn	SC pathway + layer 5 and 6 pyramidal output to LGN and SC	Saccadic pursuit tracking Preferential orienting to temporal visual field "Externality effect"
1 months	As above + inhibitory pathway to SC via BG	As above + "obligatory" attention
2 months	As above + MT (magnocellular) pathway to SC	Onset of smooth pursuit tracking and increased sensitivity to nasal visual field
3 months and over	As above + FEF (parvocellular) pathway to SC and BS	Increase in "anticipatory" tracking and sequential scanning patterns

SC, superior colliculus: LGN, lateral geniculate nucleus; BG, basal ganglia; MT, middle temporal area; FEF, frontal eye fields; BS, brain stem.

and faster reaction times to make an eye movement than in the irregular series. Haith and colleagues concluded from these results that infants of this age are able to develop expectancies for non-controllable spatiotemporal events. Canfield and Haith (1991) tested 2- and 3-month-old infants in an experiment which included more complex sequences (such as left–left–right, left–left–right, etc.). Consistent with the predictions from developmental neuroanatomy, while they failed to find significant effects with 2-month-olds, 3-month-olds were able to acquire at least some of the more complex sequences.

Given that this survey of the behavioral evidence pertaining to the development of visual orienting was broadly consistent with the predictions from developmental neurobiology (see Table 5.1 for a summary), the next step was to develop and consider marker tasks for some of these and other parts of the cortex with a role in oculomotor control. Table 5.2 shows a number of marker tasks that have recently been developed for the functioning of structures involved in oculomotor control and visual attention (next section) shifts.

Marker tasks for several cortical regions thought to play a role in oculomotor control, the parietal cortex, frontal eye fields (FEF), and dorsolateral prefrontal cortex (DLPFC), have been developed, and show rapid development between 2 and 6 months of age in human infants. Starting with marker tasks for the FEF, frontal cortex damage in humans results in an inability to suppress involuntary automatic saccades toward targets, and an apparent inability to control volitional saccades (Fischer & Breitmeyer, 1987; Guitton, Buchtel, & Douglas, 1985). For example, Guitton et al. (1985) studied typical participants and patients with frontal lobe

Table 5.2   Marker tasks for the development of visual orienting and attention

Brain Region	Marker Task	Studies
Superior colliculus	Inhibition of return	Clohessy Posner, Rothbart, & Vecera (1991); Simion, Valenza, Umilta, & Dalla Barba (1995)
	Vector summation saccades	Johnson, Gilmore, Tucker, & Minister (1994)
Middle temporal area	Coherent motion detection; structure from motion	Wattam-Bell (1991)
	Smooth tracking	Aslin (1981)
Parietal cortex	Spatial cueing task	Hood & Atkinson (1991); Hood (1993); Johnson (1994); Johnson & Tucker (1996)
	Eye-centered saccade planning	Gilmore & Johnson (1997)
Frontal eye fields	Inhibition of automatic saccades	Johnson (1995)
	Anticipatory saccades	Haith et al. (1988)
Dorsolateral prefrontal cortex	Oculomotor delayed response task	Gilmore & Johnson (1995)

lesions or temporal lobe lesions in a so-called "anti-saccade" task. In this task participants are instructed to *not* look at a briefly flashed cue, but rather to make a saccade in the opposite direction (Hallett, 1978). Guitton et al. (1985) reported that while typical participants and patients with temporal lobe damage could do this task with relative ease, patients with frontal damage, in particular those with damage around the FEF, were severely impaired. Patients with frontal damage had particular difficulty in suppressing unwanted saccades toward the cue stimulus.

I have developed a version of the anti-saccade task for use with infants (Johnson, 1995). Clearly, one cannot give verbal instruction to a young infant to look to the opposite side from where the cue stimulus appears. Instead, infants are motivated by making the second stimulus reliably more dynamic and colorful than the first. Thus, after a number of such trials infants may learn to inhibit their tendency to make a saccade to the first stimulus (the cue) when it appears, in order to respond as rapidly as possible to the more attractive second stimulus (the target). A group of 4-month-old infants showed a significant decrease in their frequency of looking to the first (cue) stimulus over a number of such trials (Johnson, 1995). A second experiment demonstrated that this decrement was not due to differential habituation to the simpler stimulus. A more refined version of this saccade inhibition task tailored to individual differences between infants has recently been published (Holmboe, Fearon, Csibra, Tucker, & Johnson, 2008). Since 4-month-olds are able to inhibit saccades to a peripheral stimulus, it is reasonable to infer that their frontal eye field circuit is functioning by this age.

Other tasks recently conducted with infants are consistent with an increasing prefrontal cortex endogenous control over shifts of attention and saccades around 6 months of age. For example, Funahashi, Bruce, and Goldman-Rakic (1989, 1990) devised an oculomotor delayed response paradigm to study the properties of neurons in the DLPFC of macaque monkeys. In this task the monkey plans a saccade toward a particular spatial location, but has to wait for a period (usually between 2 and 5 seconds) before actually executing the saccade. Single-unit recording in the macaque indicates that some cells in the DLPFC code for the direction of the saccade during the delay. Further, reversible microlesions to the area result in selective amnesia for saccades to a localized part of the visual field. A subsequent PET study on human participants has confirmed the involvement of DLPFC (and parietal cortex) in this task (Jonides et al., 1993).

Gilmore and Johnson (1995) devised an infant version of the oculomotor delayed response task: a marker task for DLPFC (see Figure 5.5). The results obtained to date indicate that 6-month-old human infants can perform delayed saccades successfully with delays of up to 5 seconds, suggesting some influence of the prefrontal cortex on eye movement control by this age.

In terms of the three viewpoints on human functional brain development outlined earlier, the Johnson (1990) model of the development of visual orienting could be described as a maturational hypothesis. The emphasis of this model was on how maturational changes in neuroanatomy cause or allow new brain pathways to become active.

FURTHER READING   Johnson (2002); Richards (2008).

Data collected more recently suggest that the original model requires some modification, and that it may be beneficial also to consider skill learning perspectives. A more direct assessment of the hypotheses advanced in the Johnson model can be provided by event-related potential measures (time-locked to the initiation of the eye movements: Balaban & Weinstein, 1985; Csibra, Johnson, & Tucker, 1997). By time-locking to the onset of eye movements we can examine the brain events that precede the production of this simple action. In adults such experiments reveal characteristic pre-saccadic components recorded over the parietal cortex prior to the execution of saccades. The clearest of these components is the pre-saccadic "spike potential" (SP), a sharp positive-going deflection which precedes the saccade by 8–20 ms (Csibra et al., 1997). The spike potential is observed in most saccade tasks in adults, and is

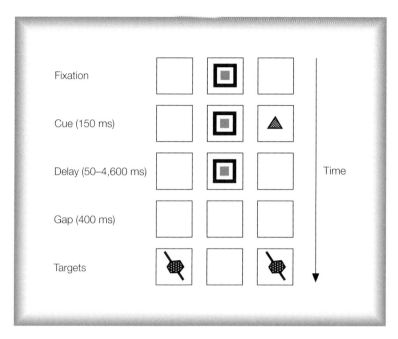

Figure 5.5   The oculomotor delayed response task as designed for use with infants. Infant subjects face three computer screens on which brightly colored moving stimuli appear. At the start of each trial a fixation stimulus appears on the central screen. Once the infant is looking at this stimulus, a cue is briefly flashed up on one of the two side screens. Following the briefly flashed cue, the central stimulus stays on for between 1 and 5 seconds, before presentation of two targets on the side screens. By measuring delayed looks to the cued location prior to the target onset, Gilmore and Johnson (1995) established that infants can retain information about the cued location for several seconds.

therefore thought to represent an important stage of cortical processing required to generate a saccade.

Csibra, Tucker, and Johnson (1998) investigated whether there are pre-saccadic potentials recordable over parietal leads in 6-month-old infants. Given the prediction that by this age infants have essentially the same pathways active for saccade planning as do adults, we were surprised to find no evidence of this component (see Figure 5.6) in our infant participants (see also Vaughan & Kurtzberg, 1989). This finding suggests that the target-driven saccades performed by 6-month-olds in our study were controlled largely by subcortical routes for visually guided responses mediated by the superior colliculus.

Because this result was surprising, we decided to conduct two follow-up studies. In one of these we tested 12-month-olds with the same procedure. These older infants did show a spike potential like that observed in adults though somewhat smaller in amplitude (see Figure 5.6). The other study explored whether the dorsal pathway could be activated in very young infants through a more demanding saccade task. Specifically, we compared ERPs before reactive (target-elicited) and anticipatory (endogenous) saccades in 4-month-old infants (Csibra, Tucker, & Johnson, 2001).

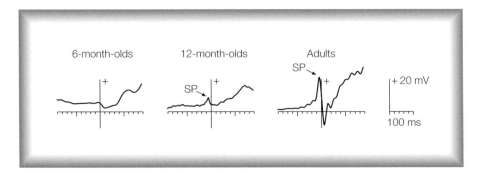

Figure 5.6 Grand-average saccade-locked potentials at Pz in (a) 6-month-old infants, (b) 12-month-old infants, and (c) adults. The vertical bar marks the saccade onset, a spike potential is evident in adults and 12-month-olds, but not at 6 months.

We were not able to record any reliable posterior activity prior to either reactive or anticipatory eye movements. Thus, even when the saccade is generated by cortical computation of the likely location of the next stimulus, as in the case of anticipatory eye movements, posterior cortical structures do not seem to be involved in the planning of this action.

In all these infant ERP studies, while there was a lack of evidence for posterior cortical control over eye movements in our experiments with 6-month-olds, we observed effects recorded over frontal leads. These saccade-related effects were consistent with the frontal eye field disinhabition of subcortical (collicular) circuits when a central foveated stimulus is removed (Csibra et al., 1998, 2001). In brief, we interpreted these findings in terms of the frontal eye fields helping to maintain fixation on to foveated stimuli by inhibiting collicular circuits. This is consistent with the predictions of the Johnson (1990) model. However, when saccades to peripheral stimuli are made, the ERP evidence indicated that these are largely initiated by collicular circuits, sometimes as a consequence of inhibition being released by the frontal eye fields. In a converging line of thinking, Canfield and colleagues argued on the basis of behavioral and further neuroanatomical evidence that the FEF pathway would precede the more posterior pathways developmentally (Canfield, Smith, Brezsnyak, & Snow, 1997). This early involvement of the FEF pathway could be consistent with a skill learning hypothesis in which more anterior structures get activated earlier than posterior circuits. By this interpretation, there is greater involvement of frontal cortex circuitry in infants because they are still acquiring the skill of planning and executing eye movements.

The third perspective on functional brain development, interactive specialization, could also be brought to bear on this data. From this perspective, the pathways involved in visual orienting are initially less distinct from both surrounding tissue and each other (see Iliescu & Dannemiller, 2008). Further, rather than the onset of a new ability being associated with the onset of functioning in a "new" area, the interactive specialization approach encourages the view that there will be widespread changes across one or more pathways associated with new abilities. In a study where functional activity in children and adults was assessed by fMRI during the onset of demanding saccade tasks, multiple cortical and subcortical areas appeared to change their response pattern (Luna et al., 2001), rather than one or two previously silent regions becoming active (mature).

One cortical area involved in oculomotor control for which a more experience-dependent approach has been taken is the parietal cortex. This is a region of the primate cortex which has been implicated in aspects of saccade planning in monkey cellular recording studies, human functional neuroimaging studies, and neuropsychological studies of brain-damaged patients. It is also a region of cortex that undergoes marked developmental changes between 3 and 6 months of age, as demonstrated in both neuroanatomical studies of postmortem brains (Conel, 1939–1967) and PET (Chugani et al., 2002). Andersen and colleagues (2000) have recorded from single cells in parts of the macaque monkey parietal cortex, and many of these cells code for saccades within an eye- or head-centered frame of reference. In other words, their receptive fields respond to combinations of eye or head position, on the one hand, and retinal distance from the fovea to the target, on the other. This is in contrast to parts of the superior colliculus in which cells commonly respond according to the retinal distance and direction of the target from the fovea.

Zipser and Andersen (1988; Andersen & Zipser, 1988) constructed a connectionist model in which the hidden layer units developed response properties which closely resembled those observed within regions of the primate parietal cortex. While the details of this neuroconnectionist model need not concern us here, the fundamental point to note is that the representations for generating saccades within an eye- or head-centered frame of reference emerged as a result of training, and did not require to be "hard-wired" into the network. An important question that remains is whether infants only develop the ability to use extra-retinal coordinates to plan saccades during postnatal life. If they do, this would be consistent with the assumption underlying the model that representations controlling eye- or head-centered action need to be constructed postnatally, and result from constraints imposed by the network structure and its interaction with the external environment.

With Rick Gilmore, I conducted several experiments designed to ascertain whether the ability of infants to use extra-retinal frames of reference to plan saccades emerges over the first few months of life. In one of these experiments we exposed 4- and 6-month-old infants to two simultaneously flashed targets on a large monitor screen. The targets were flashed so briefly that they were gone before the infant started to make a saccade to them. We then studied the saccades which infants made in response to these targets (see Figure 5.7). In many trials they made two saccades, the first of these being to the location of one of the two targets. Having made a saccade to one of the two targets, we examined whether the second saccade that they made was to the actual location of the second target, or whether it was to the retinal location (the location on the retina at which that target had originally appeared). To make the second saccade to the correct spatial location requires infants to be able to take into account the fact that their eyes had shifted position, and then compute the saccade necessary given the new eye position. The results indicated that for 4-month-olds the

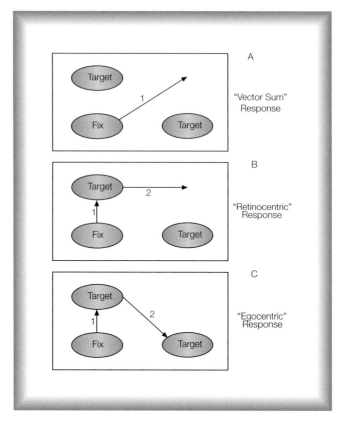

Figure 5.7 Three types of saccades made by young infants in response to two targets briefly flashed as shown. (A) A "vector summation" saccade in which eye movement is directed between the two targets. (B) A "retinocentric" saccade in which the second saccade is directed to the location corresponding to the retinal error when the flash occurred. (C) An "egocentric" saccade which corresponds to the use of extra-retinal information to plan the second saccade. Between birth and 6 months, infants shift from the first two types of response to the third.

majority of second saccades were directed to the retinal location in which the target had appeared. In contrast, for the 6-month-olds, the majority of second saccades were made to the correct spatial location for the other target. These results suggest that the ability to use extra-retinal cues to plan saccades emerges through the first six months of life. However, saccades based on retinal location (and thought to be subcortical in origin) are probably present from birth (Gilmore & Johnson, 1997).

FURTHER READING   Johnson, Mareschal, & Csibra (2008).

In sum, while even newborns are capable of simple target-driven saccades, oculomotor skills continue to develop throughout the first year. Influential maturational models have been only partially supported by recent ERP and neuroim aging evidence. In particular, the finding that frontal regions may be more important than more posterior areas presents a challenge to the maturational approach. It is possible that in early development these pathways are initially less segregated than is observed in adults, and therefore may interact and process information in quite different ways (Iliescu & Dannemiller, 2008).

5.3   Visual Attention

Our discussion so far has concerned *overt* shifts of attention due to eye and head movements. However, as adults we are also capable of shifting our attention *covertly* (i.e. without moving the eyes or other sensory receptors). This allows us to enhance our processing of some spatial locations or objects within our visual field, to the exclusion of others.

One way in which evidence for covert attention has been provided in adults is by studying the effect on detection of cueing saccades to a particular spatial location. A briefly presented cue serves to draw covert attention to the location, resulting in the subsequent facilitation of detection of targets at that location (Maylor, 1985; Posner & Cohen, 1980). While detection of and responses to a covertly attended location are *facilitated* if the target stimulus appears very shortly after the cue offset, with longer latencies between cue and target, saccades toward that location are *inhibited*. This latter phenomenon, referred to as "inhibition of return" (Posner, Rafal, Choate, & Vaughan, 1985), may reflect an evolutionarily important mechanism which prevents attention returning to a recently processed spatial location. In adults facilitation is reliably observed when targets appeared at the cued location within about 150 ms of the cue, whereas targets appearing between 300 and 1300 ms after a peripheral (exogenous) cue result in longer detection latencies (e.g., Maylor, 1985; Posner & Cohen, 1980, 1984).

Following lesions to the posterior parietal lobe, adults show severe neglect of the contralateral visual field. According to Posner and colleagues, this neglect is due to damage to the "posterior attention network." This refers to a brain circuit which includes not only the posterior parietal lobe, but also the pulvinar and superior colliculus (Posner, 1988; Posner & Petersen, 1990; see Figure 5.4 for all but the pulvinar). Damage to this circuit is postulated to impair participants' ability to shift covert attention to a cued spatial location. The involvement of these regions in shifts of visual attention has been confirmed by PET studies. As mentioned above, both neuroanatomical (Conel, 1939–1967) and PET (Chugani et al., 1987) evidence from the human infant indicate that the parietal lobe is undergoing substantive and rapid development between 3 and 6 months after birth. The question arises, therefore, as to whether infants become capable of covert shifts of attention during this time.

Since infants do not accept verbal instruction and are poor at motor responses used to study spatial attention in adults, such as a key press, the only response available to demonstrate facilitation and inhibition of a cued location is eye movements. That is, overt shifts are used to study *covert* shifts of attention by examining the influence of a cue stimulus (which is presented so briefly that it does not normally elicit an eye movement) on infants' subsequent saccades toward conspicuous target stimuli. Using these methods, Hood and Atkinson (1991; see Hood, 1995) reported that 6-month-old infants have faster reaction times to make a saccade to a target when it appears immediately after a brief (100 ms) cue stimulus than when it appears in an uncued location. A group of 3-month-old infants did not show this effect. Johnson (1994; Johnson & Tucker, 1996) employed a similar procedure in which a brief (100 ms) cue was presented on one of two side screens, before bilateral targets were presented either 100 ms or 600 ms later. It was hypothesized on the basis of the adult findings that the 200 ms stimulus onset asynchrony (SOA) would be short enough to produce facilitation, while the long SOA trials should result in preferential orienting toward the opposite side (inhibition of return). This result was obtained with a group of 4-month-old infants, suggesting the possibility that infants are capable of covert shifts of attention at this age. Consistent with the previous findings, these effects were not observed in a group of 2-month-old infants.

Another manifestation of covert attention concerns so-called "sustained" attention. Sustained attention refers to the ability of participants to maintain the direction of their attention toward a stimulus even in the presence of distracters. Richards (2001, 2003) has developed a heart rate marker for sustained attention in infants. The heart-rate-defined period of sustained attention usually lasts for between 5 and 15 seconds after the onset of a complex stimulus (see Figure 5.8).

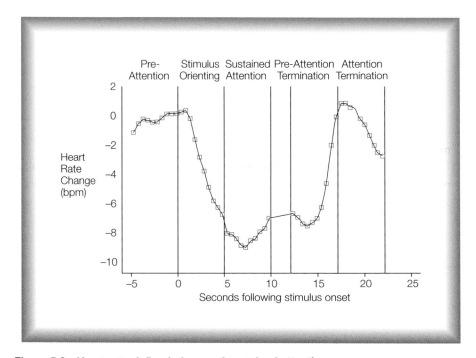

Figure 5.8   Heart-rate-defined phases of sustained attention.

In order to investigate the effect of sustained attention on the response to exogenous cues, Richards (2001, 2003) used an "interrupted stimulus method" in which a peripheral stimulus (a flashing light) is presented while the infant is gazing at a central stimulus (a TV screen with a complex visual pattern). By varying the length of time between the onset of the TV image and the onset of the peripheral stimulus, he was able to present the peripheral stimulus either within the period of sustained covert attention, or outside it. Richards found that during the periods when heart rate was decreased (sustained endogenous attention) it took twice as long for the infant to shift their gaze toward the peripheral stimulus as when heart rate had returned to pre-stimulus levels (attention termination). Further, those saccades that are made to a peripheral stimulus during sustained attention are less accurate than normal, and involve multiple hypometric saccades, a characteristic of collicular-generated saccades (Richards, 1991). Thus, the lack of distractibility during periods of sustained attention is likely to be due to cortically mediated pathways inhibiting collicular mechanisms.

FURTHER READING Richards (2008).

A number of studies have traced developments in visual attention during childhood using purely cognitive methods, but have described the continuation of similar transitions to those observed in early infancy. Three transitions that have been described are the greater ability to expand or constrict a field of attention (e.g., Chapman, 1981; Enns & Girgus, 1985), the greater ability to disengage attention from distracting information or invalid cueing (Akhtar & Enns, 1989; Enns & Brodeur, 1989), and a faster speed of shifting attention (Pearson & Lane, 1990).

Enns and Girgus (1985) tested school-age children and adults in speeded classification tasks involving a stimulus composed of two elements that varied in distance (visual angle). Participants had to classify stimuli on the basis of one of the two elements. Younger children (6–8 years) experienced more interference when the elements were closely spaced than did older children (9–11 years) and adults. The same stimuli were used for a second task in which both of the elements had to be taken into account. In this task the younger children had difficulty when the elements were separated by large visual angles. The authors conclude that younger children have problems in contracting and expanding the size of attentional focus. An ERP study of auditory attention also concluded that there is a development in the ability to narrow attentional focus during childhood (Berman & Friedman, 1995).

An observation that may be related is that older children and adults are often reported as being able to shift their attention more rapidly than younger ones. For example, Pearson and Lane (1990) using a spatial cueing paradigm observed that younger infants took longer to covertly shift their attention to more peripheral targets, whereas they were almost as fast as adults to shift to targets very close to fixation. This indicates that it is the speed of shifting, rather than the latency to elicit a covert shift, which improves with age. The increasing speed of shifting attention with age has also been reported during infancy (Johnson & Tucker, 1996), indicating that this developmental transition may be a gradual one that begins early in life.

In several studies, younger children and infants have been argued to have greater difficulty in disengaging from distracting stimuli or invalid spatial cues. For example, Enns and Brodeur (1989) used a spatial cueing paradigm to cue either neutrally (all locations cued), unpredictably (random cueing), or predictably (cue predicts target presentation). The results from participants aged 6, 8, and 20 years indicated that while all age groups automatically oriented attention to the cued location, the children processed targets in non-cued locations more slowly than did adults, and did not take advantage of the predictability of the cues. Thus the costs and benefits of cueing were greater in the younger participants due to an increased cost imposed by invalid cueing. Tipper, Bourque, Anderson, and Brehaut (1989) suggest that these deficits are due to the relative inability to inhibit irrelevant stimuli, a conclusion that is consistent with more recent findings (Brodeur & Boden, 2000; Wainwright & Bryson, 2002). Once again, similar developmental trends have been observed in infancy experiments where younger infants are more likely to fail to disengage from competing stimuli, such as obligatory attention described earlier.

Research on the neural basis of the development of covert attention in childhood has only just begun, and has been based on three topics: (a) ERP studies, (b) effects of early cortical damage, and (c) developmental disorders of genetic origin. Richards (2003) describes several experiments in which he has used the spatial cueing procedure while recording ERPs from infants in order to detect neural signatures of covert attention. In one study he examined the "P1 validity effect" in young infants. The P1 is a large positive ERP component that occurs around 100 ms after stimulus presentation. Studies with adult participants have shown that the P1 is enhanced in scale in valid trials (where the cue correctly predicts the target) (Hillyard, Mangun, Woldorff, & Luck, 1995). This is of interest since this short-latency component reflects early stages of visual processing, demonstrating that shifts of covert attention modulate early sensory processing of the target. Richards (2003) reports that while there was little ERP evidence for covert attention shifts in 3-month-old infants, by 5 months the pattern of ERP data resembled that in adults, indicating that infants at this age were shifting attention to the cued location covertly.

Another way to examine the neural basis of covert orienting in development has been to assess the consequences of perinatal damage to the cerebral cortex. In collaboration with Joan Stiles and colleagues, we examined spatial cueing in infants who had unfortunately suffered perinatal damage to one of four quadrants of the cortex (Johnson, Tucker, Stiles, & Trauner, 1998). The results were somewhat surprising in that the posterior lesions that would normally cause deficits in adults had no effect on the infants. In contrast, frontal damage did have a measurable effect on spatial cueing. While surprising, these results fit well with work from other laboratories. For example, Craft, Schatz, and colleagues have studied the consequences of perinatal brain injury (sometime associated with sickle cell anemia) on performance in spatial cueing tasks during childhood. In several studies deficits were observed following anterior (frontal) damage, and not (or less) with posterior damage (Craft, White, Park, & Figiel, 1994; Schatz, Craft, Koby, & DeBaun, 2000; Schatz, Craft, White, Park, & Figiel, 2001).

A third way to address the neurodevelopment of covert attention is to study disorders of this process in groups of atypically developing children. ADHD (attention deficit/hyperactivity disorder) is characterized by inattention, hyperactivity, and impulsivity beginning before 7 years of age (Karatekin, 2001). Estimates for its prevalence run as high as 3–5% of school children in the USA, although this figure varies enormously across cultures. Despite the title of the disorder, there is no general agreement about specific deficits in components of attention in these children. Rather, they appear to have mild difficulties in some tests of sustained and selective attention that may reflect difficulties in processing attended stimuli and/or in maintaining attention in tasks that make demands on cognitive resources (see Karetekin, 2001, for review).

Another disorder that has been linked to deficits in attention is autism (see Chapter 2 for an introduction to autism). One of the key symptoms of autism in children and adults is atypical attention. For example, Courchesne and colleagues (Akshoomoff & Courchesne, 1994; Townsend & Courchesne, 1994) have tested individuals with autism on a variety of spatial cueing and attention switching tasks. They report, on the basis of autopsy and structural MRI data, that most participants with autism have developmental damage to their cerebellum. In a number of tasks they have associated this damage with reduced ability to switch attention, and a slower shifting of covert spatial attention. Another neural deficit observed in at least some participants with autism is bilateral parietal damage. Townsend and Courchesne (1994) have proposed that this damage gives rise to a narrowed focus of spatial attention, such that targets presented within the narrowed "spotlight" are detected more rapidly than normal. In contrast, targets presented at small eccentricities from fixation that would be responded to rapidly by typical participants are responded to much more slowly by autistic participants since they are outside the narrow attentional focus.

As with other symptoms of autism that are evident following diagnosis, the question arises as to whether deviant patterns of attention are a compounded symptom of original deficits in other domains, such as in social cognition (see Chapter 7), or whether initial problems with attention actually cause some of the other symptoms of the condition (Elsabbagh & Johnson, 2007). One way to address this issue is to study babies at risk for a later diagnosis of autism by virtue of having an older sibling already diagnosed. Converging findings from different groups indicate that during the first year of life infants at risk behave differently from groups of control babies in simple visual orienting paradigms (Elsabbagh et al., 2009), and may even identify those particular infants who will go on to be diagnosed when they are 2 or 3 years old (Zwaigenbaum et al., 2005).

FURTHER READING Cornish and Wilding (2010).

5.4   General Summary and Conclusions

This chapter began with a discussion of the contribution of peripheral systems (retinal) development in the emergence of basic visual functions. Retinal development can only partially explain improvements in basic visual functions, indicating that brain changes are important also. With regard to binocular vision, neuroanatomical and computational modeling evidence highlights the importance of the segregation of inputs to layer 4 cells in the primary visual cortex. This increased segregation of inputs from the two eyes can be viewed as the result of a self-organizing neural network constrained by certain intrinsic and extrinsic factors.

Moving from sensory processing to sensorimotor integration, we proceeded to describe an attempt to use the developmental neuroanatomy of the cortex to make predictions about developmental changes in visual orienting in infants. A number of behavioral marker tasks for cortical regions involved in oculomotor control were reviewed and discussed in relation to the maturational model. Recent neuroimaging and behavioral studies require modifications to the original model, and suggest that an interactive specialization view may eventually prove more fruitful.

Finally, experiments concerned with the development of covert (internal) attention shifts in infants and children were described. A number of changes in the flexibility and speed of shifting attention were shown to originate in infancy but continue into childhood. Some developmental disorders, such as autism, may involve deficits in shifting overt or covert attention.

Key Issues for Discussion

- What experiments or populations could be studied to ascertain the degree to which experience is important in the formation of ocular dominance columns in humans?
- To what extent do maturational models explain changes in the development of visual orienting abilities over the first year?
- Are attention problems in autism likely to be a cause or a consequence of difficulties in other domains?

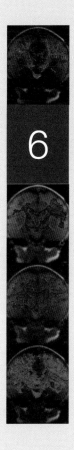

6

Perceiving and Acting on the Physical World: Objects and Number

Objects are special in our sensory world since they are both recognized and manipulated. Neuroscience evidence suggests that these two functions are computed by two different pathways: a ventral recognition pathway and a dorsal sensorimotor action pathway. Preliminary attempts to relate these two pathways to human development are discussed, and simple computational models are presented. Bursts of high-frequency neural oscillations have been related to the binding of features to compose objects and to the retention of objects following occlusion.

Objects can be counted, and two number-relevant systems in the primate brain are discussed. One of these is an analog- magnitude system similar to that active in time or length judgments, while the other is a system engaged by tracking small numbers of objects (object-files). Both systems appear to be active in young infants, and may underlie their ability to perform simple numerical computations with small numbers of objects. Some suggest that more sophisticated computations with large numbers require language-mediated integration between these two systems.

Developmental Cognitive Neuroscience (Third Edition) Mark H. Johnson with Michelle de Haan
© 2011 Mark H. Johnson

Physical objects are special in our sensory world since—unlike landscapes, faces, and sounds—they are not only recognized and categorized, but are also often manipulated using our hands and feet. As adults, perceiving and acting on everyday objects seems easy. However, further consideration reveals that complex computations and rich representations need to underlie these processes. For example, objects have to be recognized from multiple different viewpoints, and under conditions where they are partially obscured (partial occlusion) or in front of complex backgrounds (object parsing). Our fingers and hands have to be adjusted according to the anticipated size and weight of the object, and our wrists oriented appropriately to let us grasp the object in the appropriate place and correct orientation. While there have been many behavioral studies conducted on object processing in infants and young children, only recently has evidence from cognitive neuroscience been used to inform and constrain theories of this domain of cognitive development.

6.1   The Dorsal and Ventral Visual Pathways

In Chapter 5 we discussed several pathways that underlie visual orienting and attention. There is now a substantive body of evidence that visual information processing about objects is divided into two relatively separate streams in the brain. The detailed connectivity of these cortical routes is very complex (see van Essen, Anderson, & Felleman, 1992), but, in simplified terms, one pathway (the ventral route) extends from the primary visual cortex through to parts of the temporal lobe, while the other pathway (the dorsal route) goes from the primary visual cortex to the parietal cortex (see Figure 6.1). The exact point at which the routes separate is still debated. For reasons we will discuss below, the ventral route is sometimes called the *What* or *Perception* pathway, while the dorsal route is often called the *Where* or *Action* pathway. We will start our discussion with the dorsal route.

   All visually guided actions take place in space, but the spatial processing required will differ according to the action to be performed. Evidence for multiple spatial systems can be seen in the spatial coding shown by neurons in the dorsal stream. For example, as we saw in Chapter 5, some cells in the parietal cortex anticipate the retinal consequences of saccadic eye movements and update the cortical (body-centered) representation of visual space to provide continuously accurate coding of the location of objects in space. Other cells have gaze-dependent responses. That is, they mark where the animal is looking with respect to eye-centered coordinates systems. Both of these provide egocentric spatial codings that are only useful over very short periods of time since every time the animal moves the coordinates have to be recomputed.

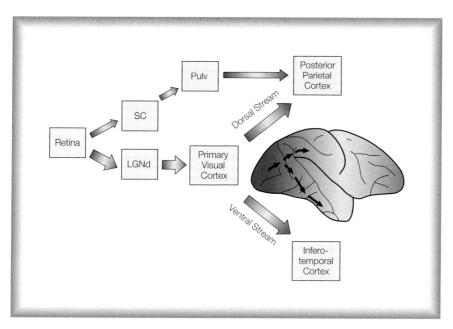

Figure 6.1 Major routes whereby retinal input reaches the dorsal and ventral streams. The diagram of the brain on the right of the figure shows the approximate routes of the projections from primary visual cortex to posterior parietal and the inferotemporal cortex, respectively. LGNd: lateral geniculate nucleus, pars dorsalis; Pulv: pulvinar; SC: superior colliculus.

In the real world target objects are often moving. Hence, it is not only necessary for us to track that motion in order to localize the object in space, but it is also necessary to anticipate the object's movement. Some cells in the parietal cortex appear to be involved in the tracking of moving objects. Moreover, many of these cells continue to respond after the stimulus has disappeared (Newsome, Wurtz, & Komatsu, 1988). In addition, there is selectivity in other parts of the dorsal stream for relative motion and size changes when an object moves toward or away from the viewer. Many neurons on the dorsal pathway are also driven by large-scale optical flow fields, suggesting that self-motion is being computed. Cells in the dorsal pathway also code size, shape, and orientation, which are necessary for the proper reaching for and grasping of an object.

There is also evidence suggesting that the different spatial-temporal systems described above are partially segregated into different regions and routes within the dorsal pathway. Thus the dorsal stream could be viewed as a pathway with many parallel computations of different spatial-temporal properties occurring at once. Different streams compute different-spatial temporal analyses in different coordinate systems, possibly with different effector systems in mind. Milner and Goodale (1995) argue that the cells of the parietal cortex are neither sensory nor motor, but rather sensorimotor. They are involved in transforming retinal information (sensory) into motor coordinates (motor), and in transducing perceptual input into motor actions.

The properties of neurons in the adult ventral stream seem complementary to those in the dorsal stream. As one proceeds along the ventral stream, cells respond to more and more complex clusters of features. At the higher levels, the complex cells show remarkable selectivity in their firing. These neurons are all selective to the figural and surface properties of objects (i.e. the internal object features). More importantly, many of the cells have very large receptive fields on the retina. That means that, although they can process feature information, they lose much of their spatial resolution on the retina. In effect, these cells develop spatially invariant representations of objects by responding to the presence of a consistent feature cluster independently of its position. Some cells seem to respond maximally to a preferred object orientation (independently of position) thereby computing a "view-centered representation." Other cells respond equally to an object in any orientation. That is, they have developed a transformation-invariant representation. Thus, the properties of neurons along the ventral pathway are entirely consistent with what would be expected of a system concerned with recognizing objects, scenes, and individuals with enduring characteristics rather than the moment-to-moment changes in the visual array that occur in a natural setting. Transformation-invariant representations could provide the basic raw material for recognition memory and other long-term representations of the visual world.

Why should such different streams of processing be present in adult primates? If the representations in the dorsal stream are closely linked to the functions of the motor system, then it is not surprising that spatial-temporal information is at a premium down this pathway. Motor actions involve localizing targets within a three-dimensional spatial-temporal world. In contrast, recognition or identification of objects requires that spatial-temporal variability be minimized. Early work in machine vision found that view-invariant recognition (i.e. the ability to recognize an object as the same independently of orientation and location) was a very difficult computational problem. One of the most efficient ways of doing this is to factor out spatial variability. However, removing spatial information from the object representation is completely at odds with the requirements of the motor system. Hence the need for two distinct object classes of object representations.

FURTHER READING Atkinson and Braddick (2003); Iliescu and Dannemiller (2008); Johnson, Mareschal, and Csibra (2008).

The three approaches discussed in Chapter 1 cast a different light on developmental hypotheses about the dorsal and ventral pathways. According to a maturational viewpoint, we need to consider which of the pathways develops first, and whether this can explain aspects of behavioral development of object processing. For example, Atkinson (1998) argued, on the basis that infants and children can perceive coherent forms prior to judging motion coherence, that the dorsal pathway develops later than the ventral. However, evidence from developmental neuroanatomy in human infants is not compelling in this regard. For example, in resting (with no task) PET studies of glucose uptake, virtually identical overall patterns of developmental change are seen in the temporal and parietal cortex (Chugani et al., 2002). Resting blood flow measurements and structural neuroanatomy studies cannot inform us directly about function. In Chapter 5 we reviewed several functional imaging studies with young infants showing activity in primary visual and some ventral pathway structures. However, these tasks involved passive viewing of 2D visual patterns or faces and were thus unlikely to evoke dorsal pathway activity even in adults. In non-human primates, there is evidence of ventral pathway functioning from as young as 6 weeks of age. Rodman and colleagues (Rodman, Skelly, & Bross, 1991) established that neurons within the superior temporal sulcus were activated by complex visual stimuli, including faces, from the earliest age at which they could record—6 weeks. Unfortunately, equivalent data are not available for dorsal pathway functions, and so no comparison is possible. Thus, there is currently very little direct evidence relevant to the question available (but see Iliescu & Dannemiller, 2008).

From a skill learning perspective, we need to inquire into the acquisition of perceptual recognition skills in the ventral pathway, and the emergence of senso-rimotor integration skill in the dorsal pathway. Further, we might investigate whether interactions between processing in the two pathways is acquired during development. The third perspective outlined in Chapter 1, interactive specialization, suggests yet another theoretical possibility for the dorsal and ventral visual pathways: that as the two pathways become more specialized, and acquire representations appropriate for either recognition or action, they become less interactive and tend to be co-activated less often. This view would also predict that the two pathways initially begin inter-mixed and hard to dissociate, but with development the dissociation becomes more complete. Further, from this perspective, the complementary spe-cialization of the two pathways emerges during the development of the individual.

6.2   Hidden Objects

It was Jean Piaget who originally noticed some unusual "errors" in the way that young children thought about, and acted on, objects that were out of view. Specifically, Piaget (1954) reported that infants fail to retrieve objects partly occluded by a surface until 7–8 months, fail to search manually for fully occluded objects until several months later, and fail to trace the spatial-temporal trajectory of a hidden object to its final destination until 1½ years of age. Piaget proposed that these developmental changes reflect a conceptual revolution in the first years of life that results in the construction of the first true object representation: an "object concept."

More recently, studies of the early development of object perception have qualified Piaget's original account. Experiments that rely on measures of looking, rather than manual reaching, have shown that even 4-month-olds perceive that a partly occluded object continues behind its occluder. For example, after familiarization with an object moving behind a central occluder, infants generalized to (i.e. looked less at) a fully visible complete object relative to a fully visible display with a gap where the occluder had been (Johnson & Aslin, 1996; Johnson & Nanez, 1995; Kellman & Spelke, 1983; Slater, Mattock, & Brown, 1990). Two-month-old human infants were not found to perceive complete objects over occlusion when tested with the displays used with 4-month-olds, but they performed like the older infants when tested with enhanced displays in which the occlusion and motion relationships were easier to detect (Johnson & Aslin, 1995). In recent studies using even more enhanced displays, abilities to perceive the complete shapes of partly occluded displays have been extended to 3-week-old human infants (Kawabata, Gyoba, Inoue, & Ohtsubo, 1999).

These findings provide evidence that human perceptual systems rapidly come to detect one kind of invariance in natural scenes: the invariant shape of an object over changing patterns of occlusion and background. Experiments in psychophysics and in cognitive neuroscience provide evidence that adults detect many other invariant properties of objects as well, including the invariant view-dependent shape of an object over changes in object size and position (e.g., Grill-Spector et al., 1998). These abilities also appear to have their roots in infancy, where some evidence for size and shape constancy has been obtained even with newborn infants (Slater, Morison, & Rose, 1982). All these findings cast doubt on Piaget's claim that the ability to perceive objects depends on a process akin to scientific reasoning. They raise the question whether infants might also be able to represent objects that they cannot see, when they are tested with looking methods. Evidence from several laboratories indicate that in looking tasks infants represent fully occluded objects long before they pass Piaget's object permanence tasks (e.g., Baillargeon, 1993; Spelke, Breinlinger, Macomber, & Jacobsen, 1992), although scattered negative findings also have been reported using this method (see Haith & Benson, 1998, for review). Given that different results are obtained with looking methods compared to other infant behavioral testing paradigms, several groups have turned to cognitive neuroscience theories and methods to resolve this paradox. Studies in cognitive neuroscience suggest several potential answers to this issue that are currently under active investigation: (a) the extent of integration of the dorsal and ventral visual pathways, (b) the changing strength of representations of objects in the brain, and (c) the possible inability of infants to plan the necessary actions to retrieve hidden objects. Since the second of these possibilities is discussed in Chapter 12, and the third in Chapter 10, we will focus here on explanations associated with the dorsal and ventral visual pathways.

Mareschal and colleagues chose to explore the hypothesis that the discrepancy between looking and reaching tasks is due to a relative lack of integration between the dorsal and ventral visual pathways in early infancy (Mareschal, Plunkett, & Harris, 1999). The logic behind this hypothesis is that object-directed action toward hidden objects requires a degree of interaction between the two pathways. This idea was initially explored through a connectionist model designed to simulate some of the computational properties and development of the dorsal and ventral pathways.

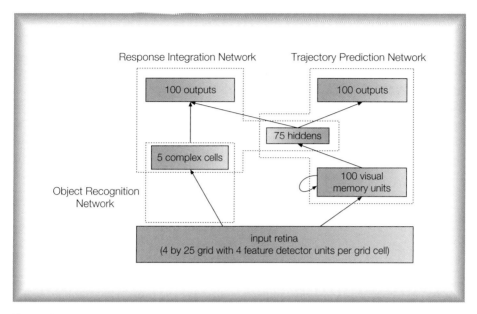

Figure 6.2 A diagram showing the object processing model of Mareschal et al. (1999).

Figure 6.2 shows a schematic outline of this "dual route" processing model. Consistent with the neurophysiology reviewed above, the model has an object recognition route (equivalent to the ventral pathway) and a trajectory prediction route (dorsal pathway). The former route develops a spatially invariant representation of an object to which it is exposed (using the unsupervised learning algorithm developed by Foldiak, 1996), while the latter learns to predict the next "retinal" position of the object. Through recurrent connections, both pathways have some degree of memory. A third component of the model is a response integration network that corresponds to the infant's ability to coordinate and use the information it has about object position and object identity. This network integrates the internal representations generated by the two pathways as required by a retrieval response task.

The model embodies the basic architectural constraints on visual cortical pathways revealed by contemporary neuroscience: an object recognition network that develops spatially invariant feature representations of objects; a trajectory prediction network that is blind to surface features and computes appropriate spatial-temporal properties even if no actions are undertaken towards the object; and a response module that integrates information from these two networks for use in voluntary actions.

A prediction of the above model has recently been tested (Mareschal & Johnson, 2003). In this behavioral experiment infants viewed an array presented on a video monitor in which two different objects moved behind, and then reappeared from behind, an occluding surface. In some conditions these objects were potentially graspable toys, while other conditions involved stimuli more likely to engage ventral pathway function such as faces (see Chapter 7). When the objects reappeared following removal of an occluder, the objects concerned could have either their features switched (e.g., color, or the identity of a face), or their spatial location, or both. If infants were surprised (looked longer) when just features were changed, this was taken to indicate ventral (recognition) pathway processing, whereas if surprise was shown when only the location of the objects changed, this was taken to indicate dorsal pathway retention. The results indicated that infants were able to encode either the surface features, or the spatial location, but not both. This suggests that infants are only capable of activating either the dorsal or the ventral pathway, but, unlike adults, not both at the same time. As yet, behavioral evidence such as this does not conclusively decide between the view that there is increasing integration between the two visual pathways, or the contrary idea that there may be increasing dissociation between the two pathways (Jacobs, Jordan, & Barto, 1991; O'Reilly, 1998).

The ideas behind the Mareschal model have also been extended by Kaufman, Mareschal, and Johnson (2003), who reviewed some of the apparently inconsistent findings from behavioral experiments on object perception in infants in terms of the potential graspability or other properties of the objects involved. The logic behind this analysis was that behavioral tasks that involve objects that are the appropriate size, shape, and distance to be grasped are more likely to activate the dorsal pathway. Thus, the information that infants encode about these objects relates to their spatial location and shape, and not their color or other surface features. In contrast, tasks that involve objects that are too large, or too far away, to be grasped by the infant may lead to object processing centered on the surface features important for visual recognition. Future work to explore these ideas will require ERP, event-related oscillations (see below), or other forms of functional imaging.

6.3   Neural Oscillations and Object Processing

A third general direction for understanding object processing and permanence in the infant brain comes from animal and human research on neural oscillations. A number of electrophysiological studies in animals and scalp-recorded EEG studies in humans have identified sharply timed bursts of high-frequency oscillatory activity that relate to aspects of visual processing and cognition (see Singer & Gray, 1995, for review). For example, Tallon-Baudry and colleagues found a burst of "gamma" frequency EEG oscillations (around 40 Hz) when adults had to bind together spatially separate features to compose a single object (Tallon-Baudry, Bertrand, Peronnet, & Pernier, 1998). This team proposed that such bursts of Gamma EEG reflect the computational process of "perceptual binding."

The question of at what age infants are able to bind together separate features to compose a unitary object has been controversial based on behavioral experiments (e.g., Kavsek, 2002). Therefore, with my colleagues, we set out to determine when infants will show a Gamma burst when viewing a Kanisza figure (a well-known illusory figure; Csibra et al., 2000). We found that a group of 8-month-old infants showed a clear burst of Gamma activity over left frontal channels at around the same time after the beginning of stimulus presentation as we would expect to see it in adults. This burst was not evident to the control, "pacmen," stimulus, which could not be bound into a single object. We also tested a group of younger infants who showed a general tendency for higher Gamma EEG in response to the Kanisza stimulus, but this was not structured as a single burst and seemed to be smeared over a long time period of brain computation.

Given the possible role of Gamma EEG in object processing, a further question that can be asked is whether these high-frequency oscillations are sustained when an object is being "kept in mind." This may entail the brain keeping active a representation of an object through oscillatory neural activity (for computationally minded readers, a recurrent network). This issue was addressed by recording EEG while presenting infants with visual arrays in which objects appeared or disappeared behind occluders (Kaufman, Csibra, & Johnson, 2003). A sustained Gamma response over temporal lobe channels was observed when infants saw an object pass behind an occluder without reappearing (see Figure 6.3 in the color plate section). Interestingly, results suggest that this response was enhanced when an occluder was removed and the object had unexpectedly disappeared. The finding suggests the possibility that active object representations are enhanced (at least temporarily) when the visual pathways of the brain are faced with conflicting visual input. By this view sustained Gamma is a neural signature of an "active" object representation that needs to be strengthened or weakened depending on the extent to which it conflicts with the current visual input. If Gamma EEG lives up to its early promise as a marker for stages of object processing in the infant brain, it will be worthwhile to explore the two visual pathways with this method.

6.4   Number

Alongside language, number processing and mathematical thinking offer the most likely candidates for uniquely human abilities. They are also topics within developmental cognitive neuroscience that potentially offer application to education and remediation of developmental disorders. Research by comparative psychologists and animal behavior experts reveals two systems for representing number in several animal species. First, a diverse collection of animals, including birds, rodents, and primates, have been found, in laboratory training studies, to represent the approximate numerosity of large sets of objects and to respond to changes in numerosity when other continuous variables are controlled (see Dehaene, 1997; Gallistel, 1990, for reviews). This ability has been termed "analog-magnitude" representation, and is thought to represent quantity by a representation that reflects physical magnitude proportional to the items being enumerated. In such a system, "numerical" comparisons are made in a similar way to length or time comparisons. Three signatures of these analog-magnitude representations are: (a) that discriminability is proportional to magnitude, in accord with Weber's Law (e.g., 1 and 2 are more discriminable than 7 and 8); (b) that successful representations are formed only when all members of a set are perceptually available at once (for visual/spatial arrays) or in immediate succession (for sequences of lights or sounds); and (c) that these representations can be transferred both across modalities (auditory and visual) and across formats (spatial and temporal). With regard to the latter point, it is striking that the same mental magnitude system may represent number, time, and the surface area of objects (see Cordes & Brannon, 2008, for review). Thus, while the system is number-relevant, it is probably not specific to the domain of number.

Second, both trained and untrained birds and primates have been found to represent the exact numerosity of very small sets of objects (e.g., Hauser, MacNeilage, & Ware, 1996). Some have suggested that this system is an "object-file" system that originally evolved to allow us to track up to about four moving objects at a time (Carey, 2001). Three signatures of these exact number representations are (a) that they are limited to set sizes of 3 or 4, (b) that successful representations can be formed and maintained even when different members appear successively and then are occluded, and (c) that these representations are as abstract as large number representations, for they are impaired by simultaneous variation in continuous quantitative variables such as area or contour length (Carey & Spelke, in press).

FURTHER READING Carey (2001); Cordes & Brannon (2008).

While both of the above systems are number-domain-relevant, they are not domain-specific in that they can be engaged by non-numerical tasks. Behavioral studies of human infants provide evidence that both these systems exist in humans and emerge early in development (see Cordes & Brannon, 2008, for review). By 6 months of age, infants discriminate between large numerosities when all other continuous variables are controlled, both in visual spatial arrays and in auditory temporal arrays. Like other animals, infants discriminate between large numerosities only when the ratio difference is large: they discriminate arrays of 8 versus 16 dots or sequences of 8 versus 16 sounds but fail, in each case, to discriminate 8 from 12 elements (Lipton & Spelke, 2003; Xu & Spelke, 2000).

Experiments from several laboratories indicate that young infants discriminate between small numbers of objects exactly, both in visible arrays and in arrays in which each object is successively revealed and occluded (see Wynn, 1998, for review). For example, young infants and even newborns can discriminate between 2 and 3 dots, sounds, or objects, and 5-month-olds can track simple transformations of object arrays, such as addition and subtraction (Wynn, 1992). However, like monkeys, human infants fail to discriminate between large approximate numerosities when elements are successively revealed and occluded, fail to discriminate numerosities exactly for arrays of more than 3–4 objects (Chiang & Wynn, 2000), and they form representations that are robust over variations in continuous quantities for large but not small numerosities (Feigenson, Carey, & Spelke, 2002). These findings suggest that both infants and other animals have separate systems for representing large approximate numerosity and small exact numerosity. It is important to note that some of the human infant experiments remain open to alternative (non-numerical) explanations (e.g., see Cohen & Marks, 2002; Cordes & Brannon, 2008), and that the capacity for successful behavior in small exact numerosity tasks may depend on a system that, while domain-relevant, is not necessarily domain-specific (see Carey, 2001).

There is evidence that both the analog-magnitude and the object-file systems exist in human adults and are associated with bilateral activity in the inferior parietal lobes. This finding is consistent with the sensitivity of the dorsal pathway to the spatial-temporal aspects of object processing. Evidence for the analog-magnitude system comes from experiments in which adults must rapidly (i.e. without counting) discriminate between numerosities in visual spatial arrays, visual sequences (light flashes), or auditory sequences. In these types of tasks, discriminability follows Weber's Law and is independent of stimulus modality, as found in animals (Barth, Kanwisher, & Spelke, 2003; Whalen, Gallistel, & Gelman, 1999). Evidence for the object-file system comes from experiments in which adults must enumerate or attentively track several objects (Pylyshyn & Storm, 1988; Trick & Pylyshyn, 1994). In these studies of object-files there is usually a limit of four objects, and performance is unimpaired by occlusion, as in studies of infants and animals (see Carey, 2001).

Recently, the first neuroimaging studies of number processing in children have been published. Cantlon and colleagues (Cantlon, Brannon, Carter & Pelphrey, 2006) presented adults and 4-year-old children with sequences of visual arrays that varied either in the number of stimuli or in their local shapes. During these presentations participants' brains were scanned using functional MRI. Adults showed greater activity around their intra-parietal sulcus when the arrays deviated in the number of elements, than when they deviated in the shape of the elements, a result consistent with previous scanning studies that have linked non-symbolic and symbolic numerical processing. Interestingly, 4-year-old children with considerably less symbolic knowledge of number showed very similar patterns of activation, showing that the cortical tissue sensitive to non-symbolic numerical representations exists in early childhood, and provides a neural basis for the acquisition of symbolic number representations during education.

When children attend school and learn elementary arithmetic, however, they must work with a different system of number representation: a system that does not have an upper limit, that is not constrained by the Weber fraction, that is not constrained by perception, and that can be related to language including number words. This system has been termed an "integer-list" representation (Carey, 2001). Studies of highly trained birds and primates so far provide no evidence that any non-human animal can acquire such a system (although some animals impressively expand their ability to use the two building-block systems described above: see, e.g., Brannon & Terrace, 2000; Matsuzawa, 1985, 1991; Pepperberg, 1987). How do human children construct this system?

One idea, advanced by Elizabeth Spelke and Susan Carey, is that children construct a new concept of number and gain arithmetic skills by bringing together their two initial systems of number representation, and that language—the number words and the verbal counting routine—plays a central role in orchestrating these systems. There are several lines of evidence in support of this view. First, when children learn the number words and the counting routine, they first map "one" to the object-file system and all other number words to the analog-magnitude system indiscriminately: for example, they respond correctly when they are presented with arrays of one and of four objects and are asked to point to the array with "one" versus "four", but they respond at chance when presented with arrays of two versus four or eight objects and asked to point to the array with "two" versus "four" or "eight" (Wynn, 1992). Next, children coordinate the systems together to learn the meanings of "two" and "three," while continuing to use all other number words indiscriminately to mean, roughly, "some" (Condry, Smith, & Spelke, 2000; Wynn, 1992). Finally, children surmise that each word in the count sequence refers to an array that includes one more entity, and a larger overall set size, than the array picked out by the previous word in the count sequence (Wynn, 1992).

Further evidence that the natural number concepts result from the coordination, through the language of counting, of the analog-magnitude and object-file systems comes from studies of human adults. When adults make judgments about number words or symbols (e.g., whether a given number word is larger or smaller than five), they activate analog-magnitude representation as well as exact numerosity, and therefore judge more quickly numbers that are more distant from the comparison number (Dehaene, 1997). This finding, and many other findings from behavioral studies of typical adults, behavioral studies of neuropsychological patients, and neuroimaging studies of typical adults, provides evidence that approximate number representations are activated in tasks requiring representations of the number concepts picked out by the counting words (see Dehaene, 1997, for review). Moreover, when bilingual adults learn new information about exact numerosity, their learning is language-specific: there is a cost in response time when the information is queried in the language not used in training. In contrast, when the same adults learn new information about exact numerosity, their learning shows full transfer across languages. This finding, and parallel findings from neuroimaging studies, provides evidence that representations of large, exact numerosities depend on language for adults, whereas representations of large approximate numerosities do not (Dehaene, Spelke, Pinel, Stanescu, & Tsivkin, 1999).

Problems with number come in several forms. Sometimes children with otherwise normal intelligence show particular problems with arithmetic. This is usually called "dyscalculia," and contrasts with cases where deficits in mathematical abilities co-occur with low IQ and other cognitive problems that result from genetic disorders. Some suggest that dyscalculia may not be as specific as originally supposed since it often co-occurs with dyslexia and attention deficit disorders (see Ansari & Karmiloff-Smith, 2002, for review). In genetic disorders such as Williams syndrome, numeracy deficits are quite commonly observed (Ansari & Karmiloff-Smith, 2002). Further, performance in number tasks is often worse than reading scores, suggesting that number may be a particularly vulnerable cognitive domain in the atypically developing child. Other authors suggest that dyscalculia may be a specific developmental syndrome (Butterworth, 2006) that can even be artifically induced in typical people by electrical stimulation to relevant parts of the parietal lobe (Cohen-Kadosh et al., 2007).

FURTHER READING Ansari (2008).

6.5   General Summary and Conclusions

In adults, there is evidence that the dorsal and ventral visual pathways perform different computations on objects, with the ventral pathway involved in identification and recognition, and the dorsal pathway in actions on objects. Preliminary attempts to relate these two pathways to changes in infant behavior were discussed, and a simple computational model of the changing degree of integration between the pathways was presented. While models such as this can account for some behavioral data, further progress will depend on functional imaging studies. Bursts of high-frequency neural oscillations have been related to the binding of features to compose objects and to the retention of objects following occlusion. Recent studies have used these neural oscillations to study object processing in infants, and may provide a direct marker for active representations of occluded objects in infants.

Two number-relevant systems in the primate brain were discussed. One of these is an analog-magnitude system similar to that active in time or length judgments, while the other is a system engaged by tracking small numbers of objects (object-files). Both systems appear to be active in young infants, and may underlie their ability to perform simple numerical computations with small numbers of objects. Some suggest that more sophisticated computations with large numbers require language-mediated integration between these two systems. Overall, the research to date on number suggests that mathematical thinking, and perhaps other forms of uniquely human thinking, results from the coordination of functionally and neurologically distinct subsystems that emerge early in human development and have homologs in other animals. This in turn suggests that developmental disabilities in the domain of mathematics may result either from impairments to one of the subsystems or from impairments to the system, related to language, that coordinates their functioning. Continued investigations, using the newly emerging tools of developmental cognitive neuroscience, may yield major insights into both normal and impaired cognitive functioning through continued investigation of the building-block systems in humans and other animals and through investigation, in developing children, of the processes by which these building blocks are assembled into mature cognitive skills.

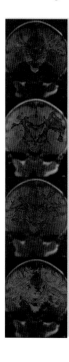

Key Issues for Discussion

- How can we best characterize the relative development of the dorsal and ventral visual pathways?
- How does recent neuroscience evidence inform Piaget's claim that objects out of sight are out of mind for young infants?
- To what extent does the evidence suggest that number processing is an innate ability?

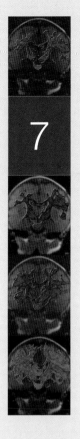

7 Perceiving and Acting on the Social World

Cognitive neuroscience studies in adults have revealed a network of structures involved in the perception and processing of social stimuli, including interpreting the thoughts and intentions of other humans. However, considerable debate remains about the developmental origins of this brain network. Perhaps the most basic aspect of the visual social brain is the perception of faces. One extreme view is that there is an innate cortical module for face processing (maturational view). At the opposite extreme is the view that expertise for faces is acquired in the same way as visual expertise for non-social stimuli (skill-learning view). By considering evidence from an animal model (chicks), behavior, and neuroimaging, I argue that a primitive bias ensures that infants orient frequently to faces. This early exposure to faces allows this stimulus to capture dedicated regions of neural tissue. This process of specialization for faces appears to take months or years. The remainder of the chapter addresses other aspects of social cognition such as perceiving and acting on information from the eyes, and attributing intentions or goals to other humans. Evidence from two developmental disorders, autism and Williams syndrome, initially appears to provide support for a social module that can be selectively impaired (autism) or spared in the face of other deficits (Williams syndrome). On closer inspection, however, it becomes apparent that such a clean dissociation is not borne out by the evidence, and that social information processing emerges as a result of constraints from interactions with other conspecifics, initial biases toward social stimuli, and the basic architecture of the brain.

Developmental Cognitive Neuroscience (Third Edition)   Mark H. Johnson with Michelle de Haan
© 2011 Mark H. Johnson

7.1   The Social Brain

One of the major characteristics of the human brain is its social nature. As adults, we have areas of the brain specialized for processing and integrating sensory information about the appearance, behavior, and intentions of other humans. Sometimes this processing is also extended to other species, such as the family cat, or even to inanimate objects such as our desktop computer. A variety of cortical areas have been implicated in the "social brain," including the superior temporal sulcus (STS), the "fusiform face area" (FFA—see further below), and orbitofrontal cortex (see Figure 7.1; for reviews, see Adolphs, 2003; Bauman & Amaral, 2008). One of the major debates in cognitive neuroscience concerns the origins of the "social brain" in humans, and theoretical arguments abound about the extent to which this is acquired through experience. Mentalistic understanding of others' behavior ("theory of mind") has been associated with various neural structures, including the amygdala and the temporal pole, the superior temporal gyrus and the temporo-parietal junction, and parts of the prefrontal cortex (mainly orbitofrontal and medial areas). According to Frith and Frith (2003), the neural activity in these regions may reflect different aspects of mental state understanding: the amygdala is involved in understanding emotions through empathy; parts of the temporal lobe represent biological motion and actions; and regions of the frontal cortex play a role in understanding "intentional" referential mental states, including mental states of the

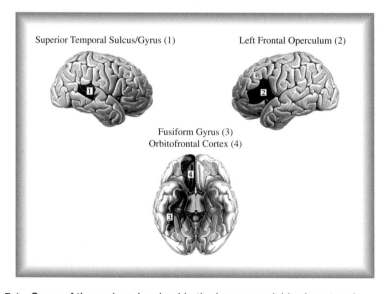

Figure 7.1   Some of the regions involved in the human social brain network.

self. The question I will address in this chapter is how these regions develop their functionality and become parts of the human social brain.

The three perspectives on human functional brain development discussed in Chapter 1 lead to different expectations about the origins of the social brain. According to the maturational view, through evolution, specific parts of the brain and areas of cortex have become dedicated to processing social information. Plausibly, some of the circuits are present and functioning at birth, while other components of the network become available through maturation later in development. For example, prefrontal areas associated with "theory of mind" computations may be the last component of the social brain to mature. While the maturational timetable may be accelerated or decelerated by experience, the sequence of maturation and the domain-specific wiring patterns are not. According to the skill learning view, at least some parts of the social brain are engaged by social stimuli because these tend to be the visual inputs with which we are most experienced. In other words, we tend to develop a higher level of perceptual expertise for socially relevant visual inputs. By this view we would not expect newborns to have any specific responses to social stimuli, and we should observe parallels between the development of face processing in infancy and the acquisition of perceptual expertise for other stimuli in adults. The third view, interactive specialization, predicts that the social brain will emerge as a network that becomes increasingly finely tuned to relevant stimuli and events in an activity-dependent manner. We should anticipate interactions between more primitive brain systems, cortical areas, and the environment, to produce the end result of a social brain.

In this chapter we initially examine these issues with perhaps the most fundamental visual function of the social brain—the perception and processing of faces. In later sections we go beyond this to examine some of the evidence available on more dynamic aspects of social cognition, such as interpreting eye gaze and the actions of other humans.

7.2   Face Recognition

The ability to detect and recognize faces is commonly considered to be a good example of human perceptual abilities, as well as being the basis of our adaptation as social animals. There is a long history of research on the development of face recognition in young infants extending back to the studies of Fantz more than forty years ago (e.g., Fantz, 1964). Over the past decade numerous papers have addressed the cortical basis of face processing in adults, including identifying areas that may be specifically dedicated to this purpose (Kanwisher, McDermott, & Chun, 1997; but see Haxby et al., 2001). Despite these bodies of data, until recently surprisingly little was known about the developmental cognitive neuroscience of face processing.

Face recognition skills may be divided into a number of components, including the ability to recognize a face as such, the ability to recognize the face of a particular individual, the ability to identify facial expressions, and the ability to use the face to interpret and predict the behavior of others. In a review of the available literature in the late 1980s, Johnson and Morton (1991) revealed two apparently contradictory bodies of evidence: while the prevailing view, and most of the evidence, supported the idea that infants gradually learn about the arrangement of features that compose a face over the first few months of life (for reviews, see also Maurer, 1985; Nelson & Ludemann, 1989), the results from at least one study indicated that newborn infants, as young as 10 minutes old, will track a face-like pattern further than various "scrambled" face patterns (Goren, Sarty, & Wu, 1975). Evidence that newborns showed a preferential response to faces was used by some to bolster nativist views of infant cognition (maturational view). In contrast, the evidence for the graded development of face processing abilities over several months tended to be cited by theorists who believed that such skills need to be learned, and result from experience of the world (skill learning view). To translate these views into the framework introduced in Chapter 1, while some believed that the brain possesses innate representations of faces, others took the view that face representations resulted from the information structure of the environment.

Since the study with newborn infants remained controversial for methodological reasons, my colleagues and I attempted to replicate it (Johnson, Dziurawiec, Ellis, & Morton, 1991). As in the original study, newborn infants (this time around 30 minutes old) were required to turn their head and eyes to keep a moving stimulus in view. This measure contrasts with more standard procedures in which the infant views one or more stimuli in static locations and the length of time spent looking at the stimuli is measured. In the first experiment we conducted, three of the four stimuli used in the original Goren et al. (1975) study were used: a schematic face pattern, a symmetric "scrambled" face, and a blank face outline stimulus. While we were unable to replicate preferential head turning to follow the face pattern, we did successfully replicate the preferential response to the face using a measure of eye movements (see Figure 7.2).

This experiment confirmed that the brain of the newborn human infant contains some information about faces. Many more studies on face preferences in newborns have been published since 1991 (for review see Johnson, 2005). While there are some differences reached in the conclusions of these authors, all of the studies found some evidence for sensitivity to face-like patterns. These have led to three hypotheses about the basis of this newborn preference behavior. Further, these three hypotheses may be associated with the three perspectives on functional brain development mentioned earlier.

FURTHER READING   Bauman and Amaral (2008); De Haan (2008); Johnson (2005).

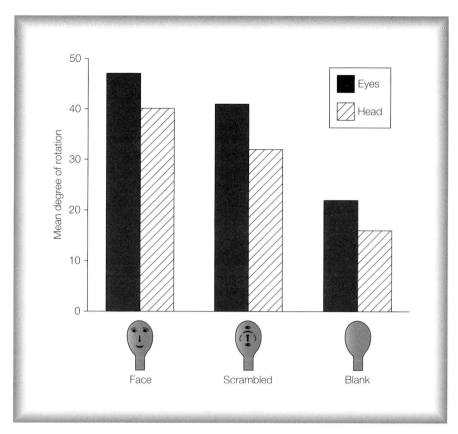

Figure 7.2   Data showing the extent of newborns' head and eye turns in following a schematic face, a scrambled face, and a blank (unpatterned) stimulus. The infants tracked the face significantly further than the other stimuli (Johnson & Morton, 1991).

The sensory hypothesis

This is the hypothesis that the visual preferences of newborns, including face preferences, are determined by low-level psychophysical properties of the stimuli. This hypothesis is consistent with the skill learning perspective since it does not assume any domain-specific bias early in life. The hypothesis that face patterns are preferred due to their amplitude spectrum better suiting the infants' visual system (Kleiner, 1993) was initially rejected since face patterns always fare better than would be predicted on the basis of amplitude alone (Johnson & Morton, 1991). However, Acerra, Burnod, and de Schonen (2002) recently suggested that minor differences in the exact schematic face stimuli used in critical experiments could regenerate the sensory hypothesis. However, Bednar and Miikkulainen (2003) have criticized this analysis, and suggested that the overall pattern of data better fits a face-biasing system (see below for details).

Newborns have complex face representations

Empirical results have led some to the hypothesis that newborns already have complex representations of faces. This hypothesis is most consistent with the maturational view of functional brain development, since it presumably requires domain-specific circuits to be established prior to experience. These findings include the preference for attractive faces, and data indicating that newborns are sensitive to the presence of eyes in a face (Batki, Baron-Cohen, Wheelwright, Connellan, & Ahluwalia, 2001), and prefer to orient toward faces with direct (mutual) eye gaze (Farroni, Csibra, Simion, & Johnson, 2002). However, inspection of images of such stimuli through the appropriate spatial frequency filters for the newborn visual system reveals that a mechanism sensitive to low-spatial frequency components corresponding to the spatial arrangement of a face (below) could account for these seemingly more complex preferences.

Face-biasing system ("Conspec")

These hypotheses argue that the newborn's brain contains a system that biases it to orient to faces. Johnson and Morton (1991) referred to such a system as "Conspec." This hypothesis is most consistent with the interactive specialization view. In contrast to the last hypothesis, the functioning of a cortical face module is not assumed. Rather, the bias is presumed to be close to the minimum necessary for picking out faces from a natural environment. In contrast to the sensory hypothesis, the spatial relations between face features are thought to be important, even though the representation underlying this preference may not exactly map on to a face (Simion, Macchi Cassia, Turati, & Valenza, 2003). In one variant of this hypothesis, Johnson and Morton (1991) argued that their "Config" stimulus (see Figure 7.3) was the minimal sufficient representation to ensure this preference. In neural network simulations, Bednar and Miikkulainen (2003) found that such a representation could account for the vast majority of documented newborn preferences between schematic and realistic face stimuli (see Figure 7.3).

In conclusion, it appears that a primitive face-biasing system (Conspec) can, at present, account for the vast majority of data currently available on face preferences with newborns (see Johnson, 2005, for review). While this does not rule out some influence of sensory factors, it does mean that a simple version of the skill-learning view is an unlikely explanation for the development of face processing.

Surprisingly, many other studies which used more conventional infant testing methods have not found a preference for face patterns over others until 2 or 3 months after birth (for review see also Maurer, 1985; Nelson & Ludemann, 1989). For example, Maurer and Barrera (1981) used a sensitive "infant control" testing procedure, in which participants view a series of singly presented static stimuli, and established that while 2-month-olds looked significantly longer at a face-like pattern than at various scrambled face patterns, 1-month-olds had no such pref-

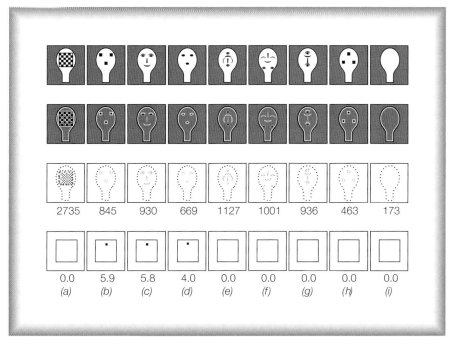

Figure 7.3   A summary of human newborn and model responses to schematic images. The top row represents some of the schematic patterns presented to both newborns and the "retina" of the neural network model. The next two rows illustrate the LGN and visual cortex stages of the models processing. The bottom row indicates the output of the model, with the prefered stimuli being b, c and d. The preferences of the model correspond well to the result obtained with newborn infants.

erence. Using the same method, Johnson, Dziurawiec, Bartrip, and Morton (1992) replicated this result and extended the original findings by including in the stimulus set the "de-focused" face arrangement stimulus used in the newborn studies earlier. The results replicated entirely the previous findings: the face was looked at longer than any of the other stimuli by 10-week-olds, but a group of 5-week-old infants showed no preference. This evidence was consistent with the alternative claim that infants gradually construct representations of faces as a result of repeated exposure to them over the first few months of life (Gibson, 1979). Clearly, these apparently contradictory findings raised a problem for theories of the development of face recognition that involved only one process (either learning or innate face representations). In an attempt to interpret this apparently conflicting behavioral data, Johnson and Morton (1991) turned to evidence from two areas of biology: ethology and brain development.

The primary source of evidence from other species (ethology) that Johnson and Morton used to interpret the human infancy results concerned filial imprinting in the domestic chick. Imprinting in chicks was selected because it is well studied both in terms of behavior and in terms of its neural basis. Filial imprinting is the process by which young precocial birds, such as chicks, recognize and develop an attachment for the first conspicuous object that they see after hatching (for reviews see Bolhuis, 1991; Johnson & Bolhuis, 1991). While imprinting has been reported in the young of a variety of species, including spiny mice, guinea pigs, chicks, and ducklings, only in precocial species (those that are mobile from birth) can we measure it using the conventional measure of preferential approach.

7.3   Filial Imprinting in Chicks

In the laboratory, 1-day-old domestic chicks will imprint onto a variety of objects such as moving colored balls and cylinders. After even a few hours of exposure to such a stimulus, chicks develop strong and robust preferences for the training object over novel stimuli. In the absence of a mother hen this learning is relatively unconstrained: virtually any conspicuous moving object larger than a matchbox will serve as an imprinting stimulus, and will come to be preferred over any other.

A particular region of the chick forebrain (thought to correspond to mammalian cortex) has been shown to be critical for imprinting, IMM (intermediate and medial part of the mesopallium—formerly called IMHV; for reviews see Horn, 1985; Horn & Johnson, 1989). Lesions to IMM placed before or after training on an object severely impair preference for that object in subsequent choice tests, but do not affect several other types of visual and learning tasks (Johnson & Horn, 1986, 1987; McCabe, Cipolla-Neto, Horn, & Bateson, 1982). Similar size lesions placed elsewhere in the chick forebrain do not result in significant impairments of imprinting preference (Johnson & Horn, 1987; McCabe et al., 1982).

The next step in analyzing the neural basis of imprinting was to study the microcircuitry of the region involved. Although the bird forebrain lacks the laminar organization of the mammalian cortex, the relation of the forebrain to subcortical structures is similar following the basic higher vertebrate brain design (Chapter 4). Evidence from a variety of vertebrate species supports the suggestion that the avian forebrain is a site of plasticity, and not the location of inbuilt, automatic, types of behavior which are located in other structures (Ewert, 1987; MacPhail, 1982). Figure 7.4 illustrates the location of IMM within the chick brain. The area occupies about 5% of total forebrain volume. Its main inputs come from visual projection areas, and some of its projections go to regions of the bird brain thought to be involved in motor control. Thus, the area is well placed to integrate visual inputs and motor outputs.

After identifying features of the basic microcircuitry of IMM, the next step was to take a synthetic approach and build a computational model of the circuit concerned (Bateson & Horn, 1994; O'Reilly & Johnson, 1994). In one of these models, Randall O'Reilly and I constructed a connectionist model based on two characteristics of

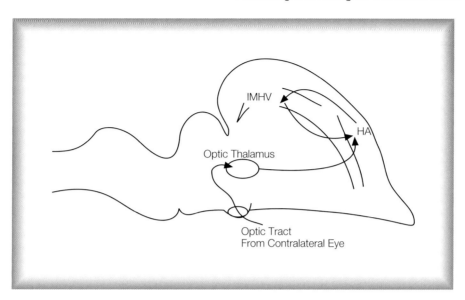

Figure 7.4   Outline sagittal view of the chick brain showing the main visual pathway to IMM (formerly known as IMHV; HA, hyperstriatum accessorium). There are other routes of visual input to IMM which are not shown in this figure (see Horn, 1985). The brain of a 2-day-old chick is approximately 2 cm long.

the cytoarchitectonics of IMM: the existence of positive feedback loops between the excitatory principle neurons, and the extensive inhibitory circuitry mediated by the local circuit neurons.

FURTHER READING   Horn (2004); O'Reilly & Johnson (2002).

In the laboratory a wide range of objects, such as moving red boxes and blue balls, are as effective for imprinting as are more naturalistic stimuli, such as a moving stuffed hen. However, in the wild, precocial birds such as chicks invariably imprint on their mother, and not on other moving objects. These observations raise the question as to what constraints ensure that this plasticity in the chick brain is normally guided to encode information about conspecifics (the mother hen), rather than other objects in its environment.

An answer to this question became evident from the results of a series of experiments in which stimulus-dependent effects of IMM lesions were observed (Horn & McCabe, 1984). Groups of chicks trained on an artificial stimulus such as a rotating red box were severely impaired by IMM lesions placed either before or after training on an object. However, groups of chicks exposed to a stuffed hen were only mildly impaired in their preference. Other neurophysiological manipulations also show differences between the hen-trained and box-trained birds (see Table 7.1). For example, administration of the neurotoxin DSP4, which depletes forebrain levels of

Table 7.1   Stimulus-dependent effects of neurophysiological manipulations

Treatment	Hen-trained Chicks	Box-trained Chicks
Bilateral IMHV lesions	Mild impairment	Severe impairment
DSP4 treatment	Mild impairment	Severe impairment
Plasma testosterone levels	Correlated with preference	No correlation with preference
Multicellular recording in IMHV	No correlation	Correlated

the neurotransmitter norepinephrine (see Chapter 4), resulted in a severe impairment of preference in birds trained on the red box, but only a mild impairment in birds trained on the stuffed hen (Davies, Horn, & McCabe, 1985). In contrast, plasma levels of the hormone testosterone correlate with preference for the stuffed hen, but not preference for the red box (Bolhuis, McCabe, & Horn, 1986).

These results led Johnson and Horn (1988) to seek experimental evidence for an earlier suggestion (Hinde, 1961) that naturalistic objects such as hens may be more effective at eliciting attention in young chicks than are other objects. A series of experiments were therefore conducted in which dark-reared chicks were presented with a choice between a stuffed hen and a variety of test stimuli created from cutting up and jumbling the pelt of a stuffed hen. Johnson and Horn (1988) concluded from these experiments that chicks have an untrained tendency, or predisposition, to attend toward features of the head and neck region of the hen. While this untrained preference seemed to be specific to the correct arrangement of features of the face/head, it was not specific to the species. For example, the head of a duck was as attractive as that of a hen.

The results of these and several other experiments led to the proposal that there are two independent brain systems that control filial preference in the chick (Horn, 1985; Johnson, Bolhuis, & Horn, 1985). The first of these controls a specific predisposition making newly hatched chicks orient toward objects resembling a mother hen. In contrast to non-specific color and size preferences in the chick (see Johnson & Bolhuis, 1991), this predisposition system appears to be specifically tuned to the correct spatial arrangement of elements of the head and neck region. While the stimulus configuration triggering the predisposition is not species- or genus-specific, it is sufficient to pick out the mother hen from other objects the chick is likely to be exposed to in the first few days after hatching. Although the neural basis for this predisposition is currently unknown, the optic tectum, the homolog of the mammalian superior colliculus, is one likely candidate.

The second brain system acquires information about the objects to which the young chick attends and is supported by the forebrain region IMM. In the natural environment, it has been argued, the first brain system guides the second system to acquire information about the closest mother hen. Biochemical, electrophysiological, and lesion evidence all support the conclusion that these two brain systems have largely independent neural substrates (for review see Horn, 1985). For example, while selective lesions to IMM impair preferences acquired through exposure to an object, they do not impair the specific predisposition (Johnson & Horn, 1986).

There are, of course, a number of different ways in which the predisposition could constrain the information acquired by the IMM system. For example, the information in the predisposition could act as a sensory "filter" or template through which information had to pass before reaching the IMM system. The evidence available at present is consistent with the view that the two systems influence the preference behavior of the chick independently, that is, there is no internal informational exchange between them. Instead, it appears that the input to the IMM system is selected simply as a result of the predisposition biasing the chick to orient toward any hen-like objects in the environment. Given that the species-typical environment of the chick includes a mother hen in close proximity, and that the predisposition includes adequate information to pick the hen out from other objects in the early environment, the input to the learning system will be highly selected.

One benefit of this well-studied animal model for developmental cognitive neuroscience is that it allows us to examine the plausibility of the three perspectives on human functional brain development (while bearing in mind the possibility of species differences). The chick imprinting story is inconsistent with the skill learning view in that the predisposition is present without prior training, and the learning involves self-terminating plasticity. The chick model is also somewhat inconsistent with the maturational view in that the IMM is relatively unconstrained in its learning, and appears to emerge from surrounding tissue as a result of experience. The evidence reviewed in this section suggests that the emergence of a simple vertebrate social brain is consistent with the interactive specialization view in that brain plasticity was constrained by simple biases, neural architecture and the early environment.

7.4   Brain Development and Face Recognition

The other source of biological data that Johnson and Morton used to generate an account of human infant face recognition came from the postnatal development of the cerebral cortex. As previously mentioned (Chapter 5), both neuroanatomical and neurophysiological data indicate that visually guided behavior in the newborn infant is largely (though not exclusively) controlled by subcortical structures such as the superior colliculus and pulvinar, and that it is not until several months of age that cortical circuitry comes to dominate subcortical control over behavior. Consistent with these arguments is the position that visually guided behavior in human infants, like that in domestic chicks, is based on activity in two or more distinct brain systems.

If these systems have distinct developmental time courses, then they may differentially influence behavior in infants of different ages.

There is much evidence that the recognition of individual faces in adults involves cortical areas and pathways. This evidence comes from three main sources: (a) neuropsychological patients with brain damage who are unable to recognize faces (prosopagnosia); (b) neuroimaging studies of face perception; and (c) single- and multi-cellular recording studies with non-human primates. To briefly review this literature, prosopagnosia commonly results from damage to the region of cortex that lies between the temporal and occipital (visual) cortex, although the exact neuropathology required is still controversial and may vary between participants. Some cases have suggested that only a right-hemisphere lesion is necessary, while others suggest bilateral lesions are required (see Farah, 1990, for a review). The deficit resulting from these lesions can be fairly specific. Although prosopagnosic patients have difficulty recognizing individual faces, they sometimes seem to be able to identify other objects. Of course, exceptions to this have been noted, with some patients having difficulty identifying other complex objects. However, not all face processing is entirely abolished in these patients. For example, some prosopagnosic patients seem to have intact facial emotion processing (e.g., Bruyer et al., 1983), and many show "covert" recognition of familiar faces as indicated by sensitive measures such as galvanic skin responses (Tranel & Damasio, 1985).

Evidence from neuroimaging studies of human adults has demonstrated the involvement of a number of regions of cortex. A range of cortical regions within the social brain, including regions of the fusiform gyrus, lateral occipital area, and superior temporal sulcus, have all been implicated in neuroimaging studies as being face-specific regions involved in encoding or detecting facial information. The stimulus specificity of response has been most extensively studied for the "fusiform face area" (FFA), a region which is more activated by faces than by many other comparison stimuli, including houses, textures, and hands (Kanwisher et al., 1997). While the greater activation of the FFA to faces than other objects has led some to propose it is a face module (Kanwisher et al., 1997), others call this view into question. In particular, investigations demonstrating that (a) the distribution of response across the ventral cortex may be more stimulus-specific than the strength of response of a particular region such as FFA (Haxby et al., 2001; Ishai, Ungerleider, Martin, Schouten, & Haxby, 1999; but see Spiridon & Kanwisher, 2002), and (b) that activation of the FFA increases with increasing expertise in discriminating members of non-face categories (Gauthier et al., 1999), together suggest that the region may play a more general role in object processing. However, the observations do remain that faces more than any other object activate the FFA, and that the distribution of activity over the ventral cortex for faces differs from other objects in that it is more focal and less influenced by attention (Haxby et al., 2001).

FURTHER READING   de Haan (2008).

Thus, there is considerable evidence for specific cortical involvement in face processing among adults. However, there is also evidence for a face preference in newborn infants, whose behavior, as discussed in the previous chapter, is thought to be guided largely by subcortical sensorimotor pathways. Consideration of this evidence led Morton and me to propose a two-process theory of infant face preferences analogous to that in chicks. We argued that the first process consists of a system accessed via the subcortical visuomotor pathway (but possibly also involving some of the deeper, earlier developing, cortical layers) that is responsible for the preferential tracking of faces in newborns. However, the influence of this system over behavior declines (possibly due to inhibition by developing cortical circuits) during the second month of life. The second brain system depends upon a degree of cortical maturity, and exposure to faces over the first month or two, and begins to control infant orienting preferences from around 2 or 3 months of age. By extension with the evidence on chicks, we (Johnson & Morton, 1991) argued that the newborn preferential orienting system biases the input set to developing cortical circuitry. This circuitry is configured in response to a certain range of input, before it starts to gain control over the infant's behavior. Once this occurs, the cortical system has acquired sufficient information about the structure of faces to ensure that it continues to acquire further information about them. Like in the chick, the proposal is that a specific, early developing brain circuit acts in concert with the species-typical environment to bias the input to later developing brain circuitry. A number of strands of evidence are consistent with this theory. First, let us consider evidence about the neural basis of the face bias in newborns.

Johnson and Morton (1991) speculated that the face bias ("Conspec") was mediated largely, but not necessarily exclusively, by subcortical visuomotor pathways. This proposal was made for several reasons: (a) that the newborn preference declined at the same age as other newborn reflexes assumed to be under subcortical control; (b) evidence from the maturation of the visual system indicating later development of cortical visual processing, and (c) evidence from another species (the domestic chick). Owing to the continuing difficulty in successfully using functional imaging with healthy awake newborns, this hypothesis has, as yet, only been indirectly addressed. First, de Schonen and colleagues examined face preferences in a number of infants with perinatal damage to regions of cortex. Even in cases of damage to the visual cortex, the bias to orient to faces remained (see Mancini et al., 1998). The second line of evidence used the fact that the nasal and temporal visual fields feed differentially into the cortical and subcortical visual pathways. Specifically, Simion and colleagues predicted that the face bias would be found in the temporal visual field, but not the nasal visual field. This prediction was confirmed (Simion, Valenza, Umilta, & Dalla Barba, 1998). A third line of evidence comes from a large number of adult neuropsychological and neuroim-aging studies showing evidence for a subcortical "quick and dirty" route for face processing (see Johnson, 2005, for review). Analysis of these studies reveals that the adult subcortical route rapidly processes low spatial frequency "coarse" information about faces, and then modulates activity in the face-sensitive cortical areas that process fine detailed information about faces. The visual stimuli which maximally elicit

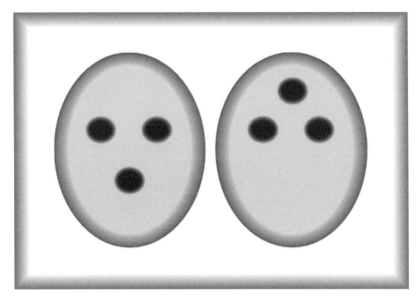

Figure 7.5 Schematic illustration of the stimuli that might be optimal for eliciting a face-related preference in human newborns. These hypothetical representations were created by integrating the results from several experiments with newborns.

activity in the adult subcortical route are strikingly similar to those to which newborns preferentially orient, strongly suggesting that this route is the basis for newborn behavior (see Figure 7.5).

While Johnson and Morton (1991) identified the superior colliculus as a major visuomotor structure that could be involved in determining Conspec preferences, another candidate structure is the pulvinar. Our knowledge of this brain structure has increased dramatically over the past decade, and the description of its function now makes it a candidate for involvement in newborn visual preferences. Specifically, portions of pulvinar receive input directly from the superior colliculus (as well as from the retina and, at least in adults, striate and extrastriate visual cortex). Additionally, in adults there are reciprocal connections to frontal, temporal, and parietal regions and to the anterior cingulate and amygdala. The advent of new technology suitable for studying the neural correlates of behavior in newborns may allow further investigation of this issue.

We now turn to the neurodevelopment of face processing during infancy and childhood. To recap, the three perspectives on human functional brain development discussed earlier make differing predictions about how this specialization arises. By a maturational view we expect to see the gradual addition of new brain modules relating to aspects of face processing ability. From a skill learning perspective, the fusiform face area should become active as the perceptual skill of face processing is acquired. From an interactive specialization view, we expect to observe the increasing neural specialization and more restricted localization of face processing with development. With these different predictions in mind, let us review some of the evidence from developmental cognitive neuroscience.

Several labs have examined changes in event-related potentials (ERPs) as adults view faces. In particular, interest has focused on an ERP component termed the "N170" (because it is a negative-going deflection that occurs after around 170 ms), which has been strongly associated with face processing in a number of studies on adults (see de Haan, Johnson, & Halit, 2003, for review). Specifically, the amplitude and latency of this component vary according to whether or not faces are present in the visual field of the adult volunteer under study. An important aspect of the N170 in adults is that its response is highly selective. For example, the N170 shows a different response to human upright faces than to very closely related stimuli such as inverted human faces and upright monkey faces (de Haan, Pascalis, & Johnson, 2002). While the exact underlying neural generators of the N170 are currently still debated, the specificity of response of this component can be taken as an index of the degree of specialization of cortical processing for human upright faces. For this reason de Haan and colleagues undertook a series of studies on the development of the N170 over the first weeks and months of postnatal life.

The first issue addressed in these developmental ERP studies was when does the face-sensitive N170 emerge? In a series of experiments a component in the infant ERP that has many of the properties associated with the adult N170, but that is of a slightly longer latency, was identified (240–90 ms; de Haan et al., 2002; Halit, de Haan, & Johnson, 2003; Halit, Csibra, Volein, & Johnson, 2004). In studying the response properties of this component at 3, 6, and 12 months of age we have discovered that (a) the component is present from at least 3 months of age (although its development continues into middle childhood), and (b) the component becomes more specifically tuned to human upright faces with increasing age. To expand on the second point, we found that while 12-month-olds and adults showed different ERP responses to upright and inverted faces, 3- and 6-month-olds did not (de Haan et al., 2002; Halit et al., 2003). Thus, the study of this face-sensitive ERP component is consistent with the idea of increased specialization of cortical processing with age, a result also consistent with some behavioral results (see below).

The interactive specialization view predicts increases in both the degree of specialization and localization of face-evoked activity in the cortex during development. This stands in contrast to a maturational perspective prediction that face processing in the child's brain should be limited to a subset of the areas that can be activated by faces in adults. Recently, several studies have used fMRI to investigate the neurodevelopment of face processing in children (see Cohen-Kadosh & Johnson, 2007, for review). Several of these studies have yielded support for the dynamic changes predicted by the interactive specialization hypothesis. As far as face processing in general is concerned, all fMRI studies to date were able to show that certain regions of the cortex show reliable activation to faces from at least mid-childhood. However, two studies are of particular importance as they specifically address both the localization and the specialization predictions. Scherf and colleagues (Scherf, Behrmann, Humphreys, & Luna, 2007) used naturalistic movies of faces, objects, buildings, and navigation scenes in a passive viewing task with children (5–8 years), adolescents (11–14 years) and adults (see Figure 7.6 in the color plate section). They found that the children exhibited similar patterns of activation of the face processing areas commonly reported in adults (such as the FFA). However, this activation was not selective for the category of face stimuli; the regions were equally strongly activated by objects and landscapes. Moreover, this lack of fine-tuning of classical face processing areas stood in contrast to distinct preferential activation patterns for other object categories (occipital object areas and the parahippocampal place area).

In a similar study, Golarai and colleagues (Golarai et al., 2007) tested children (7–11 years), adolescents (12–16 years) and adults with static object categories (faces, objects, places, and scrambled abstract patterns). They found substantially larger right FFA and left parahippocampal volumes of selective activation in adults than in children. While this increase in functionally defined areas with development may initially appear to contradict predictions of the interactive specialization view, it is important to note that the contrasts employed defined the increase as an expansion of the area of category-specific activation of FFA. The developmental changes observed in these recent studies thus provide strong support for interactive specialization as a framework within which to interpret functional brain development (Cohen-Kadosh & Johnson, 2007).

Similar conclusions can be drawn from a PET study conducted on 3-month-old infants, in which a large network of cortical areas were activated when infants viewed faces as compared to a moving dot array (Tzourio-Mazoyer et al., 2002). This study involved the "subtraction" of the activation resulting from a complex dynamic stimulus from that elicited by photographs of a female face. The resulting areas of activation corresponded to those regions activated by face processing in adults, namely bilateral activation of the superior and middle temporal gyrus (though the regions activated in infants may be more anterior than those in adults). Despite a low baseline of overall metabolic activity in the frontal lobes (in agreement with the Chugani et al., 2002, study reviewed in Chapter 4), there was a significant increase in activity in the left orbito-frontal cortex and Broca's area in the face condition.

Another area of face-processing research that could potentially contribute to our understanding of the developmental trajectory of face-specialized cortical areas is the work on developmental prosopagnosia. Developmental prosopagnosia refers to individuals who never develop typical adult face-processing abilities (Duchaine & Nakayama, 2006), and in particular facial identity recognition skills. This condition can occur in the absence of any obvious sensory or intellectual deficit (Avidan, Hasson, Malach, & Behrmann, 2005; Behrmann & Avidan, 2005; Yovel & Duchaine, 2006). Moreover, while there are cases of developmental prosopagnosia that arise from brain trauma early in life, there is increasing evidence for cases in which typical adult-like face processing skills fail to develop in the absence of any known acquired injury (Duchaine & Nakayama, 2006). Some of these individuals have family members that are also affected, and it is tempting to speculate on a genetic cause. However, since nothing is currently known about the early rearing and social interaction environment of these families, the specificity or directness of this genetic effect remains unknown.

Functional MRI studies have generally shown that developmental prosopagnosics activate face-sensitive regions of the cortex (for review see Duchaine & Nakayama, 2006). However, the degree of selectivity of this response remains in doubt, and a plausible interpretation of these results is that while adult developmental prosopagnosics show activation in face-sensitive regions, they may also show the lack of specificity in this response reported earlier for typically developing children. Moreover, a recent fMRI study (Avidan et al., 2005) showed that in four developmental prosopagnosics face perception recruited additional brain areas (e.g., the inferior frontal gyrus) that were not commonly found in typical adults. Interestingly, however, inferior frontal gyrus activation has been observed in children in several of the developmental neuroimaging studies reported above (Gathers, Bhatt, Corbly, Farley, & Joseph, 2004; Passarotti et al. 2003; Passarotti, Smith, DeLano & Huang, 2007; Scherf et al., 2007). Thus, both components of the interactive specialization account (localization and specialization) may accommodate data from developmental prosopagnosia. If this account of developmental prosopagnosia is correct, then with sufficient training on faces the selectivity of the response of cortical areas, and their inter-connectivity, should change toward the typical pattern. This was tested in a recent training study with a developmental prosopagnosic patient that showed that as behavioral performance improved the selectivity of cortical processing of faces (as measured by the N170 component) increased (DeGutis, Bentin, Robertson, & D'Esposito, 2007). Further, these authors also observed increased functional connectivity between face-selective regions as measured by fMRI, particularly the right occipital face area and the right fusiform face area.

Converging evidence about the increasing specialization of face processing during development comes from a behavioral study that set out to test the intriguing idea that as processing "narrows" (Nelson, 2003) to human faces, then infants will lose their ability to discriminate non-human faces (Pascalis, de Haan, & Nelson, 2002). Pascalis and colleagues demonstrated that while 6-month-olds could discriminate between individual monkey faces as well as human faces, 9-month-olds and adults could only discriminate the human faces. These results are particularly compelling since they demonstrate a predicted competence in young infants that is not evident in adults.

The lines of evidence reviewed above are hard to reconcile with a strictly maturational view that posits the addition of new components of processing with development. Rather, the evidence available to date suggests "shrinkage" of the cortical activity associated with face processing during development. While increased specialization and localization are specifically predicted by the interactive specialization view, these changes are not necessarily inconsistent with skill learning (Gauthier & Nelson, 2001). Thus, with regard to face perception, the available evidence from newborns allows us to rule out the skill learning hypothesis, while the evidence on the neurodevelopment of face processing over the first months and years of life is consistent with the kinds of dynamic changes in processing expected from the interactive specialization, and not the maturational, approach.

Before leaving the topic of face and individual face recognition, I should note that there is some evidence that infants in the first week of life are able to identify their mother (e.g., Pascalis, de Schonen, Morton, Deruelle, & Fabre-Grenet, 1995). At first sight this evidence seems to conflict with the view that cortical face processing does not emerge until at least the second month. However, this discriminative ability in newborns is based only on the general shape of the head and hair, and not on facial configuration or features. De Schonen and Mancini (1995) argue that this "third system" is a non-specific visual pattern learning ability which has also been evident from studies with visual patterns of many other kinds. Johnson and de Haan have modified the original two-process theory to take account of early hippocampal-based learning (see Chapter 8).

FURTHER READING   de Haan (2008).

7.5   Perceiving and Acting on the Eyes

Moving beyond the relatively simple perception of faces, a more complex attribute of the adult social brain is processing information about the eyes of other humans. There are two important aspects of processing information about the eyes. The first of these is being able to detect the direction of another person's gaze in order to direct your own attention to the same object or spatial location. Perception of averted gaze can elicit an automatic shift of attention in the same direction in adults (Driver et al., 1999), allowing the establishment of "joint attention" (Butterworth & Jarrett, 1991). Joint attention to objects is thought to be crucial for a number of aspects of cognitive and social development, including word learning. The second critical aspect of gaze perception is the detection of direct gaze, enabling mutual gaze with the viewer. Mutual gaze (eye contact) provides the main mode of establishing a communicative context between humans, and is believed to be important for typical social development (e.g., Kleinke, 1986; Symons, Hains, & Muir, 1998). It is commonly agreed that eye gaze perception is important for mother–infant interaction, and that it provides a vital foundation for social development (e.g., Jaffe, Stern, & Peery, 1973; Stern, 1977).

With regard to the social brain network, the superior temporal sulcus (STS) has been identified in several adult imaging studies of eye gaze perception and processing (for review see Adolphs, 2003). As with cortical face processing above, in adults the response properties of this region are highly tuned (specialized) in that the region responds only to non-biological motion (Puce, Allison, Bentin, Gore, & McCarthy, 1998). While we cannot directly capture the functioning of STS in infants, a number of behavioral experiments have been conducted to determine the specificity or otherwise of gaze cueing in infants.

Several studies have demonstrated that gaze cues are able to trigger an automatic and rapid shifting of the focus of the adult viewer's visual attention (Driver et al, 1999; Friesen & Kingstone, 1998; Langton & Bruce, 1999). All these studies used variants of the spatial cueing paradigm (see Chapter 5), where a central or peripheral cue directs attention to one of the peripheral locations. When the target appears in the same location where the cue was directed (the congruent position), the participant is faster to look at that target compared to another target at an incongruent position relative to the previous cue. Human infants start to discriminate and follow adults' direction of attention at least from the age of 3 or 4 months (Hood, Willen, & Driver, 1998; Vecera & Johnson, 1995). In our studies we examined further the visual properties of the eyes that enable infants to follow the direction of the gaze. We tested 4-month-olds using a cueing paradigm adapted from Hood et al. (1998). Each trial began with the stimulus face's eyes blinking (to attract attention), before the pupils shift to either the right or the left for a period of 1,500 ms (see Figure 7.7). A target stimulus was then presented either in the same direction as the

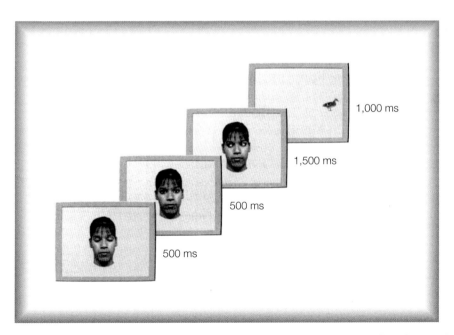

Figure 7.7   Example of the edited video image illustrating the stimulus for Experiment 1 in Farroni et al. (2000). In this trial the stimulus target (the duck) appears on the side incongruent with the direction of gaze.

stimulus face's eyes were looking (congruent position) or in a location incongruent with the direction of gaze. By measuring the saccadic reaction time of infants to orient to the target we demonstrated that the infants were faster to look at the location congruent with the direction of gaze of the face.

In a series of experiments using this basic paradigm, we have established that it is only following a period of mutual gaze with an upright face that cueing effects are observed. In other words, mutual gaze with an upright face may engage mechanisms of attention such that the viewer is more likely to be cued by subsequent motion. In summary, the critical features for eye gaze cueing in infants are (a) lateral motion of elements and (b) a brief preceding period of eye contact with an upright face.

Evidence from functional neuroimaging indicates that a network of cortical and subcortical regions are engaged in eye gaze processing in adults (Senju & Johnson, 2009). This network of structures overlaps with, but does not completely duplicate, the patterns of activation seen in the perception of motion, and the perception of faces in general. While it may be important to activate the whole network for eye gaze processing, one region in particular, the "eye area" of the superior temporal sulcus, appears to be critical. The finding that infants are as effectively cued by non-eye motion (Farroni, Johnson, Brockbank, & Simion, 2000) provides preliminary evidence that their STS may be less finely tuned than in adults.

Following the surprising observation that a period of direct gaze is required before cueing can be effective in infants, several authors have investigated the developmental roots of eye contact detection. It is already known that human newborns have a bias to orient toward face-like stimuli (see earlier), prefer faces with eyes opened (Batki et al., 2001), and tend to imitate certain facial gestures (Meltzoff & Moore, 1977). Preferential attention to faces with direct gaze would provide the most compelling evidence to date that human newborns are born prepared to detect socially relevant information. For this reason we recently investigated eye gaze detection in humans from birth. We (Farroni et al., 2002) tested healthy human newborn infants by presenting them with a pair of stimuli, one a face with eye gaze directed straight at the newborns, and the other with averted gaze (see Figure 7.8). Videotapes of the baby's eye movements throughout the trial were analyzed by the two recorders. The dependent variables we used were the total fixation time and the number of orienting responses. Results showed that the fixation times were significantly longer for the face with the direct gaze. Further, the number of orientations was higher with the straight gaze than with the averted gaze.

In a second experiment, we attempted to gain converging evidence for the differential processing of direct gaze in infants, by recording event-related potentials (ERPs) from the scalp as infants viewed faces. We studied 4-month-old babies with the same stimuli as those used in the previous experiment with newborns, and found a difference between the two gaze directions at the face-sensitive component of the infant ERP discussed earlier (Farroni et al., 2002). Our conclusion from the second study is that direct eye contact enhances the perceptual processing of faces in 4-month-old infants.

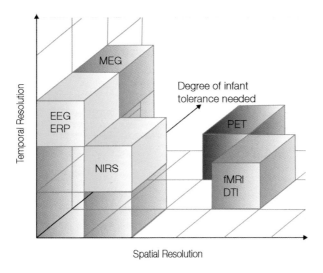

Figure 2.1 An illustration of the relative strengths and weaknesses of different functional brain imaging methods used with infants and children.

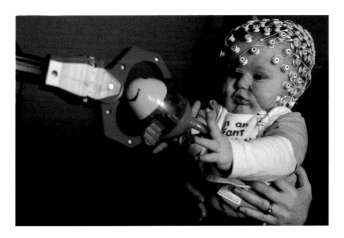

Figure 2.2 An infant wearing a high-density ERP/EEG system (EGI Geodesic Sensor Net) during a study on the "mirror neuron system". The sensor net consists of damp sponge contacts that rest gently on the scalp.

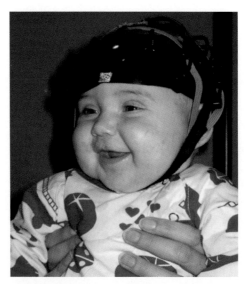

Figure 2.3 An infant engaged in an optical imaging (NIRS) study. Light emitters and detectors are incorporated into a cloth head cap.

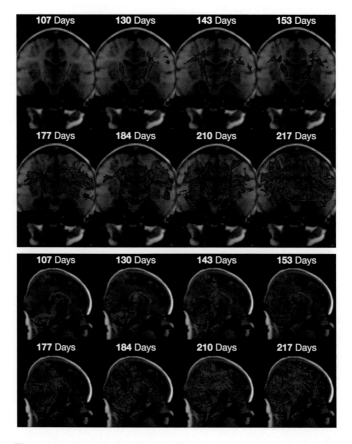

Figure 2.4 The expansion of myelinated fibers over early postnatal development as revealed by a new structural MRI technique.

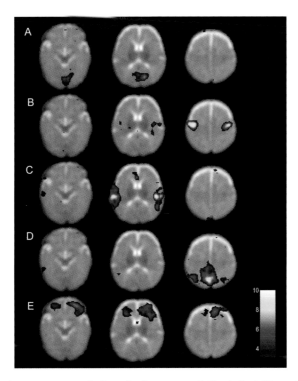

Figure 4.7 Resting state networks in a single representative infant. Rows A to E each show one resting state network at three axial sections.

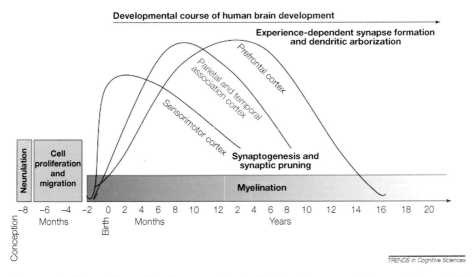

Figure 4.8 Figure illustrating the approximate timeline for some of the most important changes in human brain development, including the characteristic rise and fall of synaptic density.

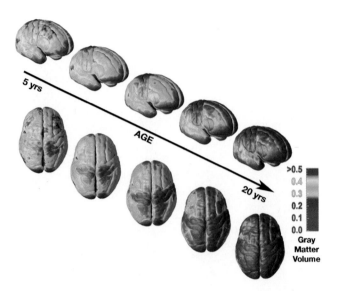

Figure 4.10 A colour-coded map of changes in cortical gray matter with development. The maps illustrate regional variations in decreases in gray matter density between the ages of 5 and 20 years. Reprinted by permission of Dr. Arthur W. Toga and Dr. Paul M. Thompson, Laboratory of NeuroImaging at UCLA.

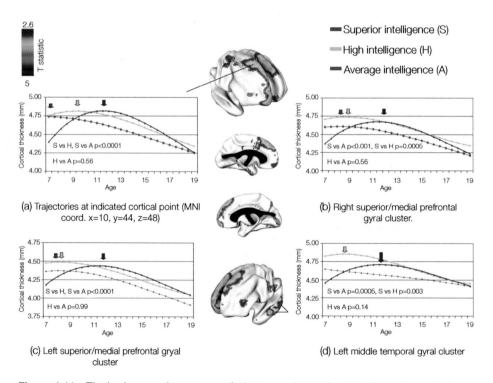

(a) Trajectories at indicated cortical point (MNI coord. x=10, y=44, z=48)

(b) Right superior/medial prefrontal gyral cluster.

(c) Left superior/medial prefrontal gryal cluster

(d) Left middle temporal gyral cluster

Figure 4.11 The brain maps (centre panel) show prominent clusters where "superior" and "average" intelligence groups differ significantly in the trajectories of cortical development. The graphs show the developmental trajectories for these regions. The age of peak cortical thickness is arrowed for each of the three groups in each region.

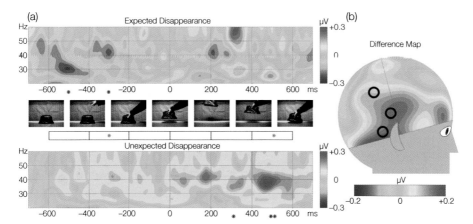

Figure 6.3 Gamma-band EEG activity recorded from infants in the Kaufman, Csibra, and Johnson (2003) experiment. (a) Time-frequency analysis of the average EEG at three electrodes over the right temporal cortex (around T4) during the phase in which the tunnel was lifted showed higher activations when the object should have been below the tunnel. Black asterisks below the maps indicate a significant difference from baseline; red asterisks indicate a significant difference between conditions in the average gamma activity in 200 ms-long bins. (b) A topographical map of the between-condition difference of Gamma-band (20–60 Hz) activity during the occlusion-related peak gamma activity (from −400 to −200 ms) revealed a right-temporal focus. Circles signify right-temporal electrode sites.

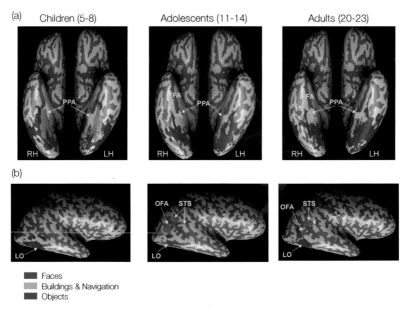

Figure 7.6 Differential activation for each stimulus category mapped onto an inflated brain: (a) ventral view and (b) a lateral view of the right hemisphere for all three age groups. In contrast to older groups, young children showed no face-selective activation in face-related areas. However, objects and buildings or navigation yielded similar patterns of selective activation at all ages. Abbreviations: FFA, fusiform face area; LO, Lateral occipital object area; OFA, occipital face area; PPA, parahippocampal place area; STS, superior temporal sulcus.

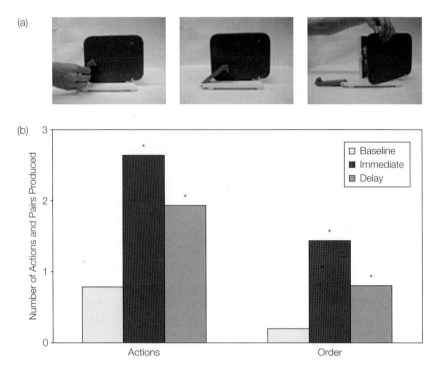

Figure 8.2 (a) Example of a sequence to be imitated. (b) The number of actions and ordered pairs of actions produced by 20-month-old infants in a baseline period, at immediate recall after the sequence is demonstrated, and after a two-week delay.

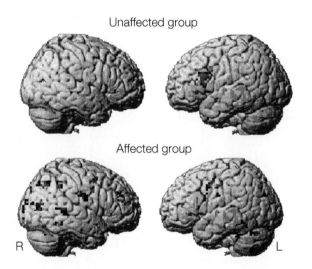

Figure 9.3 Covert language task: group average fMRI activation in the unaffected and affected members of the KE family. Activated regions are projected onto the surface rendering of a typical 3D individual brain, displayed at a statistical threshold of $p < .05$, corrected for multiple comparisons. L, left hemisphere; R, right hemisphere.

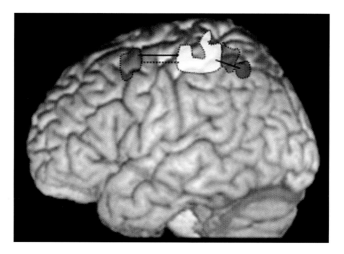

Figure 10.1 A summary of the superior frontal-intraparietal network involved in the development of visuo-spatial working memory. Regions in red show a correlation between brain activity and development of working memory capacity, and regions in white show a correlation between white matter maturation and development.

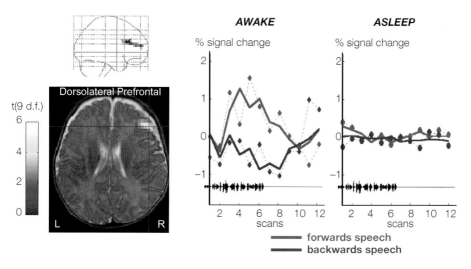

Figure 10.2 Interaction between wakefulness and the linguistic nature of the stimuli. This comparison isolated a right dorsolateral prefrontal region that showed greater activation by forward speech than by backward speech in awake infants, but not in sleeping infants.

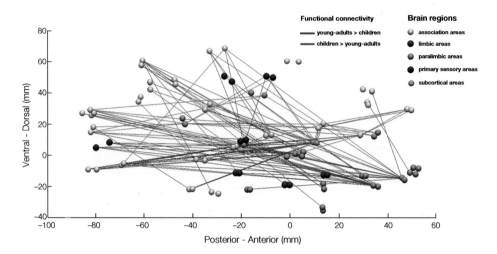

Figure 12.3 Developmental changes in interregional functional connectivity. A graphical representation of developmental changes in functional connectivity along the posterior-anterior and ventral-dorsal axes of the brain highlighting higher subcortical connectivity and lower paralimbic connectivity in children compared to young adults.

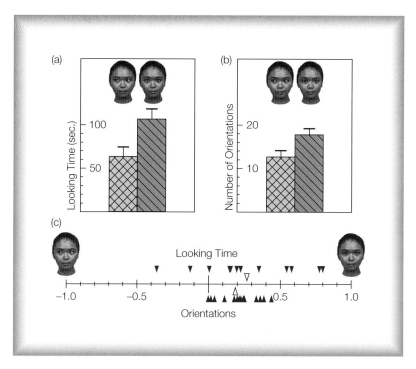

Figure 7.8 Results of the Farroni et al. 2002 preferential looking study with newborns. (A) Mean looking times (and Standard Error) spent at the two stimulus types. Newborns spent significantly more time looking at the face with direct gaze than looking at the face with averted gaze. (B) Mean number of orientations toward each type of stimulus. (C) Filled triangles indicate reference scores for the direct gaze over the averted gaze for each individual newborn. Open triangles indicate average preference scores.

This conclusion was reinforced by recent experiments analyzing high-frequency EEG bursting in the gamma (40 Hz) range (Grossman, Johnson, Farroni, & Csibra, 2007). Gamma oscillations are of interest partly because they correlate with the BOLD response used in fMRI (see Chapter 2). Grossmann et al. (2007) predicted a burst of gamma oscillation over prefrontal sites to direct gaze if gamma oscillations are indeed related to detecting eye contact or the perception of communicative intent as suggested by adult fMRI work (Schilbach et al., 2006). The data revealed that gamma oscillations varied as a function of gaze direction only in the context of an upright face, which extended the previous ERP results. As predicted, direct gaze within an upright face also elicited a late (300 ms) induced gamma burst over right prefrontal channels. A similar result was also obtained with a different imaging method, NIRS, and we observed a striking convergence in results between the two methods in individual infants (Grossmann et al., 2008).

The empirical evidence gathered on the development and neural basis of eye gaze processing in infants is consistent with the interactive specialization view.

Specifically, the same primitive representation of high-contrast elements ("Conspec") as underlies the face bias in newborns may also be sufficient to direct them toward faces with direct eye contact. Therefore, the more frequent orienting to the direct gaze in newborns could be mediated by the same mechanism that underlies newborns' tendency to orient to faces in general. A face with direct gaze would better fit the spatial relation of elements in this template than one with gaze averted, suggesting that the functional role of this putative mechanism is more general than previously supposed. This primitive bias ensures a biased input of human faces with direct gaze to the infant over the first days and weeks of life, a bias that helps to lay a further foundation stone for the emerging social brain (Senju & Johnson, 2009).

FURTHER READING Johnson (2005); Senju and Johnson (2009).

According to the interactive specialization view, a network as a whole becomes specialized for a particular function. Therefore, I suggest that the "eye region" of the STS does not develop in isolation, or in a modular fashion, but that its functionality emerges within the context of interacting regions involved in either general face processing or in motion detection. Viewed from this perspective, STS may be a region that integrates motion information with the processing of faces (and other body parts). While STS may be active in infants, it may not yet efficiently integrate motion and face information. In other words, while the 4-month-old has good face processing and general motion perception, it has not yet integrated these two aspects of perception together into adult eye gaze perception. By this account, making eye contact with an upright face fully engages face processing, which then facilitates the orienting of attention by lateral motion. At older ages, eye gaze perception becomes a fully integrated function where even static presentations of averted eyes are sufficient to facilitate gaze.

7.6   Understanding and Predicting the Behavior of Others

Beyond face processing and eye gaze detection there are many more complex aspects of the social brain, such as the coherent perception of human action and the appropriate attribution of intentions and goals to other humans. Traditionally, one way in which these issues have been addressed is through behavioral studies with infants, toddlers, and children. However, in recent years developmental cognitive neuroscience investigations have also begun to make inroads. In addition to its sensitivity to eyes, in adults the STS responds to moving biological stimuli (but does not respond as well to non-biological similar moving stimuli, or to static pictures of biological stimuli—Puce et al., 1998). Does this specialization emerge during postnatal development in accord with predictions from the interactive specialization view?

Functional MRI studies with children (Mosconi, Mack, McCarthy, & Pelphrey, 2005) have shown that the STS can be activated by dynamic social stimuli from mid-childhood. Carter and Pelphrey (2006) used fMRI to test the specificity of response of the STS and other regions in 7- and 10-year-old children while they viewed a variety of biological motion and related stimuli (such as walking robots). They observed that, consistent with predictions from the interactive specialization view, the STS became increasingly specific in its response properties to biological motion with increasing age.

A recent optical imaging (NIRS) study with 5-month-old infants (Lloyd-Fox et al., 2009) also found patterns of activation consistent with STS activity when they viewed dynamic social stimuli (an actress moving her hands, eyes, and mouth) as compared to dynamic non-social stimuli (moving machinery). However, the precise degree of specialization of this response during infancy remains to be determined. In general, while research on the STS is not as advanced as that on the FFA, the evidence currently available suggests that similar processes of emerging functional specialization may occur.

One of the most intriguing recent discoveries in neuroscience is that the perception of others' actions induces subthreshold motor activity in the adult observer, a phenomenon recorded in both monkeys and humans, and often attributed to a "mirror neuron system" (MNS; Rizzolatti & Craighero, 2004). A MNS is one in which the same cells and circuits are involved both in generating a motor action, and in processing the visual input that arises from watching someone else performing a similar action. There has been much speculation and controversy about the importance or otherwise of motor mirroring for the perception of action. A promising way to elucidate the function of motor system activation during action observation is to investigate the ontogeny of this phenomenon (Kilner & Blakemore, 2007). As one's own particular motor abilities and skills are a determinant of whether the motor system is recruited during action observation (Calvo-Merino, Glaser, Grèzes, Passingham, & Haggard, 2005), the limited motor repertoire of infants means that they can shed light on which capacities are modulated by motor system recruitment (van Elk, van Schie, Hunnius, Vesper, & Bekkering, 2008).

Until very recently there was little clear evidence about whether young infants do activate their motor system when they observe someone else perform similar actions. One way to observe the functional role of motor activation in the perception of action is to use recordings of sensorimotor alpha EEG activity. However, to make a convincing case for a MNS it is important that this activity be recorded during *both* action and perception in the same participants. Showing changes in one or other task only is not sufficiently compelling evidence. Therefore, Southgate and colleagues (Southgate, Johnson, Osborne, & Csibra, 2009) used EEG to measure changes in sensorimotor alpha band activity during the course of observing predictably occurring repeated actions in 9-month-old infants. Studies with adults have demonstrated that sensorimotor activity is modulated both by the execution and observation of goal-directed actions (Hari *et al.*, 1998), and likely originates in primary somatosensory cortex (Hari & Salmelin, 1997). Southgate and colleagues found that infants did indeed exhibit subthreshold motor activity during action observation that matched directly the neural signal occurring during their own similar actions. Interestingly, rather than occurring only in response to an observed action, the motor activation was evident *prior to the onset of the repeated observed action* once infants could anticipate its occurrence. This finding is consistent with previous reports demonstrating that adults activate their motor system when they can predict that someone will perform an action (Kilner, Vargas, Duval, Blakemore & Sirigu, 2004), and fits with more recent proposals that motor activation during action observation may reflect a process of anticipating how an action will unfold (Csibra, 2007).

Beyond the perception of faces, eyes, and the actions of others, the developing child needs to develop neural and cognitive mechanisms for understanding the behavior of others in terms of their intentions, goals, and desires—an ability sometimes referred to as "mentalizing" or "theory of mind". As in the case of face processing presented earlier, in recent years a number of laboratories have begun to study the neural basis of children's understanding of the mental states of others by using fMRI. There is now a group of fMRI studies with children of various ages using different tasks showing that the Medial Prefrontal Cortex (MPFC) is consistently activated when children are engaged in mentalizing (Blakemore, den Ouden, Choudhury, & Frith, 2007; Kobayashi, Glover, & Temple, 2007; Ohnishi et al., 2004; Pfeifer, Lieberman, & Dapretto, 2007; Wang, Lee, Sigman, & Dapretto, 2006). In all of these studies, children recruited MPFC more extensively than adults when engaged in mentalizing tasks, even when task performance and possible baseline differences were controlled for. For example, Wang et al. (2006) employed an irony task to investigate the comprehension of communicative intentions from cartoons in adults and children (9–14 years), and found that children recruited MPFC and left inferior frontal gyrus to a greater extent than adults, whereas adults recruited the fusiform gyrus (FG), extrastriate areas and the amygdala more strongly than children. Furthermore in a correlation analysis the authors showed that, within the group of children, there was a positive correlation between age and FG activity and a negative correlation of age with extent of MPFC activity. Similarly, Blakemore et al. (2007) reported that adolescent participants (12–18 years) when thinking about intentions showed more extensive activity in MPFC than adults, whereas adults activated parts of the right STS more than adolescents. Finally, two other developmental mentalizing studies available revealed very similar patterns of findings. Pfeifer and colleagues (2007) examined brain activity during self-knowledge retrieval and found that children (10 years) engaged MPFC to a much great extent than adults. In this study, adults activated the lateral temporal complex (LTC) significantly more than children. Moreover, Kobayashi et al. (2007) presented adults and children (8–11 years) with classical theory of mind tasks and also reported that the children showed greater activity in MPFC than adults, but that adults exhibited great activity in the right amygdala than children. Taken together, these studies show that with age the extent of MPFC activation during mentalizing tasks becomes more focal with development, whereas activity in (task-dependent) posterior (temporal) cortical areas sometimes increases.

These developmental patterns generally concord with predictions from the interactive specialization view as they involve a diffuse to focal transition in prefrontal cortex functional activity during development. A second general trend is that the functional involvement of posterior (temporal) cortex may show more protracted development than that of frontal cortex (Brown et al., 2005).

With regard to the skill learning hypothesis, there is also an interesting parallel between these developmental fMRI findings on mentalizing, and studies on functional brain activation changes associated with practice and learning in adults (for a recent review, see Kelly & Garavan, 2005). For example, Sigman and colleagues (2005) found that in a visual shape discrimination task, extensive learning resulted in increased activity in the posterior visual cortex and decreased activity in the frontal and parietal cortex. These large-scale reorganizations of brain activity in the adult cortex as a result of learning have been interpreted as reduced executive control and increased automatization and may, at least in part, account for the patterns of activity observed in the developing social brain. However, skill learning alone cannot explain so-called 'age of acquisition' effects, that is, the age at which learning occurs has an effect on how a skill is acquired and which cortical mechanisms are used. These effects have been widely observed in other domains of cognition (see Hernandez & Li, 2007), and as recent research suggests, they also seem to apply to mentalizing activity in MPFC. For example, Kobayashi, Glover, and Temple (2008), comparing early and late bilinguals (Japanese who also speak English) of similar proficiency in a mentalizing task, found that early bilinguals (children 8–12 years of age) showed an overlap in brain activity between the first and second language in MPFC during a mentalizing task, whereas late bilinguals (adults 18–40 years of age) activate more dorsal MPFC in the first language mentalizing condition and more ventral MPFC during the second language mentalizing condition.

How the more widespread activation observed in children shrinks to the focal activation observed in adults remains to be studied in detail (see Chapter 12). One possibility is that parts of the MPFC that become specialized for other functions in adults are more broadly tuned in childhood and thus are also activated in mentalizing tasks. Thus, while adults may selectively activate subregions of MPFC, children may activate the whole area in response to different aspects of social cognition.

7.7   The Atypical Social Brain

Another way to study the emerging social brain is to investigate what happens when it goes awry in some developmental disorders such as autism and Williams syndrome (WS; see Chapter 2).

Many different laboratories have attempted to locate specific brain deficits in autism. Applying the adult neuropsychology model (see the causal epigenesis view in Chapter 1), it was initially assumed that there would be a focal structural deficit somewhere in the brain, and that this "hole" in the brain could be associated with a particular pattern of cognitive deficits. As we will see, although developmental deficits can result in seemingly quite specific profiles of cognitive deficit, the corresponding structural damage to the brain can be elusive, diffuse, and/or inconsistent across different individuals (see Chapter 2). In the case of autism, structural brain imaging and postmortem neuroanatomical studies have variously implicated the brain stem, cerebellum, limbic system, thalamus, and frontal lobes (for review see South et al., 2008). Several studies have reported enlargement of the ventricles, indicating atrophy in adjacent limbic and frontal structures (for review see Pennington & Welsh, 1995). However, like several of the brain atypicalities that have been reported in autism, ventricular enlargement is not specific to autism, since it is also observed in schizophrenia.

> FURTHER READING   South et al. (2008); Tager-Flusberg (2003).

Another deficit observed in several studies on autism is in the cerebellum (e.g., Courchesne, Yeung-Courchesne, Press, Hesselink, & Jernigan, 1988). At present it is unclear whether this is a postnatal effect (recall from Chapter 4 that cell migration in this region continues into postnatal life) or whether, as Courchesne et al. (1988) argue, it is caused by atypical cell migration between 3 and 5 months of gestation. Some evidence for migrational failures in the cortex has also been observed, though these do not appear to be restricted to any particular area (Piven et al., 1990). One problem in determining developmental brain damage is that it is difficult to ascertain which atypicalities are the root cause, and which are subsequent consequences of earlier atypical development. In general, it is likely that structures and areas that develop latest are most likely to be affected by earlier deviations from the normal developmental trajectory. For example, in autism the atypicalities sometimes observed in the cortex, hippocampus, and cerebellum could all possibly be the consequences of a primary deficit in the thalamus.

The latest region of the cortex to show structural changes in postnatal development, the frontal cortex, has been a favorite region of focus for studies of autism and other developmental disorders such as phenylketonuria (see Chapters 2 and 10). While atypicalities in this region may be responsible for some of the cognitive deficits observed, this does not mean that people with autism can be equated with patients with acquired prefrontal cortex damage.

While the brain damage that gives rise to autism may be diffuse and variable, the resulting cognitive profile presents a clearer picture. Many social processes observed in early childhood appear to be intact in children with autism. However, they generally show deficits in aspects of mentalizing or "theory of mind." Despite its grand title, theory of mind is a relatively basic and essential function for our understanding of, and interactions with, other people. Specifically, theory of mind refers to the ability most of us have to comprehend another person's thought processes, such as their feelings, beliefs, and knowledge. One type of task that can be used to study theory of mind abilities is the so-called "false-belief" task. For example, the following scenario can be demonstrated with dolls, puppets, or human actors (example of procedure taken from Wimmer & Perner, 1983).

> Sally has a marble that she puts in a basket. Sally then goes away for a walk. While Sally is away, Anne comes in and moves the marble from the basket to a box. The participant viewing this scenario is then asked "When Sally returns, where will she look for her marble?" If the participant simply tries to predict Sally's response on the basis of their own personal knowledge, then he or she will answer "the box". If, on the other hand, she predicts Sally's response on the basis of Sally's (false) belief, then the participant will correctly predict that Sally will look in the basket for the marble.

Another false-belief scenario involves showing the participant a container that normally holds candy well known to the child and asking the child what is in the container. The participant will reply with the name of the appropriate candy. The box is then opened and the child shown that it contains a pencil, and not candy. The child is then told that a friend will come in a moment and be shown the closed container and asked what is in it. The participant is asked what the friend will say. Once again, only if the child can infer the friend's inevitable false belief will he or she reply with the name of the candy rather than a pencil.

Baron-Cohen, Leslie, Frith and their collaborators have shown in a series of studies that many individuals diagnosed with autism, unlike those with Down's syndrome, fail these and other theory of mind tasks (for reviews see Baron-Cohen, 1995; Frith, 2003; Happé, 1994), while they are relatively unimpaired (compared to mental-age-matched controls) on a variety of related tasks. This pattern of deficit would explain why people with autism often seem to regard others as little different from inanimate objects. Thus, many believe that a deficit in theory of mind is a central cognitive deficit in autism. While there is some agreement on the nature of this cognitive deficit, there are a number of detailed variants of this view that are currently being tested.

Other theoreticians have proposed more developmental accounts, arguing that a lack of theory of mind arises from deficits in precursors of adults social cognition skills such as the infants' capacity for imitation (Rogers & Pennington, 1991) or the perception of emotion (Hobson, 1993). Thus, these authors believe that a social-cognitive deficit from birth, or very shortly thereafter, results in the later deficit of theory of mind.

With the aim of identifying the very earliest precursors of autism, several groups have begun longitudinal studies of babies at-risk for a later diagnosis of autism for family genetic reasons. So-called "baby siblings" are baby brother and sisters of older children already diagnosed and are at a higher risk of being diagnosed themselves (although it is important to note that this is still a minority). Studies with baby siblings have shown that in many cases the first signs of atypical social interaction skills become evident from 12 to 18 months of age (Zwaigenbaum et al., 2005). While observation of social behavior and interaction skills does not reveal atypicality until around the end of the first year, some neurophysiological studies have revealed group differences between babies at-risk and controls at younger ages when viewing faces with either direct or averted gaze (Elsabbagh et al., 2009). Whether these early group differences in neurophysiological measures will predict those individuals who go on to a diagnosis, or whether they are an early manifestation of the "broader phenotype" that affects many family members, is currently under investigation.

Following on from the infant siblings work, others have studied toddlers that have recently received a preliminary diagnosis of autism. For example, Dawson and colleagues studied effects of familiarity on face and object (toy) processing (Dawson et al., 2002). While a control group of young children showed ERP evidence of recognition of both categories, the potentially autistic sample did not show evidence of recognizing the faces. This suggests some degree of specificity in their neural deficit. However, as the authors point out, this deficit is probably secondary to an earlier developmental cause, such as failing to orient toward faces at birth. In a similar experiment, Grice and colleagues observed that the ERP correlates of eye gaze processing (as described earlier) appear to be developmentally delayed in young children with autism (Grice et al., 2005).

Given the somewhat mixed structural neuroimaging and neuroanatomical evidence, some research teams have tried to use the pattern of cognitive deficits to infer which brain pathways and structures are damaged in autism. Perhaps the most commonly held neuropsychological view is that the pattern of cognitive deficits observed is consistent with damage to, or dissociation of, the frontal cortex (e.g., Damasio & Maurer, 1978; Pennington & Welsh, 1995). For example, even high-functioning people with autism fail on a number of "executive function" tasks thought to be markers for frontal lobe functioning, such as the Tower of Hanoi planning task and the Wisconsin card sorting task (Ozonoff, Pennington, & Rogers, 1991). At present it is unclear whether these deficits are primary to those in theory of mind, independent of theory of mind, or dependent on the same underlying computations (see Pennington & Welsh, 1995).

The view that the deficit in theory of mind is one of several cognitive deficits which share common underlying computations is also held by those who argue for the importance of the atypicalities observed in the cerebellum (e.g., Courchesne, 1991).

By this view, theory of mind is disrupted because the cerebellum is important for the processing of complex context-dependent sequential information that unfolds over time. It is likely that future studies involving functional neuroimaging will allow the dissociation between these different neuropsychological hypotheses.

> FURTHER READING Elsabbagh and Johnson (2007); South et al. (2008).

In contrast to the specific social deficit seen in autism, WS participants appear to have the putative "social module" intact. WS (also known as infantile hypercalcemia) is a relatively rare disorder of genetic origin (see Chapter 2). Alongside surprising linguistic abilities (see Chapter 9), WS participants perform as well as controls in a face discrimination task (the Benton test; Bellugi, Bihrle, Neville, Jernigan, & Doherty, 1992), and better than typical adults on the face recognition component of a standard memory test (the Rivermead Behavioral Memory Test; Udwin & Yule, 1991). This pattern of spared abilities suggests approximately the opposite of deficits described earlier for autism, and raised the initial hypothesis that people with WS have intact a functional brain system corresponding to a "social module." Specifically, one preliminary hypothesis is that the social module remains intact in WS, while being specifically damaged in autism. As discussed earlier, one prominent account of the cognitive deficit in autism is that people with autism lack a theory of mind. Karmiloff-Smith and colleagues carried out a series of experiments with WS participants to test the hypothesis that there is "a broad cognitive module for representing and processing stimuli relevant to other individuals, including face processing, language, and theory of mind" (Karmiloff-Smith, Klima, Bellugi, Grant, & Baron-Cohen, 1995, p. 197). While only about 20% of autistic participants pass theory of mind tasks such as that described earlier, 94% of the WS participants passed these tasks, indicating that theory of mind is intact alongside aspects of language and face processing. From this result, along with some others, it is tempting to portray WS as showing approximately the opposite neurocognitive profile to autism (while acknowledging that both groups may show some general retardation). This hypothesis is enhanced by the differential cerebellar atypicalities.

> FURTHER READING Karmiloff-Smith (2008); Tager-Flusberg (2003).

However, Karmiloff-Smith et al. (1995) cite evidence from other developmental disorders that is contrary to the simplest view of an impaired or intact prespecified module. For example, in Down's syndrome, a serious deficit in face processing and in the use of morphology in language can co-occur with relatively good performance on theory of mind tasks (Baron-Cohen, Leslie, & Frith, 1985, 1986). Conversely, in an individual with hydrocephalus with associated myelomeningocele, very competent language output co-exists with serious deficits in face processing and theory of mind

(Cromer, 1992; Karmiloff-Smith, 1992). These different patterns of dissociation clearly challenge the notion of a predetermined social module in the brain.

An alternative view consistent with the interactive specialization approach (Karmiloff-Smith, 2002) is that some degree of modularization is a result of postnatal development, and not a precursor to it (see also Chapter 12). Specifically, domain-specific biases in the newborn (such as the face preference discussed earlier in this chapter and the speech discrimination abilities discussed in Chapter 9) ensure that cortical circuits are preferentially exposed to socially relevant stimuli like language and faces. With prolonged exposure to such stimuli, plastic cortical circuits develop representations appropriate for processing these inputs, eventually giving rise to an emergent superordinate system for the pragmatics of social interaction in general.

FURTHER READING   Karmiloff-Smith (2008).

If this general view of the emergence of the social brain is correct, it implies that early sensory or social deprivation may have long-term consequences. Two lines of research have pursued this issue. In the first, Maurer and colleagues have studied people who suffered visual deprivation for varying periods of time following birth as a result of uni- or bilateral cataracts. These dense cataracts prevent structured visual input until they are reversed by surgery, usually within the first year. By studying aspects of face processing in this clinical population, this research group showed that even after years of normal experience of faces some deficits remained (Le Grand, Mondloch, Maurer, & Brent, 2001). In other words, visual deprivation over the first months has detectable life-long effects on face processing. Further, by examining cases of unilateral deprivation it has been shown that these effects are more due to right hemisphere (left eye) deprivation. Data such as these present a severe challenge for the "skill learning" approach to human functional brain development, and suggest propensity of the right hemisphere for face processing from the first months.

While the cataract population can inform us about sensory deprivation, other populations have been studied that suffered from social deprivation. For example, samples of children raised in orphanages (e.g., during the Romanian communist regime) can subsequently have multiple social, cognitive, and sensorimotor problems (for review see Gunnar, 2001). While orphanage rearing can be variable in general care quality, at a minimum, stable long-term relationships with caregivers are missing (Rutter, 1998). The outcome from "good" orphanages can include problems with executive functions (see Chapter 10) and social cognition, while other aspects of sensorimotor, cognitive, and linguistic development can recover well. At the other extreme, in a sample of children raised in Romanian orphanages for at least the first 12 months, 12% exhibited features of autism, although even here these symptoms tended to diminish over time (Rutter et al., 1999).

FURTHER READING   Shackman et al. (2008).

7.8   General Summary and Conclusions

As discussed at the beginning of this chapter, the three viewpoints on functional brain development make different predictions about the development of the social brain. Evidence reviewed from the neurodevelopment of face processing appeared inconsistent with a maturational account. The long-term effects of early deprivation and the presence of face and eye gaze biases in the newborn discourage a strictly skill learning perspective. Thus, there is probably neither an innate module for social cognition, nor innate representations relating to these functions that "mature" in the cortex during postnatal life. Rather, complex representations for processing information about other people, their probable thoughts, and likely future actions emerge in the brain as an inevitable result of a combination of factors: initial biases to attend to socially relevant stimuli such as faces and language; the presence of other humans who actively seek interaction with the child; and the basic architecture of the cortex along with its regional biases and patterns of connectivity. Atypicalities in any of these factors could send the infant into a deviant path in which only some components of typical social cognitive abilities develop.

A challenge for this interactive specialization view of the emerging social brain will be to generate hypotheses about the consequences of the network of social processing areas being initially intermixed with other cortical networks. Behavioral studies with infants have demonstrated that, from at least 9 months of age, they attribute goals to appropriately moving objects even when these objects do not physically resemble biological forms (see Csibra, 2003, for review). Indeed, some have suggested that infants and toddlers may over-extend their social cognitive abilities to physical objects that adults would not (Csibra, 2003). Whether this blurring of the boundary between social and non-social perception is a byproduct of a social brain that has not yet fully emerged from the rest of the brain remains an interesting topic for future research.

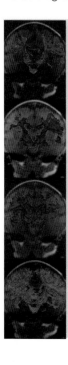

Key Issues for Discussion

- Given the complex social cognitive abilities of humans, what is the value of animal models of the developing social brain?
- In what ways might the functions of the STS differ in infants from those observed in adults, and how could this be tested empirically?
- What different factors could make the typical development of the social brain go awry?

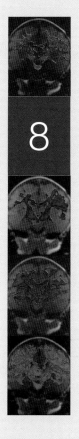

8 Learning and Long-Term Memory

Long-term memory is usually divided into different types. One important division is between an explicit form of long-term memory for information we can bring to mind, and implicit form of long-term memory involving perceptuo-motor skills. Each of these also has subtypes—explicit memory includes semantic memory for faces and episodic memory for personal events, and implicit memory includes a range of skills such as conditioning and priming. Initially it was thought that implicit memory was present from birth, while explicit memory emerged later due to the immaturity of the medial temporal lobe (MTL). More recently investigators have found that a form of explicit memory that is dependent on the MTL is also present from birth, with important improvements then occurring at about 8–10 months of age as the MTL matures. While implicit memory performance generally shows little developmental change beyond 3 years of age, explicit memory, particularly the episodic type, continues to develop throughout childhood, along with changes in connectivity of the hippocampus and increasing involvement of the frontal cortex. The expansion of cortical involvement in the neural basis of explicit memory may be due to an experience-dependent increasing specialization of cortical regions related to the hippocampus. Overall, it seems that several brain systems may be engaged by most memory tasks, a conclusion that echoes those drawn for cognitive domains reviewed in other chapters.

Memory is central to our everyday lives, allowing us to build a knowledge base of facts, rules, and skills and to store details about personal experiences that are central to our sense of who we are as individuals. Our present-day understanding of the cognitive and neural bases of memory was hugely influenced by the study of a single individual, known as HM. He suffered severe memory loss following surgical removal of a large part of both temporal lobes as treatment for medication-resistant epilepsy. After surgery HM was unable to form new long-term memories for facts or events, forgetting such things within minutes. Even so, he remained able to remember things from his life before the surgery and to form new long-term memories under some circumstances, such as when learning a motor skill. This advanced our understanding of memory in two ways: (a) by illustrating that memory is not a unitary function, and (b) by illustrating that different types of memory rely on different brain networks. In particular, his case highlighted the difference between *explicit memories* (sometimes also called declarative or cognitive memories), which are those memories that we can bring to mind, and *implicit memories* (sometimes also called non-declarative, procedural, habit or non-cognitive memories), which are memories typically expressed as changes in perceptual or motor performance; only the former type of memory is affected in HM and dependent on the medial temporal lobes (MTL; Cohen & Squire, 1980).

Additional research suggests that there are further divisions within the explicit and implicit forms of memory. Explicit memory includes semantic memory for facts that are not associated with a particular context (e.g., A car has wheels), and episodic memory for events associated with the spatial-temporal context in which we experienced them (e.g., I parked my car under a tree this morning). Explicit memory relies on a MTL (see Figure 8.1) cortical circuit, involving the hippocampus, the surrounding cortex (perirhinal, entorhinal, and parahippocampal cortices) and diencephalon. Within this system, the hippocampus is believed by many to be particularly involved in episodic memory and less involved in semantic memory (Mishkin, Suzuki, Gadian, & Vargha-Khadem, 1997; though see Squire, Stark, & Clark, 2004, for a different view). Implicit memory involves a range of different skills including motor learning, conditioning, visual discrimination learning, and priming, mediated by different though sometimes overlapping brain circuits. For example, some forms of implicit motor learning and conditioning have been linked to the basal ganglia, cerebellum, and other motor structures, while perceptual priming, which is the greater ease with which a perceptual stimulus is processed if it has been encountered before, has been linked to the sensory cortex.

The multi-system view of memory has been a dominant framework for those investigating the cognitive neuroscience of memory development. Researchers have taken advantage of the wealth of data from animal and human adult cognitive neuroscience studies on the neural bases of different learning and memory systems in the brain (for reviews see Bachevalier, 2008; Squire et al., 2004) to design tasks and develop theories of the neural bases of memory development. Nevertheless, this developmental cognitive neuroscience approach to memory faces a number of challenges:

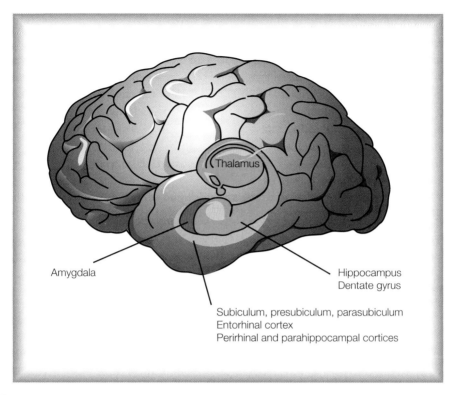

Figure 8.1   The medial temporal lobe memory system.

- Behavioral development in a memory task may be due to the emergence of function in non-memory-related brain systems. For example, improvements in motor or verbal skills may allow better expression of the contents of memory even if these themselves have not changed. Further, at the molecular and cellular level, development and learning often share common mechanisms, making the distinction between them unclear.
- As discussed above, behavioral neuroscience and neuropsychological investigations have revealed that there are multiple brain systems supporting different types of memory. Even in the adult these various systems have proved difficult to disentangle and there is still some debate as to whether it is really appropriate to apply this same framework to the developing system.
- Some forms of "explicit" memory in human adults involve conscious awareness of information, something that is difficult to ascertain in preverbal infants.

Despite these difficulties, we will see in this chapter that considerable progress has been made by adopting a cognitive neuroscience approach to the development of memory. As a starting point, most researchers have turned to studies of the neural basis of various memory systems in adults and animals. They have then attempted to develop marker tasks for the functioning of these systems, often speculating that deficits in memory abilities in young infants and children may be due to the differential development of neural systems supporting particular types of memory function.

8.1   Development of Explicit Memory

One of the first cognitive neuroscience hypotheses about memory development was put forward by Schacter and Moscovitch (1984), who speculated that the brain mechanisms necessary for the long-term storage of information, most probably in the medial temporal lobe are not functional for the first year or two of life. A related hypothesis was put forward by Bachevalier and Mishkin (1984), who pointed out similarities between the amnesic syndrome, in which medial temporal system damage in adults results in deficits in recognition memory but no deficits in learning stimulus–response "habits," and the profile of memory abilities in infants. Mishkin and colleagues had earlier demonstrated that a similar pattern of deficits to that observed in human amnesic syndrome patients could be seen in adult monkeys following surgical lesions to portions of the limbic system. These observations led to the proposal that infants initially relied on implicit memory, with emerging explicit memory later.

FURTHER READING Bachevalier (2008); Bachevalier and Vargha-Khadem (2005).

To test the hypothesis that the putative "cognitive memory" and "habit" systems show a different ontogenetic timetable, Bachevalier and Mishkin (1984) tested infant monkeys aged 3, 6, and 12 months on two types of tasks. The first task was a visual recognition task that involved the infant monkey learning to reach for the novel object of a pair following the earlier presentation of the familiar one (delayed non-match to sample). This task involved just a single presentation of the to-be-learned object and was thought to require a "cognitive memory" system as it could only be successfully performed by bringing to mind what had been observed in the single learning episode. In the second task, a visual discrimination habit task, the infant monkey was sequentially exposed to the same 20 pairs of objects every day. Every day the same object of each pair was baited with a food reward, even though their relative positions were varied. The monkeys had to learn to displace the correct object in each pair. This task was thought to involve the "habit" memory system as it could be successfully performed by learning the association between an item and reward across the repeated trials.

Infant monkeys failed to learn the "cognitive memory" task until they were approximately 4 months old, and did not reach adult levels of proficiency even by the end of the first year. In contrast, infant monkeys of 3 or 4 months old were able to learn the visual "habit" as easily as adults. Bachevalier and Mishkin suggested that this dissociation in memory abilities in infant monkeys is due to the prolonged postnatal development of the MTL system delaying the ability of recognition and association ("cognitive") memory relative to sensorimotor habit formation. This explanation could be extended to human infants since they are also unable to acquire the delayed non-match to sample task in early infancy (until around 15 months), and still have not reached adult levels of performance at 6 years old (Overman, Bachevalier, Turner, & Peuster, 1992).

A key line of evidence to challenge this view came from the visual paired comparison task. This task is a bit like the delayed non-match to sample task, as participants are first familiarized to a stimulus, and then their memories are tested by presenting the familiar stimulus alongside a novel one. However, in the visual paired comparison task, longer looking (instead of reaching) to the novel compared to the familiar stimulus provides evidence of recognition memory. Between 15 and 30 days of age, normal infant rhesus monkeys develop a strong preference for looking toward the novel stimulus, indicating recognition of the familiar one. This preference was not found in monkeys that received MTL lesions including the hippocampus in early infancy. These surprising results suggest that medial temporal structures do make a significant contribution to visual recognition memory even at this very early age. This also suggests that factors other than MTL immaturity might contribute to the more prolonged development of memory performance on the delayed non-match to sample task. For example, slower development of the ability to learn the rule ("Choose the novel object") or associate an object with a reward might be responsible.

Human infants also show evidence of delayed recognition memory in visual paired comparison tasks: 3- to 4-day-olds look longer at a novel face than a familiar one even when a 2-minute delay is imposed (Pascalis & de Schonen, 1994), and 3-month-olds can do the same over a 24-hour delay (Pascalis, de Haan, Nelson, & de Schonen, 1998). These results suggest that the MTL memory circuit is functioning to some extent in human infants as well.

To account for these results, Nelson (1995; Nelson & Webb, 2003) proposed a different, but still maturational, view of early memory development. In this view, an immature form of explicit memory, called "pre-explicit memory," is present from birth, is reliant mainly on the hippocampus, and mediates novelty preferences in the visual paired comparison task. At around 8–10 months of age, developments within the hippocampus, the surrounding cortex and their connections enables a more mature form of explicit memory to emerge that supports a wider range of memory performance. Thus, Nelson believes that early-maturing components of the MTL circuit allow an immature form of explicit memory to function in the first postnatal months, but that an important advance in explicit memory abilities occurs around 8–10 months due to further maturation of the MTL circuit, probably involving the dentate gyrus of the hippocampus.

Another memory task, the deferred imitation task, provides evidence for a striking improvement in memory skills around 8–10 months. In this task, participants are first given a set of toys to play with for a baseline assessment of spontaneous actions. Then, the toys are used to model a specific sequence of target actions to produce an interesting result. The example sequence shown in Figure 8.2a (in the color plate section) involves moving a lever from the front of a door and then opening the door to reveal an infant-friendly character. Immediately or after a delay, the toys are re-presented to the participant and the number of target actions produced is noted (Figure 8.2b). Increases in the number of target actions produced in the correct order from baseline to after modeling are taken as evidence of memory. Patients with damage to the MTL show impaired performance in this task (McDonough, Mandler, McKee & Squire, 1995), even if the injury was sustained during childhood and restricted to the hippocampus (Adlam, Vargha-Khadem, Mishkin, & de Haan, 2005). Carver, Bauer and colleagues have found that only about half of typical 9-month-old infants are able to remember any actions in the correct order after a delay (Carver & Bauer, 1999), and even then they cannot retain this information longer than about 4 weeks (Carver & Bauer, 2001; Bauer et al., 2006). By 10 months there is a substantial improvement: almost all 10-month-olds are able to recall some information (Bauer et al., 2006) and they can still do so up to 6 months later (Carver & Bauer, 2001). This sudden improvement in memory skill is attributed to the maturation occurring around this time in the MTL.

FURTHER READING   Bauer (2008).

However, this view is not without its opponents. Most notably, Rovee-Collier (Rovee-Collier & Cuevas, 2009) has argued that: (a) infant memory is unitary and does not consist of multiple systems that develop at different rates, and (b) memory development is a continuous process, with no transition occurring at 9–10 months. Evidence in favor of the last point comes from her studies using the mobile conjugate reinforcement task. In this task, there is a learning phase where a ribbon is used to connect the infant's ankle to a mobile so that the mobile moves when the infant kicks. During baseline and memory tests, the ribbon is disconnected. Changes in the kicking response are then used as a way of measuring what the infant remembers (e.g., characteristics of the mobile or the context in which it is seen): more kicking than in baseline indicates they recognize the mobile. Using this task, and a similar task modified for older infants, Rovee-Collier has found a linear increase in how long information is remembered over the first 18 months of postnatal life, with no indication of a sudden improvement at 9–10 months (Hartshorn et al., 1998). Proponents of the multi-system view, in turn, refute this evidence by arguing that the mobile conjugate reinforcement task is a motor skill and thus an implicit memory task reliant on the cerebellum and subcortical structures (Nelson, 1995). Seen this way, the continuous development of performance of the task is unsurprising and not damaging to the multi-system view, as it would expect implicit memory functions to develop early and continuously. Since the neural correlates of infants' memory in the mobile conjugate reinforcement task have not been directly studied, this debate remains unresolved.

FURTHER READING   Rovee-Collier (1997); Rovee-Collier and Cuevas (2009).

Explicit memory continues to develop beyond infancy. In particular, episodic memory appears to show a protracted course of development, attributed to continued development of the MTL circuit and its connections with the frontal lobes. Since episodic memory is defined as memory associated with the spatio-temporal context in which it was encoded, it is commonly studied by investigating how well people can remember details about the "source" of their memories. Drummey and Newcombe (2002) tested children of 4, 6, and 8 years of age in a source memory paradigm adapted from those previously used with adults. In this task the children were first presented with ten facts (on a variety of topics) by either an experimenter or a puppet. After a delay of one week the children were asked questions on the facts ("item memory"), and also asked to identify the source of the fact (experimenter, puppet, teacher, or parent; "source memory"). Children showed a steady improvement with age in their ability to remember the facts, but showed an abrupt improvement between 4 and 6 years in their ability to monitor the source of those facts. In particular, the 4-year-olds made many errors in identifying the source of the facts. However, while 4-year-olds are less skilled than older children at recalling the sources of their memories, they are still able to do so at a level greater than chance (Sluzenski, Newcombe, & Ottinger, 2004). Improvements in source memory are probably related to developments in the frontal cortex and its connections with the MTL. This view is supported by two lines of evidence. First, performance on source memory has been found to be correlated with performance on both "frontal lobe" tasks (Drummey & New-combe, 2002; see also Chapter 10) and "MTL tasks" (such as cued recall; Sluzenski et al., 2004), pointing to the importance of both regions, and possibly their interconnections, to the development to episodic memory. Second, studies using fMRI to look at the brain correlates of episodic encoding in children have also suggested that the prefrontal cortex plays an increasing part with age (Chiu, Schmithorst, Brown, Holland, & Dunn, 2006; Menon, Boyett-Anderson & Reiss, 2005; Ofen et al., 2007).

The hippocampus itself is also critical for episodic memory development. This is clearly demonstrated by a unique group of patients who suffered bilateral damage mainly restricted to the hippocampus when they were infants or children (Vargha-Khadem et al., 1997). A report of three cases with such injury—Jon, Kate, and Beth—showed that they all had difficulty remembering information after a delay in spite of normal performance on tests of immediate memory and of memory span (see Figure 8.3). Even though they were unable to retain much information for more than a minute or so, all three children also performed in the normal range on tests of academic achievement (with the exception of spelling) and on the subtests of IQ that tap general knowledge. In other words, the children appeared to have a selective impairment in episodic memory, with relatively intact semantic memory and working memory (see Chapter 10). This pattern of memory impairment occurred together with selective, bilateral reduction of the volume of the hippocampus to a level ∼40–60% of normal size, with brain imaging also showing that even the little remaining hippocampal tissue was atypical.

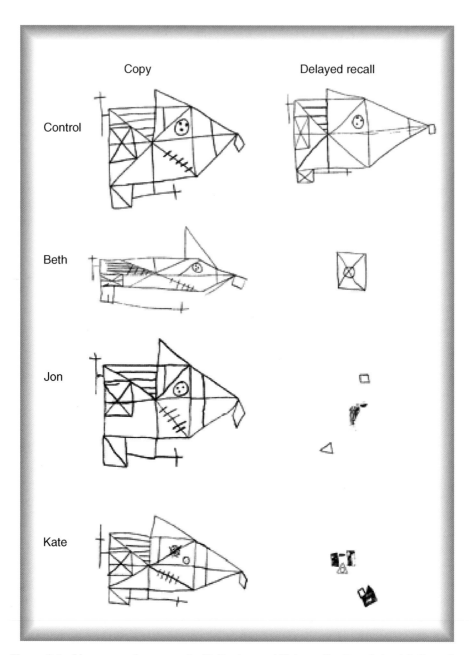

Figure 8.3 Memory performance for Beth, Jon and Kate on the Rey-Osterrieh Complex Figure. Left column shows their normal copying of the figure, while the right column show how much less they were able to recall after a 40-minute delay compared to control participants.

From a maturational viewpoint, this outcome following injury is easy to explain. The hippocampus normally mediates episodic memory, and thus if it is injured a child will fail to develop episodic memory. However, an alternate explanation is that memory outcome following paediatric hippocampal injury is the result of a reorganization of brain memory systems. Studies comparing infant and adult monkeys suggesting that connections of the temporal lobe are more widespread in infants and become more refined with age, provide a possible neuroanatomical bases for reorganization (Webster, Bachevalier, & Ungerleider, 1995). From an interactive specialization viewpoint, the loss of the hippocampus might mean that these extra connections are retained and as a consequence brain memory circuits are left more widespread and less specialized than normal. In support of this view, the patient Jon showed more widespread activation and atypical connectivity than the controls when he was using his residual episodic memory ability (Maguire, Vargha-Khadem, & Mishkin, 2001).

FURTHER READING De Haan, Mishkin, Baldeweg & Vargha-Khadem (2006).

To summarize, the maturational viewpoint has dominated research on the brain bases of explicit memory development. In the current view, components of the MTL circuit, particularly the hippocampus, are functioning to some extent soon after birth to mediate the beginning form of explicit memory. Subsequent development within the MTL and its connections with the frontal cortex mediate further improvements in explicit memory. However, it is important to note that, to date, this framework is based mainly on use of tasks whose brain bases is known in monkeys or human adults and assuming that development of human infants' or children's performance reflects maturation of these structures. More direct information about the pattern of brain activity associated with memory abilities in developing humans may force a revision of these ideas.

8.2   Implicit Memory

While there has been great debate about the development of explicit memory, there has been much more agreement about the development of implicit memory. Most investigators agree that implicit memory is in place within the first months of postnatal life, and that there is little, if any, further development in performance beyond 3 years of age. This has held true even though different forms of implicit memory, such as perceptual priming and motor sequence learning, rely on different neural substrates.

Several investigators have contrasted the development of implicit and explicit memory in children within the same task and shown that implicit memory develops earlier than explicit memory. For example, Drummey and Newcombe (1995) tested 3-year-olds' priming and recognition memory for pictures of animals from a children's book they had read 3 months earlier. While the children showed no evidence of explicit recognition of the pictures, they did show evidence of implicit priming by identifying blurred images of the animals more quickly (perceptual facilitation) than control children who had not previously read the book. A second experiment showed that explicit memory improved between 3–5 years whereas priming did not.

Studies using a different type of implicit memory task, the serial reaction time task, have reached similar conclusions. In this task, participants must learn the association between a set of response keys and a corresponding set of locations on a display screen, so that they press the correct button when a location is cued. The participant does not know that the locations are actually cued in a repeating sequence. The classic result is that participants' get faster at pressing the button as they do the task, even though they are not explicitly aware that there is a pattern. Studies with children show that these changes in reaction time are observed at the youngest ages tested (4–6 years) and do not change with increasing age (e.g., Meulemans, Van der Linden, & Perruchet, 1998; Thomas & Nelson, 2001). However, there is an increase with age in children's ability to explicitly report on the sequence (Thomas & Nelson, 2001).

A neuroimaging study does suggest that the neural correlates of implicit memory in the serial reaction time task may change with age. Thomas and colleagues (2004) found a similar network of cortical and subcortical structures, including the striatum, activated in adults and 7- to 11-year-old children. At both ages, activity in the right striatum correlated with implicit memory performance. However, there were also differences in activation between adults and children: children showed greater subcortical activation and adults greater cortical activation.

While the studies described above suggest that implicit memory abilities are largely in place by 3 years of age, they do not provide insight into how this accomplishment is achieved. Tasks such as the serial reaction time task and other tasks used to assess implicit memory in children are often not suitable for use with infants and toddlers. However, some attempts have been made to bridge this gap by using tasks that are suitable over a wider age span or by drawing analogies between tasks used in older children and those suitable for infants. Another challenge is that few studies with human infants have used tasks whose brain bases have been investigated. In several of the explicit memory tasks outlined above, infants have been tested in behavioral tasks that are close analogues of the monkey and adult tasks, which allowed inferences to be made about the neural bases of infants' performance. In contrast, with implicit forms of memory there has been little attempt to develop marker tasks for infants that closely correspond to tasks used with animals, neuropsychological patients, or functional brain imaging.

One exception is the conditioned eye blink, a paradigm in which a harmless puff of air blown on to the eye, or a gentle tap on the forehead, causes the infant (or animal) to blink. In a conditioning procedure, the forehead tap, or airpuff can come to be predicted by an unrelated sensory stimulus such as auditory tone. Studies with animals point to the importance of the cerebellum for this type of implicit memory. The early development of the cerebellum may be responsible for the fact that between 10 and 30 days the human infant starts to show the conditioned eyeblink response (see Dziurawiec, 1996; Lipsitt, 1990).

In other cases, analogies between tasks are drawn. For example, the visual expectancies paradigm (discussed in Chapter 5), in which infants of 3 months and older start to anticipate the location where the next target in a fixed sequence will appear, resembles some motor sequence learning tasks thought to involve the striatum (such as the serial reaction time task discussed above). While there is little evidence on the development of human striatum, it seems likely from the evidence reviewed in Chapter 4 that this structure is functional by around birth. A further constraint on the emergence of infant visual expectation abilities, however, may be the control of eye movements by the frontal eye fields (see Chapter 5). However, the ability to learn auditory sequences of tones can provide converging evidence. For example, Saffran, Johnson, Aslin, and Newport (1999) examined the response of 8-month-olds to sequences of pure tones, and showed that the infants could group these tones based solely on their distributional properties within a sequence. Whether such abilities are present nearer to birth is currently unknown.

FURTHER READING   Aslin and Hunt (2001).

Priming has also been investigated in infants using event-related potentials. In adults, repeating an image after a series of intervening items leads to a priming effect at about 200–600 ms after stimulus onset (Henson, Rylands, Ross, Vuilleumier & Rugg, 2004; Webb & Nelson, 2001). Webb and Nelson found that 6-month-olds showed a priming effect in a similar time window, though the shape of the component influenced by priming and its location on the scalp differed compared to adults. Importantly, they found no priming effects for the infant late slow wave, which has been linked to recognition memory (Nelson, 1995) and is thought to be generated by the temporal lobes (Reynolds & Richards, 2005). The absence of modulation of the slow wave in this priming task is consistent with the idea that infants were not using the MTL circuit in this task, though it is not clear from this study which brain circuits were mediating the priming effect.

8.3   General Summary and Conclusions

While there is some capacity for explicit memory in the newborn, this expands over the first year of life. Currently, the predominant views emphasize the importance of maturation of components of the MTL circuit and its connections with the frontal lobe for the development of memory skills. However, it is important to consider the limitations of this view as it tends to impose the adult organization of memory systems onto infants and young children, which may not be appropriate. Future studies which take fuller advantage of neuroimaging techniques to allow a better, more direct characterization of brain memory systems in developing human infants and children will help to evaluate the validity of this viewpoint and also better explore how the interactive specialization framework applies. For example, at the neural level memory development may involve regions of the temporal cortex becoming coordinated with the hippocampus through a process of input-dependent increasing specialization.

It is clear that several types of procedural or habit memory, probably dependent on subcortical structures such as the cerebellum and basal ganglia, are present from birth or shortly thereafter. There are currently few marker tasks that allow the direct comparison of cognitive neuroscience data to developmental findings, but this seems a promising area for future research.

From the discussion above it is evident that most memory tasks likely engage multiple memory systems, in a similar way to the partially independent brain pathways that are engaged in eye movement control and attention shifts. A lack of maturity in one or other pathway may be masked in some tasks due to compensatory activity in other pathways. Possibly it is the extent of integration between different memory pathways that is the most significant change with postnatal development. If this is the case, it is not until we have a more integrative account of the relations between different brain memory pathways that we will be able to make sense of the developmental data.

Key Issues for Discussion

- How does the phenomenon of infantile amnesia (the fact that most adults have few memories from the period of life before 3-4 years of age) challenge neurobiological models of memory development?
- How might modern neuroimaging techniques help test the hypothesis that early selective bilateral hippocampal injury leads to an atypical widespread (less focal) cortical memory network?
- Since we are able to learn and form new memories throughout the lifespan, how is it possible to define a mature learning and memory network in the brain?

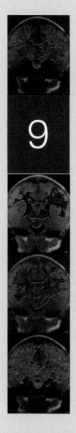

9   Language

This chapter starts with the question of whether language is "biologically special." This issue refers to the extent to which the human infant's brain is predisposed to learn about language. Cognitive neuroscience approaches to this question are outlined. First, studies from early brain damage indicate that different regions of the cortex are capable of supporting nearly normal language acquisition. Second, ERP studies with congenitally deaf participants show that regions which normally support oral language can also support other functions. While these two lines of evidence indicate that there are no innate language representations in the cortex, there is strong functional neuroimaging evidence that the left temporal lobe is efficient at processing speech input from shortly after birth.

An increasing number of studies have examined how experience with language shapes the development of brain language systems. Studies of perceiving speech sounds of the native language, learning the meanings of single words, and reading the printed word together are consistent with the idea that the brain activity related to language becomes more specific and focalized as processing of language becomes more efficient and automatic.

A number of neural correlates of stages of normal language acquisition are outlined. In some developmental disorders, such as Williams syndrome, language can be relatively proficient as compared to other domains of cognition. In others, such as specific language impairment (SLI), language appears to be deficient alongside normal scores in other domains. While these apparent dissociations have sometimes been characterized as evidence for an "innate language module," they are also consistent with an interactive specialization view.

Developmental Cognitive Neuroscience (Third Edition) Mark H. Johnson with Michelle de Haan
© 2011 Mark H. Johnson

9.1   Introduction

Language is a system for communicating with other people using sounds, symbols, and words to express a meaning, idea, or thought. A network of regions of the adult cortex has been typically associated with language functions, and this network is illustrated along with the putative functions of each region in Figure 9.1. Language includes both primary functions, such as perception and processing of incoming speech and production of meaningful speech output, and secondary functions such as reading and writing. Primary language functions normally seem to emerge without much effort as children develop, whereas mastery of secondary language functions

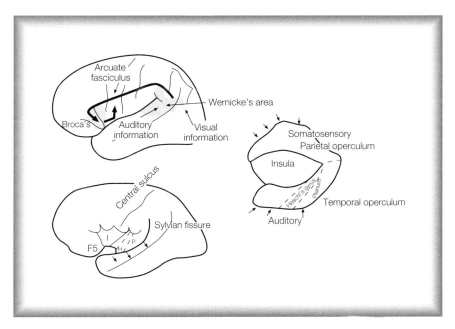

Figure 9.1 Some of the key structures involved in language processing. Top left: Schematic view of information flow from posterior sensory areas to frontal response areas through the inferior temporofrontal loop. The dotted regions show where brain damage causes fluent (Wernicke's) and non-fluent (Broca's) aphasia. These regions are conceptual rather than anatomical. Bottom left: The Sylvian fissure has been pulled out and down in the direction of the arrows to reveal the insula (I) and the auditory cortex (H, P) on the superior surface of the temporal lobe. The region of the frontal operculum indicated as F5 contains mirror neurons in the monkey. It is thought that these neurons play a crucial role in imitation learning. Right: Enlarged view of Heschl's gyrus and planum temporal.

requires extensive practice. Within primary language functions, it is important to distinguish between speech perception, which involves the complex sensory processing required to discriminate between and analyze the sound patterns of an incoming speech stream, and language processing, which refers to a variety of skills including understanding word meaning and applying of rules for grammar. The majority of theorists believe that there is a developmental relation between the two skills, with early speech perception abilities providing the foundation for later construction of successful language processing (e.g., Kuhl, 2000; Werker & Tees, 1999).

A challenge for developmental cognitive neuroscientists studying language acquisition is that it is not possible to use animal models to directly study an aspect of cognition unique to humans. This is not to say that animal studies have not made any contribution to our understanding of language acquisition. For example, there is work on the auditory aspects of language, such as speech perception in species including chinchillas and song birds (see e.g., Marler, 2002) and there is work on the genes involved in language, such as FOXP2, in mice and other species (see e.g., Fisher & Scharff, 2009). However, the bulk of our understanding about the brain bases of language development has come from studies of humans including studies of functional neuroimaging during speech and language processing, studies of infants with focal brain damage, studies of congenital atypicalities, and correlations between phases of language acquisition and neuroanatomical development. An implicit or explicit motivating question for many researchers in this field has been the extent to which language is "biologically special." This issue refers to the extent to which the human child is predisposed to learn language. To translate this question into the framework presented in Chapter 1, does a region of the cortex have innate representations for language, or are language representations the emergent result of a variety of constraints, including the basic architecture of the cortex?

FURTHER READING   Marler (2002); Werker and Vouloumanos (2001).

Two cognitive neuroscience approaches to this question have been pursued. The first of these has been to investigate whether there are particular parts of the cortex critical for language processing or acquisition. If particular parts of the cortex are critical for language, some assume that this region(s) contains innate language-specific representations. In contrast, if several regions of cortex can support language acquisition, this suggests that the representations involved will emerge given the combination of language input and basic cortical architecture. The second cognitive neuroscience approach has been to attempt to identify neural correlates of language-related processing abilities very early in life. I start by reviewing evidence relevant to the first of these approaches.

9.2   Are Some Parts of Cortex Critical for Language Acquisition?

Language acquisition has become a focal point for studies designed to investigate the extent to which particular cortical areas are prespecified to support specific functions. Two complementary directions have been taken, with one set of studies examining the extent to which language functions can be supported by other regions of the cortex, and another group of studies concerned with whether other functions can "occupy" regions that normally support language. The first of these lines of research has asked whether children suffering from perinatal lesions to "language areas" can still acquire language. The second line of research has involved testing congenitally deaf children to see what functions occupy regions of cortex that are normally (spoken) language areas, and also by studying the consequences of brain damage on the ability to produce sign language in a previously fluent signer.

If particular cortical regions are uniquely prespecified to support language, then it is reasonable to assume that early damage to such regions will impair the acquisition of language. This implicit hypothesis has motivated a large body of research, the conclusions of which still remain somewhat controversial. In an influential book, Lenneberg (1967) argued persuasively that if localized left-hemisphere damage occurred early in life, it had little or no effect on subsequent language acquisition. This contrasted both with the effect of similar lesions in adults or older children, and with several congenital atypicalities in which language is delayed or never emerges (see Chapter 2). Lenneberg's view lost adherents in the 1970s, as evidence accumulated from studies of children with hemispherectomies suggesting that left-hemisphere removal always leads to selective subtle deficits in language, especially for syntactic and phonological tasks (e.g., Dennis & Whitaker, 1976). Similar results were also reported for children with early focal brain injury due to strokes (Vargha-Khadem, Isaacs, & Muter, 1994). These findings were compatible with studies of typical infants indicating a left-hemisphere bias at birth in processing speech and other complex sounds (see below), and led some researchers to the conclusion that functional asymmetries for language in the human brain are established at birth, and cannot be reversed. Unfortunately, some of the secondary sources that summarized the work on hemispherectomies and/or early focal injury failed to note that the deficits shown by these children are far more subtle than the frank aphasias displayed by adults with homologous forms of brain damage (see Bishop, 1983, for a critique of the Dennis & Whitaker, 1976, study). Indeed, most of the children with left-hemisphere injury who have been studied to date fall within the normal range, attend normal age-appropriate schools (Stiles, Bates, Thal, Trauner, & Reilly, 2002), and do far better than adults with equivalent damage.

While most studies to date have involved assessing language competence in children who acquired perinatal lesions many years beforehand, Bates, Stiles and their colleagues have, over the past 20 years, carried out *prospective* studies of language and spatial cognition in children who have suffered a single unilateral injury to either the right or the left hemisphere, prenatally or before 6 months, confirmed by at least one radiological technique (Bates & Roe, 2001; Stiles & Thal, 1993; Stiles et al., 2002). Children in these studies were identified prior to the onset of measurable language skills and were examined longitudinally. This team has now studied more than twenty cases between 8 and 31 months of age, all with unilateral lesions that occurred before language development would normally begin. Regardless of the lesion site, infants with focal brain lesions were delayed, suggesting, not surprisingly, that there is a general non-specific cost to early brain injury. However, the prospective study of these infants also produced a number of rather surprising results. Based on the adult aphasia literature, delays in word comprehension would be expected to be most severe in children with damage to left posterior sites. In contrast to this, it appears that comprehension deficits are actually more common in the right-hemisphere infant group. Such a deficit is rarely reported in adults with right-hemisphere damage. This and other findings led these authors to suggest that the regions responsible for first-language learning in children are not necessarily the regions responsible for language use and maintenance in the adult.

FURTHER READING Bates and Roe (2001); Leonard (2003); Stiles et al. (2002).

Another complicating factor revealed by prospective studies of infants with focal lesions came from a study of language production by Reilly, Bates and Marchman (1998). This study used the same population with pre- or perinatal lesions just discussed. Reilly and colleagues looked at many different aspects of lexical, grammatical, and discourse structure in a storytelling task, in children with focal lesions and typically developing controls between 3 and 8 years of age. In this study (like many others within this age range), there were no significant differences between the left- and right-hemisphere groups on any of the language measures. However, the infants with focal lesions as a whole performed worse than typically developing controls on several measures of morphology, syntax, and narrative structure. Each of these disadvantages appeared to resolve over time in the children with focal lesions group, but each time the child moved on to the next level of development (in language acquisition), differences between the infants with focal lesions and typically developing infants reappeared. Thus, functional recovery does not appear to be a one-off event, but rather may reoccur at several critical points during acquisition.

More recently, investigators have used functional neuroimaging to understand how brain language systems reorganize following injury early in life. In other words, if the brain regions that normally subserve language are injured, what brain regions then take on language function? Several studies have now looked at this question by studying brain activation during language processing in children with injury to Broca's area due to stroke or epilepsy (Guzzetta et al., 2008; Liégeois et al., 2004). One pattern of reorganization that has been reported is for activation to be observed in the right hemisphere in areas homologous to those that would normally be activated in the left hemisphere. For example, Guzzetta and colleagues studied five children all of whom had damage to Broca's area in the left hemisphere due to perinatal stroke. Brain activation was measured while children carried out a task involving generating a rhyme in response to a cue word. All five children showed activation in the right hemispheres in areas that were homologous to those activated in the left hemisphere in a healthy control group. Another pattern of reorganization that has been reported is for activation to be observed in the left hemisphere in the tissue surrounding Broca's area. For example, Liégeois and colleagues (2004) found that in four out of five of their cases with injury in or near Broca's area, language activation occurred not in the right hemisphere but in the left hemisphere cortex surrounding the lesioned area. Studies to date have not conclusively identified what factors determine where reorganization takes place within the damaged hemisphere or in the intact hemisphere. A final interesting point to note from such studies is that they have also indicated that activity may be more widely distributed in patients compared to healthy controls. For example, Tillema and colleagues (2008) found that children with left hemisphere stroke showed language-related activation not only in the right-hemisphere homologues but also showed more bilateral activation in the anterior cingulate cortex and more activation in the primary visual cortex. Overall, these studies demonstrate that brain regions other than the traditional left-hemisphere "language areas" can support language function and suggest that, following left-hemisphere injury, language processing may be less focally represented in the brain. This pattern is consistent with an interactive specialization view, where the ultimate brain correlates of language will be determined by interaction among brain areas during development so that alternate patterns can emerge following injury. However, as the interactive specialization model suggests, brain representation of cognitive processes may be more distributed and less focal following brain injury.

To summarize, the effects of early focal lesions on language acquisition are complex. However, in general the evidence supports the following conclusions:

1. Most children with early left-hemisphere damage go on to acquire language abilities within the normal range (although often at the lower end).
2. In general, there is no significant difference in language outcomes when direct comparisons are made between children with early left- versus right-hemisphere damage.
3. Different regions of the cortex may be involved in the actual acquisition of language from those that are important for language use in adults.
4. Functional compensation may have to reoccur at several points in language acquisition, and is not a one-off event.
5. Functional compensation may involve a within-hemisphere or across-hemisphere neural reorganization.

Another approach to studying the extent to which the cortical areas supporting language are prespecified is to ascertain whether other functions can occupy the cortical regions that normally support aspects of language. Such experiments would be analogous in logic to the neurobiological studies mentioned in Chapter 4 in which input to a developing region of cortex was "rewired" such that representations generated from a new sensory modality were produced.

Neville and Bavelier (2002) have used ERPs (Chapter 2) to examine cortical plasticity related to inter-sensory competition. Evidence from visual and spatial tasks in deaf participants suggests that visual processing in the cortex is different in individuals reared in the absence of auditory input. Specifically, the congenitally deaf seem more sensitive to events in the peripheral visual field than are hearing participants. ERPs recorded over classical auditory regions, such as portions of the temporal lobe, are two or three times larger for deaf than for hearing participants following peripheral visual field stimulation. Thus, the lack of auditory input has resulted in a normally auditory area becoming at least partially allocated to visual functions.

FURTHER READING Neville and Bavelier (2002).

Thus, the evidence described so far indicates that regions of the cortex are not prespecified for language processing, and that other functions may be able to "capture" areas that normally end up processing language. However, it is still possible that small variations on the basic architecture of the cortex may be sufficient to "attract" language processing to some regions during normal functional brain development.

Some evidence for this view comes from studies of deaf signers with acquired focal brain lesions. After reviewing evidence that sign language has most of the same formal properties as spoken languages, Bellugi, Poizner, and Klima (1989) found that deaf signers with left-hemisphere lesions acquired in adulthood were aphasic for sign language, while showing intact performance on several visuospatial tasks. Adult patients with recently acquired right-hemisphere lesions, on the other hand, showed the reciprocal pattern of performance. In this latter group, signing was fluent even to the extent of being able to sign fluently about the contents of their room while showing gross spatial distortion in their description of its contents! This, and other evidence, led Bellugi and colleagues to propose that it is the computations required for linguistic processing, rather than its modality, that determine cortical localization.

This conclusion received partial support from a more recent fMRI study in which hearing and deaf participants were scanned while reading sentences in either English or American Sign Language (ASL; Neville et al., 1998; see Neville & Bavelier, 2002).

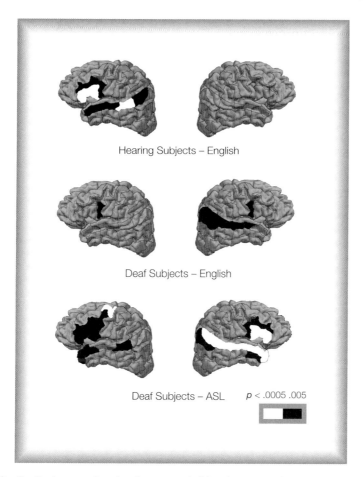

Hearing Subjects – English

Deaf Subjects – English

Deaf Subjects – ASL $p < .0005 .005$

Figure 9.2   Cortical areas showing increases in blood oxygenation on fMRI when normal hearing adults read English sentences (top), when congenitally deaf native signers read English sentences (middle), and when congenitally deaf native signers view sentences in their native sign language (American Sign Language).

The top of Figure 9.2 shows patterns of cortical activation when hearing adults read English. Consistent with previous research, there was robust activation within some classical left-hemisphere language areas, such as Broca's area. No such activation was observed in the right hemisphere. When deaf people viewed an ASL signer performing the same sentences (bottom of figure), they showed activation of most of the left-hemisphere regions identified for the hearing participants. Since ASL is not sound-based, but does have all of the other characteristics of language, including a complex grammar (Klima & Bellugi, 1979), these data suggest that some of the neural systems that mediate language can do so regardless of the modality and structure of the language acquired. Having said this, there were also some clear differences between the hearing and deaf activations, with the deaf group activating some similar regions in the right hemisphere. One interpretation of the right-hemisphere activation is that it is evoked by the biological motion inherent in sign, but not spoken, language.

FURTHER READING MacSweeney, Capek, Campbell, and Woll (2008).

9.3   Neural Basis of Speech Processing in Infants

The second general approach to investigating the extent to which language is "biologically special" involves attempting to identify speech-processing-relevant processes in the brains of very young infants. A further question then concerns how specific to speech these correlates are. The logic here is that if there are specific neural correlates of speech processing observable very early in life, this may indicate language-related neural processing prior to significant experience.

One example of this approach concerns the ability to discriminate speech-relevant sounds such as phonemes. Behavioral experiments have revealed that young infants show enhanced (categorical) discrimination at phonetic boundaries used in speech such as/ba/,/pa/. That is, a graded phonetic transition from/ba/to/pa/is perceived as a sudden categorical shift by infants. These observations initially caused excitement as evidence for a speech-perception-specific detection mechanism in humans. However, over the past decade it has become clear that other species, such as chinchillas, show similar acoustical discrimination abilities, indicating that this ability may merely reflect general characteristics of the mammalian auditory processing system, and not an initial spoken-language-specific mechanism (see Werker & Vouloumanos, 2001). However, Werker and Polka (1993) have reported that while young human infants can discriminate between a very wide range of phonetic constructs, including those not found in the native language (e.g., Japanese infants, but not Japanese adults, can discriminate between "r" and "l" sounds), this ability becomes restricted to the phonetic constructs of the native language around 10 months of age.

FURTHER READING Aslin, Clayards, and Bardhan (2008); Friederici (2008).

If brain correlates of this process could be identified, it might be possible to study the mechanisms underlying this speech-specific selective decrease of sensitivity. As mentioned in Chapter 1, ERPs offer a good opportunity to study the neural correlates of cognition in typical infants in a non-invasive manner. The excellent temporal resolution of ERPs can be complemented by some spatial resolution through the use of high-density ERPs (HD-ERP). When components of ERP differ in both latency (following the event) and spatial resolution, we may be confident that different neural circuitry is being activated. An example of this approach comes from a HD-ERP study of phonetic discrimination in 3-month-old infants.

Dehaene-Lambertz and Dehaene (1994) presented their participants with trials in which a series of four identical syllables (the standard) was followed by a fifth that was either identical or phonetically different (deviant). They time-locked the ERP to the onset of the syllable and observed two peaks with different scalp locations. The first peak occurred around 220 ms after stimulus onset and did not habituate to repeated presentations (except after the first presentation) or dishabituate to the novel syllable. Thus the generators of this peak, probably primary and secondary auditory areas in the temporal lobe, did not appear to be sensitive to the subtle acoustical differences that encoded phonetic information.

The second peak reached its maximum around 390 ms after stimulus onset and again did not habituate to repetitions of the same syllable, except after the first presentation. However, when the deviant syllable was introduced, the peak recovered to at least its original level. Thus, the neural generators of the second peak, also in the temporal lobe but in a distinct and more posterior location, are sensitive to phonetic information. Further studies have found that such mismatch responses are also found for vowel discriminations even in newborns (Cheour-Luhtanen et al., 1995).

More recently, researchers have used two methods with better spatial resolution to investigate early correlates of speech perception. Dehaene-Lambertz, Dehaene, and Hertz-Pannier (2002) measured brain activation with fMRI in awake and sleeping healthy 3-month-olds while they listened to forwards and backwards speech in their native tongue (French). The authors assumed that forward speech would elicit stronger activation than backward speech in areas related to the segmental and suprasegmental processing of language, while both stimuli would activate mechanisms for processing fast temporal auditory transitions (see Werker & Vouloumanos, 2001, for a discussion of the appropriate control stimuli for human speech). Compared to silence, both forward and backward speech activated widespread areas of the left temporal lobe, which was greater than the equivalent activation on the right for some areas (planum temporale). This activation pattern is consistent with the ERP experiment described above. However, forward speech activated some areas that backward speech did not, including the angular gyrus and mesial parietal lobe (precuneus) in the left hemisphere. The authors suggest that these findings demonstrate an early functional asymmetry between the two hemispheres. However, they acknowledge that their results cannot discriminate between an early bias for speech perception, or a greater responsivity of the left temporal lobe for processing auditory stimuli with rapid temporal changes (both of which could start during the final trimester in utero). Further, in awake infants only, the right dorsolateral prefrontal cortex showed greater activation to forward speech, an observation that we will return to in Chapter 10.

The general conclusions from the above studies are reinforced by converging results from a new methodology—near infrared spectroscopy (NIRS; Chapter 2). In this experiment, Mehler and colleagues (Pena et al., 2003) played normal infant-directed speech or the same utterances played in reverse while they measured changes in the concentration of total hemoglobin over the right and left hemisphere. They observed that left temporal areas showed significantly more activation when infants were exposed to normal speech than to backwards speech or silence, leading them to conclude that neonates are born with a left-hemisphere bias for speech processing.

Taken together, the experiments on speech perception just described provide perhaps the best example in developmental cognitive neuroscience of the power of converging methodology. It is encouraging that similar conclusions can be drawn from experiments using behavioral, ERP, fMRI, and NIRS methods.

9.4 Influence of Experience on Brain Language Processing

Whether or not there are biologically "special" areas for processing language in the brain, language inputs must play some role in shaping the brain's response to language. Children grow up hearing a specific language(s) in their environment and develop expertise for that language.

Studies of infants' processing of speech sounds (see above) have demonstrated not only that infants can discriminate these sounds early in life, but that the type of language they hear in their environment subsequently shapes how infants perceive speech sounds. More specifically, behavioral experiments show that infants younger than about 6 months can discriminate speech sounds that are present in their native language, as well as those that are not. However, by about 10 months, their ability to discriminate non-native contrasts diminishes. ERP studies have shown similar results. For example, Rivera-Gaxiola, Silva-Pereyra and Kuhl (2005) found that American infants showed discrimination of both English (native) and Spanish (non-native) consonant contrasts at 7 months in the N250-550 response, whereas 11-month-olds did so only for native contrasts. Moreover, they found that there was an increase in response to native contrasts only from 7 to 11 months of age. These early discriminative capabilities are related to later language abilities. For example, one ERP study showed infants who at 7½ months of age showed a larger ERP to deviant than standard native speech sounds produced a larger number of words at 18 and 24 months, had faster vocabulary growth from 14–30 months, produced more complex sentences at 24 months than infants who did not show this response (Kuhl et al., 2008). These ERP measures of speech processing early in life may thus be useful for the early detection of infants at risk for later language disorder (Benasich & Tallal, 2002).

FURTHER READING Kuhl and Rivera-Gaxiola (2008).

Learning words is another aspect of language that involves inputs from the child's environment. Infants tend to initially learn words relatively slowly, but at about 18–20 months infants typically show a rapid increase in the production of words, often called the vocabulary spurt or "naming explosion." Some researchers have speculated that this sudden increased ability is related to changes in organization of language-relevant brain regions (Mills, Coffey-Corina, & Neville, 1993). One study used ERPs to investigate the neural correlates of processing of known and unknown words in children before and after the vocabulary spurt. The results showed that before the vocabulary spurt, the amplitudes of ERPs from 200–400 ms were larger to known than unknown words. These ERP differences were broadly distributed over anterior and posterior regions of both the left and right hemispheres. In contrast, for 20-month-olds, who had vocabularies over 150 words, ERP differences from 200–400 ms were more focally distributed over temporal and parietal regions of the left hemisphere. A subsequent analysis that compared children with different vocabulary sizes but age held constant showed that this shift in brain response was related to vocabulary, not age.

FURTHER READING   Mills & Conboy (2009).

Yet another aspect of language that involves experience is learning to read. Reading involves linking the visual word form with the sound structure of language and interpreting its meaning. The development of reading poses a somewhat different challenge than the development of the ability to perceive and produce spoken language. Unlike the latter abilities, which seem to unfold without special effort as children develop, reading is a relatively recent development in human history that is acquired through explicit teaching and much practice. In this way, studying the acquisition of reading provides an interesting opportunity for investigating how experience impacts brain function during development.

One brain area that has been intensively studied in this respect is the "visual word form area" (VWFA). The visual word form area is a region in the left occipito-temporal cortex, centered on the mid-fusiform gyrus, that shows a preferential response to visual words compared to other complex visual stimuli. The VWFA appears to be involved in perceptual expertise for word recognition that allows words to be perceived and processed quickly and automatically in skilled readers. This echoes the role of another region of the fusiform gyrus that is also involved in perceptual expertise, the fusiform face area (see Chapter 7). Important changes have been observed in activation of the VWFA over the years when children begin to learn to read. Functional MRI studies have shown that VWFA is typically bilateral in beginning readers, but shifts to the mature pattern of left-lateralization with age and increasing reading skill (Schlaggar et al., 2002).

ERP studies have also been employed to investigate the development of the VWFA, as this region is believed to contribute to the N170 ERP component elicited by visual words. In adults, the N170 for visual words is left-lateralized, and this spatial distribution of the response is believed to be a signature of perceptual expertise of visual words as opposed to other forms of perceptual. Preschoolers' N170s for words are slow and do not show sensitivity to words or letters (Maurer, Brem, Bucher, & Brandeis, 2005); however, after a year and a half of reading instruction, reading fluency correlated with the degree to which the N170 showed an adult-like response (Maurer et al., 2006). Overall, these findings are consistent with the idea that perceptual expertise for recognizing visual words involves a process whereby brain occipito-temporal brain activity elicited to words becomes more specific to words and more focalized to the left hemisphere.

FURTHER READING   Schlaggar and McCandliss (2007).

To summarize, language input from spoken and printed words has an important input to the neural bases of language. Generally speaking, the findings discussed above are consistent with the interactive specialization view that the brain activity underlying language functions becomes more focal with experience, as language skills become more efficient and automated.

9.5   Dyslexia

Dyslexia was one of the first developmental disorders to be associated with a particular underlying neural atypicality. In 1907, Hinshelwood postulated that it was a developmental version of alexia (failure to recognize words) and associated it with atypicality of the left angular gyrus of the cortex (Hinshelwood, 1907). Key symptoms of dyslexia are difficulties in learning to read and spell, sometimes with letter and number reversals, and unusual errors. These correlated deficits (such as in naming and verbal short-term memory) are thought to be due to primary cognitive deficit in the phonological coding of spoken language. There is both structural and physiological evidence from the brains of dyslexics consistent with Hinshelwood's original proposal that developmental atypicalities in the left hemisphere are important.

The structural evidence comes from the work of Galaburda and colleages (e.g., Galaburda, Sherman, Rosen, Aboitiz, & Geschwind, 1985), who conducted autopsies on the brains of several dyslexic individuals. They observed symmetry (between the right and left side) of a particular part of the temporal lobe of the cortex, the planum temporale (see Figure 9.1). This region is part of the so-called Wernicke's area, which has been implicated in phonological processing. Galaburda and colleagues also observed malformations in the clustering of neurons in this region and, to a lesser extent, elsewhere in the cortex of these individuals. These cellular atypicalities are not evident in structural MRI or CT scanning, indicating that developmental atypicalities at the cellular or molecular level will not always be evident in terms of gross brain structure.

More recent efforts have also been made to identify structural asymmetries linked to dyslexia. In a study examining the brain images of a group of children and adults with reading and language disorders, Leonard and Eckert (2008) found two patterns of contrasting anatomical and reading profiles. One pattern was characterized by small, symmetrical brains and was related to deficits in several domains of written and spoken language. The second pattern was characterized by larger, asymmetrical brain structures and was related to isolated phonological deficits as in dyslexia.

Turning to functional studies of the brain, Wood, Flowers, Buchsbaum, and Tallal (1991) described studies from blood flow, PET, and scalp-recorded evoked responses in individuals with dyslexia. Consistent with the postmortem studies, they concluded that people with dyslexia showed atypical processing in the left temporal lobe in both phonemic discrimination and orthographic tasks. Similar conclusions were reached by Paulesu and colleagues (1996), who compared people with dyslexia to a control group during a rhyming task and a short-term memory (for visually presented letters) task. The results showed that only a subset of the regions normally active during these tasks were activated in the individual with dyslexia. Specifically, unlike in the control group, Broca's area and Wernicke's area were never activated together, possibly because they were not functionally connected via the insula.

Research by Tallal and colleagues has suggested that the ability to process the rapid temporal information necessary for phonemic discrimination (see previous section) may be critical for normal language acquisition (e.g., Tallal & Stark, 1980; see Merzenich et al., 2002). Specifically, children with oral language delay often, but not always, have deficits in the perception and discrimination of rapidly changing acoustic information (Tallal, Stark, Clayton, & Mellits, 1980). The inability to discriminate some phonemes with rapid temporal transitions, such as/ba/and/da/, may have consequences for oral speech recognition. Tallal, Merzenich and colleagues have produced preliminary evidence that the inability to process rapid temporal transitions in children with language delay can be rectified by training with adapted speech in which the temporal transitions are extended (Merzenich et al., 2002; Tallal et al., 1996). Whether such remediation can be successfully extended to a wider range of language and reading disorders remains to be seen. However, some reports have indicated that children with language delay frequently develop reading problems symptomatic of some types of dyslexia.

Researchers have also examined the role of the VWFA (see above) in dyslexia. Several studies have reported an underactivation of the VWFA in adults or adolescents with dyslexia (e.g., Maurer et al., 2007). A recent study investigated young children with dyslexia with just a few years' reading experience, and examined the VWFA as well as other regions of the visual-word form pathway along the left occipito-temporal cortex (van der Mark et al., 2009). The results showed the children with dyslexia activated the same basic brain reading network as controls. However, there were differences in the specialization of this activation. They found that only control children showed a differential pattern of activation for print compared to false fonts, with greater activation to print in anterior regions but the opposite in posterior regions. Moreover, they also found that only control children showed an "orthographic familiarity effect," whereby responses in the pathway were greater for unfamiliar than familiar word forms. These results thus show a dysfunction and lack of specialization of the VWFA and related regions in children with dyslexia soon after they begin to read, though they do not make clear to what extent this dysfunction is a cause versus consequence of the reading difficulties.

FURTHER READING Eden and Flowers (2008); Merzenich et al. (2002).

The above studies are all broadly consistent with involvement of the left temporal lobe in both phonemic discrimination and dyslexia. However, it is important to stress that there is considerable controversy about the exact nature of the cognitive deficits observed in dyslexia (e.g., Eden & Flowers, 2008; Pennington & Welsh, 1995) and that there is also evidence for atypicalities elsewhere in the brain (e.g., Livingstone, Rosen, Drislane, & Galaburda, 1991). Further, the putative involvement of the left temporal lobe in this disorder need not be interpreted in terms of a causal epigenesis pathway. It is tempting to infer that a neural deficit or atypicality in the left temporal lobe gives rise to a failure to process the rapid temporal transitions necessary for phonemic discrimination, and that in some cases this might be related to subtypes of dyslexia. However, the evidence on cortical development and plasticity discussed in Chapter 4, and the apparent initial success of the training studies by Merzenich et al. (2002), suggest a more probabilistic epigenetic view.

Broadly speaking, this view is that regions of the left temporal lobe are engaged by inputs that require rapid temporal processing. This is due to having an architecture slightly different from the basic structure common to the rest of the cortex. This makes this region the best, but not the only, possible "home" for speech processing. If this region is damaged, other parts of the cortex can also support these representations, though perhaps not quite as efficiently. Processing speech within this region influences its synaptic and dendritic microstructure through some of the mechanisms discussed in Chapter 4. Through interaction with a certain type of input it thus becomes increasingly specialized and different from other regions. Some degree of plasticity may remain during development, resulting in a reconfiguration of the microcircuitry of the region following specific training. Differences in neural structure between this region in adults with dyslexia and controls would reflect this deviant developmental pathway, much of which may have occurred postnatally. Thus, a slight initial bias can be enhanced through development into greater anatomical and functional specialization.

9.6   Neural Correlates of Typical and Atypical Language Acquisition

Bates, Thal, and Janowsky (1992) reviewed and identified a number of correlations between neuroanatomical developments in the human cerebral cortex and "landmarks" in language acquisition. Such correlations cannot be used to establish firm links between neural events and cognitive ones. However, the approach is useful for identifying specific hypotheses that can then be tested with more direct methodologies.

Consistent with the findings reviewed so far in this chapter, Bates et al. (1992) suggested that the evidence for some neuroanatomical differences between the right and left hemispheres at birth may set up computational differences that "bias" language toward the left hemisphere. As discussed in Chapter 2, it is likely that these differences between the hemispheres are due to differential timing of development, rather than a genetic encoding of a specific architecture. Bates et al. (1992) identify a peak transition in both behavioral and neural development at around 8–9 months after birth. They discuss the establishment of long-range connections (especially from the frontal cortex) and the onset of an adult distribution of metabolic activity (from the PET study of Chugani, 1994, reviewed in Chapter 4) at this age, and suggest that these neural developments enable the onset of a number of language-related skills such as word comprehension, and the inhibition of non-native speech contrasts.

Around 16–24 months there is a "burst" in vocabulary and grammar, and Bates and colleagues argue that this correlates with a steep increase in synaptic density in many relevant cortical regions. The increased synaptic density, they speculate, enables a larger capacity for storage and information processing. At around 4 years of age most typical children have acquired the basic morphological and syntactic structures of their native language, and thus have reached the end of the "grammar burst." Bates and colleagues point out that this "stabilization" of language coincides with the decline in overall brain metabolism and synaptic density (although, as mentioned in Chapter 4, the peaks of these two measures may not coincide exactly).

Developmental disorders involving language can also be informative about the neurodevelopmental basis of these abilities. Some authors have argued that developmental disorders in which language is relatively deficient, despite a lack of problems in other domains, constitute evidence for an innate language module. Conversely, cases where language is supposedly intact, despite impairment in other domains, could provide powerful converging evidence. An example of the former kind that has attracted much scientific and media interest in recent years concerns three generations of the KE family and the "FOXP2" gene. As reviewed in Chapter 3, while initial reports suggested that about half of the members of this unfortunate family had an inherited specific impairment in grammar (Gopnik, 1990), claims for a "grammar gene" have been diluted by the finding that the deficits in the affected family members are much broader than grammar alone. Varghha-Khadem and colleagues have conducted extensive work on the family and found deficits in coordinating complex mouth movements (orofacial dyspraxia), timing of rhythmic motor movements, various aspects of language outside grammar (e.g., lexical decision), with IQ scores 18–19 points below unaffected members of the same family (Vargha-Khadem et al., 1995). Moreover, there is not a clear association of mutations of the FOXP2 gene with developmental language disorders. For example, one study of 270 four-year-old children with poor language functioning found that none had a mutation of the FOXP2 gene (Meaburn, Dale, Craig, & Plomin, 2002).

Nevertheless, the relatively simple single-gene basis of the condition, and its association with language, make it worthy of further study (see Marcus & Fisher, 2003, for further discussion). One such study has involved fMRI during verb generation and repetition tasks (Liégeois et al., 2003). This study demonstrated that affected members of the family showed significant underactivation mainly in two regions: Broca's area and the putamen. However, as can be seen in Figure 9.3 in the color plate section, the affected members also showed greater activation than did controls in a variety of other cortical regions, suggesting widespread adjustment of cortical networks in response to the aberrant gene.

While the KE family may not have turned out to have the specific deficits initially hypothesized, similar claims about the specificity of language deficits have been made for so-called "specific language impairment" (SLI). While there is much controversy about the behavioral specificity or otherwise of this condition (see Bishop, 1997), most neuroanatomical studies have tended to focus on the particular regions thought to be important for language as discussed above. Thus, it is difficult to know whether or not regions outside the adult classical language regions are atypical as well. However, a recent study set out to examine the whole brain of "SLI" participants with MRI (Herbert et al., 2003). Compared to controls, these children showed a substantial increase (more than 10%) in cerebral white matter throughout the brain. This atypical pattern was no more severe in the classical language areas than anywhere else in the brain, suggesting to the authors that the population they studied had a "generalized systems impairment" that differentially affected language.

A case where language is supposedly spared relative to other domains of impairment is Williams syndrome (WS). In WS (see Chapters 2 and 7), language can be strikingly proficient, despite severe deficits in other domains. Several studies have demonstrated that linguistic and face-processing skills are surprisingly good in WS participants, despite low IQs (typically in the 50s–60s) and serious deficits on visuospatial, number, motor, planning, and problem-solving tasks (see Karmiloff-

Smith, 2008, for review). The linguistic ability of these participants is not just superficial (such as repetition of previously heard sentences), but is generative in the sense that they can create new sentences with appropriate grammatical structure. The depth of this linguistic knowledge is currently the subject of debate. In certain cases the dissociation between linguistic ability and other abilities can be very marked. For example, the following is the spontaneous speech of a 21-year-old WS participant (studied by Karmiloff-Smith and colleagues) with performance equivalent to a mental age of $5^{1}/_{2}$ years as assessed on a standardized spatial cognition task (Ravens Matrices):

[talking about her job at the hospital where she helps with the catering staff]

Well sometimes I do and sometimes I don't. They just tell you how many cups you put on the tray and the saucers and how many (um) spoons and sugars and creams you put on the tray and how many sandwiches they want for how many people.

[EXPERIMENTER: But do you count them yourself, the cups?]

No, they count them and I just put them on the trays. So, I put them in with clingfilm on top so they don't get wet.

In this example, while this participant is unable to count relatively small numbers (the number of cups on a tray), she is able to express herself grammatically and has a fairly wide vocabulary. While it seems initially attractive to account for such cases of isolated proficient language in terms of innate representations for language, the evidence on cortical development in Chapter 4 should make us wary of jumping to this conclusion. A better way to view such cases is that some deviation from the normal trajectory of brain development results in a slightly maladaptive architecture in some structures (Karmiloff-Smith, 2008). This slightly deviant aspect of neural architecture has much more effect on some domains of processing than others. Once early postnatal development deviates from the normal trajectory, then it is likely that this deviation will be amplified by atypical interactions with the environment.

9.7   General Summary and Conclusions

The degree to which the acquisition of language is "biologically special" has been hotly contested on the basis of linguistic and behavioral data. While the addition of cognitive neuroscience data has not resolved this debate, it has illuminated some of the constraints and biases that ensure that most adults acquire a specialized brain network for the production and processing of language. For example, converging evidence from several cognitive neuroscience methods indicates that, from birth or even earlier, regions of the left temporal lobe are engaged by, and process, auditory inputs that require rapid temporal processing. While these regions may be the ideal "home" for speech processing, if they are damaged early in life then other parts of the cortex can also support this function, though perhaps not quite as efficiently. In accord with the interactive specialization view, it is likely that processing speech within this region from early in life influences its synaptic and dendritic micro-structure, resulting in it becoming increasingly specialized and different from other regions. Some degree of plasticity may remain during development, resulting in a reconfiguration of the microcircuitry of the region following specific training. Interestingly, recent studies have also focused more attention on the white matter tracts connecting brain language regions. For example, the dorsal pathway projecting from Broca's area to the superior temporal region appears to be especially important for higher-language functions and is weaker in non-human primates compared to humans, as well as in human children compared to adults (reviewed in Friederici, 2009). Better understanding of such pathways may also provide new insights into the brain bases of reorganization, since the interactive specialization view indicates that interactions among brain regions are important in this process.

Developmental disorders in which language functions are supposedly selectively impaired, or remain "intact" in the face of other deficits, have been used as examples in support of claims for an "innate language module." Closer examination of such cases reveals that they are better viewed as deviations from the typical trajectory of brain development that have more effect on some domains of processing than others. Once early postnatal development deviates from the typical trajectory, then it is likely that this deviation will be amplified by atypical interactions with the environment.

Language acquisition and speech perception have been some of the most active areas of developmental cognitive neuroscience. The use of converging methodologies, and frequent comparisons between typical and atypical trajectories of development, make it the general domain most likely to see major breakthroughs over the next decade.

Key Issues for Discussion

- What methods and approaches are likely to be most successful for revealing the genetic contribution to language acquisition?
- To what extent are there parallels between the emergence of functional specialization of the fusiform face area (Chapter 7) and in the visual word form area?
- How does speech perception contribute to language acquisition and its dbe seenisorders?

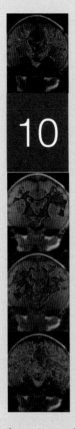

10 Prefrontal Cortex, Working Memory, and Decision-Making

The prefrontal cortex shows a prolonged course of development compared to most other cortical regions. This chapter outlines two approaches to understanding the role of this part of cortex in cognitive development. In the first of these, the maturational approach links structural development of the prefrontal cortex to the emergence of specific cognitive skills. One example is work linking maturation of the dorsolateral prefrontal cortex with developments in working memory. Perseverative errors of young infants on object permanence tasks have been linked with maturation of the dorsolateral prefrontal cortex by means of data from human infants, infant monkeys, and adult prefrontal-cortex-lesioned monkeys, and working memory capacity in children and adolescents has been linked with maturation of lateral prefrontal cortex by means of data from structural and functional neuroimaging. This maturational account will require some modification in the light of recent evidence suggesting that a broader neural network is involved in working memory and highlighting the role of experience in shaping this network. A second example of the maturational approach has involved associating the differential rate of development of prefrontal cortex compared with other cortical and subcortical regions with increases in risky decision-making and mental illness observed in adolescence. This has involved neuroimaging studies demonstrating less activation of prefrontal control systems in adolescents compared to adults or children. The mismatch between the slowly maturing prefrontal regulation systems and the earlier-maturing emotion-processing systems is said to account for adolescents' increased vulnerability to risky decision-making and mental illness. This view may need modification in light of evidence indicating that the dichotomy between prefrontal control systems and subcortical systems is an oversimplification.

A second view of the role of the prefrontal cortex in cognitive development is that it is needed for skill learning and plays an important and early role in brain organization. Studies of electroencephalography (EEG) coherence suggest a role for prefrontal regions in the cyclical reorganization of cortical representations during cognitive development. Some of the problems with this approach are outlined. It is concluded that the specificity of prefrontal cortex functioning probably arises from a combination of initial neurochemical and connectivity biases, and the relatively protracted plasticity of the region.

Developmental Cognitive Neuroscience (Third Edition) Mark H. Johnson with Michelle de Haan
© 2011 Mark H. Johnson

10.1   Introduction

As discussed in Chapter 4, the prefrontal cortex shows a prolonged period of postnatal development, with detectable changes in grey matter volume, white matter volume and cortical thickness throughout childhood and into the teenage years (Giedd et al., 1999; Gogtay et al., 2004; Shaw et al., 2008). For this reason, it has been the part of the brain most commonly associated with developments in cognitive abilities during childhood.

Two major unresolved issues concerning frontal cortex development are as follows:

- Are the specialized computations performed by the frontal cortex due to a unique neuroanatomy/neurochemistry, or to other factors?
- How are we to align evidence for prefrontal cortex functioning within the first 6 months of life, with evidence for the continuing neuroanatomical development of the region until the teenage years?

These issues will be revisited at the end of the chapter. First, the chapter will describe two alternative views that have been taken of the relation between prefrontal cortex structural development and increases in cognitive ability in childhood. The first of these is that structural developments in the prefrontal cortex occur at a particular age, allowing certain increases in cognitive ability. This view is in line with the maturational perspective outlined in Chapter 1. Two examples of this view will be presented, one highlighting the role of the prefrontal cortex in development of object permanence and working memory, and the other examining the role of the prefrontal cortex in the increased vulnerability to risky behaviors and mental illness observed in adolescence. A different view is that the prefrontal cortex is consistently involved in acquisition of new skills and knowledge from very early in life, and may also play a role in organizing other parts of the cortex (e.g., Thatcher, 1992). By this second view, regions of prefrontal cortex play a fundamental role in cognitive transitions primarily because of the region's involvement in the acquisition of *any* new skill or knowledge. A corollary of this hypothesis is that prefrontal involvement in a particular task or situation may decrease with experience of the task. This perspective on prefrontal cortex development is inspired by the skill learning model of functional brain development outlined in Chapter 1. With regard to prefrontal cortex development, many of the predictions from this model overlap with those from the interactive specialization view. Consequently, these two perspectives will only be differentiated at the end of the chapter.

10.2   Prefrontal Cortex, Object Permanence and Working Memory

One of the most comprehensive attempts to relate a cognitive change to underlying brain development has concerned the emergence of object permanence in infants. In particular, Diamond, Goldman-Rakic, and colleagues (Diamond, 1991; Diamond & Goldman-Rakic, 1989; Goldman-Rakic, 1987) have argued that the maturation of prefrontal cortex during the last half of the human infant's first year of postnatal life accounts for both Piaget's (1954) observations about object permanence and a variety of other transitions in related tasks, which involve working memory and the inhibition of prepotent responses (e.g., Diamond, Werker, & Lalonde, 1994).

The region of the frontal lobe anterior to the primary motor and premotor cortex, commonly called the prefrontal cortex, accounts for almost one-third of the total cortical surface in humans (Brodmann, 1909, 1912) and is considered by most investigators to be the locus of control for many abilities central to higher level cognition. Extensive clinical (Milner, 1982) and experimental observations of the effects of injury to this region have also supported the notion that the prefrontal cortex supports important aspects of cognition (for reviews see Duncan, 2001; Owen, 1997). While there are no universally accepted theories of frontal cortex functioning, some particular forms of cognitive processing that have been consistently linked to the prefrontal cortex in adults pertain to the planning or carrying out of sequences of action, the maintenance of information "on-line" during short temporal delays, and the ability to inhibit a set of responses that are appropriate in one context but not another.

It was Piaget who first observed that infants younger than around 7 months fail to accurately retrieve a hidden object after a short delay period if the object's location is changed from one where it was previously and successfully retrieved. In particular, infants of this age make a particular perserverative error. That is, they often reach to the hiding location where the object was found on the immediately preceding trial. This characteristic pattern of error, called "A not B," was cited by Piaget (1954) as evidence for the failure of infants to understand that objects retain their existence or permanence when moved from view. Between 7½ and 9 months, infants begin to succeed in the task at successively longer delays of 1 to 5 seconds (Diamond, 1985, 2001). However, their performance is unreliable: infants continue to make the A not B error up to about 12 months if the delay between hiding and retrieval is incremented as the infant's age increases (Diamond, 1985).

FURTHER READING   Benes (2001); Diamond (2001, 2002).

Diamond and Goldman-Rakic (1989) tested monkeys in a version of Piaget's object permanence task. In the object permanence task, participants are shown an object hidden at location A and are permitted to retrieve it. After a predetermined number of successful retrievals at location A (usually three), the object is then hidden at location B. Infant monkeys failed to retrieve the hidden object at location B when the delay between hiding and retrieval was 2 seconds or more. Diamond and Goldman-Rakic (1989) found that animals with damage to the parietal cortex, a brain region closely associated with spatial processing, did not show this performance deficit; nor did animals with lesions to the hippocampal formation, a region known to be crucial for other memory-related tasks (Diamond, Zola-Morgan, & Squire, 1989). However, damage to the dorsolateral prefrontal cortex severely impaired the adult monkeys' performance when a delay was imposed between hiding and search, indicating that this region plays a central role in delayed response tasks that require the maintenance of spatial information over temporal delays.

Developmental evidence that links maturation in frontal cortical regions to the emergence of working memory abilities comes from studies (Diamond & Goldman-Rakic, 1986, 1989) showing that infant monkeys initially fail the A not B task in ways similar to monkeys with prefrontal cortex damage. However, between the ages of 1½ to 4 months, the infant monkeys show a similar progression as that seen in human infants between 7½ and 12 months, with both becoming able to succeed in the task and to withstand longer and longer delays. Lesions to the dorsolateral prefrontal cortex in infant monkeys who have acquired the ability to succeed on the task abolish this skill, confirming the importance of this region in the task. In humans, noninvasive imaging methods have also been used to link maturation of the prefrontal cortex to development of infants' performance in the A not B task. In one series of studies, increases in frontal EEG responses in human infants have been shown to correlate with the ability to respond successfully over longer delays in delayed response tasks (Fox & Bell, 1990; Bell, 1992a, 1992b; Bell & Fox, 1992). Another study using optical imaging (NIRS) showed a correlation between behavioral demonstration of object permanence and blood oxygenation in the prefrontal cortex (Baird et al., 2002).

In Diamond's (1991) view, the emergence of the ability to demonstrate knowledge about an object's permanence results from the maturation of dorsolateral prefrontal cortical regions between the ages of 5 and 12 months. Diamond proposed that this region of the cortex is important when a participant has to both retain information over spatial delays and inhibit prepotent (previously reinforced) responses. Let's briefly review the evidence for this position. Infants younger than 7½ months fail to retrieve hidden objects when any delay is imposed between hiding and retrieval. In this sense, human infants behave like the adult monkeys with dorsolateral prefrontal lesions and infant monkeys, as discussed previously. Human infants of this age make similar retrieval errors in both the A not B task, in which the side of hiding is switched after several repeated hidings on one side, and in an object retrieval task when the side of hiding is varied randomly (Diamond & Doar, 1989). This suggests that Piaget's observations about object permanence reflect the state of development of one or more underlying neural mechanisms common to performance on both the object permanence and retrieval tasks. Since successful performance on these tasks requires both memory for the most recently hidden location and the inhibition of an incorrect reach to the last rewarded location, the underlying neural mechanism must subserve both computations. Extensive neurobiological evidence implicates the prefrontal cortex in spatial working memory performance, and lesions of this region frequently reveal patterns of behavior in which the inhibition of inappropriate responses is impaired. Consequently, Diamond and colleagues have presented a strong case for the importance of dorsolateral prefrontal cortex development.

The maturational approach to prefrontal cortex development has also been extended to later childhood and adolescence. The results from a variety of behavioral tasks designed to tap into advanced prefrontal cortex functions have demonstrated that adult levels of performance are not reached until adolescence or later (see Fabiani & Wee, 2001; Luciana, 2003). For example, participants from 3 to 25 years old were tested on the CANTAB (Cambridge Neuropsychological Testing Automated Battery), a well-established and -validated battery of tests previously used on adult human and animal populations (Fray, Robbins, & Sahakian, 1996). This battery assesses several measures, including working memory skills, self-guided visual search, and planning. Importantly for developmental studies, the battery is administered with touch-screen computer technology, and does not require any verbal or complex manual responses. Using the CANTAB, Luciana and Nelson (1998, 2000; Luciana, 2003) found that, while measures that depend on posterior brain regions (such as recognition memory) were stable by 8 years, measures of planning and working memory had not yet reached adult levels by age 12.

FURTHER READING Olson and Luciana (2008).

While such behavioral measures are useful as marker tasks, it is even better to use functional imaging while children perform tasks likely to engage prefrontal cortical regions. Several fMRI studies by Klingberg and colleagues (summarized in Klingberg, 2006) document that the dorsolateral prefrontal cortex (in particular, the superior frontal sulcus) is involved in working memory in both children and adults, but also show that it is activated as part of a network also involving the intraparietal cortex (see Figure 10.1 in the color plate section). These studies show that stronger activation of the fronto-parietal network is related to greater working memory capacity, and that activation of the network also increases with age, independent of performance (Klingberg, Forssberg, & Westerberg, 2002). Development of white matter tracts connecting the frontal and parietal regions seems to play a role in this process: maturation of these tracts relates to working memory (but not reading) performance, and to the degree of cortical activation in the frontal and parietal grey matter (Olesen, Nagy, Westerberg, & Klingberg, 2003). At a cellular level, computational modeling indicates that stronger synaptic connectivity between the prefrontal and parietal regions, and not faster transmission of neural signals or stronger connections within each region, can by itself account for observed changes in brain activity associated with the development of working memory in childhood (Edin, Macoveanu, Olesen, Tegner, & Klingberg, 2007).

FURTHER READING   Klingberg (2006, 2008).

While this body of evidence is convincing, it also suggests that the prefrontal cortex maturation hypothesis is not the whole story, and that some modification or elaboration of the original account will be required. A further line of evidence that can potentially challenge the maturational view comes from studies showing how experience can influence working memory capacity and prefrontal activation. Traditionally, working memory capacity was thought to be a fixed, unchangeable trait once we become adults. More recent studies show greater flexibility in working memory capacity. For example, one study showed that after 5 weeks of training on a working memory task, adults showed both an increased working memory capacity and increased working memory-related brain activity in the fronto-parietal network (Olesen, Westerberg, & Klingberg, 2004). These findings also have potential implications for understanding the development of working memory. The maturational viewpoint would argue that development of the fronto-parietal network enables improvements in working memory performance. However, the training study suggests an alternative viewpoint: experience using working memory and/or the increased demands on working memory as children develop might drive changes in the brain network underlying this ability, a view more consistent with the interactive specialization and skill learning perspectives.

Another line of evidence suggests that the neural bases of infant working memory may be more broadly based than initially thought. For example, EEG studies have reported that in 6-month-old infants there is a burst of high-frequency EEG activity over right temporal regions during the period of maintenance of the representation of the object, after it disappears and before it reappears (Kaufman, Csibra, & Johnson, 2003, 2005; see Chapter 6). Another EEG study found that, in infancy, working memory was associated with changes in EEG power from baseline to task across all brain regions, whereas by 4 years of age working memory was associated with changes in EEG at frontal regions only (Bell & Wolfe, 2007). A recent study of the development of working memory in infants born preterm, showed that neonatal hippocampal volumes correlated with working memory ability at 2 years of age but cortical volumes, even from the dorsolateral prefrontal region, did not (Beauchamp et al., 2008). Findings such as these hint that the neural network underlying working memory may be different, possibly more diffuse, in infants, and become increasingly focused on the fronto-parietal network with development (Kaldy & Sigala, 2004), a pattern consistent with the interactive specialization view.

10.3   Prefrontal Cortex, Social Decision-Making and Adolescence

Another domain in which the prefrontal cortex is believed to play an important role is in decision-making. Recently investigators have been particularly interested in understanding how maturation of the prefrontal cortex contributes to social decision-making in adolescence. Adolescence is a period of clear gains in intellect and cognitive skills, but it also marks a period of intense emotions and impulsive behavior that seem not to reflect these cognitive improvements, as well as a time when there is a clear increase in incidence of antisocial and risky behaviors and mental illnesses including depression, anxiety and mood disorders, eating disorders, and substance abuse.

Several investigators have argued that this profile of behavior can be explained by the differential rate of maturation of the prefrontal cortex compared to other brain regions. One specific model of this general idea is the Social Information Processing Network (SIPN) model (Nelson, Leibenluft, McClure, & Pine, 2005). In this model, social behavior involves three interacting "nodes": (a) a detection node which detects social information, involving mainly the occipito-temporal cortex; (b) an affective node which processes the emotional significance of a social stimulus and influences the behavioral and emotional responses to it, involving subcortical structures and the orbito-frontal cortex; and (c) a cognitive regulatory node which is important for goal-directed behavior, impulse control, and theory of mind, involving much of the prefrontal cortex. According to this model, the three nodes mature at different rates, with the detection node maturing very early in life, the affective node maturing in early adolescence, and the cognitive regulatory node maturing much more slowly than the other two nodes. This mismatch in maturation among the nodes creates a vulnerability in adolescence, when strong emotional responses to social stimuli are not yet properly moderated by the as-yet immature cognitive-regulatory system. This vulnerability then accounts for the rise in risky decision-making.

In order to study decision-making more systematically, Bechara and colleagues developed a task called the Iowa Gambling Task (Bechara, Damasio, Damasio, & Anderson, 1994). This task is meant to tap into the type of decision-making we are often faced with in everyday life, when we must choose between options that have different short-term and long-term advantages. In the task, participants are asked to choose cards one at a time from four decks, two of which can result in immediate big rewards and two of which result in immediate smaller rewards. The twist in the game is in how punishment is delivered. The two decks that result in high rewards are also accompanied by large delayed punishment and thus are not advantageous in the long term as they will result in a net loss. By contrast, the decks that result in low immediate reward are accompanied by small delayed punishment and so are more advantageous as they result in a net gain in the long term. Participants are not told about the differences between the decks and must discover the differences themselves as they choose cards and receive the resulting rewards and punishments. Healthy adults come to learn that it is best to choose from the advantageous decks during the course of the task, whereas patients with damage to prefrontal cortex keep selecting from the disadvantageous decks that give short-term reward but result in a loss over the long term. Thus, they seem to be influenced more by the immediate reward and fail to consider the longer-term consequences of their actions and regulate their choices accordingly (Bechara, Damasio, Tranel, & Damasio, 1997). This description is quite similar to that often applied to adolescents, who are often said to have difficulty in seeing the future consequences of their actions.

Crone and colleagues have carried out studies of children and adolescents using a similar task, and found that there is a slow course of development, with children not consistently learning to make advantageous choices until they are 16–18 years old. Brain imaging studies suggest that this behavioral pattern relates to an adolescent imbalance between subcortical reward-processing systems and frontal control systems: adolescents are more driven by reward systems, leading to suboptimal choices in social decision-making tasks (Crone & Westenberg, 2009).

FURTHER READING   Crone and van der Molen (2008); Crone and Westenberg (2009).

While these findings are promising, the maturational view may need modification. One reason is in light of evidence showing that rewards are also processed cortically, and that control systems also rely on subcortical regions (Phillips, Drevets, Rauch, & Lane, 2003). Thus, the processes involved in decision-making are more broadly based and thus developments at the behavioral level may not only be attributable to maturation of a specific component. A recent case study also demonstrated that problems with emotion regulation and attention engagement begin in the first months of life following perinatal prefrontal injury (Anderson et al., 2007), indicating that prefrontal systems may already be involved in regulation of behavior from early in postnatal life.

10.4   Prefrontal Cortex, Skill Learning, and Interactive Specialization

An alternative approach to understanding the role of the prefrontal cortex in cognitive development has been advanced by several authors who have suggested that the region plays a critical role in the *acquisition* of new information and tasks. From this perspective, the challenge to the infant brain in, for example, learning to reach for an object is equivalent in some respects to that of the adult's brain when facing complex motor skills like learning to drive a car. Three concomitants of this general view are that (a) the cortical regions crucial for a particular task will change with the stage of acquisition, (b) the prefrontal cortex plays a role in organizing information within or allocating it to other regions of cortex, and (c) that development involves the establishment of hierarchical control structures, with the frontal cortex maintaining the currently highest level of control. Three recent lines of evidence indicating the importance of prefrontal cortical activation early in infancy have given further credence to this view: (a) fMRI and PET studies, (b) psychophysiological evidence, and (c) the long-term effects of perinatal damage to the prefrontal cortex.

The limited number of fMRI and PET studies that have been conducted with infants have often surprisingly revealed functional activation in the prefrontal cortex, even when this would not be predicted from adult studies. For example, in an fMRI study of speech perception in 3-month-olds, Dehaene-Lambertz and colleagues (2002) observed a right dorsolateral prefrontal cortex activation that discriminated (forward) speech in awake, but not sleeping, infants (see Figure 10.2 in the color plate section and Chapter 9). Similar activation of DLPFC was found in response to faces at the same age (Tzourio-Mazoyer et al., 2002). While this is evidence for activation of at least some of the prefrontal cortex in the first few months, it remains possible that this activation is passive as it may not play any role in directing the behavior of the infant. Two other recent lines of evidence, however, suggest that this is not the case.

Developmental ERP studies have often recorded activity changes over frontal leads in infants, and some recent experiments suggest that this activity has important consequences for behavioral output. These experiments involve examining patterns of activation that precede the onset of a saccade (Chapter 5). In one example, Csibra and colleagues (1998, 2001) observed that presaccadic potentials that are usually recorded over more posterior scalp sites in adults are observed in frontal channels in 6-month-old infants. Since these potentials are time-locked to the onset of an action, it is reasonable to infer that they are the consequence of computations necessary for the planning or execution of the action.

Further evidence for the developmental importance of the prefrontal cortex from early infancy comes from studies of the long-term and widespread effects of perinatal damage to the area. In several of the previous chapters we have seen how selective perinatal damage to the relevant regions activated in adults often has, at worst, mild effects on infants, with subsequently almost complete recovery of function. In contrast, perinatal damage to frontal and prefrontal cortical regions often results in long-term difficulties that can become increasingly apparent with development. This generalization from several domains suggests that the prefrontal cortex plays an important structuring or enabling role from very early in postnatal development. One example of this theoretical approach to functional prefrontal cortex development has been advanced by Thatcher (1992) and Case (1992) (for another, related approach see Stuss, 1992).

Thatcher (1992) and colleagues have analyzed EEG data from a large number of participants at various ages between 2 months and 18 years. During recording, the participants sat quietly and, as far as can be ascertained, were not responding to any stimuli. From 16 leads placed evenly across the scalp the spontaneous EEG rhythms of the brain were recorded before being subjected to a complex analysis that ascertained the extent to which the recordings from each lead "cohered" (roughly speaking, correlated in their activity) with other leads. From the large amount of raw data that such an analysis generates, the major factors (i.e. which leads cohere) could be adduced for each age group, and the age "peaks" of rate of increase in coherence for these leads could be computed. Thatcher then added two working assumptions to this data, namely that scalp electrode locations provide reasonable indications of underlying cortical activity, and that the extent of correlation between the activity of regions (leads) reflects the strength of neural connections between them. The result was a hypothesis about recurring cycles of cortical reorganization orchestrated by the frontal cortex.

Figure 10.3 illustrates the hypothesis put forward by Thatcher on the basis of a complex analysis of a subset of his data. The lines in between points indicate the leads that show the greatest rate of increase in cohesion at that age. Thatcher's claim is that there are cycles of cortical reorganization which begin with microcycles involving reorganization of short-range connections in the left hemisphere. Following this, longer-range frontal connections become important, at first only on the left side, but then bilaterally. The cycle is then completed by reorganization of short-range connections on the right-hand side. According to Thatcher, a complete cycle of this kind takes approximately four years, though subcycles and microcycles provide the basis for shorter-term periods of stability and transition. By virtue of the longer-range connections related to the frontal cortex, Thatcher suggests that this part of the cortex plays an integral role in the reorganization of the cortex as a whole.

Case (1992) attempted to use these EEG findings to relate brain reorganizations to cognitive change by arguing (a) that cognitive change has a similarly "recursive" character, and (b) that many limitations on cognitive performance are due to functions such as working memory commonly associated with the frontal cortex. One example used to illustrate that neural and cognitive changes may both be manifestations of a common underlying process is the rate of change in EEG coherence between a particular pair of leads (frontal and parietal) and the rate of

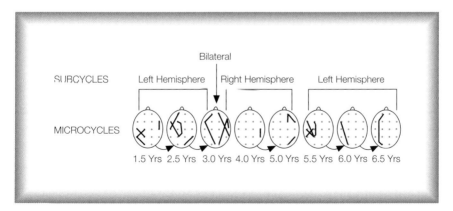

Figure 10.3 Summary of the sequence and anatomical distribution of the coherence patterns reported by Thatcher (1992). Lines connecting electrode locations indicate a measure of strong coherence. "Microcycles" are a developmental sequence that involves a lateral-medial rotation that cycles from the left hemisphere to bilateral to right hemisphere in approximately four years. Note the hypothesized involvement of the frontal cortex in the "bilateral" subcycle.

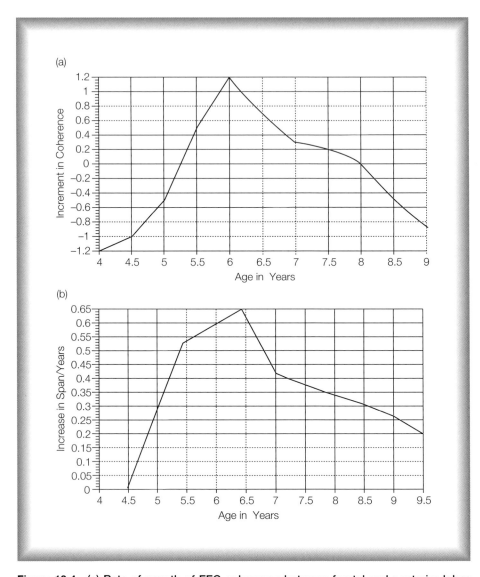

Figure 10.4 (a) Rate of growth of EEG coherence between frontal and posterior lobes during middle childhood (F 7–P 3). (Thatcher, 1992). (b) Rate of growth of working memory (counting span and spatial span) during the same age range.

growth in working memory span during the same ages (see Figure 10.4). While the change in the rate of growth in the two variables may seem compelling at first glance, there are a number of reasons why it cannot be regarded as more than suggestive at present. One of these is that there is no clear rationale for choosing the particular pair of electrodes presented—there are, after all, 56 possible pairs to select from, and there are always likely to be a few that show peaks in growth at similar ages to some developing cognitive function.

Even assuming that watertight correlations between the peaks in rates of increase in cognitive abilities and EEG coherence could be obtained, this association between brain and cognition would still be based only on temporal correlation, a form of evidence which, when taken in isolation, is not very compelling. Hopefully, in the future this approach will attempt to consider the fact that EEG coherence shows phases of significant decreases of coherence as well as increases, which may be associated with "dips" in performance at the behavioral level, and more dynamic, as opposed to stage-based, accounts of cognitive change.

Another potential criticism for the skill-learning view is the findings from individuals with early prefrontal lesions. While there are many reports documenting long-term social and cognitive difficulties in such cases, intellectual abilities can develop in the normal range (Anderson et al., 2007). This would be unexpected if the prefrontal cortex were critical for acquiring new knowledge and skills, and instead a more profound cognitive delay might be expected.

10.5   General Summary and Conclusions

Two different viewpoints on the development of the prefrontal cortex have been reviewed in this chapter. The view that the maturation of regions of the prefrontal cortex enables particular cognitive functions is, of course, a *causal epigenesis* type of account (maturational view, Chapter 1), and such accounts will always be vulnerable to demonstrations of partial functioning of the region in question at earlier ages. On the other hand, the second approach discussed, in which the frontal lobes are a critical part of the cyclical self-organization of cortex, still remains relatively unspecified, with only preliminary evidence to support it at the moment. Nevertheless, bearing in mind the evidence for these two approaches, we can return to the unresolved issues raised at the start of the chapter.

The first of these issues concerned whether the specialized computations performed by the frontal cortex are due to a unique neuroanatomy and/or neurochemistry, or to other factors. The view put forward in Chapter 2 was that while the cerebral cortex provides architectural constraints on the representations that emerge during ontogeny, there are no innate representations. However, it seems likely that graded differences in neurotransmitter densities, and differences in patterns of interconnectivity to other regions of cortex, will provide initial biases that may subsequently lead to some regional differences in microcircuitry. In addition, however, the relatively delayed developmental trajectory of the frontal cortex means that it is likely to develop representations which capture invariances in the structure of the external world, and interactions with the external environment, at greater spatial and temporal distances than other regions of cortex. In other words, it will tend to integrate information over larger time and space intervals than will other regions of the cortex. Thus, a combination of small intrinsic biases and relatively delayed development may give rise to the unique information-processing properties of this region of cortex. Whether this region plays a role in orchestrating the specialization of other regions of cortex, as Thatcher claims, is an exciting topic for research in the future.

The second unresolved issue concerned how to reconcile evidence for continuing neuroanatomical development in the frontal cortex until the teenage years, on the one hand, and evidence for some functioning in the region as early as the first few months of age, on the other. The evidence for early functioning of the prefrontal cortex provides perhaps the biggest challenge to the maturational approach. One possible resolution to this issue is that representations that emerge within this region of the cortex are initially weak, and sufficient only to control some types of output, such as saccades, but not others, such as reaching (Munakata, McClelland, Johnson & Siegler, 1994). Other plausible resolutions of this issue come from Diamond's (1991) proposal that different regions of frontal cortex are differentially delayed in their development, and Thatcher's (1992) suggestion that prefrontal regions may have a continuing role in the cyclical reorganization of the rest of the cortex. Whether these hypotheses work out or not, there is a good reason why some degree of prefrontal cortical functioning is vital from the first weeks of postnatal life, or even earlier (Fulford et al., 2003; Hykin et al., 1999; Moore et al., 2001): the ability to form and retain goals, albeit for short periods, is vital for generating efforts to perform actions such as reaching for objects. Early, and often initially unsuccessful, attempts to perform motor actions provide the essential experience necessary for subsequent development.

Key Issues for Discussion

- How useful is the concept of "maturation" to account for the development of the prefrontal cortex, and what objective criteria could be used to establish functional or structural maturity?
- Why do several different developmental disorders involve symptoms of prefrontal cortex dysfunction?
- Recent evidence suggests that it is possible to train better working memory abilities in both children and adults. What types of brain changes would we expect to accompany these improvements in behavioral performance?

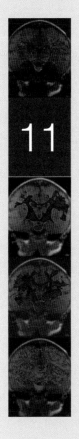

11 Cerebral Lateralization

A major feature of human brain function is the differential specialization of the two cerebral hemispheres. Three developmental models of hemispheric specialization of function are presented: "biased gene" models, "biased brain" models, and "biased head/uterus" models. Some of these models also address the relation between manual lateralization and hemispheric specialization for cognitive functions. A variety of genetic models of handedness and laterality have been put forward. While these models are increasing in their complexity, none of them have yet achieved universal acceptance, and there are remaining doubts about the heritability of handedness. Biased brain models are designed to account for neuroanatomical evidence of hemispheric specialization in newborns. Consequently, no firm conclusions can be drawn about prespecified computational properties of the two hemispheres. Biased head models argue that motor biases in the newborn, such as the tendency to turn the head to the right when lying on their backs, result in some visual inputs being biased to one visual field. Thus motor lateralization may indirectly initiate hemispheric specialization.

Within the first year of life, hemispheric specialization emerges for cognitive functions such as language and face processing. Several authors have proposed that these specializations are not due to prespecified computations (innate representations), but rather due to an initial difference in developmental timing between the two hemispheres. Such an initial difference in developmental state could result in certain types of inputs being more readily processed by one hemisphere. Subsequent dynamic inhibition between the hemispheres could increase this functional lateralization to such an extent that the other hemisphere can no longer take over processing the inputs in question following damage to the opposite side. Thus, slight differences in timing between the hemispheres may mean that the detailed architecture of one side is engaged more readily by certain inputs. Processing these inputs increases the specialization of these circuits to the extent that other cortical regions eventually cannot replace them.

Developmental Cognitive Neuroscience (Third Edition)   Mark H. Johnson with Michelle de Haan
© 2011 Mark H. Johnson

A major feature of biological organisms is symmetry around a central axis (e.g., we have two hands, two eyes, two lungs). In their general morphology, the two cerebral hemispheres of the brain are very similar, and initially appear to be symmetric. However, a number of domains of adult cognition seem to be differentially processed in the two hemispheres, such as face recognition, language, and spatial cognition. In developmental neuropsychology debate has ensued about the extent to which such hemispheric specialization is prespecified (generally equated with being present from birth), as opposed to it being an emergent product of differential timing of development. This debate has been further complicated by the fact that empirical studies of hemispheric functional and structural specialization during postnatal development have sometimes produced apparently contradictory results, with the left hemisphere appearing to be more mature at some points of development and the right at others (Thatcher, Walker, & Giudice, 1987; Spreen et al., 1995). A further source of difficulty has concerned the extent of the interrelationship (if any) between the hemispheric specialization of cognitive functions and the lateralization of motor functions (such as handedness).

It is now generally agreed that there is some degree of neuroanatomical hemispheric lateralization present from shortly after birth in the human infant. However, there is still considerable disagreement about how this laterality arises and its relation to subsequent adult hemispheric specialization. Hopkins and Rönnqvist (1998) have discussed a number of hypotheses about the developmental origins of handedness and hemispheric laterality. They divided the range of theories into a number of types, including "biased gene" models, "biased brain" models, and "biased head/uterus" models.

"Biased gene" models provide genetic accounts of laterality. Among the most prominent of these is the "right shift theory" of Annett (1985) and the model of McManus and Bryden (1993). Briefly, the right shift theory states that the majority of individuals inherit a gene which predisposes them to left-hemisphere control of speech as a byproduct of right-handedness. The minority of individuals that do not have this "right shift gene" have their laterality determined by environmental factors. Specifically, this model accounts for the high percentage of right-handedness observed in the children of two left-handed parents. McManus and Bryden (1993) have pointed out a number of problems with the right shift theory, and proposed a more complicated alternative that incorporates the influence of a second, sex-linked, modifier gene. This modifier gene allows them to account for some of the sex differences observed (left-handedness being more common in males, and left-handed mothers giving rise to more left-handed offspring than left-handed fathers). The increasingly complex genetic models of laterality reflect the fact that the heritability of handedness remains controversial, and the effects that have been reported are subtle and interact with other factors such as sex and early experience. A further problem is that the relation between handedness and cognitive lateralization remains unclear (see below). Additionally, until the ontogenetic function of the putative genes in question is known, the behavior genetic approach is necessarily limited in its explanatory value. Finally, we need not assume that these putative genes have their effect in the central nervous system. Instead they may bias some other factor that indirectly influences brain development.

The "biased brain" models refer to neuroanatomical observations of hemispheric differences around the time of birth. A number of neuroanatomical studies have shown differences between parts of the left and right cerebral cortex in adults. For example, Geschwind and Levitsky (1968) reported that the left planum temporale, an area thought to be involved in language (see Chapter 9), was larger than the right in 65% of adult brains studied. A number of groups have looked for similar differences in infant brains. Chi, Gooling, and Gilles (1977) investigated the timing of gyral and sulcal development in the fetus. In certain cases these developed earlier on the right than on the left. In particular, a region of the temporal lobe thought to be important for language decoding and comprehension, Heschl's gyrus, was found to develop a little earlier on the right than on the left. In apparent contradiction to this finding of earlier development of the right hemisphere are several studies that report that as early as the 29th week of gestation the left planum temporale is usually larger on the left than on the right (Teszner, Tzavaras, Gruner, & Hecaen, 1972); Witelson & Pallie, 1973; Wada, Clark, & Hamm, 1975). It is important to remember, however, that these measures refer simply to the extent of folding in the cortex. As reviewed in Chapter 4, the cerebral cortex is a thin flat sheet that becomes convoluted as it grows within the skull. Gyral and sucal measures can therefore only tell us about the quantity of cortical tissue within a region (roughly speaking, the more tissue, the more folding) and cannot be used to argue for architectural prespecification. The latter can only be established by examining the detailed cytoarchitecture of the regions concerned. Until such studies are conducted with postmortem tissue from newborn infants, no definite conclusions can be reached about different computational properties of the left and right cerebral hemispheres at birth.

Even if empirical evidence for the "biased brain" hypothesis was obtained, the question of the factors responsible for this bias remains. The model of Geschwind, Behan and Galaburda (GBG; Geschwind & Behan, 1982; Geschwind & Galaburda, 1987) provided a causal account of how some of these neuroanatomical differences may arise and their consequences for later life. Briefly, these authors argued for a causal relationship between hormone levels in the uterus and the development of cerebral dominance, and a further relationship between the former and the immune system. More specifically, they argued that higher or lower levels of the hormone testosterone *in utero* can slow down or accelerate the embryological migration of neurons from the neural crest into the cortex. Raised testosterone levels, more commonly found in males, are said to delay migration specifically in the left hemisphere, resulting in "anomalous dominance" in which a reduced degree of hemispheric specialization is observed. A characterization of the GBG hypothesis is illustrated in Figure 11.1.

A number of theoretical and empirical problems with this theory have been reviewed by McManus and Bryden (1993) and Previc (1994). Among the more

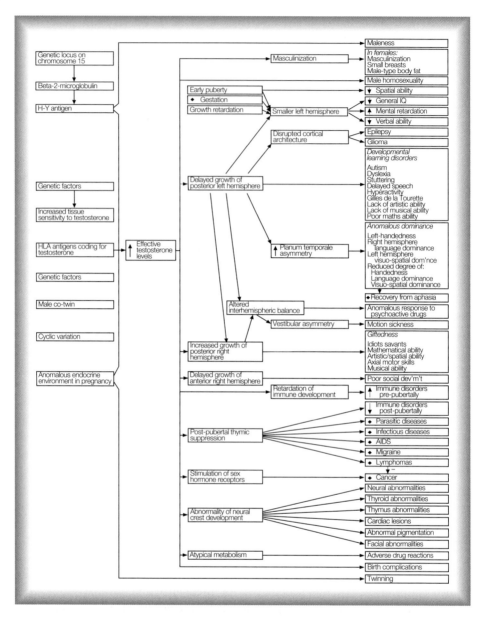

Figure 11.1 A summary diagram of the model proposed by Geschwind, Behan, and Galaburda. Arrows between boxes indicate direct causal link (McManus & Bryden, 1991).

serious problems with the theory are that it posits that those who are not right-handed are part of the "abnormal dominance" population, and such an overinclusive category does not seem likely to be clinically useful. Another problem is that the theory does not differentiate between a number of possible outcomes: for example, why does elevated testosterone sometimes lead to autism and sometimes to dyslexia?

Despite these problems, recent evidence has led to a resurgence of interest in the more general claims of the GBG model.

In one set of studies, fetal testosterone levels (as measured in amniotic fluid) have been shown to correlate strongly with social-cognitive assessments in toddlers. For example, there is a strong inverse correlation between fetal testosterone and amount of eye contact (a risk factor for autism) at 12 and 24 months, and between the size of vocabulary at 18 and 24 months postnatally (Lutchmaya, Baron-Cohen, & Raggatt, 2002a, 2002b). These studies demonstrate a prospective relationship between fetal testosterone and aspects of typical social-cognitive development, consistent with a theory that prenatal testosterone levels influence the "masculinization" of the brain and may be a causal factor in autism (if characterized as an extreme version of the male brain; Baron-Cohen, Lutchmaya & Knickmeyer, 2004). However, attempts to link prenatal testosterone to cerebral lateralization as measured by ERPs during childhood have yet to reveal positive associations (Mercure et al., 2009).

> FURTHER READING Baron-Cohen et al. (2004); Berenbaum et al. (2003); Cameron (2001).

The third class of model Hopkins and Rönnqvist (1998) refer to as the "biased head" or uterus models. These models share the assumption that laterality, and possibly also hemispheric specialization, results from a strong tendency for young infants to angle their head to one side. A number of researchers have noted that when lying on their back newborn infants commonly orient their head toward the right side (though a minority orient strongly to the left). This can be demonstrated both in spontaneous behavior and after a period in which the head is held at the midline (e.g., Turkewitz & Kenny, 1982). This head bias may be caused by the most common position in the uterus restricting the extent of possible head and hand movement to one side (Michel, 1981). These restrictions, in turn, are imposed by asymmetries in the shape of the uterus. A consequence of a bias to turn the head to one side when supine are that one hand (most commonly the right) falls into view more frequently, generating a preference for use of that hand for subsequent visually guided reaching. Alternatively, head turning preference and manual handedness may share a common neural basis. While full-term newborns have been shown to have a preference for turning and maintaining the head to the right (Hopkins, Lems, Janssen, & Butterworth, 1987), the findings of a longitudinal study from 12 weeks gestational age to term indicate that a predominant head position to the right was not achieved until 36 to 38 weeks (Ververs, de Vries, van Geijn, & Hopkins, 1994). Thus, the attainment of a biased head position is a late-occurring event in human pregnancy, but one that is sustained for some 2–3 months after birth (Hopkins et al., 1990).

Whichever of the above models of laterality turns out be most correct, it is clear that by a few months after birth infants start to show behavioral evidence for some hemispheric specialization for cognitive functions. For example, in adults the right hemisphere shows an advantage in certain kinds of face processing tasks. De Schonen and Mathivet (1989) reviewed a number of studies indicating that the right hemisphere (left visual field) has an advantage for the recognition of faces in the human infant by 4 or 5 months of age. One way to interpret these findings is that the right hemisphere has innate representations for face processing. However, de Schonen and colleagues (de Schonen & Mathivet, 1989; de Schonen & Mancini, 1995) believe that this emergent right-hemisphere specialization for face processing is a product of small biases in the detailed architecture of this hemisphere relative to the left, since other (abstract) patterns also differentially engage processing in the two hemispheres. The architectural differences are argued by these authors to arise from slightly different timing of development in the two hemispheres, with the right temporal lobe being a little ahead of its counterpart on the left. This differential timing means that the right temporal lobe processes the low spatial frequency input that carries most of the information about facial identity. Thus, by this view, differential timing of development between the two hemispheres in early infancy may be sufficient to bias each of them to process particular types of inputs.

Similar views have been expressed with regard to hemispheric specialization for language (see Chapter 7). For example, Bullock, Liederman, and Todorovic (1987) argued against Witelson's (1987) view that the left hemisphere is innately pre-specified to process language, and that the ability of the right hemisphere to support language following early damage to the left is due to specialized trauma-induced plasticity mechanisms. Bullock et al. argued instead that developmental timing differences cause an initial small bias for language to be processed on the left. This initial bias, when combined with dynamic inhibition between the hemispheres, leads to increasing lateralization of cognitive function with development. By this view, the end of the "sensitive period" within which the right hemisphere can compensate for damage to the left is a function of the extent of hemispheric specialization for language that had occurred prior to the damage.

11.1   General Summary and Conclusions

It is difficult to directly align the three theories of laterality presented in this chapter with the three perspectives of functional brain development discussed in earlier chapters. While it has to be acknowledged that one of the major contributions of functional imaging in infants has been to demonstrate a surprising degree of lateralization function within the first few months (see Chapter 9), this occurs for functions (speech and language perception) where learning in the womb is known to occur. In visual processing, patterns of laterality over the first months appear to be less consistent with considerable inter-individual variation (e.g., Lloyd-Fox et al.

2009) consistent with a pattern of emergent specialization (de Haan et al. 2002). A dynamic probabilistic epigenesis view of hemispheric specialization of function can also potentially explain data from recovery of function following early unilateral damage (Chapter 9). An interesting question currently under investigation is whether, within an individual, the degree of specialization for a right hemisphere function—such as fusiform face area (Chapter 7)—predicts or correlates with the degree of specialization of a similar region on the left—such as the visual word form area (Chapter 9). If such a correlation were found, it would be consistent with interhemispheric inhibitory connections promoting the differential specialization for functions within the two hemispheres. The comparison between the perception of faces and words is complicated by the fact that they systematically vary in their typical psychophysical properties such as spatial frequency composition (Mercure, Dick, Halit, Kaufman, & Johnson, 2008). When matched as evenly as possible, one study reported a strong *positive* correlation between an ERP measure of laterality for faces and words within individual children (Mercure et al., 2009). In other words, the evidence so far supports a general laterality bias within individuals, on top of which a right-left bias for faces and words is superimposed. Further work with fMRI will be required to explore this issue further. Indeed, an exciting decade lies ahead in which functional imaging measures of lateralization could be associated with behavioral, hormonal, and genetic information.

Key Issues for Discussion

- What are the strengths and weakness of the Geschwind, Behan and Galaburda model?
- To what extent is handedness a useful proxy measure for cerebral lateralization?
- A relative lack of lateralization has been reported in several different developmental disorders. Why might this be?

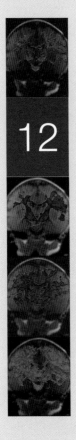

12   Interactive Specialization

In this chapter we return to the three viewpoints on human functional brain development raised in Chapter 1. It is suggested that interactive specialization provides the best framework for understanding the majority of data currently available. Interactive specialization provides an account of developmental changes in two of the major issues in cognitive neuroscience: localization (the extent of cortex activated in a given task situation) and specialization (how finely tuned the functionality of a given cortical area is). Mechanisms underlying interactive specialization are reviewed, and some of their functional consequences are explored in more detail. A variety of types of selectionist theories are outlined, but all share the common belief that the loss of synapses and circuits during postnatal development increases the specificity of neural and cognitive functioning. The loss of synaptic contacts and circuits is also invoked in a developmental mechanism called "parcellation." Parcellation is the increasing encapsulation (informational isolation) of neural circuits. This process is argued to have a number of computational consequences such as a reduction in interference, and a reduction in exchange of information between, different neural systems. To date, most research has investigated the emergence of functions in particular regions or areas. The major challenge for the next decade will be to reveal how interacting networks of regions emerge during postnatal development. We review some preliminary attempts to understand the emergence of functional brain networks during development.

Developmental Cognitive Neuroscience   (Third Edition)   Mark H. Johnson with Michelle de Haan
© 2011 Mark H. Johnson

2.1   Three Viewpoints on Human Functional Brain Development

In Chapter 1 we discussed three different perspectives on human functional brain development: the maturational view, the skill learning view, and interactive specialization. In later chapters, a number of themes emerged from surveying several domains of cognitive development. From our review of the available evidence on cortical development in Chapter 4 we concluded that while large-scale regions of cerebral cortex show graded differential patterns of gene expression, the small-scale functional areas of interest to the cognitive neuroscientist require activity-dependent processes for their specialization. In other words, most of the areal divisions of cortex arise from a combination of intrinsic spatial and timing factors and extrinsic input. However, the laminar structure of the cortex, and the particular connectional and neurochemical properties of the general region, impose architectural constraints on the representations that can emerge within these areas.

In several of the other chapters evidence from human infants and children was consistent with the general viewpoint outlined above. In most of the domains examined there was evidence that cortical representations for cognitive functions emerged postnatally, and partially under the influence of the informational structure of the input in question. In some cases where there was evidence of specific information about the world in the newborn, such as the preferential responses to face patterns (Chapter 7), subcortical circuits appeared to play an important contributory role in controlling the behavior. Thus, while the current state of the evidence does not allow definitive conclusions, of the three perspectives on functional brain development discussed in this book, I suggest that the interactive specialization approach is most consistent with the majority of data available.

Table 12.1 illustrates some of the assumptions that underlie the three approaches outlined earlier. It is a defining feature of the maturational approach that it assumes deterministic epigenesis; region-specific gene expression is assumed to effect changes in intra-regional connectivity that, in turn, allow new functions to emerge. A related assumption commonly made within the maturational approach is that there is a one-to-one mapping between brain and cortical regions and particular cognitive functions, such that specific computations come "on-line" following that maturation of circuitry intrinsic to the corresponding cortical region. In some respects, this view parallels "mosaic" development at the cellular level in which simple organisms (such as C. elegans) are constructed through cell lineages that are largely independent of each other (Elman et al., 1996). Similarly, different cortical regions are assumed to have different maturational timetables, thus enabling new cognitive functions to emerge at different ages.

In contrast to the maturational approach, interactive specialization (Johnson, 2001, 2002) has a number of different underlying assumptions. Specifically, a probabilistic epigenesis assumption is coupled with the view that cognitive functions are the emergent product of interactions between different brain regions. With

Table 12.1 Three viewpoints on human functional brain development

	Brain-cognitive Mapping	Primary Locale of Changes	Plasticity	Cause
Maturational	One-to-one mapping Static over development	Intra-region connectivity matures	A specialized mechanism invoked by stroke or injury	Brain changes cause cognitive development
Skill learning	Changes during acquisition of skill		Life-long; no clear sensitive period	
Interactive specialization	Networks/neural systems	Inter-regional connectivity changes and shapes intra-regional connectivity	An inherent property – the state of having not yet specialized	Bi-directional relations between structure and function
	Dynamic changes during development		Sensitive – period determined by state of specialization	

regard to the latter of these assumptions, interactive specialization follows recent trends in adult functional neuroimaging. For example, Friston and Price (2001) point out that it may be an error to assume that particular functions can be localized within a certain cortical region. Rather, they suggest, the response properties of a region are determined by its patterns of connectivity to other regions as well as by their current activity states. By this view, "the cortical infrastructure supporting a single function may involve many specialized areas whose union is mediated by the functional integration among them" (Friston & Price, 2001, p. 276). Similarly, in discussing the design and interpretation of adult fMRI studies, Carpenter and collaborators have argued that:

> In contrast to a localist assumption of a one-to-one mapping between cortical regions and cognitive operations, an alternative view is that cognitive task performance is subserved by large-scale cortical networks that consist of spatially separate computational components, each with its own set of relative specializations, that collaborate extensively to accomplish cognitive functions (Carpenter et al., 2001, p. 360).

Extending these ideas to development, the interactive specialization approach emphasizes changes in *inter-regional* connectivity, as opposed to the maturation of *intra-regional* circuitry. Specifically, inter-regional connectivity influences intra-regional connectivity, including the shaping of smaller-scale areas. While the maturational approach may be analogous to mosaic cellular development, the interactive specialization view corresponds to the "regulatory" development seen in higher organisms in which cell–cell interactions are critical in determining developmental fate. While mosaic development can be faster than regulatory, the latter has several advantages. Namely, regulatory development is more flexible and better able to respond to damage, and it is more efficient in terms of genetic coding. In regulatory development genes need only orchestrate cellular-level interactions to yield more complex structures (see Elman et al., 1996).

As well as the mapping between structure and function at one age, we can also consider how this mapping might change during development. When discussing functional imaging of developmental disorders, many researchers have assumed that the relation between brain structure and cognitive function is unchanging during development. Specifically, in accordance with a maturational view, when new structures come on-line, the existing (already mature) regions continue to support the same functions that they did at earlier developmental stages. The "static assumption" is partly why it is acceptable to study developmental disorders in adulthood and then extrapolate back in time to early development. Contrary to this view, the interactive specialization viewpoint suggests that when a new computation or skill is acquired, there is a reorganization of interactions between different brain structures and regions (Johnson, 2001). This reorganization process could even change how previously acquired cognitive functions are represented in the brain. Thus, the same behavior could potentially be supported by different neural substrates at different ages during development.

Stating that structure–function relations can change with development is all very well, but it lacks the specificity required to make all but the most general predictions. Fortunately, the view that there is competitive specialization of regions during development gives rise to expectations about the types of changes in structure–function relations that should be observed. Specifically, as regions become increasingly selective in their response properties during infancy, patterns of cortical activation during behavioral tasks may therefore be more extensive than those observed in adults, and involve different patterns of activation.

The basic assumption underlying the skill learning approach is that there is a continuity of the circuitry underlying skill acquisition from birth through to adulthood. This circuit is likely to involve a network of structures that retains the same basic function across developmental time (a static brain-cognition mapping). However, other brain regions may respond to training with dynamic changes in functionality similar or identical to those hypothesized within the interactive specialization framework. Another way in which the skill learning view differs from the other perspectives is with regard to the notion of "plasticity."

Plasticity in brain development is a phenomenon that has generated much controversy, with several different conceptions and definitions having been presented (Thomas & Johnson, 2008). The three perspectives we have discussed provide different viewpoints on plasticity. According to the maturational framework, plasticity is a specialized mechanism that is activated following brain injury. According to the interactive specialization approach, plasticity is simply the state during which a region's function is not yet fully specialized. That is, there is still remaining scope for developing more finely tuned responses. This definition corresponds well to the view of developmental biologists that development involves the increasing "restriction of fate." Finally, according to the skill learning hypothesis, plasticity is at least the result of specific circuitry that remains in place throughout the life span. This hypothesis, unlike the interactive specialization approach, does not claim that plasticity necessarily reduces during development.

12.2   Interactive Specialization

Interactive specialization specifically addresses two of the most fundamental issues in cognitive neuroscience: *localization* and *specialization*. In this context, *localization* refers to the extent to which a given computational function can be associated with a region or area of cortex. Specifically, the extent of cortex activated following the presentation of a given task or perceptual stimulus may change during development. *Specialization* refers to the degree of specificity of function of a given region or area of cortex. Functions may be finely tuned, such as an area that is activated only by a restricted category of visual objects or under a very narrow range of task demands, or broadly tuned, in that they are activated under a wide range of circumstances. According to the interactive specialization view, the issues of localization and specialization are two sides of the same coin, and are both consequences of the same common underlying mechanisms. These mechanisms are explored in more detail in later sections of this chapter.

To recap on the basis of the interactive specialization view, it argues that early in postnatal development many areas begin with poorly defined functions, and consequently can be partially activated by a wide variety of sensory inputs and tasks. During development, activity-dependent interactions between regions result in modifications of the intra-regional connectivity such that the activity of a given area becomes restricted to a narrower range of circumstances. As a result of becoming more finely tuned, small-scale functional areas become increasingly distinct from their surrounding cortical tissue, and this will be evident in functional imaging studies as increasing localization of function.

To briefly review some of the evidence consistent with this approach, in the development of face processing (Chapter 7) we discussed ERP and behavioral evidence consistent with the idea of increasingly finely tuned cortical processing of faces (also referred to by Nelson, 2003, as "perceptual narrowing"). For example, this narrowing process resulted in better recognition of non-human faces by younger infants (Pascalis et al., 2002). Along with these changes in specialization, fMRI work showed increasingly restricted localization of face processing when children were compared to adults in a face-matching task. Some similar findings were reported for language acquisition in Chapter 9. For example, Schlagger and McCandliss (2007) marshal evidence from neuroimaging and other sources to argue that the emergence of the cortical area specifically activated by reading words (the left hemisphere visual word form area) occurs through the interactive specialization processes of increased specialization and localization, in close association with the child learning to read. In another example, from Chapter 5, we discussed evidence that changes in visual orienting abilities as assessed by fMRI revealed multiple sites of change throughout a network of different pathways involved in oculomotor control, and not just the activation of one or two "new" functional areas. This evidence is consistent with adjustments throughout a network of regions as it accommodates to a new function. In atypical development resulting from genetic disorders, structural and functional imaging has usually revealed widespread atypical patterns of activation, and changes in the extent of white matter (connectivity) (Johnson, Halit, Grice, & Karmiloff-Smith, 2002). These latter findings are consistent with processes of interactive specialization that have gone awry, or specialized differently in an attempt to compensate for an earlier deviation or deficit.

In summary, according to the interactive specialization view, small-scale areas of cortex become tuned for certain functions as a result of a combination of factors, including (a) the suitability of the biases within the large-scale region (e.g., transmitter types and levels, synaptic density, etc.), (b) the information within the sensory inputs (sometimes partly determined by other brain systems), and (c) competitive interactions with neighboring regions (so that functions are not duplicated). In the following sections we explore in more detail the neurocomputational mechanisms that may underlie interactive specialization.

12.3   Selective Pruning

In Chapter 4 the marked postnatal loss of synaptic contacts within the cerebral cortex was reviewed. This ubiquitous observation has led some authors to speculate on the functional consequence of this selective loss process (Changeux, 1985; Changeux, Courrege, & Danchin, 1973; Edelman, 1987; Ebbesson, 1980; Gazzaniga, 1983). One of the best known "selectionist" accounts was provided by Changeux and his collaborators. They argued that connections between classes of cells are prespecified, but are initially labile. Synapses in their labile state may either become stabilized or regress, depending on the total activity of the postsynaptic cell. The activity of the postsynaptic cell is, in turn, dependent upon its input. Initially, this input may be the result of spontaneous activity in the network, but rapidly it is evoked by input to the circuit. The critical concept here is that of *selective stabilization*. In short, Changeux and colleagues proposed that "to learn is to eliminate," as opposed to learning taking place by instruction, or new growth.

Changeux and Dehaene (1989) extended and generalized the earlier neurocomputational account of selective loss. Specifically, they argued that there are definable biological levels in the brain (molecular, circuit level, and cognitive), and that selectionist theory can be used to bridge these levels. They then introduced a "Darwinian" version of selectionism. By their view, a "Darwinian" change has two stages. The first of these is a constructive process that generates a range of possible options, while the second is a mechanism for selecting among these options. At the neural level, these two stages are implemented as an exuberance of connections specified within a particular genetic envelope, followed by the selection of particular synapses, or groups of synapses, selected either as a result of patterns of spontaneous activity within neural circuitry, and/or as a result of the information structure of sensory input. Changeux and Dehaene (1989) then outlined how an analogous mechanism might operate at the cognitive level. The initial step, the generation of options, they suggest, is achieved by the presence of "prerepresentations." Prerepresentations are described as transient, dynamic, "privileged" spontaneous activity states in neural circuits. The selection process is achieved by particular prerepresentations from the set available "resonating" with particular sensory inputs. This process probably takes place in seconds or less, whereas a more prolonged time course may be necessary for the process of attrition at the neural level.

Selectionist-type mechanisms of functional brain development vary along a number of dimensions. One of these dimensions is the scale of the unit selected. For example, Edelman (1987) has proposed a similar selectionist account to that outlined above except that particular "neuronal groups" are the unit of selection rather than single synapses. (Crick, 1989, suggests that such neuronal groups will be composed of around 200–1,000 neurons, or a "mini-column.") Possibly the cognitive level of selection posited by Changeux and Dehaene (1989) could be implemented as the dynamic selection of large-scale neural circuits or pathways according to particular task demands. Most likely, selection occurs at multiple scales and time courses.

Another dimension along which selectionist theories can vary is the extent to which the selective loss is responsive to sensory input, as opposed to being determined by intrinsic factors. In the model of Changeux and colleagues, sensory input or spontaneous activity determines both the pattern and the timing of the loss. Ebbesson (1988) discussed some examples in which both the pattern and timing of connection loss is insensitive to experience, such as when it occurs prenatally. That is, not only is the initial excess of connections genetically specified, but so is the extent and pattern of loss of connectivity. This difference between the Changeux and Ebbesson selection mechanisms is not trivial, and has implications for how plasticity in a developing neural system is terminated. For Changeux the process is self-terminating, with only connections that are actively employed remaining. For Ebbesson, the end of plasticity is more rigidly determined: that is, by a given developmental stage, a certain proportion of connections *must* be lost, regardless of experience. A "hybrid" selectionist account of postnatal neural development which draws on aspects of both the Changeux and Ebbesson accounts has also been advanced (see Johnson & Karmiloff-Smith, 1992). The emphasis in this account is on a distinction between *timing* and *patterning* of loss. The hypothesis put forward was that although the timing and extent of loss of connections or neurons may be a product of interactions intrinsic to the organism (innate, by the definition in Chapter 1), the specificity or particular pattern of that loss is partly determined by interactions with the extrinsic environment. By this view there can be an intrinsically determined termination of the phase of selective loss, while the pattern of loss within the "sensitive period" may be determined by experience-driven neural activity. These different possibilities will require systematic investigation in real developing nervous systems, and their different effects at the computational level will need to be assessed through neural network modeling.

As discussed in the previous section, a number of modelers have investigated the functional consequences of different variations of link loss (Barto, Sutton, & Anderson, 1983; Jacobs, 2002; Kerszberg, Dehaene, & Changeux, 1992; Thomas & Johnson, 2006), including the interaction between activity-dependent link loss and overall network decreases in "trophic" factors (Shrager & Johnson, 1995). However, it is important to note that selective loss is only one of several aspects of postnatal neural development (see Sanes, Reh, & Harris, 2006), and so a selectionist account alone can never provide a complete account of neurocognitive development.

In an influential article, Quartz and Sejnowski (1997) criticized selectionist theories, and instead proposed that the specificity of neural connections can arise from directed dendritic growth. These authors suggest that by utilizing a constructive process of growth, as opposed to synaptic loss, development has more flexibility. Similar arguments have been made with regard to computational models of cognitive development by Shultz (2003). Quartz and Sejnowski's mechanism for directed dendritic growth involves a variation of Hebbian associative learning in which a small volume of neural tissue attracts dendritic growth by passive diffusion (possibly of nitric oxide) and without synaptic contacts. While this is a plausible computational mechanism for directed dendritic growth, there is, as yet, no compelling neurobiological evidence to support it. In addition, directed dendritic growth should be seen as an additional, rather than an alternative, mechanism for increasing the specificity of neural connections. Specifically, synaptic (connection) loss in brain development is part of a dynamic ongoing process of synaptic turn-over, with new synapses being generated at almost the same rate as they disappear.

FURTHER READING Bourgeois (2001); Greenough et al. (2002); Sanes et al. (2006); Thomas and Johnson (2008).

12.4   Parcellation and Emergent Modularity

As discussed above, the interactive specialization view predicts that cortical areas will gain increasing functional specialization during development. Another facet of this specialization may be that processing in any given area becomes increasingly separated from that of neighboring regions, a process sometimes referred to as "parcellation."

On the basis of evidence from a variety of species and neural systems, Ebbesson (1984) argued that the increasing differentiation of the brain into separate processing streams and structures during both phylogeny and ontogeny occurs as a result of the selective loss of synapses and dendrites. The result of this parcellation process is the creation of information encapsulated processing streams and structures. At the cognitive level, such systems may correspond to "modules" in the adult mind/brain (Fodor, 1983). While some authors have viewed parcellation as comparatively insensitive to the effects of experience (Ebbesson, 1984), others have viewed the process as being at least partially experience-dependent (Killackey, 1990; O'Leary, 2002). Johnson and Vecera (1996) hypothesized that certain behavioral and cognitive changes may be directly related to the increasing segregation of streams of information (i.e., parcellation) at the neuronal level. Clearly, neural parcellation occurs at a number of different levels, and both within and between cortical regions. However, Johnson and Vecera argued that in all these cases differentiation by selective loss at the neuronal level gives rise to increasingly modular information processing. (Modular here was used in its most general sense, to refer to information-processing systems that are isolated from others.) Specifically, they argued that evidence is consistent with the following consequences of a developmental increase in the extent of cortical modularization:

- less informational exchange between certain brain systems with development;
- less interference between certain brain systems with development;
- increased specificity in sensory detection.

One example of parcellation is the emergence of ocular dominance columns, discussed in Chapter 5. Recall that ocular dominance columns that received inputs exclusively from one eye emerged from a situation in which most layer 4 cells (in the primary visual cortex) received afferents from both eyes. The parcellation process would lead us to expect that the selective loss of afferents will result in components of the network becoming increasingly encapsulated and inaccessible to other parts. Held and his colleagues (see Held, 1993) tested this idea with the experiment described earlier in which they demonstrated that infants under 4 months had a form of integration between the two eyes not observed in older infants. The older infants did not show this integration between the eyes because by this age neurons in cortical layer 4 of the primary visual cortex only receive inputs from one eye.

The example of ocular dominance column formation also demonstrates that parcellation (or segregation) at one level of processing can allow for more adaptive or accurate recombination at another level of processing. Thus, while parcellation may result in a loss of a certain level of integration between systems (e.g., binocular summation in the case of ocular dominance columns), it may be followed by the acquisition of a new level of integration (e.g., binocular vision, as in the current example).

A more recent example of increased segregation with development comes from the separation of color- and motion-processing channels in adult primates (Dobkins & Anderson, 2002). Specifically, in adults, brain pathways that encode direction of object motion do not also process color (e.g. Merigan & Maunsell, 1993). This dissociation of processing means that in psychophysical experiments adults are very poor at detecting the direction of motion (as measured by directionally appropriate eye movements) of red- and green-striped color gratings. In contrast, infants of 2, 3, and 4 months were much better at detection than adults, suggesting that color input to motion processing is relatively stronger in the immature visual system. Furthermore, younger infants showed more evidence of this integration than did older ones, demonstrating a dynamic process of increasing segregation of these streams of information (Dobkins & Anderson, 2002).

Another domain in which parcellation processes were described by Johnson and Vecera (1996) was cross-modal integration (see also Maurer, 1993). While the example of ocular dominance columns concerned increasing differentiation *within* a sensory projection, it is possible that a similar process may occur *between* sensory modalities. Many mammals appear to have transient connections between different sensory cortices early in life. For example, Dehay et al. (Dehay, Bullier, & Kennedy, 1984; Dehay et al., 1988) have reported transient connections between visual, auditory, somatosensory, and motor cortices in the kitten. The loss of the connections through parcellation would presumably result in less cross-talk between sensory modalities at the level of primary sensory representations. Two consequences of increasing parcellation between sensory modalities were discussed by Johnson and Vecera: (a) sensory input should provide a broader pattern of activation across the cortex prior to parcellation, and (b) there will be more "cross-talk" between sensory modalities prior to parcellation.

With regard to the first of these predictions, Wolff, Matsumiya, Abroms, Van Velzar, and Lombroso (1974) investigated the cortical evoked response of 3- and 4-day-old infants to somatosensory and auditory stimulation. Their evidence suggested that auditory input (white noise) had a modulating effect on the somatosensory evoked responses in these very young infants. However, when a similar experiment was run with adults, no effects of auditory input on somatosensory responses was found. One interpretation of these results is that there is less inter-sensory integration at this level in adults as a result of parcellation between the auditory and somatosensory modalities.

With regard to the second prediction, it should be noted that there are likely to be multiple levels of information exchange between sensory modalities. This fact means that an infant is likely to go through a sequence of developmental stages in which he or she integrates increasingly specific forms of information across the sensory modalities. Considering this, the prediction from parcellation is that infants will go through developmental periods in which they show an apparent loss of intersensory integration within a particular cross-modal task. This may then be followed by subsequent reintegration between modalities of a more specific kind, resulting in some cases in an apparent U-shaped pattern of developmental change.

Lewkowicz (1991), when reviewing the development of intersensory functions in human infants, argues that there is strong evidence for non-specific cross-modal influences early in life. For example, Lewkowicz and Turkewitz (1981) established that the looking preferences of newborn infants for bright or dim stimuli were affected by prior exposure to auditory stimuli. Infants tested in silence looked longer at intermediate-intensity lights, whereas infants exposed to an auditory tone looked longest at the dimmest light.

Other cross-modal experiments with infants have been concerned with apparently more complex types of stimuli, such as the matching of numerical quantity (Starkey & Cooper, 1980; Starkey, Spelke, & Gelman, 1983, 1990). When infants succeed in these tasks at a young age, the results can be interpreted in one of two ways. One explanation is that infants have "intelligently" matched input in one sensory modality to input in another. The other explanation is that infants are unable to discriminate the sensory modality of the input and merely respond to some non-specific aspect of the stimulus such as intensity or quantity. In the first case the infant is viewed as having separate representations of the visual and auditory input, and then actively extracting the similarity between them. In the second case the representations from the two sensory modalities are blended within the cortex such that infants cannot discriminate between them. Rather, they just perceive a certain stimulus intensity. The parcellation conjecture predicts an initial state in which there are non-specific connections between primary sensory representations. These connections will then be pruned, resulting in the apparent loss of cross-modal influence. Subsequently, more specific cross-modal matching may emerge. This account of the development of cross-modal effects makes the counterintuitive prediction that early cross-modal influences should decline with development, a surprising prediction for which there is in fact some evidence.

Streri (1987) and Streri and Pecheux (1986) investigated whether there is intermodal transfer of shape from touch to vision (and vice versa) in infants from 2 to 5 months old. Infants were familiarized with an object visually or tactually (hand) until they habituated to it. Subsequently, the infant was presented with the same shape in the other modality and the duration of look or grasp was recorded. If the infants were capable of cross-modal habituation, then they should remain habituated to that shape and show little interest in it. Streri found no evidence for cross-modal transfer from touch to vision in 5-month-old infants, but strong evidence for such transfer in 2- and 3-month-olds. Older infants have yet to be tested in this experiment.

Meltzoff and Borton (1979) conducted a cross-modal "matching" experiment with 1-month-old infants. These authors reported cross-modal matching between the infant mouthing nubby or smooth pacifiers for 90 seconds and whether they subsequently looked more toward a picture of a nubby or smooth pacifier when presented side by side. Maurer and Stager (reported in Maurer, 1993) also found an effect with 1-month-old infants, but failed to find any effects in a group of 3-month-olds in the same experiment. This pattern of loss is consistent with the increasing parcellation of cortical sensory inputs.

Johnson and Vecera (1996) also speculated that although developmental atypicalities may have failed or deviant patterns of parcellation in the cortex, they may also have symptoms of inappropriate cross-modal integration. They then note reports of synesthesia, or multi-channel sensory experiences, in adults with autism (Cesaroni & Garber, 1991). Another area in which parcellation processes may be speculatively applied is in particular aspects of language acquisition. Johnson and Karmiloff-Smith (1992) discuss some examples on language acquisition from Karmiloff-Smith's earlier work, in which some components of the language system appear to become modularized as a result of development, in the sense that other information-processing streams no longer have access to its contents. One example of this occurs in a study of awareness of linguistic repairs within a narrative. Younger participants (11-year-olds) were able to detect one type of linguistic repair, "discourse cohesion" repairs, more frequently than were adults. Discourse cohesion repairs involved either a change from noun-phrase to pronoun (e.g., then the girl/ then she), or a change from pronoun to noun-phrase (e.g., he's got/the man's got), depending on whether the expression referred to the main or to the subsidiary character in the story, according to the "thematic participant constraint" (Karmiloff-Smith, 1985). The results showed that although participants of all ages were successful in detecting all categories of repair and could easily furnish explanations of lexical and referential repairs, they were remarkably poor at providing metalinguistic explanations of discourse cohesion repairs. Although there was some increase in correct responses between 7 and 11 years, this was followed by a decline by adulthood. Karmiloff-Smith and colleagues suggest that discourse cohesion rules can be accessed at some points in development, whereas in adulthood that access is lost. The discourse cohesion system becomes progressively more modular and cognitively impenetrable and begins to operate automatically (thereby allowing for focus on propositional content) (Karmiloff-Smith, 1985).

Although I believe that the association between neural parcellation and increasing cognitive encapsulation may be a fruitful one for further research, there are a number of limitations and complicating factors that must be acknowledged. The first of these is that refinement of neural connections also occurs at subcortical levels in structures such as the superior colliculus (Stein, 1984) and the hippocampus (Duffy & Rakic, 1983). While parcellation at the subcortical level could also have behavioral consequences, much of the parcellation in these structures appears to occur prenatally. The second caveat is that some aspects of behavioral development that Johnson and Vecera (1996) attributed to cortical-level parcellation could also be attributed to a shift from subcortical to cortical processing. For example, in the cross-modal integration studies, it is known that the superior colliculus contains many multi-sensory neurons and plays an important role in attending to and orienting toward such stimuli (e.g., Stein, 1984). Whether the superior colliculus could support the cross-modal abilities observed in human infants is not known, but this is certainly a possibility that cannot be excluded. Third, the most compelling evidence for cognitive encapsulation comes from apparent decrements in performance during development. Arguably, however, development would not involve these processes unless they led to some eventual computational benefit to the organism. Presumably, a partially modular brain is more efficient in generating behavior in some respects. Finally, the increasing encapsulation of neural systems within a brain could also involve the strengthening of connections within a system, possibly by dendritic growth mechanisms similar to that outlined by Quartz and Sejnowski (1997).

The mechanisms underlying interactive specialization can also be investigated through computational neural network modeling. For example, several groups have used simple "cortical matrix" models to investigate the factors and mechanisms responsible for cortical specialization (e.g. Kerszberg et al., 1992; Oliver, Johnson, Karmiloff-Smith, & Pennington, 2000; Shrager & Johnson, 1995). In these artificial neural networks connections between nodes are pruned according to variations of Hebbian learning: links between nodes that are often active together are strengthened, whereas links between nodes that are not often coactive get weaker and are pruned. In some of these models, the degree of pruning of connections during learning approximately matches that seen during the course of human brain development. During exposure to patterned input (roughly equivalent to sensory stimulation), nodes become more selective in their response properties, and under certain conditions clusters of nodes with similar response properties emerge. Thus, in these computational models selective pruning plays a role in the emergence of clusters of nodes (localization) that share common specific response properties (specialization) (see Figure 12.1).

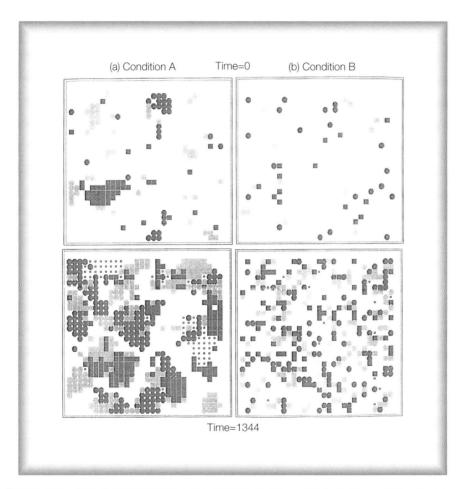

Figure 12.1 The formation of representations in the cortical matrix model under two different architectural conditions. The left upper panel shows the starting state and the left lower the final state. In the final state, "structured" representations emerge in which stimuli that have features in common tend to be clustered together (spatially aligned). With just a minor change in the architecture of the network (changing the relevant average lengths of intrinsic excitatory and inhibitory links: the right-hand side), nodes in the network fail to form structured clustered representations.

12.5   Emerging Networks

To date, the majority of the research on the emergence of specialized functions in human cortex has focused on specific regions. However, it is clear from the interactive specialization viewpoint that the next step is to understand how *networks* involving different regions, each with their own different specializations, emerge. In other words, while we are beginning to understand functional brain development at the level of individual cortical regions, we are still in the dark about how the larger scale of cortical function in terms of networks of regions develops (Johnson & Munakata, 2005). In this section we advance some initial evidence and speculation that may begin to address this intriguing issue.

Before considering the empirical evidence, we need to consider what makes a network of functional nodes more or less successful. A branch of mathematics called "graph theory" concerns itself with the relatively efficiency of different kinds of networks (see Figure 12.2). Although it may seem at first that a lattice or grid pattern is the best design for a network, formal analysis of measures of local network connectivity, and the average path length from one node to another, show that so-called "small world" networks are the most efficient. In contrast to the grid pattern of streets found in many American cities, small world networks are more like the clusters of small streets in a village that is then linked to other such villages by fast highways. Although the overall balance of the small local streets and highways can vary, most biological systems (and even the worldwide web) are small world networks. Several studies have shown the regional interconnectivity of the

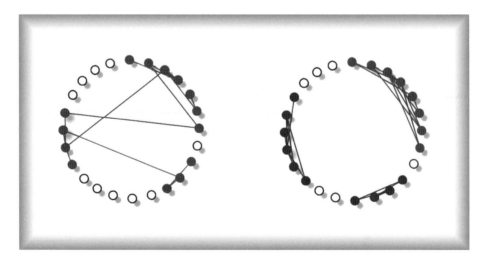

Figure 12.2 An illustration of different kinds of brain connectivity. The right hand panel shows dense local connectivity without long-range connections. The left panel shows the more optimal arrangement that balances local connectivity with some long-range connections (a "small world" network).

adult brain is a highly efficient small world network, but how does this efficient network emerge?

The first piece of the jigsaw comes from recent work by Fair et al. (2007, 2009) who used functional connectivity analyses in fMRI to study resting state "control" networks in school age children and adults. Their analysis allows them to infer the nature and strength of functional connections between 39 different cortical regions. They found that development entailed both *segregation* (i.e., decreased short-range connectivity) and *integration* (i.e., increased long-range connectivity) of brain regions that contribute to a network. In a similar study, the general developmental transition from more local connectivity to greater and stronger long-range network connectivity was confirmed using slightly different methods and 90 different cortical and subcortical regions (Supekar et al., 2009).

The decrease in short-range inter-regional functional connectivity is readily explicable in terms of the interactive specialization view. As neighboring regions of cortical tissue become increasingly specialized for different functions (e.g., objects versus faces), they will less commonly be coactivated. This process may also involve synaptic pruning and, as we heard in the last section, has been simulated in neural network models of cortex in which nodes with similar response properties cluster together spatially distinct from nodes with other response properties (Oliver, Johnson, & Shrager, 1996). Thus, decreasing functional connectivity between neighboring areas of cortex is readily predicted by models implementing the interactive specialization view. More challenging from the current perspective is to account for the increase in long-range functional connections.

A maturational explanation of the increase in long-range functional connectivity would suggest that this increase is due to the establishment or strengthening of the relevant fiber bundles. However, the increase in functional connectivity during development may occur after the relevant long-range fiber bundles are in place (see Fair et al., 2009; Supekar et al., 2009 for discussion). While increased myelination is likely to be a contributory factor, (a) myelination itself can be a product of the activity/usage of a connection (Markham & Greenough, 2004) and (b) a general increase in myelin does not in itself account for the specificity of inter-regional activity into functional networks that support particular computations (but see Nagy, Westerberg, & Klingberg, 2004). Thus, the strengthening and maintenance of long-range brain connections is likely to also be an activity-dependent aspect of brain development. This raises the question of why and how do particular anatomically distant brain regions begin to cooperate in a functional network?

A key to answering this question may lie in scaling up the basic mechanisms of Hebbian learning. Instead of "cells that fire together wire together" we are seeing regions that tend to be coactivated in a given task context strengthening or maintaining the neural pathways between them. While each region is becoming individually specialized for a particular function, this intraregion change in tuning is modulated and influenced by its presence within an emerging network of coactivated structures. For example, in a task that requires visually guided action, a variety of visual and motor areas will be coactivated along with multimodal integration areas. If the task is repeated sufficiently often then these patterns of coactivation will be strengthened, and specialization of individual regions will proceed within this context of overall patterns of activation.

A second source of coactivation in the developing human brain is commonly overlooked—spontaneous activity during the resting state (with no task demands). Although there has been great interest in the resting state or "default network" in adults, only recently has this been studied using fMRI in children (although, as mentioned in Chapter 2 there is a long history of studying resting EEG in children). We learned earlier (Chapter 4) about the importance of spontaneous activity during prenatal development in shaping aspects of cortical structure and function. It seems likely that the oscillatory resting activity of the brain, which possibly occupies more waking hours than any specific tasks, may play a key role in strengthening and pruning the basic architecture of long-range connections.

A third reason why anatomically distant regions may strengthen and maintain their connectivity relates to the fact that most of the long-range functional connections studied by Fair et al. (2007) involved links to parts of the prefrontal cortex. As mentioned earlier (Chapter 10), this part of the cortex is generally considered to have a special role during development in childhood and skill acquisition in adults (Gilbert & Sigman, 2007; Thatcher, 1992). In earlier chapters we reviewed a number of studies consistent with the idea that the prefrontal cortex (PFC) may play a role in orchestrating the collective functional organization of other cortical regions during development. While there are several neural network models of PFC functioning in adults (e.g., O'Reilly, 2006), few if any of these have addressed development. However, another class of model intended to simulate aspects of development may be relevant both to PFC and to the issue of how networks of specialized regions come to coordinate their activity to support cognition. Knowledge-based cascade correlation (KBCC; Shultz, Rivest, Egri, Thivierge, & Dandurand, 2007) involves an algorithm and architecture that recruits previously learned functional networks when required during learning. Computationally, this dynamic neural network architecture has a number of advantages over other learning systems. Put simply, it can learn many tasks faster, or learn tasks that other networks cannot, because it can recruit the "knowledge" (computational abilities) of other self-contained networks as and when required. In a sense, it selects from a library of available computational systems to orchestrate the best combination for the learning problem at hand. While this class of model is not intended to be a detailed model of brain circuits (Shultz & Rivest, 2001; Shultz et al., 2007), it has been used to characterize frontal systems (Thivierge, Titone, & Schultz, 2005) and may capture important elements of the emerging interactions between PFC and other cortical regions at an abstract level. In addition, it offers initially attractive accounts of (a) why PFC is required for the acquisition of new skills, (b) why PFC is active from early in development, but also shows prolonged developmental change, and (c) why early damage to PFC can have widespread effects over many domains.

Although much work remains to be done to understand in more detail the factors that lead to the emergence of long-range networks, the graph theory analyses of changes during the school-age years are generating important insights. While, as described earlier, there are differences in the balance of short and long connections between children and adults, it is important to note that the network organization of children's brains is as efficient as that of adults. In other words, while children's brains are wired differently from those of adults (Figure 12.3 in the color plate section), they are still optimally geared for the rapid and high-fidelity transmission of information. Whether the same is true in infancy and early childhood remains unknown.

Aside from the shift from local to long-range connectivity, another change in network structure observed using graph theory analysis during development is in the hierarchical structure. Adult networks have a more hierarchical structure that is optimally connected to support top-down relations between one part of the network and another (Supekar et al., 2009). Although hierarchical networks have a number of computational advantages to be discussed below, they are known to be less plastic and more vulnerable to damage or noise in the particular nodes at the top of the hierarchy. Thus, the network arrangement of children may be more flexible and plastic in response to unusual or atypical sensory input or environmental context. Further, the response to focal brain damage, particularly in the prefrontal cortex (Chapter 10), may be more clearly understood in the light of these different network structures.

One of the features of a hierarchical network is the capacity for one region to feed back highly processed sensory or motor input to the earlier stages of processing. In much the same way as we hypothesized that lateral interregional interactions help shape the intrinsic connectivity of areas to result in functional specialization, interactions between regions connected by feedback and feed-forward connections may also help to shape the specialization of the areas involved. Top-down effects play an important role in sensory information processing in the adult brain (e.g., Siegel, Körding, & König, 2000). For example, during perception, information propagates through the visual processing hierarchy from primary sensory areas to higher cortical regions, while feedback connections convey information in the reverse direction. In a neurocomputational model of feedback in visual processing in the adult brain, Spratling and Johnson (2004) demonstrated that a number of different phenomena associated with visual attention, figure/ground segmentation, and contextual cueing could all be accounted for by a common mechanism underlying cortical feedback. Extending these ideas to development, there are potentially two important implications of feedback that will benefit from future exploration. The first of these will be to examine how the specialization of early sensory areas is shaped by top-down feedback, and vice versa, during development. The second topic for investigation will be to examine the consequences of relatively poor or diffuse cortical feedback in the immature cortex. For example, possibly some of the failures in object processing in infants (Chapter 6) can be explained by a lack of adequate top-down feedback.

Top-down feedback from PFC may also have a direct role in shaping the functional response properties of posterior cortical areas. In cellular recording studies from both humans and animals, evidence has accrued that the selectivity of response of neurons in areas such as the fusiform cortex may increase in realtime following the presentation of a stimulus. For example, McCarthy and colleagues (Puce, Allison, & McCarthy, 1999) measured local field potentials in face-selective regions of the lateral fusiform cortex in human adults and found that responses of these neurons go from being face-selective at around 200 ms after stimulus presentation, to being face identity or emotion-selective at later temporal windows. This suggests that top-down cortical feedback pathways, in addition to their importance in attention and object processing (Spratling & Johnson, 2004, 2006) may increase the degree of specialization and localization in realtime, as well as in developmental time. Thus, some of the changes in functional specialization and localization seen in face-sensitive regions may reflect the increasing influence of interregional coordination with other regions, including the PFC.

A final aspect of the transition from the child brain network to the adult one is the greater connectivity between cortical and subcortical structures seen at younger ages (Supekar et al., 2009). This observation may be fundamental for our understanding of the emergence of the social brain (Chapter 7) and memory systems (Chapter 8) as it implies that the specialization of some cortical areas may be initially more dominated by structures such as the amygdala and hippocampus. As we approach adulthood, more networks become intrinsic to the cortex and develop a complex hierarchical structure more dominated by PFC.

12.6   General Summary and Conclusions

In this chapter we focused on the interactive specialization view of human functional brain development. Interactive specialization provides an account of developmental changes in two of the major issues in cognitive neuroscience: localization (the extent of cortex activated in a given task situation) and specialization (how finely tuned the functionality of a given cortical area is). Mechanisms of selective pruning underlying interactive specialization were reviewed, and some of their functional consequences were explored in more detail. The loss of synaptic contacts and circuits was also invoked in parcellation (the increasing encapsulation of neural circuits). This process was argued to have a number of computational consequences, such as a reduction in interference, and a reduction in informational exchange, between neural systems. These principles are now being applied to the emergence of functional networks of regions in the human brain. Evidence from formal analyses of network structure show that with development from mid-childhood, cortical networks change from more local to more long-range connectivity, become less interconnected with subcortical regions, and develop a more hierarchical structure. Nevertheless, at least by school age, brain networks are as efficient in the processing and transmission of information as in adults. How brain networks emerge over the early years remains perhaps the greatest challenge for developmental cognitive neuroscience over the next decade.

Key Issues for Discussion

- How would the three different viewpoints on human functional brain development account for the emergence of integrated functional networks of brain regions?
- Discuss the evidence for the process of parcellation from two of the domains covered in previous chapters.
- How might graph theory analyses be applied to developmental disorders?

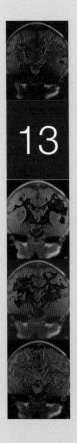

13 Toward an Integrated Developmental Cognitive Neuroscience

This final chapter attempts to tie together some themes of the book, and points out some future directions. The first issue discussed is the value of the molecular genetic analysis of cognitive development. It is suggested that the role of genes in functional development can only be interpreted from within a developmental cognitive neuroscience approach. Next, I expound the value of a level of neural network modeling that can make contact with both neural and cognitive data. It is suggested that this approach can also be extended to developmental disorders, and to assessing the effects of developmental changes in levels of neuromodulators. General guidelines for developing theory within the field are proposed. Implications and applications of developmental cognitive neuroscience for issues of societal and educational importance are presented. Finally, I stress the need for applying multiple methods to cognitive transitions, and for training a future generation of developmental cognitive neuroscientists.

Developmental Cognitive Neuroscience (Third Edition)   Mark H. Johnson with Michelle de Haan
© 2011 Mark H. Johnson

13.1   Introduction

The earlier chapters of this book have introduced the reader to the newly emerging field of developmental cognitive neuroscience. No doubt it is evident that there is a long way to go before the field becomes a cohesive and well-integrated area of inquiry. However, the extent to which previously disparate fragments of information are coming together encourages optimism for the future. In this final chapter some conclusions and recommendations are presented which may help progress the field.

13.2   Genes and Cognitive Development

The first issue concerns the relation between genes and cognition. In Chapter 3 we reviewed how molecular biological techniques will have a major impact on our understanding of genetic contributions to cognitive change. However, it is important to remember that genes do not "code for" functional components of cognition in any direct sense. We are never likely to discover a "gene for language" for the same reason as there is not a single gene for the big toe. Both language and big toes are the result of complex interactions between many genes, their products, and multiple levels of environments. Similarly, with regard to brain structure it is likely that most relevant genes have widespread effects throughout several or all brain regions, and commonly other organs (such as the heart). As attractive as the notion may seem at first sight, patterns of gene expression do not neatly localize to small-scale functional areas of the cerebral cortex. Since brain structure is not directly "coded for" in genes, but rather is the product of complex self-organizing interactive processes, providing causal accounts of cognitive change purely in terms of gene action is certain to be inadequate. Rather, expression of particular genes will have to be located within a developmental cognitive neuroscience framework that includes some account of the interactions at molecular, cellular, and organism–environment levels. Ultimately, development is the path from genotype to phenotype, and no cognitive "function" for a gene can be attributed without some account of this mapping. In other words, attempting to "explain" a cognitive developmental change purely in terms of gene expression will miss out much that should be of core interest to the developmental cognitive neuroscientist.

3.3   Relations Between Brain Structure and Function in Development

Another issue that surfaced in several of the preceding chapters was the apparent discrepancy between structural and functional development. For example, with regard to the prefrontal cortex, there is evidence of neuroanatomical changes occurring until the teenage years, yet infants as young as 6 months appear to pass some behavioral marker tasks of prefrontal cortex functioning and show activation in functional imaging experiments. These findings are, however, only a problem for a causal epigenesis (maturational) view (Chapter 1) in which cause operates in a single direction from brain development to cognitive change. The data can be resolved by taking a probabilistic epigenesis view, in which there are two-way interactions between brain and cognitive development. In fact, there are several ways that they can be reconciled. One way is to invoke the graded development of representations in which input helps to tune the fine structure of a network over time (Chapter 10). Another is the view advanced by Thatcher (1992) and others that there are dynamic changes in the connectivity between cortical regions which lead to a reorganization of representations at several points in development. Finally, the interactive specialization view predicts that detailed structural changes in postnatal development will be a consequence of increasing functional specialization.

Throughout this book I have made use of comparisons to connectionist-style neural network models. The use of these models does not necessarily commit one to an empiricist (behaviorist) viewpoint on development, as some critics have suggested. Rather, as we have seen in this book, these models are excellent research tools for exploring interactions between intrinsic and extrinsic information during the emergence of representations, and interpreting the functional consequence of partial or weak representations. When information about brain structure is added to the network architecture, neural network models can potentially provide a theoretical bridge between neurobiology and cognitive psychology.

FURTHER READING   Elman et al. (1996); Mareschal et al. (2007).

Combining these two applications of connectionist modeling, we can devise models in which aspects of postnatal developmental neuroanatomy can be simulated, such as the selective loss of synapses, and the interacting effects of different variables studied. In my opinion, for such models to be useful they need to be pitched at an appropriately abstract level to make contact with both neural and cognitive data. Such models are only just beginning to be developed. Similarly, some network models of neural development are pitched at a detailed cellular level and thus do not allow any inferences about cognitive representations. In order to study the possible functional consequence of developments in neural structure, we need models that make contact with both sets of data. Other types of non-linear models, such as those derived from dynamic systems theory (Thelen & Smith, 1994), may be useful in certain contexts, such as motor development. However, while these models tend to give good descriptions of the shape of development change in a given task or behavior, they do not always address the fundamental (in my view) issue of representational transformation (see Karmiloff-Smith & Johnson, 1994). Conse-quently, they may as yet be of limited utility for studying some types of cognitive transitions during development (but see Spencer, Thomas & McClelland 2009).

FURTHER READING   Spencer et al. (2009).

One of the general assumptions that pervades this book is that an understanding of cognitive change during ontogeny will be best achieved at a neurocomputational level. Looking for mechanisms of cognitive change at this level does not imply a maturationist, empiricist, or reductionist viewpoint. It does, however, require a belief that a level of explanation closer to neural mechanisms will bring benefits. While this belief remains largely untested, it is no less plausible than the widely held assumption that cognitive models, unconstrained by neural evidence, can provide the best explanation of behavioral change.

13.4   Neuroconstructivism

In the previous chapter I suggested that the interactive specialization approach to human functional brain development is likely to be more productive than the maturational or skill learning views. Interactive specialization is a specific example of a broader approach to brain and cognitive development sometimes called neuro-constructivism (Mareschal et al., 2007). Neuroconstructivism differs in several ways from more traditional unidisciplinary approaches to behavioral and cognitive development. One difference is that the organism's interaction with its current external environment is taken into account. Taking this more "ethological" view of cognitive development changes the types of representations we consider in our models of cognitive development in two ways. First, it inclines the researcher to consider the entire neurocognitive path from input to output. This is done because the nature of the input representations, and the nature of the representations necessary for certain outputs, severely restrict the possible intermediate representa-tions. In other words, there is a need for models that, while less detailed, attempt to capture the functioning of several brain systems within a given domain. The second, and related, difference in an ethological approach is that taking into account the structure of the external environment in which the organism develops means that the information contained in mental representations can be relatively impoverished, but still be adaptive. In other words, the representation need only be as detailed as that which is sufficient for adaptive behavior in a given context. For example, in Chapter 7 I reviewed the hypothesis that the face representation possessed by newborn infants is merely a primitive "sketch" of the face—something like three blobs corresponding to the eyes and mouth (Johnson & Morton, 1991). This somewhat impoverished representation is sufficient for adaptive behavior, however, given that faces engage this representation, and that the early environment of the infant is guaranteed to have faces present. Few naturally occurring stimuli (other than those generated by developmental psychologists for experiments!) are likely to engage the same representation.

Neuroconstructivism also has implications for developmental disorders. The developmental disorders discussed in this book are those in which the most research has been done in attempting to link cognitive and neural deficits (see Chapter 2). However, even in these cases the mapping from neural to cognitive system remains far from clear. In some cases multiple brain regions have been implicated despite apparently focal cognitive deficits. In my opinion, a number of factors contribute to the complexity of this mapping:

- If a region that develops relatively early in the course of brain development is atypical, then this is likely to have knock-on consequences for later developing regions. For example, if the projections from the thalamus to the cortex are atypical, then the subsequent parcellation of the cortex into areas will be disturbed. Further, it is likely that cognitive deficits result from a combination of primary and secondary neural atypicalities. Indeed, it is possible that the primary cognitive deficits arise from secondary neural effects.
- It is likely that the most devastating forms of brain injury in development are those that affect a major brain system, rather than, for example, a particular cortical area. In most cases of genetic atypicality, or insult early in gestation, the neural consequences are likely to be widespread. Thus they are more likely to disturb whole brain systems than are focal lesions acquired in later life. Focal lesions commonly result in compensation at neural and cognitive levels in primate infants.
- It is possible that a number of different types of developmental brain damage can result in the same cognitive profiles. This could be because the same brain system is ultimately affected, and/or because the self-organizing and adaptive nature of brain development channels deviant developmental trajectories to one of a small number of adaptive outcomes. This consideration highlights the importance of taking an "emergent" as opposed to a "static" approach to developmental disorders (see Chapter 1). Developmental disorders are unlikely to yield to the same types of neuropsychological analysis as applied to adults with acquired brain damage (Karmiloff-Smith, 1998).

Given that conventional "static" neuropsychological analysis can only provide, at best, a preliminary analysis of the neural basis of developmental disorders, what could the neuroconstructivist approach provide? At present there are still few attempts at computational modeling of developmental trajectories (but see Thomas & Karmiloff-Smith, 2003). As a preliminary attempt to study the ways in which the "normal" formation of structured representations in the cortex can go wrong, Oliver et al. (2000) developed simulations with a simple cortical matrix model (see Chapter 12) in which one or other of the parameters known to be important was deliberately changed. The results of one such simulation are illustrated in Figure 12.1 (see Chapter 12). In this case, when we manipulated an aspect of the intrinsic structure of the network, the relative length of excitatory and inhibitory links, we totally disrupted the formation of structured representations. In other simulations, representations can emerge, but distorted in different ways relative to the "normal" case. By developing a taxonomy of the ways that structured representations can go awry, we hope to be able to shed light on some developmental disorders.

Within the same general constructivist viewpoint we can also consider developmental disorders in terms of Waddington's intuitive conceptualization of developmental trajectories in the form of an epigenetic landscape (see Chapter 1; Figure 1.3). In the epigenetic landscape, a perturbation to the trajectory early in development (possibly corresponding to prenatal) will lead to an entirely different pathway (valley) being taken. However, a variety of different sources of perturbation could lead to the same alternative path being taken, and therefore the same behavioral phenotype could result. This corresponds to the fact that there are probably several sources of perturbation that can result in autistic symptoms, for example. Waddington's analysis would, however, predict that these perturbations occur around the same developmental stage. Perturbations to development that occur later in development when the organism is in a chreod (possibly corresponding to perinatal or early postnatal) are compensated for by self-regulatory (adaptive) processes which ensure that the same behavioral phenotype results. I suggest that this corresponds to the effects of perinatal and early postnatal acquired cortical damage. As we have seen, if perinatal damage is limited to regions of the cortex, there is often a degree of functional compensation not seen in adults and older children. For example, lesions to the left temporal lobe early in life do not have a devastating effect on language acquisition (Chapter 9). The effects are subtle and affect other domains of cognition also. Thus, in these cases the injured brain adapts to preserve the patterns of specialization which results from typical development. Obviously, major perturbations, such as the loss of most of the cortex, or prolonged rearing in darkness or social isolation, are likely to push the child into a different phenotype.

13.5   Criticisms of Developmental Cognitive Neuroscience

Now that development cognitive neuroscience has become established as an interdisciplinary field in its own right it has become time to evaluate and question the directions in which we are going. One of the most common criticisms leveled at the newly emerging field is that it is primarily being driven forward by the powerful new methods for imaging brain structure and function in an infant and child-friendly way (as well as new techniques for genetic analyses), and that it lacks the theory-driven approach that characterizes much of the best work in, for example, the neighboring field of cognitive development. Similar concerns are expressed, albeit less directly, by students who can be daunted by the somewhat fragmentary islands of data we have acquired to date about human functional brain development. Where is the overarching theory or framework within which they can make sense of disparate observations? A related concern sometimes expressed by those in cognitive science is that the hypotheses which are presented in developmental cognitive neuroscience are reductionist, or otherwise impoverished as a proper cognitive explanation of infant or child behavior. In other words, this criticism is that what hypotheses and theories there are in the field are of the wrong type, and do not offer a satisfactory explanation of behavioral change in development.

Starting with the criticism of a relative lack of theories in developmental cognitive neuroscience, we have to acknowledge that, at least compared to the parent discipline of cognitive development, work in our field generally tends to be less theory-driven (with several notable exceptions to this generality duly noted). Why is this? A large part of the explanation I believe to be due to the sudden increase in the volume and diversity of data due to the new methods that have become available. Many theories that successfully accounted for sets of behavior observations in child development founder on the rocks when we also try to account for neuroscience data relating to the same behavioral tasks. For one thing, when you more than double the *quantity of data* to be accounted for then many previously successful theories will no longer offer a satisfactory explanation, simply because the chance of observing refuting evidence is much higher. Bringing powerful new methods into a field is analogous to a catastrophic environmental change during evolution—the majority of species (theories) simply cannot adapt and therefore die off. It takes generations for the better adapted species to emerge.

A second issue is that of accommodating to *new types of data*. When you begin to study brain function directly, the first thing that hits you is the complexity of the processes involved. For example, neuroscience evidence indicates that the brain has at least three partially independent routes for executing eye movements (Chapter 5). Although these routes may have slightly different attributes, duplication of computations and (apparent) redundancy seems to be a basic feature of how the brain does things. Thus, at a sweep, simple single-route cognitive models appear less plausible. Add to this the complexity of feedback routes interacting with sensory-driven information (Chapter 12), and the undoubted importance of temporal synchrony, and many existing theories of cognitive development start to look hopelessly simplistic. Of course, a common reaction to this is that theories of cognitive development are not intended to account for neuroscience data—that is merely a matter of implementation. However, this argument implies that you are not interested in doing cognitive neuroscience, and I would argue that satisfactory explanations of development necessitate bridging between levels of observation (Chapter 1).

This leads us to the second common criticism of theory in developmental science. This criticism is that the theories are of the *wrong type* to be of relevance for explaining the development of human behavior. Commonly, the view is expressed that theories in developmental cognitive neuroscience are reductionist and therefore do not offer good explanations of cognitive change. Cognition, it is argued following Marr (1982), is a level of explanation independent from the underlying neuroscience. A simple analogy sometimes given is that computer software could, in theory, be run on a variety of different hardwares. Recent directions in neuroscience suggest that, to the contrary, there is a large degree of interdependence between levels in real complex biological systems such as the brain. This has led to the proposal that we should be seeking theories that are *consistent* between different levels of explanation (see Mareschal et al., 2007, for a detailed discussion of this point). Ultimately, theories that are consistent with both behavioral and brain development evidence will have greater explanatory power than those confined to one level of observation.

In considering the issues above, the current dearth of plausible theories in developmental cognitive neuroscience seems unsurprising. After all, new fields in the biological sciences (in contrast to some physical sciences) often go through a "natural history" phase in which collection of basic data is the priority. However, since I share the view that we need to strive to bring more adequate and appropriate theories into the field, I offer three positive suggestions for hallmarks of a good theory in developmental cognitive neuroscience.

1. The theory advanced should genuinely relate neural observations to behavioral ones, and can be equally well tested (and refuted) by either neural or behavioral level observations. I suspect that a variety of different types of theories will emerge to serve this bridging function, but that they are unlikely to look like many existing cognitive development theories. Theories that have been developed purely on the basis of behavioral data are unlikely to naturally map onto brain imaging data, and there is a danger in seeking only confirmatory data. Ideally, we should develop theories of functional brain development that are equally compatible with brain and behavioral observations.
2. Theories in developmental science should involve mechanisms of change. This suggestion is not new (e.g. Mareschal & Thomas, 2007), but it is still surprisingly common to see theories that explain the state of affairs before and after a developmental transition, but that do not specify the mechanisms of the transition itself (other than using the terms "maturation" or "learning"). Theories of development need to be theories focused on change.
3. Given that theories in developmental cognitive neuroscience are accounting for several levels of observation, and that they also need be compatible with undoubtedly complex and dynamic aspects of neural processing, we need to find ways to elucidate and present those theories so that they are both comprehensible and clarifying. This is the attraction and importance of formal computational modeling, be it symbolic, connectionist or hybrid (see Mareschal et al., 2007). While theories may initially develop as informal ideas, ultimately we should aim to implement them as computational models.

Finally, a caution against being too prescriptive. In the long term it is probably good for the field to have a heterogeneous mix of different types of theories and let the data, and time, select those with the best fit to reality. After all, despite their prolonged domination, the dinosaurs did not inherit the globe.

13.6   Applications of Developmental Cognitive Neuroscience

Developmental cognitive neuroscience has been identified by several national and international grant agencies as one of the most significant growth areas in all of the neurosciences, partly because an understanding of human functional brain development has fundamental implications for social, educational, and clinical policies and strategy. In several chapters of this book we have heard how some developmental disorders can be characterized as a deviation from the typical trajectory of postnatal human brain development (Karmiloff-Smith, 1998). For example, according to the interactive specialization view, biases in attention and processing in early infancy are reinforced by differential patterns of experience subsequently resulting in the patterns of specialization observed in adults. Thus, some adult patterns of cortical functional specialization are an inevitable consequence of interacting factors in typical development (Johnson, 2001). A corollary to this is that disruption of one or more of these factors can lead to failure to develop the typical degree or patterns of cortical specialization. Further, an initial slight deviance, for example in mother–infant interaction, can lead to increasingly compounded patterns of deviance as others alter their natural behavior. However, the positive side of the interactive specialization view of atypical development is that remediation strategies may be effective in alleviating some symptoms in at least some cases as long as it is started early in life, before the compounding of symptoms into a more complex syndrome. Thus, on the agenda for the next decade will be attempts to intervene in the course of development before major symptoms in some disorders (such as autism) have become compounded.

In many cases developmental disorders arise from atypical genetics, but atypical early environments can also lead to adverse outcomes. Evidence from several sources indicates that childhood, and particularly infancy, within a low income (low social economic status) family context has a surprisingly strong relationship to later cognitive ability as measured by IQ and school achievement. Although there are multiple correlated factors such as diet, parental drug abuse, and life stress, being raised in a poor family itself correlates with a variety of cognitive differences in language, working memory, spatial cognition, and attention. In particular, lower language abilities and specific differences in prefrontal and executive functions have been consistently identified (for review see Hackman & Farah, 2009). Governments have acknowledged how crucial the level of cognitive development during the early years is for the later educational and life outcomes. As a consequence of this a number of pilot intervention programs have been funded, some of which involved weekly home visits by well-trained teachers and extra school hours, over periods of 1–3 years. Most of these programs proved that there are economic gains of early interventions, in terms of a decreased number of individuals requiring benefits or ending up in prison (Heckman, 2007). However, to date, none of these programs have been specifically designed based on current knowledge about cognitive and brain development. Because most programs have been fairly generic (e.g., targeting both cognitive and noncognitive factors, such as access to better health care), and measured different outcomes at different ages it is difficult to make a comparative analysis of their results and to assess which were the intervening factors that led to their success or otherwise. Nevertheless, a challenge for the application of developmental cognitive neuroscience over the next decade will be developing theoretically motivated and evidence-based early interventions for children raised in poverty.

Another potential area of application for developmental cognitive neuroscience that has caused great interest recently is school education. Education presents serious challenges for cognitive neuroscience because it concerns learning what other people have learned, whereas the domain of most neuroscience has been what the learner discovers through interaction with their own environment. Equally, neuroscience challenges the discipline of education to make use of the research on the neural and genetic factors now known to influence the effectiveness of learning. Until recently these two disciplines have proceeded in parallel with little or no collaboration. The vacuum between the disciplines was often filled by commercial products based on a folk-level understanding of the brain and its processes. However, advances in both disciplines are leading to greater precision in the understanding of fundamental issues, and this in turn creates the possibility of a new disciplinary field sometimes called "educational neuroscience". One example of this nascent approach comes from the recent interest in understanding the basic mechanisms of learning about number and number systems (Chapter 7). For the next decade we need examples of where issues of educational need are taken up by the developmental cognitive neuroscience laboratory, and then the principles and processes revealed are used to inform classroom practice.

3.7   Concluding Remarks

The past decade has seen developmental cognitive neuroscience grow from newborn to toddler. The next steps will be dependent on successful collaboration between developmental neuroscientists, cognitive developmentalists, and computational modelers. New methods and new theoretical approaches will be equally important. In the longer term we will depend on the next generation, who will need some familiarity with all of these fields, and will become true developmental cognitive neuroscientists.

Key Issues for Discussion

- What are the prospects for a neuroscience approach to education, and what major barriers to progress need to be overcome?
- What domains of cognition have yet to be approached by a developmental cognitive neuroscience approach, and why have these been neglected to this point?
- What new (or old) methods will be most useful for advancing developmental cognitive neuroscience in the future, and why?

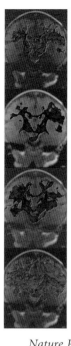

References

Acerra, F., Burnod, Y., & de Schonen, S. (2002). Modelling aspects of face processing in early infancy. *Developmental Science*, *5* (1), 98–117.

Adlam, A. L., Vargha-Khadem, F., Mishkin, M., & de Haan, M. (2005). Deferred imitation of action sequences in developmental amnesia. *Journal of Cognitive Neuroscience*, *17*, 240–248.

Adolphs, R. (2003). Cognitive neuroscience of human social behaviour. *Nature Reviews Neuroscience*, *4* (3), 165–178.

Akhtar, N., & Enns, J. T. (1989). Relations between covert orienting and filtering in the development of visual attention. *Journal of Experimental Child Psychology*, *48* (2), 315–334.

Akshoomoff, N.-A., & Courchesne, E. (1994). ERP evidence for a shifting attention deficit in patients with damage to the cerebellum. *Journal of Cognitive Neuroscience*, *6* (4), 388–399.

Alexander, G. E., DeLong, M. R., & Strick, P. L. (1986). Parallel organization of functionally segregated circuits linking basal ganglia and cortex. *Annual Review of Neuroscience*, *9*, 357–382.

Andersen, R. A., Batista, A. P., Snyder, L. H., Buneo, C. A., & Cohen, Y. E. (2000). Programming to look and reach in the posterior parietal cortex. In M. S. Gazzaniga (Ed.), *The new cognitive neurosciences* (2nd ed., pp. 515–524). Cambridge, MA: MIT Press.

Andersen, R. A., & Zipser, D. (1988). The role of the posterior parietal cortex in coordinate transformations for visual-motor integration. *Canadian Journal of Physiology & Pharmacology*, *66*, 488–501.

Anderson, S. W., Aksan, N., Kochanska, G., Damasio, H., Wisnowski, J., & Afifi, A. (2007). The earliest behavioral expression of focal damage to human prefrontal cortex. *Cortex*, *43*, 806–816.

Annett, M. (1985). *Left, right, hand and brain: The right shift theory*. London: Lawrence Erlbaum.

Ansari, D. (2008). Effects of development and enculturation on number representation in the brain. *Nature Reviews Neuroscience*, *9*, 278–291.

Ansari, D., & Karmiloff-Smith, A. (2002). Atypical trajectories of number development. *Trends in Cognitive Sciences*, *6* (12), 511–516.

Aslin, R. N. (1981). Development of smooth pursuit in human infants. In D. F. Fisher, R. A. Monty, & J. W. Senders (Eds.), *Eye movements: Cognition and visual perception* (pp. 31–51). Hillsdale, NJ: Erlbaum.

Developmental Cognitive Neuroscience (Third Edition) Mark H. Johnson with Michelle de Haan
© 2011 Mark H. Johnson

Aslin, R. N. (2007). What's in a look? *Developmental Science, 10*, 48–53.

Aslin, R. N., Clayards, M. A., & Bardhan, N. P. (2008). Mechanisms of auditory reorganization during development from sounds to words. In C. A. Nelson & M. Luciana (Eds.), *Handbook of developmental cognitive neuroscience* (2nd ed., pp. 97–116). Cambridge, MA: MIT Press.

Aslin, R. N., & Hunt, R. H. (2001). Development, plasticity and learning in the auditory system. In C. A. Nelson & M. Luciana (Eds.), *Handbook of developmental cognitive neuroscience* (pp. 205–220). Cambridge, MA: MIT Press.

Atkinson, J. (1984). Human visual development over the first six months of life: A review and a hypothesis. *Human Neurobiology, 3*, 61–74.

Atkinson, J. (1998). The "where and what" or "who and how" of visual development. In F. Simion & G. Butterworth (Eds.), *The development of sensory, motor and cognitive capacities in early infancy: From perception to cognition* (pp. 3–20). Hove: Psychology Press.

Atkinson, J., & Braddick, O. (2003). Neurobiological models of normal and abnormal visual development. In M. de Haan & M. H. Johnson (Eds.), *The cognitive neuroscience of development* (pp. 43–71). Hove: Psychology Press.

Avidan, G., Hasson, U., Malach, R., & Behrmann, M. (2005). Detailed exploration of face-related processing in congenital prosopagnosia: Functional neuroimaging findings. *Journal of Cognitive Neuroscience, 17*, 1150–1167.

Bachevalier, J. (2008). Nonhuman primate models of memory development. In C. A. Nelson & M. Luciana (Eds.), *Handbook of developmental cognitive neuroscience* (2nd ed, pp. 499–508). Cambridge, MA: MIT Press.

Bachevalier, J., & Mishkin, M. (1984). An early and a late developing system for learning and retention in infant monkeys. *Behavioral Neuroscience, 98*, 770–778.

Bachevalier, J., & Vargha-Khadem, F. (2005). The primate hippocampus: ontogeny, early insult and memory. *Current Opinion in Neurobiology, 15*, 168–174.

Baillargeon, R. (1993). The object concept revisited: New directions in the investigation of infants' physical knowledge. In C. E. Granrud (Ed.), *Visual perception and cognition in infancy* (pp. 265–315). Hillsdale, NJ: Lawrence Erlbaum.

Baird, A. A., Kagan, J., Gaudette, T., Walz, K. A., Hershlag, N., & Boas, D. A. (2002). Frontal lobe activation during object permanence: Data from near-infrared spectroscopy. *NeuroImage, 16*, 1120–1126.

Balaban, C. D., & Weinstein, J. M. (1985). The human pre-saccadic spike potential: Influences of a visual target, saccade direction, electrode laterality and instruction to perform saccades. *Brain Research, 347*, 49–57.

Banks, M. S., & Shannon, E. (1993). Spatial and chromatic visual efficiency in human neonates. In C. E. Granrud (Ed.), *Visual perception and cognition in infancy* (pp. 1–46). Hillsdale, NJ: Lawrence Erlbaum.

Baron-Cohen, S. (1995). *Mindblindness: An essay on autism and theory of mind*. Cambridge, MA: MIT Press.

Baron-Cohen, S., Leslie, A. M., & Frith, U. (1985). Does the autistic child have a "theory of mind"? *Cognition, 21*, 37–46.

Baron-Cohen, S., Leslie, A. M., & Frith, U. (1986). Mechanical, behavioural and intentional understanding of picture stories in autistic children. *British Journal of Developmental Psychology, 4*, 113–125.

Baron-Cohen, S., Lutchmaya, S., & Knickmeyer, R. (2004). *Prenatal testosterone in mind: Amniotic fluid studies*. Cambridge, MA: MIT Press.

Barth, H., Kanwisher, N., & Spelke, E. (2003). The construction of large number representations in adults. *Cognition*, *86* (3), 201–221.

Barto, A. G., Sutton, R. S., & Anderson, C. W. (1983). Neuronlike adaptive elements that can solve difficult learning control problems. *Institute of Electrical Engineers Transactions on System, Man and Cybernetics*, *15*, 835–846.

Bates, E. A., & Roe, K. (2001). Language development in children with unilateral brain injury. In C. A. Nelson & M. Luciana (Eds.), *Handbook of developmental cognitive neuroscience* (pp. 281–307). Cambridge: MA: MIT Press.

Bates, E., Thal, D., & Janowsky, J. S. (1992). Early language development and its neural correlates. In I. Rapin & S. Segalowitz (Eds.), *Handbook of neuropsychology* (Vol. 7). Amsterdam: Elsevier.

Bateson, P., & Horn, G. (1994). Imprinting and recognition memory: A neural net model. *Animal Behaviour*, *48*, 695–715.

Batki, A., Baron-Cohen, S., Wheelwright, S., Connellan, J., & Ahluwalia, J. (2001). How important are the eyes in neonatal face perception? *Infant Behavior and Development*, *23*, 223–229.

Bauer, P. J. (2006). Constructing a past in infancy: A neuro-developmental account. *Trends in Cognitive Sciences*, *10*, 175–181.

Bauer, P. J. (2008). Toward a neuro-developmental account of the development of declarative memory. *Developmental Psychobiology*, *50*, 19–31.

Bauer, P. J., Wiebe, S. A., Carver, L. J., Lukowski, A. F., Haight, J. C., Waters, J. M., & Nelson, C. A. (2006). Electrophysiological indexes of encoding and behavioural indexes of recall: Examining relations and developmental change late in the first year of life. *Developmental Neuropsychology*, *29*, 293–320.

Bauman, M. D., & Amaral, D. G. (2008). Neurodevelopment of social cognition. In C. A. Nelson & M. Luciana (Eds.), *Handbook of developmental cognitive neuroscience* (2nd ed., pp. 161–185). Cambridge, MA: MIT Press.

Beauchamp, M. H., Thompson, D. K., Howard, K., Doyle, L. W., Egan, G. F., Inder, T. E. et al. (2008). Preterm infant hippocampal volumes correlate with later working memory deficits. *Brain*, *131*, 2986–2994.

Bear, M. F., & Singer, W. (1986). Modulation of visual cortical plasticity by acetycholine and noradrenaline. *Nature*, *320*, 172–176.

Bechara, A., Damasio, A. R., Damasio, H., & Anderson, S. W. (1994). Insensitivity to future consequences following damage to human prefrontal cortex. *Cognition*, *50*, 7–15.

Bechara, A., Damasio, H., Tranel, D., & Damasio, A. R. (1997). Deciding advantageously before knowing the advantageous strategy. *Science*, *275*, 1293–1295.

Becker, L. E., Armstrong, D. L., Chan, F., & Wood, M. M. (1984). Dendritic development on human occipital cortex neurones. *Brain Research*, *315*, 117–124.

Bednar, J. A., & Miikkulainen, R. (2003). Learning innate face preferences. *Neural Computation*, *15*, 1525–1557.

Behrmann, M., & Avidan, G. (2005). Congenital prosopagnosia: Face blind from birth. *Trends in Cognitive Sciences*, *9*, 180–187.

Bell, M. A. (1992a). *A not B task performance is related to frontal EEG asymmetry regardless of locomotor experience*. Paper presented at the Proceedings of the Eighth International Conference on Infant Studies, Miami Beach, FL.

Bell, M. A. (1992b). *Electrophysiological correlates of object search performance during infancy*. Paper presented at the Proceedings of the Eighth International Conference on Infant Studies, Miami Beach, FL.

Bell, M. A., & Fox, N. A. (1992). The relations between frontal brain electrical activity and cognitive development during infancy. *Child Development, 63* (5), 1142–1163.

Bell, M. A., & Wolfe, C. D. (2007). Brain reorganization from infancy to early childhood: Evidence from EEG power and coherence during working memory tasks. *Developmental Neuropsychology, 31,* 21–38.

Bellugi, U., Bihrle, A., Neville, H., Jernigan, T., & Doherty, S. (1992). Language, cognition and brain organization in a neurodevelopmental disorder. In M. Gunnar & C. Nelson (Eds.), *Developmental behavioral neuroscience* (pp. 201–232). Hillsdale, NJ: Lawrence Erlbaum.

Bellugi, U., Poizner, H., & Klima, E. S. (1989). Language, modality and the brain. *Trends in the Neurosciences, 12,* 380–388.

Benasich, A. A., & Tallal, P. (2002). Infant discrimination of rapid auditory cues predicts later language impairment. *Behavioral and Brain Research, 136,* 31–49.

Benes, F. M. (1994). Development of the corticolimbic system. In G. Dawson & K. W. Fischer (Eds.), *Human behavior and the developing brain* (pp. 176–206). New York: Guilford Press.

Benes, F. M. (2001). The development of prefrontal cortex: The maturation of neurotransmitter systems and their interactions. In C. A. Nelson & M. Luciana (Eds.), *Handbook of developmental cognitive neuroscience* (pp. 79–92). Cambridge, MA: MIT Press.

Berenbaum, S. A., Moffat, S., Wisniewski, A., & Resnick, S. (2003). Neuroendocrinology: Cognitive effects of sex hormones. In M. de Haan & M. H. Johnson (Eds.), *The cognitive neuroscience of development* (pp. 207–236). Hove: Psychology Press.

Berman, S., & Friedman, D. (1995). The development of selective attention as reflected by event-related brain potentials. *Journal of Experimental Child Psychology, 59,* 1–31.

Bishop, D. V. M. (1983). Linguistic impairment after hemidecortication for infantile hemiplegia? A reappraisal. *Quarterly Journal of Experimental Psychology, 35A,* 199–207.

Bishop, D. V. M. (1997). *Uncommon understanding: Development and disorders of language comprehension in children.* Hove: Psychology Press.

Bishop, D. V. M., Canning, E., Elgar, K., Morris, E., Jacobs, P., & Skuse, D. (2000). Distinctive patterns of memory function in subgroups of females with Turner syndrome: Evidence for imprinted loci on the X-chromosome affecting neurodevelopment. *Neuropsychologica, 38,* 712–721.

Blakemore, S. -J., & Choudhury, S. (2006). Development of the adolescent brain: Implications for executive function and social cognition. *Journal of Child Psychiatry and Psychology, 47,* 296–312.

Blakemore, S. -J., den Ouden, H., Choudhury, S., & Frith, C. (2007). Adolescent development of the neural circuitry for thinking about intentions. *Social Cognitive and Affective Neuroscience, 2,* 130–139.

Blass, E. (1992). Linking developmental and psychobiological research. *Society for Research in Child Development Newsletter,* January, pp. 3–10.

Bloom, F., Nelson, C. A., & Lazerson, A. (2001). *Brain, mind, and behavior* (3rd ed.). New York: Worth Publishers.

Bolhuis, J. J. (1991). Mechanisms of avian imprinting: A review. *Biological Reviews, 66,* 303–345.

Bolhuis, J. J., McCabe, B. J., & Horn, G. (1986). Androgens and imprinting: Differential effects of testosterone on filial preferences in the domestic chick. *Behavioral Neuroscience, 100,* 51–56.

Born, P., Rostrup, E., Leth, H., Peitersen, B., & Lou, H C. (1996). Change of visually induced cortical activation patterns during development. *Lancet, 347* (9000), 543.

Born, A. P., Rostrup, E., Miranda, M. J., Larsson, H. B. W., & Lou, H. C. (2002). Visual cortex reactivity in sedated children examined with perfusion MRI (FAIR). *Magnetic Resonance Imaging, 20* (2), 199–205.

Bourgeois, J. P. (2001). Synaptogenesis in the necortex of the newborn: The ultimate frontier for individuation? In C. A. Nelson & M. Luciana (Eds.), *Handbook of developmental cognitive neuroscience* (pp. 23–34). Cambridge, MA: MIT Press.

Braddick, O. J., Atkinson, J., Hood, B., Harkness, W., Jackson, G., & Vargha-Khadem, F. (1992). Possible blindsight in infants lacking one cerebral hemisphere. *Nature, 360*, 461–463.

Brannon, E. M., & Terrace, H. S. (2000). Representation of numerosities 1–9 by rhesus macaques (Macaca mulatta). *Journal of Experimental Psychology – Animal Behaviour Processes, 26*, 31–49.

Brodal, A. (1981). *Neurological anatomy in relation to clinical medicine*. Oxford: Oxford University Press.

Brodeur, D. A., & Boden, C. (2000). The effects of spatial uncertainty and cue predictability on visual orienting in children. *Cognitive Development, 15*, 367–382.

Brodmann, K. (1909). *Vergleichende Lokalisationslehre der Grosshirnrinde in ihren Prinzipien dargestellt auf Grund des Zellenbaues*. Leipzig: Barth.

Brodmann, K. (1912). Neue Ergebnisse über die vergleichende histologische Lokalisation der Grosshirnrinde mit besonderer Berücksichtigung des Stirnhirns. *Anatomischer Anzeiger (Suppl.), 41*, 157–216.

Bronson, G. W. (1974). The postnatal growth of visual capacity. *Child Development, 45*, 873–890.

Bronson, G. W. (1982). *The scanning patterns of human infants: Implications for visual learning*. Norwood, NJ: Ablex.

Brooksbank, B. W. L., Atkinson, D. J., & Balasz, R. (1981). Biochemical development of the human brain: II. Some parameters of the GABA-ergic system. *Developmental Neuroscience, 1*, 267–284.

Brown, T. T., Lugar, H. M., Coalson, R. S., Miezin, F. M., Petersen, S. E., & Schlaggar, B. L. (2005). Maturational changes in human cerebral functional organization for word generation. *Cerebral Cortex, 15*, 275–290.

Bruinink, A., Lichtensteinger, W., & Schlumpf, M. (1983). Pre- and postnatal ontogeny and characterization of dopaminergic D2, serotonergic S2, and spirodecan one binding sites in rat forebrain. *Journal of Neurochemistry, 40*, 1227–1237.

Bruyer, R., Laterre, C., Serron, X., Feyereisn, P., Strypstein, E., Pierrand, E. et al. (1983). A case of prosopagnosia with some preserved covert remembrance of familiar faces. *Brain and Cognition, 2*, 157–281.

Bullock, D., Liederman, J., & Todorovic, D. (1987). Reconciling stable asymmetry with recovery of function: An adaptive systems perspective on functional plasticity. *Child Development, 58*, 689–697.

Butterworth, B. (2006). *The mathematical brain*. London: Macmillan.

Butterworth, G., & Jarrett, N. (1991). What minds have in common is space: Spatial mechanisms serving joint visual attention in infancy. *British Journal of Developmental Psychology, 9*, 55–72.

Bystron, I., Blakemore, C., & Rakic, P. (2008). Development of the human cerebral cortex: Boulder Committee revisited. *Nature Reviews Neuroscience, 9*, 110–122.

Calvo-Merino, B., Glaser, D. E., Grèzes, J., Passingham, R. E., & Haggard, P. (2005). Action observation and acquired motor skills: An fMRI study with expert dancers. *Cerebral Cortex, 15*, 1243–1249.

Cameron, J. L. (2001). Effects of sex hormones on brain development. In C. A. Nelson & M. Luciana (Eds.), *Handbook of developmental cognitive neuroscience* (pp. 59–78). Cambridge, MA: MIT Press.

Canfield, R. L., & Haith, M. M. (1991). Young infants' visual expectations for symmetric and asymmetric stimulus sequences. *Developmental Psychology, 27*, 198–208.

Canfield, R. L., Smith, E. G., Brezsnyak, M. P., & Snow, K. L. (1997). Information processing through the first year of life: A longitudinal study using the Visual Expectation Paradigm. *Monographs of the Society for Research in Child Development, 62* (2), 1–145.

Cantlon, J. F., Brannon, E. M., Carter, E. J., & Pelphrey, K. A. (2006). Functional imaging of numerical processing in adults and 4-y-old children. *PLoS Biology, 4*, e125.

Carey, S. (2001). Bridging the gap between cognition and developmental neuroscience: The example of number presentation. In C. A. Nelson & M. Luciana (Eds.), *Handbook of developmental cognitive neuroscience* (pp. 415–432). Cambridge, MA: MIT Press.

Carey, S., & Spelke, E. (in press). On the very possibility of conceptual change: The integer-list representation of number. In *Conceptual development: A reappraisal*. Cambridge, MA: MIT Press.

Carpenter, P. A., Just, M. A., Keller, T., Cherkassky, V., Roth, J. K., & Minshew, N. (2001). Dynamic cortical systems subserving cognition: fMRI studies with typical and atypical individuals. In J. L. McClelland & R. S. Siegler (Eds.), *Mechanisms of cognitive development* (pp. 353–386). Mahwah, NJ: Lawrence Erlbaum.

Carroll, S. B. (2005). Evolution at two levels: On genes and form. *PLoS Biology, 3*, e245.

Carter, E. J., & Pelphrey, K. (2006). School-aged children exhibit domain-specific responses to biological motion. *Social Neuroscience, 1*, 396–411.

Carver, L. J., & Bauer, P. J. (1999). When the event is more than the sum of its parts: 9-month-olds' long-term ordered recall. *Memory, 7*, 147–174.

Carver, L. J., & Bauer, P. J. (2001). The dawning of a past: The emergence of long-term explicit memory in infancy. *Journal of Experimental Psychology General, 130*, 726–745.

Casanova, M. F., & Trippell, J. (2006). Regulatory mechanisms of cortical laminar development. *Brain Research Reviews, 51*, 72–84.

Case, R. (1992). The role of the frontal lobes in the regulation of human development. *Brain and Cognition, 20*, 51–73.

Casey, B. J., Tottenham, N., Liston, C., & Durston, S. (2005). Imaging the developing brain: What have we learned about cognitive development? *Trends in Cognitive Sciences, 9*, 104–110.

Cesaroni, L., & Garber, M. (1991). Exploring the experience of autism through firsthand accounts. *Journal of Autism and Developmental Disorders, 21*, 303–313.

Changeux, J. -P. (1985). *Neuronal man: The biology of mind*. New York: Pantheon Books.

Changeux, J. -P., Courrege, P., & Danchin, A. (1973). A theory of the epigenisis of neuronal networks by selective stabilization of synapses. *Proceedings of the National Academy of Sciences of the United States of America, 70*, 2974–2978.

Changeux, J.-P., & Dehaene, S. (1989). Neuronal models of cognitive functions. *Cognition, 33*, 63–109.

Chapman, M. (1981). Dimensional separability or flexibility of attention? Age trends in perceiving configural stimuli. *Journal of Experimental Child Psychology, 31*, 332–349.

Cheour-Luhtanen, M., Alho, K., Kujala, T., Sainio, K., Reinikainen, K., Renlund, M., Aitonen, O., Eorela, O., & Naatanen, R. (1995). Mismatch negativity indicates vowel discrimination in newborns. *Hearing Research*, 82, 53–58.

Chi, J. G., Gooling, E., & Gilles, F. H. (1977). Gyral development of the human brain. *Annals of Neurology*, 1, 86.

Chiang, W.-C., & Wynn, K. (2000). Infants' representation and tracking of multiple objects. *Cognition*, 77, 169–195.

Chiu, C. Y., Schmithorst, V. J., Brown, R. D., Holland, S. K., & Dunn, S. (2006). Making memories: A cross-sectional investigation of episodic memory encoding in childhood using fMRI. *Developmental Neuropsychology*, 29, 321–240.

Chugani, D. C. (2000). Autism. In M. Ernst & J. M. Rumsey (Eds.), *Functional neuroimaging in child psychiatry* (pp. 171–188). Cambridge: Cambridge University Press.

Chugani, H. T. (1994). Development of regional brain glucose metabolism in relation to behavior and plasticity. In G. Dawson & K. W. Fischer (Eds.), *Human behavior and the developing brain* (pp. 153–175). New York: Guilford Press.

Chugani, H. T., Hovda, D. A., Villablanca, J. R., Phelps, M. E., & Xu, W. F. (1991). Metabolic maturation of the brain: A study of local cerebral glucose utilization in the developing cat. *Journal of Cerebral Blood Flow and Metabolism*, 11 (1), 35–47.

Chugani, H. T., & Phelps, M. E. (1986). Maturational changes in cerebral function in infants determined by [18] FDG positron emission tomography. *Science*, 231, 840–843.

Chugani, H. T., Phelps, M. E., & Mazziotta, J. C. (1987). Positron emission tomography study of human brain functional development. *Annals of Neurology*, 22, 487–497.

Chugani, H. T., Phelps, M. E., & Mazziotta, J. C. (2002). Positron emission tomography study of human brain functional development. In M. H. Johnson, Y. Munakata, & R. Gilmore (Eds.), *Brain development and cognition: A reader* (2nd ed., pp. 101–116). Oxford: Blackwell.

Clancy, B., Darlington, R. B., & Finlay, B. L. (2000). The course of human events: Predicting the timing of primate neural development. *Developmental Science*, 3 (1), 57–66.

Clohessy, A. B., Posner, M. I., Rothbart, M. K., & Vecera, S. P. (1991). The development of inhibition of return in early infancy. *Journal of Cognitive Neuroscience*, 3 (4), 345–350.

Cohen, L. B., & Marks, K. S. (2002). How infants process addition and subtraction events. *Developmental Science*, 5 (2), 186–201.

Cohen, N. J., & Squire, L. R. (1980). Preserved learning and retention of pattern analyzing skill in amnesia: Dissociation of knowing how and knowing what. *Science*, 210, 207–209.

Cohen-Kadosh, K., & Johnson, M. H. (2007). Developing a cortex specialized for face perception. *Trends in Cognitive Science*, 11, 367–369.

Cohen-Kadosh, R., Cohen-Kadosh, K., Schuhmann, T., Kaas, A., Goebel, R., Henik, A., & Sack, A. T. (2007). Virtual dyscalculia induced by parietal lobe TMS impairs automatic magnitude processing. *Current Biology*, 17, 689–693.

Condry, K. F., Smith, W. C., & Spelke, E. S. (2000). Development of perceptual organization. In F. Lacerda, C. von Hofsten, & M. Heimann (Eds.), *Emerging cognitive abilities in early infancy* (pp. 1–28). Hillsdale, NJ: Erlbaum.

Conel, J. L. (1939–1967). *The postnatal development of the human cerebral cortex, Vols. I–VIII*. Cambridge, MA: Harvard University Press.

Cooper, N. G. F., & Steindler, D. A. (1986). Lectins demarcate the barrel subfield in the somatosensory cortex of the early postnatal mouse. *Journal of Comparative Neurology*, 249, 157–169.

Cordes, S., & Brannon, E. M. (2008). Quantitative competencies in infancy. *Developmental Science, 11*, 803–808.

Cornish, K., & Wilding, J. (2010). *Genes, cognition and early brain development.* Oxford: Oxford University Press.

Courchesne, E. (1991). *The theory of mind deficit in autism: Possible biological bases.* Paper presented at the Society for Research in Child Development, Seattle, WA.

Courchesne, E., Yeung-Courchesne, R., Press, G. A., Hesselink, J. R., & Jernigan, T. L. (1988). Hypoplasia of cerebellar vermal lobules VI and VII in autism. *The New England Journal of Medicine, 318*, 1349–1354.

Coyle, J. T., & Molliver, M. (1977). Major innervation of newborn rat cortex by monoaminergic neurons. *Science, 196*, 444–447.

Craft, S., White, D. A., Park, T. S., & Figiel, G. (1994). Visual attention in children with perinatal brain injury: Asymmetric effects of bilateral lesions. *Journal of Cognitive Neuroscience, 6*, 165–173.

Crick, F. (1989). Neural Edelmanism. *Trends in the Neurosciences, 12*, 240–248.

Crick, F. H. C., & Watson, J. D. (1953). A structure for deoxyribose nucleic acid. *Nature, 171*, 737–738.

Cromer, R. E. (1992). A case study of dissociation between language and cognition. In H. Tager-Flusberg (Ed.), *Constraints on language acquisition: Studies of atypical children* (pp. 141–153). Hillsdale, NJ: Lawrence Erlbaum.

Crone, E. A., & van der Molen, M.W. (2008). Neurocognitive development of performance monitoring and decision making. In C. A. Nelson & M. Luciana (Eds.), *Handbook of developmental cognitive neuroscience* (2nd ed., pp. 883–896). Cambridge, MA: MIT Press.

Crone, E. A., & Westenberg, P. M. (2009). A brain-based account of developmental changes in social decision making. In M. de Haan & M.R. Gunnar (Eds.), *Handbook of developmental social neuroscience* (pp. 378–398). New York: Guilford Press.

Csibra, G. (2003). Teleological and referential understanding of action in infancy. *Philosophical Transactions of the Royal Society of London, Series B, Biological Sciences, 358*, 447–458.

Csibra, G. (2007). Action mirroring and action interpretation: An alternative account. In P. Haggard, Y. Rosetti, & M. Kawato (Eds.), *Sensorimotor foundations of higher cognition: Attention and performance XXII* (pp. 435–459). Oxford: Oxford University Press.

Csibra, G., Davis, G., Spratling, M. W., & Johnson, M. H. (2000). Gamma oscillations and object processing in the infant brain. *Science, 290*, 1582–1585.

Csibra, G., & Johnson, M. H. (2007). Investigating event-related oscillations in infancy. In M. de Haan (Ed.), *Infant EEG and event related potentials* (pp. 289–304). Hove: Psychology Press.

Csibra, G., Johnson, M. H., & Tucker, L. A. (1997). Attention and oculomotor control: A high-density ERP study of the gap effect. *Neuropsychologia, 35* (6), 855–865.

Csibra, G., Kushnerenko, G., & Grossmann, T. (2008). Electrophysiological methods in studying infant cognitive development. In C. A. Nelson & M. Luciana (Eds.), *Handbook of developmental cognitive neuroscience* (2nd ed., pp. 247–262). Cambridge, MA: MIT Press.

Csibra, G., Tucker, L. A., & Johnson, M. H. (1998). Neural correlates of saccade planning in infants: A high-density ERP study. *International Journal of Psychophysiology, 29*, 201–215.

Csibra, G., Tucker, L. A., & Johnson, M. H. (2001). Differential frontal cortex activation before anticipatory and reactive saccades in infants. *Infancy, 2* (2), 159–174.

Damasio, A. R., & Maurer, R. G. (1978). A neurological model for childhood autism. *Archives of Neurology, 35,* 777–786.

Davies, D. C., Horn, G., & McCabe, B. J. (1985). Noradrenaline and learning: The effects of noradrenergic neurotoxin DSP4 on imprinting in the domestic chick. *Behavioral Neuroscience, 99,* 652–660.

Dawson, G., Carver, L. J., Meltzoff, A. N., Panagiotides, H., McPartland, J., & Webb, S. J. (2002). Neural correlates of face and object recognition in young children with autism spectrum disorder, developmental delay, and typical development. *Child Development, 73,* 700–717.

Deb, S., & Thompson, B. (1998). Neuroimaging in autism. *British Journal of Psychiatry, 173,* 299–302.

DeGutis, J. M., Bentin, S., Robertson, L. C., & D'Esposito, M. (2007). Functional plasticity in ventral temporal cortex following cognitive rehabilitation of a congenital prosopagnosic. *Journal of Cognitive Neuroscience, 19,* 1790–1802.

De Haan, M. (2008). Neurocognitive mechanisms for the development of face processing. In C. A. Nelson & M. Luciana (Eds.), *Handbook of developmental cognitive neuroscience* (2nd ed., pp. 509–520). Cambridge, MA: MIT Press.

De Haan, M., Johnson, M. H., & Halit, H. (2003). Development of face-sensitive event-related potential components during infancy. *International Journal of Psychophysiology, 51,* 45–58.

De Haan, M., Mishkin, M., Baldeweg, T., & Vargha-Khadem, F. (2006). Human memory development and its dysfunction after early hippocampal injury. *Trends in Neurosciences, 29,* 374–381.

De Haan, M., Pascalis, O., & Johnson, M. H. (2002). Specialization of neural mechanisms underlying face recognition in human infants. *Journal of Cognitive Neuroscience, 14,* 199–209.

Dehaene, S. (1997). *The number sense: How the mind creates mathematics.* New York: Oxford University Press.

Dehaene, S., Spelke, E., Pinel, P., Stanescu, R., & Tsivkin, S. (1999). Sources of mathematical thinking: Behavioural and brain-imaging evidence. *Science, 284,* 970–974.

Dehaene-Lambertz, G., & Dehaene, S. (1994). Speed and cerebral correlates of syllable discrimination in infants. *Nature, 370,* 292–295.

Dehaene-Lambertz, G., Dehaene, S., & Hertz-Pannier, L. (2002). Functional neuroimaging of speech perception in infants. *Science, 298* (5600), 2013–2015.

Dehay, C., Bullier, J., & Kennedy, H. (1984). Transient projections from the frontoparietal and temporal cortex to areas 17, 18, and 19 in the kitten. *Experimental Brain Research, 57,* 208–212.

Dehay, C., Horsburgh, G., Berland, M., Killackey, H., & Kennedy, H. (1989). Maturation and connectivity of the visual cortex in monkey is altered by prenatal removal of retinal input. *Nature, 337,* 265–267.

Dehay, C., & Kennedy, H. (2007). Cell-cycle control and cortical development. *Nature Reviews Neuroscience, 8,* 438–450.

Dehay, C., & Kennedy, H. (2009). Transcriptional regulation and alternative splicing make for better brains. *Neuron, 62,* 455–457.

Dehay, C., Kennedy, H., & Bullier, J. (1988). Characterization of transient cortical projections from auditory somatosensory and motor cortices to visual areas 17, 18, and 19 in the kitten. *Journal of Comparative Neurology, 272,* 68–89.

Dennis, M., & Whitaker, H. (1976). Language acquisition following hemidecortication: Linguistic superiority of the left over the right hemisphere. *Brain and Language, 3,* 404–433.

De Schonen, S., & Mancini, J. (1995). *About functional brain specialization: The development of face recognition.* Developmental Cognitive Neuroscience Technical Report No. 95.1.

De Schonen, S., & Mathivet, E. (1989). First come, first served: A scenario about the development of hemispheric specialization in face recognition during infancy. *Current Psychology of Cognition, 9* (1), 3–44.

Diamond, A. (1985). Development of the ability to use recall to guide action, as indicated by infants' performance on AB. *Child Development, 56,* 868–883.

Diamond, A. (1991). Neuropsychological insights into the meaning of object concept development. In S. Carey & R. Gelman (Eds.), *The epigenesis of mind: Essays on biology and cognition* (pp. 67–110). Hillsdale, NJ: Lawrence Erlbaum.

Diamond, A. (2001). A model system for studying the role of dopamine in the prefrontal cortex during early development in humans: Early and continuously treated phenylketonuria. In C. A. Nelson & M. Luciana (Eds.), *Handbook of developmental cognitive neuroscience* (pp. 433–472). Cambridge, MA: MIT Press.

Diamond, A. (2002). A model system for studying the role of dopamine in prefrontal cortex during early development in humans. In M. H. Johnson, Y. Munakata, & R. Gilmore (Eds.), *Brain development and cognition: A reader* (2nd ed., pp. 441–493). Oxford: Blackwell.

Diamond, A., & Doar, B. (1989). The performance of human infants on a measure of frontal cortex function, the delayed response task. *Developmental Psychobiology, 22* (3), 271–294.

Diamond, A., & Goldman-Rakic, P. S. (1986). Comparative development of human infants and infant rhesus monkeys of cognitive functions that depend on prefrontal cortex. *Neuroscience Abstracts, 12,* 274.

Diamond, A., & Goldman-Rakic, P. S. (1989). Comparison of human infants and infant rhesus monkeys on Piaget's AB task: Evidence for dependence on dorsolateral prefrontal cortex. *Experimental Brain Research, 74,* 24–40.

Diamond, A., Werker, J. F., & Lalonde, C. (1994). Toward understanding commonalities in the development of object search, detour navigation, categorization and speech perception. In G. Dawson & K. W. Fisher (Eds.), *Human Behavior and the Developing Brain* (pp. 380–426). New York: Guilford Press.

Diamond, A., Zola-Morgan, S., & Squire, L. R. (1989). Successful performance by monkeys with lesions of the hippocampal formation on AB and object retrieval, two tasks that mark developmental changes in human infants. *Behavioral Neuroscience, 103* (3), 526–537.

Diebler, M. F., Farkas-Bargeton, E., & Wehrle, R. (1979). Developmental changes of enzymes associated with energy metabolism and synthesis of some neurotransmitters in discrete areas of human neocortex. *Journal of Neurochemistry, 32,* 429–435.

Dobkins, K. R., & Anderson, C. M. (2002). Color-based motion processing is stronger in infants than in adults. *Psychological Science, 13* (1), 75–79.

Driver, J., Davis, G., Ricciardelli, P., Kidd, P., Maxwell, E., & Baron-Cohen, S. (1999). Gaze perception triggers reflexive visuo-spatial orienting. *Visual Cognition, 6,* 509–540.

Drummey, A., & Newcombe, N. (1995). Remembering versus knowing the past: Children's explicit and implicit memories for pictures. *Journal of Experimental Child Psychology, 59,* 549–565.

Drummey, A. B., & Newcombe, N. S. (2002). Developmental changes in source memory. *Developmental Science*, 5, 502–513.

Duchaine, B., & Nakayama, K. (2006). Developmental prosopagnosia: A window to content-specific face processing. *Current Opinion in Neurobiology*, 16, 166–173.

Duffy, C. J., & Rakic, P. (1983). Differentiation of granule cell dendrites in the dentate gyrus of the rhesus monkey: A quantitative Golgi study. *Journal of Comparative Neurology*, 214, 224–237.

Duncan, J. (2001). An adaptive coding model of neural function in prefrontal cortex. *Nature Reviews Neuroscience*, 2, 820–829.

Dziurawiec, S. (1996). Blink reflex modification in neonates and its relationship to maturational indices. *Infant Behavior & Development*, 19, 67.

Ebbesson, S. O. (1980). The parcellation theory and its relation to interspecific variability in brain organization, evolutionary and ontogenetic development, and neuronal plasticity. *Cell and Tissue Research*, 213, 179–212.

Ebbesson, S. O. (1984). Evolution and ontogeny of neural circuits. *Behavioral and Brain Sciences*, 7, 321–366.

Ebbesson, S. O. (1988). Ontogenetic parcellation: Dual processes. *Behavioral and Brain Sciences*, 11, 548–549.

Edelman, G. M. (1987). *Neural Darwinism: The theory of neuronal group selection*. New York: Basic Books.

Eden, G. F., & Flowers, D. L. (2008). Learning, skill acquisition, reading and dyslexia. *Annals of New York Academy of Sciences*, 1145, ix–xii.

Edin, F., Macoveanu, J., Olesen, P., Tegner, J., & Klingberg, T. (2007). Stronger synaptic connectivity as a mechanism behind development of working memory-related brain activity during childhood. *Journal of Cognitive Neuroscience*, 19, 750–760.

Elman, J., Bates, E., Johnson, M. H., Karmiloff-Smith, A., Parisi, D., & Plunkett, K. (1996). *Rethinking innateness: A connectionist perspective on development*. Cambridge, MA: MIT Press.

Elsabbagh, M., & Johnson, M. (2007). Infancy and autism: Progress, prospects, and challenge. *Progress in Brain Research*, 164, 355–382.

Elsabbagh, M., Volein, A., Tucker, L., Holmboe, K., Csibra, G., Baron-Cohen, S., Bolton, P., Charman, T., Baird, G., & Johnson, M. (2009). Visual orienting in the early broader autism phenotype: Disengagement and facilitation. *Journal of Child Psychology & Psychiatry*, 50, 637–642.

Enns, J. T., & Brodeur, D. A. (1989). A developmental study of covert orienting to peripheral visual cues. *Journal of Experimental Child Psychology*, 48, 171–189.

Enns, J. T., & Girgus, J. S. (1985). Developmental changes in selective and integrative visual attention. *Journal of Experimental Child Psychology*, 48, 315–334.

Ewert, J.-P. (1987). Neuroethology of releasing mechanisms: Prey-catching in toads. *Behavioral and Brain Sciences*, 10 (3), 337–405.

Fabiani, M., & Wee, E. (2001). Age-related changes in working memory function: A review. In C. Nelson & M. Luciana (Eds.), *Handbook of developmental cognitive neuroscience* (pp. 473–488). Cambridge, MA: MIT Press.

Fair, D. A., Cohen, A. L., Power, J. D., Dosenbach, N. U. F., Church, J. A., Miezin, F. M. et al. (2009). Functional brain networks develop from a "local to distributed" organization. *PLoS Computational Biology*, 5, e1000381.

Fair, D. A., Dosenbach, N. U. F., Church, J. A., Cohen, A. L., Brahmbhatt, S., Miezin, F. M. et al. (2007). Development of distinct control networks through segregation and integration. *Proceedings of the National Academy of Sciences, USA, 104,* 13507–13512.

Fan, J., Fossella, J., Sommer, T., Wu, Y., & Posner, M. I. (2003). Mapping the genetic variation of executive attention onto brain activity. *Proceedings of the National Academy of Sciences of the United States of America, 100,* 7406–7411.

Fantz, R. L. (1964). Visual experience in infants: Decreased attention to familiar patterns relative to novel ones. *Science, 46,* 668–670.

Farah, M. J. (1990). *Visual agnosia.* Cambridge, MA: MIT Press.

Farroni, T., Csibra, G., Simion, F., & Johnson, M. H. (2002). Eye contact detection in humans from birth. *Proceedings of the National Academy of Sciences of the United States of America, 99,* 9602–9605.

Farroni, T., Johnson, M. H., Brockbank, M., & Simion, F. (2000). Infants' use of gaze direction to cue attention: The importance of perceived motion. *Visual Cognition, 7* (6), 705–718.

Feigenson, L., Carey, S., & Spelke, E. S. (2002). Infants' discrimination of number vs. continuous extent. *Cognitive Psychology, 44,* 33–66.

Filipek, P. A. (1999). Neuroimaging in the developmental disorders: The state of the science. *Journal of Child Psychology and Psychiatry, 40* (1), 113–128.

Filipek, P. A., Kennedy, D. N., & Caviness, V. S. J. (1992). Neuroimaging in child neuropsychology. In I. Rapin & S. J. Segalowitz (Eds.), *Handbook of neuropsychology, Vol. 6: Child neuropsychology* (pp. 301–309). New York: Elsevier Science.

Finlay, B. L., & Darlington, R. B. (1995). Linked regularities in the development and evolution of mammalian brains. *Science, 268* (5217), 1578–1584.

Fischer, B., & Breitmeyer, B. (1987). Mechanisms of visual attention revealed by saccadic eye movements. *Neuropsychologia, 25,* 73–83.

Fisher, S. E., & Scharff, C. (2009). FOXP2 as a molecular window into speech and languages. *Trends in Genetics, 25,* 166–177.

Fodor, J. A. (1983). *The modularity of mind.* Cambridge, MA: MIT Press.

Foldiak, P. (1996). Learning constancies for object perception. In V. Walsh & J. Kulikovski (Eds.), *Perceptual constancy: Why things look as they do* (pp. 144–172). Cambridge: Cambridge University Press.

Fosse, V. M., Heggelund, P., & Fonnum, F. (1989). Postnatal development of glutamatergic, GABA-ergic and cholinergic neurotransmitter phenotypes in the visual cortex, lateral geniculate nucleus pulvinar and superior colliculus in cats. *Journal of Neuroscience, 9,* 426–435.

Fox, N. A., & Bell, M. A. (1990). Electrophysiological indices of frontal lobe development. In A. Diamond (Ed.), *The development and neural bases of higher cognitive functions* (Vol. 608, pp. 677–698). New York: New York Academy of Sciences.

Fox Keller, E. (2002). *The century of the gene* Cambridge, MA: Harvard University Press.

Fransson, P., Skiöld, B., Horsch, S., Nordell, A., Blennow, M., Lagercrantz, H., & Aden, U. (2007). Resting-state networks in the infant brain. *Proceedings of the National Academy of Sciences, USA, 104,* 15531–15536.

Fray, P. J., Robbins, T. W., & Sahakian, B. J. (1996). Neuropsychiatric applications of CANTAB. *International Journal of Geriatric Psychiatry, 11,* 329–336.

Friederici, A. D. (2008). Brain correlates of language processing during the first years of life. In C. A. Nelson & M. Luciana (Eds.), *Handbook of developmental cognitive neuroscience* (2nd ed., pp. 117–126). Cambridge, MA: MIT Press.

Friederici, A. D. (2009). Pathways to language: Fiber tracts in the human brain. *Trends in Cognitive Sciences, 13,* 175–181.

Friesen, C. K., & Kingstone, A. (1998). The eyes have it! Reflexive orienting is triggered by nonpredictive gaze. *Psychonomic Bulletin and Review, 5,* 490–495.

Friston, K. J., & Price, C. J. (2001). Dynamic representation and generative models of brain function. *Brain Research Bulletin, 54* (3), 275–285.

Frith, U. (2003). *Autism: Explaining the enigma* (2nd ed.). Oxford: Blackwell.

Frith, U., & Frith, C. D. (2003). Development and neurophysiology of mentalising. *Philosophical Transactions of the Royal Society of London, Series B, Biological Sciences, 358,* 459–473.

Frost, D. O. (1990). Sensory processing by novel, experimentally induced crossmodal circuits. *Annals of the New York Academy of Sciences, 608,* 92–109.

Fulford, J., Vadeyar, S. H., Dodampahala, S. H., Moore, R. J., Young, P., Baker, P. N. et al. (2003). Fetal brain activity in response to visual stimulus. *Human Brain Mapping, 20,* 239–245.

Funahashi, S., Bruce, C. J., & Goldman-Rakic, P. S. (1989). Mnemonic coding of visual space in the monkey's dorsolateral prefrontal cortex. *Journal of Neurophysiology, 61* (2), 331–349.

Funahashi, S., Bruce, C. J., & Goldman-Rakic, P. S. (1990). Visuospatial coding in primate prefrontal neurons revealed by oculomotor paradigms. *Journal of Neurophysiology, 63* (4), 814–831.

Galaburda, A. M., & Bellugi, U. (2000). Multi-level analysis of cortical neuroanatomy in Williams syndrome. *Journals of Cognitive Neuroscience, 12* (Supplement), 74–88.

Galaburda, A. M., & Pandya, D. N. (1983). The intrinsic architectonic and connectional organization of the superior temporal region of the rhesus monkey. *Journal of Comparative Neurology, 221,* 169–184.

Galaburda, A. M., Sherman, G. F., Rosen, G. D., Aboitiz, F., & Geschwind, N. (1985). Development dyslexia: Four consecutive patients with cortical anomalies. *Annals of Neurology, 18,* 222–232.

Galaburda, A. M., Wang, P. P., Bellugi, U., & Rosen, M. (1994). Cytoarchitectonic anomalies in a genetically based disorder: Williams syndrome. *Cognitive Neuroscience and Neuropsychology, Neuroreport, 5,* 753–757.

Gallistel, C. R. (1990). *The organization of learning.* Cambridge, MA: MIT Press.

Galvan, A., Hare, T., Voss, H., Glover, G., & Casey, B. J. (2006). Risk-taking and the adolescent brain: Who is at risk? *Developmental Science, 10,* F8–F14.

Gathers, A. D., Bhatt, R., Corbly, C. R., Farley, A. B., & Joseph, J. E. (2004). Developmental shifts in cortical loci for face and object recognition. *NeuroReport, 15,* 1549–1553.

Gauthier, I., & Nelson, C. (2001). The development of face expertise. *Current Opinion in Neurobiology, 11,* 219–224.

Gauthier, I., Tarr, M. J., Anderson, A. W., Skudlarski, P., & Gore, J. C. (1999). Activation of the middle fusiform "face area" increases with expertise in recognizing novel objects. *Nature Neuroscience, 2,* 568–573.

Gazzaniga, M. (1983). Right-hemisphere damage following brain bisection. *American Psychologist, 25,* 549.

Geschwind, N., & Behan, P. (1982). Left-handedness: Association with immune disease, migraine and developmental learning disorder. *Proceedings of the National Academy of Sciences of the United States of America, 79,* 5097–5100.

Geschwind, N., & Galaburda, A. (1987). *Cerebral lateralization: Biological mechanisms, associations, and pathology.* Cambridge, MA: MIT Press.

Geschwind, N., & Levitsky, W. (1968). Human brain: Left–right asymmetries in temporal speech region. *Science, 161* (837), 186–187.

Gibson, J. J. (1979). *The ecological approach to visual perception.* Boston: Houghton Mifflin.

Giedd, J. N., Blumenthal, J., Jeffries, N. O., Castellanos, F. X., Lui, H., Zijdenbos., A., Paus, T., et al. (1999). Brain development during childhood and adolescence: A longitudinal MRI study. *Nature Neuroscience, 2,* 861–863.

Gilbert, C., & Sigman, M. (2007). Brain states: Top-down influences in sensory processing. *Neuron, 54,* 677–696.

Gilles, F. H., Shankle, W., & Dooling, E. C. (1983). Myelinated tracts: Growth patterns. In F. H. Gilles, A. Leviton, & E. C. Dooling (Eds.), *The developing human brain: Growth and epidemiological neuropathology* (pp. 117–183). Boston: John Wright-PSG.

Gilmore, R. O., & Johnson, M. H. (1995). Working memory in infancy: Six-month-olds' performance on two versions of the oculomotor delayed response task. *Journal of Experimental Child Psychology, 59,* 397–418.

Gilmore, R. O., & Johnson, M. H. (1997). Egocentric action in early infancy: Spatial frames of reference for saccades. *Psychological Science, 8,* 224–230.

Gogtay, N., Giedd, J. N., Lusk, L., Hayashi, K. M., Greenstein, D., Vaituzis, C. et al. (2004). Dynamic mapping of human cortical development during childhood through early adulthood. *Proceedings of the National Academy of Science, USA, 101,* 8174–8179.

Golarai, G., Ghahrmani, D. G., Whitfield-Gabrieli, S., Reiss, A., Eberhardt, J. L., Gabrieli, D. E. et al. (2007). Differential development of high-level visual cortex correlates with category-specific recognition memory. *Nature Neuroscience, 10,* 512–522.

Goldman-Rakic, P. S. (1987). Development of cortical circuitry and cognitive function. *Child Development, 58,* 601–622.

Goldman-Rakic, P. S. (1994). Introduction. In G. Dawson & K. W. Fischer (Eds.), *Human behavior and the developing brain* (pp. 1–2). New York: Guilford Press.

Goldman-Rakic, P. S., & Brown, R. M. (1982). Postnatal development of monoamine content and synthesis in the cerebral cortex of rhesus monkeys. *Brain Research, 256,* 339–349.

Gopnik, M. (1990). Feature-blind grammar and dysphasia. *Nature, 344,* 715.

Goren, C. C., Sarty, M., & Wu, P. Y. K. (1975). Visual following and pattern discrimination of face-like stimuli by newborn infants. *Pediatrics, 56,* 544–549.

Gottlieb, G. (1992). *Individual development and evolution.* New York: Oxford University Press.

Gottlieb, G. (2007). Probabilistic epigenesis. *Developmental Science, 10,* 1–11.

Greenberg, F. (1990). Introduction to special issue on Williams syndrome. *American Journal of Medical Genetics Supplement, 6,* 85–88.

Greenough, W. T., Black, J. E., & Wallace, C. S. (2002). Experience and brain development. In M. H. Johnson, Y. Munakata, & R. Gilmore (Eds.), *Brain development and cognition: A reader* (2nd ed., pp. 186–216). Oxford: Blackwell.

Grice, S. J., Halit, H., Farroni, T., Baron-Cohen, S., Bolton, P., & Johnson, M. H. (2005). Neural correlates of eye-gaze detection in young children with autism. *Cortex, 41,* 342–353.

Grill-Spector, K., Kushnir, T., Edelman, S., Avidan, G., Itzchak, Y., & Malach, R. (1998). Differential processing of objects under various viewing conditions in the human lateral occipital complex. *Neuron, 24* (1), 187–203.

Grossmann, T., Johnson, M. H., Farroni, T., & Csibra, G. (2007). Social perception in the infant brain: Gamma oscillatory activity in response to eye gaze. *Social Cognitive & Affective Neuroscience, 2*, 284–291.

Grossmann, T., Johnson, M. H., Lloyd-Fox, S., Blasi, A., Deligianni, F., Elwell, C., & Csibra, G. (2008). Early cortical specialization for face-to-face communication in human infants. *Proceedings of the Royal Society B, 275*, 2803–2811.

Guitton, H. A., Buchtel, H. A., & Douglas, R. M. (1985). Frontal lobe lesions in man cause difficulties in suppressing reflexive glances and in generating goal-directed saccades. *Experimental Brain Research, 58*, 455–472.

Gunnar, M. (2001). Effects of early deprivation: Findings from orphanage-reared infants and children. In C. A. Nelson & M. Luciana (Eds.), *Handbook of developmental cognitive neuroscience* (pp. 617–630). Cambridge, MA: MIT Press.

Guzetta, A., Pecini, C., Biagi, L., Tosetti, M., Brizzolara, D., Chilosi, A., Cipriani, P., Petacchi, E., & Cioni, G. (2008). Language organization in left perinatal stroke. *Neuropediatrics, 39*, 157–163.

Hackman, D. A., & Farah, M. J. (2009). Socioeconomic status and the developing brain. *Trends in Cognitive Neuroscience, 13*, 65–73.

Haith, M. M., & Benson, J. B. (1998). Infant cognition. In D. Kuhn & R. Siegler (Eds.), *Handbook of child psychology: Cognition, perception, and language* (5th ed., Vol. 2, pp. 199–254). New York: Wiley.

Haith, M. M., Hazan, C., & Goodman, G. S. (1988). Expectation and anticipation of dynamic visual events by 3.5-month-old babies. *Child Development, 59*, 467–479.

Halit, H., de Haan, M., & Johnson, M. H. (2003). Cortical specialisation for face processing: Face-sensitive event-related potential components in 3- and 12-month-old infants. *NeuroImage, 19*, 1180–1193.

Halit, H., Csibra, G., Volein, A., & Johnson, M. H. (2004). Face-sensitive cortical processing in early infancy. *Journal of Child Psychology and Psychiatry, 45*, 1228–1234.

Hallett, P. E. (1978). Primary and secondary saccades to goals defined by instructions. *Vision Research, 18*, 1270–1296.

Hamasaki, T., Leingartner, A., Ringstedt, T., & O'Leary, D. D. M. (2004). EMX2 regulates sizes and positioning of the primary sensory and motor areas in neocortex by direct specification of cortical progenitors. *Neuron, 43*, 359–372.

Happé, F. (1994). *Autism: An introduction to psychological theory*. London: UCL Press.

Happé, F., Ronald, A., & Plomin, R. (2006). Time to give up on a single explanation of autism. *Nature Neuroscience, 9*, 1218–1220.

Hari, R., Forss, N., Avikainen, S., Kirveskari, E., Salenius, S., & Rizzolatti, G. (1998). Activation of human primary motor cortex during action observation: A neuromagnetic study. *Proceedings of National Academy of Sciences, USA, 95*, 15061–15065.

Hari, R., & Salmelin, R. (1997). Human cortical oscillations: A neuromagnetic view through the skull. *Trends in Neuroscience, 20*, 44–49.

Hartshorn, K., Rovee-Collier, C., Gerhardstein, P., Bhatt, R. S., Wondoloski, T. L., Klein, P., Glich, J., Wurtzel, M., & Campos-de-Carvalho, M. (1998). The ontogeny of long-term memory over the first year and a half of life. *Developmental Psychobiology, 32*, 69–89.

Hauser, M. D., MacNeilage, P., & Ware, M. (1996). Numerical representations in primates. *Proceedings of the National Academy of Sciences of the United States of America, 93*, 1514–1517.

Haxby, J. V., Gobbini, M. I., Furey, M. L., Ishai, A., Schouten, J. L., & Pietrini, P. (2001). Distributed and overlapping representations of faces and objects in ventral temporal cortex. *Science, 293,* 2425–2430.

Heckman, J. J. (2007). The economics, technology and neuroscience of human capability formation. *Proceedings of the National Academy of Sciences, 104,* 13250–13255.

Held, R. (1985). Binocular vision: Behavioral and neuronal development. In J. Mehler & R. Fox (Eds.), *Neonate cognition: Beyond the blooming, buzzing confusion* (pp. 37–44). Hillsdale, NJ: Lawrence Erlbaum.

Held, R. (1993). Development of binocular vision revisited. In M. H. Johnson (Ed.), *Brain development and cognition: A reader* (pp. 159–166). Oxford: Blackwell.

Hellige, J. B. (1993). *Hemispheric asymmetry: What's right and what's left.* Cambridge, MA: Harvard University Press.

Henson, R. N., Rylands, A., Ross, E., Vuilleumier, P., & Rugg, M. D. (2004). The effect of repetition lag on electrophysiological and hameodynamic correlates of visual object priming. *Neuroimage, 21,* 1674–1689.

Herbert, M. R., Ziegler, D. A., Makris, N. B., Dakardjiev, A., Hodgson, J., Adrien, K. T. et al. (2003). Larger brain and white matter volumes in children with developmental language disorder. *Developmental Science, 6* (4), F11–F22.

Hernandez, A., & Li, P. (2007). Age of acquisition: Its neural and computational mechanisms. *Psychological Bulletin, 133,* 638–650.

Hillyard, S. A., Mangun, G. R., Woldorff, M. G., & Luck, S. J. (1995). Neural systems mediating selective attention. In M. S. Gazzaniga (Ed.), *The cognitive neurosciences* (pp. 665–681). Cambridge, MA: MIT Press.

Hinde, R. A. (1961). The establishment of parent–offspring relations in birds, with some mammalian analogies. In W. H. Thorpe & O. L. Zangwill (Eds.), *Current problems in animal behaviour* (pp. 175–193). Cambridge: Cambridge University Press.

Hinde, R. A. (1974). *Biological bases of human social behaviour.* New York: McGraw-Hill.

Hinshelwood, J. (1907). Four cases of congenital word-blindness occurring in the same family. *British Medical Journal, 2,* 1229–1232.

Hobson, R. P. (1993). Understanding persons: The role of affect. In S. Baron-Cohen, H. Tager-Flusberg, & D. J. Cohen (Eds.), *Understanding other minds* (pp. 204–227). Oxford: Oxford University Press.

Holmboe, K., Fearon, P. R. M., Csibra, G., Tucker, L. A., & Johnson, M. H. (2008). Freeze-frame: A new infant inhibition task and its relation to frontal cortex tasks during infancy and early childhood. *Journal of Experimental Child Psychology, 100,* 89–114.

Hood, B. (1993). Inhibition of return produced by covert shifts of visual attention in 6-month-old infants. *Infant Behavior and Development, 16,* 245–254.

Hood, B. (1995). Shifts of visual attention in the human infant: A neuroscientific approach. In C. Rovee-Collier & L. Lipsitt (Eds.), *Advances in infancy research* (Vol. 9, pp. 163–216). Norwood, NJ: Ablex.

Hood, B., & Atkinson, J. (1991). *Shifting covert attention in infants.* Paper presented at the Abstracts of the Society for Research in Child Development, Seattle, WA.

Hood, B. M., Willen, J. D., & Driver, J. (1998). Adult's eyes trigger shifts of visual attention in human infants. *Psychological Science, 9,* 131–134.

Hopkins, B., Lems, W., Janssen, B., & Butterworth, G. (1987). Postural and motor asymmetries in newlyborns. *Human Neurobiology, 6,* 153–156.

Hopkins, B., Lems, Y. L., van Wulfften Palthe, T., Hoeksma, J. B., Kardound, O., & Butterworth, G. (1990). Development of head position preference during early infancy: A longitudinal study in the daily life situation. *Developmental Psychobiology*, *23*, 39–53.

Hopkins, B., & Rönnqvist, L. (1998). Human handedness: Developmental and evolutionary perspectives. In F. Simmion & G. Butterworth (Eds.), *The development of sensory, motor, and cognitive capacities in early infancy: From perception to cognition* (pp. 191–236). Hove: Psychology Press.

Horn, G. (1985). *Memory, imprinting, and the brain: An inquiry into mechanisms.* Oxford: Clarendon Press.

Horn, G. (2004). Pathways of the past: The imprint of memory. *Nature Reviews Neuroscience*, *5*, 108–120.

Horn, G., & Johnson, M. H. (1989). Memory systems in the chick: Dissociations and neuronal analysis. *Neuropsychologia*, *27* (Special Issue: Memory), 1–22.

Horn, G., & McCabe, B. J. (1984). Predispositions and preferences: Effects on imprinting of lesions to the chick brain. *Brain Research*, *168*, 361–373.

Huang, Z. J., Di Cristo, G., & Ango, F. (2007). Development of GABA innervation in the cerebral and cerebellar cortices. *Nature Reviews Neuroscience*, *8*, 673–686.

Huffman, K. J., Molnár, Z., Van Dellen, A., Kahn, D. M., Blakemore, C., & Krubitzer, L. (1999). Formation of cortical fields on a reduced cortical sheet. *The Journal of Neuroscience*, *19* (22), 9939–9952.

Huttenlocher, P. R. (1990). Morphometric study of human cerebral cortex development. *Neuropsychologia*, *28*, 517–527.

Huttenlocher, P. R. (1994). Synaptogenesis, synapse elimination, and neural plasticity in human cerebral cortex: Threats to optimal development. In C. A. Nelson (Ed.), *The Minnesota Symposia on Child Psychology* (Vol. 27, pp. 35–54). Hillsdale, NJ: Lawrence Erlbaum.

Huttenlocher, P. R. (2002). Morphometric study of human cerebral cortex development. In M. H. Johnson, Y. Munakata, & R. Gilmore (Eds.), *Brain development and cognition: A reader* (2nd ed., pp. 117–128). Oxford: Blackwell.

Huttenlocher, P. R., & Dabholkar, J. C. (1997). Developmental anatomy of prefrontal cortex. In N. A. Krasnegor, G. R. Lyon, & P. S. Goldman-Rakic (Eds.), *Development of the prefrontal cortex: Evolution, neurobiology, and behavior* (pp. 69–84). Baltimore, MD: Paul. H. Brookes:

Huttenlocher, P. R., de Courten, C., Garey, L. G., & Van der Loos, H. (1982). Synaptogenesis in human visual cortex: Evidence for synapse elimination during normal development. *Neuroscience Letter*, *33*, 247–252.

Hykin, J., Moore, R., Duncan, K., Clare, S., Baker, P., Johnson, I. et al. (1999). Fetal brain activity demonstrated by functional magnetic resonance imaging. *The Lancet*, *354*, 645–646.

Iliescu, B. F., & Dannemiller, J. L. (2008). Brain-behavior relationships in early visual development. In C. A. Nelson and M. Luciana (Eds.), *Handbook of developmental cognitive neuroscience* (2nd ed., pp. 127–146). Cambridge, MA: MIT Press.

Ishai, A., Ungerleider, L. G., Martin, A., Schouten, J. L., & Haxby, J. V. (1999). Distributed representation of objects in the human ventral visual pathway. *Proceedings of the National Academy of Sciences of the United States of America*, *96* (16), 9379–9384.

Jacobs, R. A. (2002). What determines visual cue reliability? *Trends in Cognitive Sciences*, *6*, 345–350.

Jacobs, R. A., Jordan, M. I., & Barto, A. G. (1991). Task decomposition through competition in a modular connectionist architecture: The what and where vision tasks. *Cognitive Science, 15,* 219–250.

Jaffe, J., Stern, D. N., & Perry, J. C. (1973). "Conversational" coupling of gaze behavior in prelinguistic human development. *Journal of Psycholinguistic Research, 2,* 321–329.

Jernigan, T. L., & Bellugi, U. (1994). Neuroanatomical distinctions between Williams and Down syndromes. In S. Broman & J. Grafman (Eds.), *Atypical cognitive deficits in developmental disorder: Implications for brain function* (pp. 57–66). Hillsdale, NJ: Lawrence Erlbaum.

Johannsen, W. (1911). The genotype concept of heredity. *The American Naturalist, 45,* 129–159.

Johnson, M. B., Imamura Kawasawa, Y., Mason, C. E., Krsnik, Z., Coppola, G., Bogdanovic, D. et al. (2009). Functional and evolutionary insights into human brain development through global transcriptome analysis. *Neuron, 62,* 494–509.

Johnson, M. H. (1990). Cortical maturation and the development of visual attention in early infancy. *Journal of Cognitive Neuroscience, 2,* 81–95.

Johnson, M. H. (1994). Visual attention and the control of eye movements in early infancy. In C. Umilta & M. Moscovitch (Eds.), *Attention and performance. XV: Conscious and nonconscious information processing* (pp. 291–310). Cambridge, MA: MIT Press.

Johnson, M. H. (1995). The inhibition of automatic saccades in early infancy. *Developmental Psychobiology, 28,* 281–291.

Johnson, M. H. (2001). Functional brain development in humans. *Nature Reviews Neuroscience, 2,* 475–483.

Johnson, M. H. (2002). The development of visual attention: A cognitive neuroscience perspective. In M. H. Johnson, Y. Munakata, & R. Gilmore (Eds.), *Brain development and cognition: A reader* (pp. 134–150). Oxford: Blackwell.

Johnson, M. H. (2005). Sub-cortical face processing. *Nature Reviews Neuroscience, 6,* 766–774.

Johnson, M. H., & Bolhuis, J. J. (1991). Imprinting, predispositions and filial preference in the chick. In R. J. Andrew (Ed.), *Neural and behavioral plasticity* (pp. 133–156). Oxford: Oxford University Press.

Johnson, M. H., Bolhuis, J. J., & Horn, G. (1985). Interaction between acquired preferences and developing predispositions during imprinting. *Animal Behaviour, 33,* 1000–1006.

Johnson, M. H., de Haan, M., Oliver, A., Smith, W., Hatzakis, H., Tucker, L. A. et al. (2001). Recording and analyzing high-density event-related potentials with infants using the Geodesic Sensor Net. *Developmental Neuropsychology, 19* (3), 295–323.

Johnson, M. H., Dziurawiec, S., Bartrip, J., & Morton, J. (1992). The effects of movement of internal features on infants' preferences for face-like stimuli. *Infant Behavior and Development, 15,* 129–136.

Johnson, M. H., Dziurawiec, S., Ellis, H. D., & Morton, J. (1991). Newborns' preferential tracking of face-like stimuli and its subsequent decline. *Cognition, 40,* 1–19.

Johnson, M. H., Gilmore, R. O., Tucker, L. A., & Minister, S. L. (1996). Cortical development and saccadic control: Vector summation in young infants. *Brain and Cognition, 32,* 237–243.

Johnson, M. H., Halit, H., Grice, S., & Karmiloff-Smith, A. (2002). Neuroimaging of typical and atypical development: A perspective from multiple levels of analysis. *Development and Psychopathology, 14,* 521–536.

Johnson, M. H., & Horn, G. (1986). Is a restricted brain region of domestic chicks involved in the recognition of individual conspecifics? *Behavioural Brain Research, 20,* 109–110.

Johnson, M. H., & Horn, G. (1987). The role of a restricted region of the chick forebrain in the recognition of individual conspecifics. *Behavioural Brain Research, 23,* 269–275.

Johnson, M. H., & Horn, G. (1988). The development of filial preferences in the dark-reared chick. *Animal Behaviour, 36,* 675–683.

Johnson, M. H., & Karmiloff-Smith, A. (1992). Can neural selectionism be applied to cognitive development and its disorders? *New Ideas in Psychology, 10,* 35–46.

Johnson, M.H., Mareschal, D., & Csibra, G. (2008). The development and integration of the dorsal and ventral visual pathways in object processing. In C. A. Nelson & M. Luciana (Eds.), *Handbook of Developmental Cognitive Neuroscience* (2nd ed., pp. 467–478). Cambridge: MIT Press.

Johnson, M. H., & Morton, J. (1991). *Biology and cognitive development: The case of face recognition.* Oxford: Blackwell.

Johnson, M. H., & Munakata, Y. (2005). Processes of change in brain and cognitive development. *Trends in Cognitive Science, 9,* 152–158.

Johnson, M. H., Munakata, Y., & Gilmore, R. (Eds.) (2002). *Brain development and cognition: A reader* (2nd ed.). Oxford: Blackwell.

Johnson, M. H., Posner, M. I., & Rothbart, M. K. (1991). Components of visual orienting in early infancy: Contingency learning, anticipatory looking, and disengaging. *Journal of Cognitive Neuroscience, 3* (4), 335–344.

Johnson, M. H., & Tucker, L. A. (1996). The development and temporal dynamics of spatial orienting in infants. *Journal of Experimental Child Psychology, 63,* 171–188.

Johnson, M. H., Tucker, L. A., Stiles, J., & Trauner, D. (1998). Visual attention in infants with perinatal brain damage: Evidence of the importance of anterior lesions. *Developmental Science, 1,* 53–58.

Johnson, M. H., & Vecera, S. P. (1996). Cortical differentiation and neurocognitive development: The parcellation conjecture. *Behavioural Processes, 36,* 195–212.

Johnson, M. K., Hashtroudi, S., & Lindsay, D. S. (1993). Source monitoring. *Psychological Bulletin, 114* (1), 3–28.

Johnson, S. P., & Aslin, R. N. (1995). Perception of object unity in 2-month-old infants. *Developmental Psychology, 31,* 739–745.

Johnson, S. P., & Aslin, R. N. (1996). Perception of object unity in young infants: The roles of motion, depth and orientation. *Cognitive Development, 11,* 161–180.

Johnson, S. P., & Nanez, J. (1995). Young infants' perception of object unity in two-dimensional displays. *Infant Behavior & Development, 18,* 133–143.

Johnston, M. V., McKinney, M., & Coyle, J. T. (1979). Evidence for a cholinergic projection to neocortex from neurons in basal forebrain. *Proceedings of the National Academy of Sciences of the United States of America, 76,* 5392–5396.

Johnston, T. D. (1988). Developmental explanation and the ontogeny of birdsong: Nature/nurture redux. *Behavioral and Brain Sciences, 11,* 617–663.

Jonides, J., Smith, E. E., Koeppe, R. A., Awh, E., Minoshima, S., & Mintun, M. A. (1993). Spatial working memory in humans as revealed by PET. *Nature, 363,* 623–625.

Just, M. A., Cherkassky, V. L., Keller, T. A., Kana, R. K., & Minshew, N. J. (2007). Functional and anatomical cortical underconnectivity in autism: Evidence from an fMRI study of an executive function task and corpus callosum morphometry. *Cerebral Cortex, 17,* 951–961.

Kaldy, Z., & Sigala, N. (2004). The neural mechanisms of object working memory: What is where in the infant brain? *Neuroscience and Biobehavioral Reviews, 28,* 113–121.

Kalsbeek, A., Voorn, P., Buijs, R. M., Pool, C. W., & Uylings, H. B. (1988). Development of the dopaminergic innervation in the prefrontal cortex of rat. *Journal of Comparative Neurology, 269,* 58–72.

Kanwisher, N., McDermott, J., & Chun, M. M. (1997). The fusiform face area: A module in human extrastriate cortex specialized for face perception. *The Journal of Neuroscience, 17* (11), 4302–4311.

Karatekin, C. (2001). Developmental disorders of attention. In C. A. Nelson & M. Luciana (Eds.), *Handbook of developmental cognitive neuroscience.* (pp. 561–576). Cambridge, MA: MIT Press.

Karatekin, C. (2008). Eye tracking studies of normative and atypical development. In C. A. Nelson & M. Luciana (Eds.), *Handbook of Developmental Cognitive Neuroscience* (2nd ed., pp. 263–300). Cambridge, MA: MIT Press.

Karmiloff-Smith, A. (1985). Language and cognitive processes from a developmental perspective. *Language and Cognitive Processes, 1,* 61–85.

Karmiloff-Smith, A. (1992). *Beyond modularity: A developmental perspective on cognitive science.* Cambridge, MA: MIT Press/Bradford Books.

Karmiloff-Smith, A. (1998). Development itself is the key to understanding developmental disorders. *Trends in Cognitive Sciences, 2,* 389–398.

Karmiloff-Smith, A. (2008). Research into Williams syndrome: The state of the art. In C. A. Nelson & M. Luciana (Eds.), *Handbook of developmental cognitive neuroscience* (2nd ed., pp. 691–700). Cambridge, MA: MIT Press.

Karmiloff-Smith, A., Grant, J., Ewing, S., Carette, M. J., Metcalfe, K., Donnai, D. et al. (2003). Using case study comparisons to explore genotype/phenotype correlations in Williams syndrome. *Journal of Medical Genetics, 40,* 136–140.

Karmiloff-Smith, A., & Johnson, M. H. (1994). Thinking on one's feet (review of *A dynamic systems approach to the development of cognition and action,* by Esther Thelan and Linda Smith). *Nature, 372,* 53–54.

Karmiloff-Smith, A., Klima, E., Bellugi, U., Grant, J., & Baron-Cohen, S. (1995). Is there a social module? Language, face processing and theory of mind in individuals with Williams syndrome. *Journal of Cognitive Neuroscience, 7,* 196–208.

Kasamatsu, T., & Pettigrew, J. W. (1976). Depletion of brain catecholamines: Failure of monocular dominance shift after monocular conclusion in kittens. *Science, 194,* 206–209.

Kaufman, J., Csibra, G., & Johnson, M. H. (2003). Representing occluded objects in the human infant brain. *Proceedings of the Royal Society B: Biology Letters,* doi: 10.1098/rsbl.2003.0067.

Kaufman, J., Csibra, G., & Johnson, M. H. (2003). Oscillatory activity in the infant brain reflects object maintenance. *Proceedings of National Academy of Sciences USA, 102,* 15271–15274.

Kaufman, J., Mareschal, D., & Johnson, M. H. (2003). Graspability and object processing in infants. *Infant Behavior and Development, 26* (4), 516–528.

Kavsek, M. J. (2002). The perception of static subjective contours in infancy. *Child Development, 73* (2), 331–344.

Kawabata, H., Gyoba, J., Inoue, H., & Ohtsubo, H. (1999). Visual completion of partly occluded grating in infants under one month of age. *Vision Research, 39,* 3586–3591.

Kellman, P. J., & Spelke, E. S. (1983). Perception of partly occluded objects in infancy. *Cognitive Psychology, 15* (4), 483–524.

Kelly, C. A. M., & Garavan, H. (2005). Human functional neuroimaging of brain changes associated with practice. *Cerebral Cortex, 15,* 1089–1102.

Kennedy, H., & Dehay, C. (1993). The importance of developmental timing in cortical specification. *Perspectives on Developmental Neurobiology, 1* (2), 93–99.

Kerszberg, M., Dehaene, S., & Changeux, J.-P. (1992). Stabilization of complex input–output functions in neural clusters formed by synapse selection. *Neural Networks, 5,* 403–413.

Killackey, H. P. (1990). Neocortical expansion: An attempt toward relating phylogeny and ontongeny. *Journal of Cognitive Neuroscience, 2,* 1–17.

Killgore, W. D. S., Oki, M., & Yurgelun-Todd, D. A. (2001). Sex-specific developmental changes in amygdala response to affective faces. *Neuroreport, 12,* 427–433.

Kilner, J. M., & Blakemore, S. J. (2007). How does the mirror neuron system change during development? *Developmental Science, 10,* 524–526.

Kilner, J. M., Vargas, C., Duval, S., Blakemore, S. J., & Sirigu, A. (2004). Motor activation prior to observation of a predicted movement. *Nature Neuroscience, 7,* 1299–1301.

Kingsbury, M. A., & Finlay, B. L. (2001). The cortex in multidimensional space: Where do cortical areas come from? *Developmental Science, 4,* 125–142.

Kinsbourne, M., & Hiscock, M. (1983). The normal and deviant development of functional lateralization of the brain. In M. Haith & J. Campos (Eds.), *Handbook of Child Psychology* (pp. 157–280). New York: Wiley.

Kleiner, K. A. (1993). Specific vs non-specific face recognition device. In B. de Boysson-Bardies, S. de Schonen, P. Jusczyk, P. MacNeilage, & J. Morton (Eds.), *Developmental neurocognition: Speech and face processing in the first year of life* (pp. 103–108). Dordrecht: Kluwer.

Kleinke, C. L. (1986). Gaze and eye contact; A research review. *Psychological Bullatin, 100,* 78–100.

Klima, E., & Bellugi, U. (1979). *The signs of language.* Cambridge, MA: Harvard University Press.

Klingberg, T. (2006). Development of a superior frontal-intraparietal network for visuo-spatial working memory. *Neuropsychologia, 44,* 2171–2177.

Klingberg, T. (2008). White matter maturation and cognitive development during childhood. In C. A. Nelson and M. Luciana (Eds.), *Handbook of developmental cognitive neuroscience* (2nd ed., pp. 237–244). Cambridge, MA: MIT Press.

Klingberg, T., Forssberg, H., & Westerberg, H. (2002). Increased brain activity in frontal and parietal cortex underlies the development of visuospatial working memory capacity during childhood. *Journal of Cognitive Neuroscience, 14,* 1–10.

Kobayashi, C., Glover, G., & Temple, E. (2007). Cultural and linguistic effects on neural bases of "Theory of Mind" in American and Japanese children. *Brain Research, 1164,* 95–107.

Kobayashi, C., Glover, G., & Temple, E. (2008). Switching language switches mind: linguistic effects on developmental neural bases of "Theory of Mind". *Social Cognitive Affective Neuroscience, 3,* 62–70.

Kostović, I., Petanjek, Z., & Judaš, M. (1993). Early areal differentiation of the human cerebral cortex: Entorhinal area. *Hippocampus, 3* (4), 447–458.

Kostović, I., Judaš, M., & Petanjek, Z. (2008). Structural development of the human prefrontal cortex. In C. A. Nelson and M. Luciana (Eds.), *Handbook of developmental cognitive neuroscience* (2nd ed., pp. 213–235). Cambridge, MA: MIT Press.

Kozorovitskiy, Y., & Gould, E. (2008). Adult neurogenesis in the hippocampus. In C. A. Nelson and M. Luciana (Eds.), *Handbook of developmental cognitive neuroscience* (2nd ed., pp. 51–62). Cambridge, MA: MIT Press.

Krubitzer, L. A. (1998). What can monotremes tell us about brain evolution? *Philosophical Transactions of the Royal Society of London, Series B, Biological Sciences, 353,* 1127–1146.

Kuhl, P. K. (2000). A new view of language acquisition. *Proceedings of the National Academy of Science, 97,* 11850–11857.

Kuhl, P. K., Conboy, B. T., Coffey-Corina, S., Padden, D., Fivera-Gaxiola, M., & Nelson, T. (2008). Phonetic learning as a pathway to language: New data and native language magnet theory expanded (NLM-e). *Philosophical Transactions of the Royal Society, B, 363,* 979–1000.

Kuhl, P. K., & Rivera-Gaxiola, M. (2008). Neural substrates of language acquisition. *Annual Reviews of Neuroscience, 31,* 511–534.

Lai, C. S. L., Fisher, S. E., Hurst, J. A., Vargha-Khadem, F., & Monaco, A. P. (2001). A forkhead-domain gene is mutated in a severe speech and language disorder. *Nature, 413,* 519–523.

Langton, S. R. H., & Bruce, V. (1999). Reflexive visual orienting in response to the social attention of others. *Visual Cognition, 6,* 541–567.

Leamey, C. A., Glendining, K. A., Kreiman, G., Kang, N.-D., Wang, K. H., Fassler, R. et al. (2008). Differential gene expression between sensory neocortical areas: potential roles for Ten_m3 and Bc16 in patterning visual and somatosensory pathways. *Cerebral Cortex, 18,* 53–66.

Leonard, C. M., & Eckert, M. A. (2008). Asymmetry and dyslexia. *Developmental Neuropsychology, 33,* 663–681.

Le Grand, R., Mondloch, C. J., Maurer, D., & Brent, H. P. (2001). Early visual experience and face processing. *Nature, 410,* 890.

Lenneberg, E. (1967). *Biological foundations of language.* New York: Wiley.

Leonard, C. M. (2003). Neural substrate of speech and language development. In M. de Haan & M. H. Johnson (Eds.), *The cognitive neuroscience of development* (pp. 127–155). Hove: Psychology Press.

Lewis, T. L., Maurer, D., & Milewski, A. (1979). The development of nasal detection in young infants. *Investigative Opthalmology and Visual Science Supplement, 271.*

Lewkowicz, D. J. (1991). Development of intersensory functions in human infancy: Auditory/visual interactions. In M. J. Salomon Weiss & P. Zelazo (Eds.) *Newborn attention: Biological constraints and the influence of experience* (pp. 308–338). Norwood, NJ: Ablex.

Lewkowicz, D. J., & Turkewitz, G. (1981). Intersensory interaction in newborns: Modification of visual preferences following exposure to sound. *Child Development, 52,* 827–832.

Liégeois, F., Baldeweg, T., Connelly, A., Gadian, D. G., Mishkin, M., & Vargha-Khadem, F. (2003). Language fMRI abnormalities associated with FOXP2 gene mutation. *Nature Neuroscience, 6* (11), 1230–1237.

Liégeois, F., Connelly, A., Helen Cross, J., Boyd, S. G., Gadian, D. G., Vargha-Khadem, F., & Baldeweg, T. (2004). Language reorganization in children with early onset lesions of the left hemisphere: An fMRI study. *Brain, 127,* 1229–1236.

Lipsitt, L. P. (1990). Learning processes in the human newborn: Sensitization, habituation, and classical conditioning. *Annals of the New York Academy of Sciences, 608,* 113–127.

Lipton, J. S., & Spelke, E. (2003). Origins of number sense: Large-number discrimination in human infants. *Psychological Science, 14* (5), 396–401.

Livingstone, M. S., Rosen, G. D., Drislane, F. W., & Galaburda, A. M. (1991). Physiological and anatomical evidence for a magnocellular defect in developmental dyslexia. *Proceedings of the National Academy of Sciences of the United States of America, 88*, 7943–7947.

Lloyd-Fox, S., Blasi, A., & Elwell, C. E. (2010). Illuminating the developing brain: The past, present and future of functional near infrared spectroscopy. *Neuroscience and Biobehavioural Reviews, 34* (3), 269–284.

Lloyd-Fox, S., Blasi, A., Volein, A., Everdell, N., Elwell, C., & Johnson, M. H. (2009). Social perception in infancy: A near infrared spectroscopy study. *Child Development, 80*, 986–999.

Lorenz, K. (1965). *Evolution and the modification of behavior.* Chicago: University of Chicago Press.

Luciana, M. (2003). The neural and functional development of human prefrontal cortex. In M. de Haan & M. H. Johnson (Eds.), *The cognitive neuroscience of development* (pp. 157–174). Hove, UK: Psychology Press.

Luciana, M., & Nelson, C. A. (1998). The functional emergence of prefrontally-guided working memory systems in four-to-eight year-old children. *Neuropsychologia, 36* (3), 273–293.

Luciana, M., & Nelson, C.A. (2000). Neurodevelopmental assessment of cognitive function using the Cambridge Neuropsychological Testing Automated Battery (CANTAB): Validation and future goals. In M. Ernst & J. M. Rumsey (Eds.), *Functional neuroimaging in child psychiatry* (pp. 379–397). Cambridge: Cambridge University Press.

Luna, B., Thulborn, K. R., Munoz, D. P., Merriam, E. P., Garver, K. E., Minshew, N. J. et al. (2001). Maturation of widely distributed brain function subserves cognitive development. *NeuroImage, 13* (5), 786–793.

Luna, B., Garver, K. E., Urban, T. A., Lazar, N. A., & Sweeney, J. A. (2004). Maturation of cognitive processes from late childhood to adulthood. *Child Development, 75*, 1357–1372.

Lutchmaya, S., Baron-Cohen, S., & Raggatt, P. (2002a). Foetal testosterone and eye contact in 12-month-old human infants. *Infant Behavior and Development, 25* (3), 327–335.

Lutchmaya, S., Baron-Cohen, S., & Raggatt, P. (2002b). Foetal testosterone and vocabulary size in 18- and 24-month-old infants. *Infant Behavior and Development, 24* (4), 418–424.

MacPhail, E. M. (1982). *Brain and intelligence in vertebrates.* Oxford: Clarendon Press.

MacSweeney, M., Capek, C. M., Campbell, R., & Woll, B. (2008). The signing brain: The neurobiology of sign language. *Trends in Cognitive Sciences, 12*, 438–440.

Maguire, E. A., Vargha-Khadem, F., & Mishkin, M. (2001). The effects of bilateral hippocampal damage on fMRI regional activations and interactions during memory retrieval. *Brain, 124*, 1156–1170.

Mallamaci, A., Muzio, L., Chan, C. H., Parnavelas, J., & Boncinelli, E. (2000). Area identity shifts in the early cerebral cortex of Emx2 −/− mutant mice. *Nature Neuroscience, 3*, 679–686.

Mancini, J., Casse-Perrot, C., Giusiano, B., Girard, N., Camps, R., Deruelle, C., et al. (1998). Face processing development after a perinatal unilateral brain lesion. *Human Frontiers Science Foundation Developmental Cognitive Neuroscience Technical Report Series* (98.6).

Marcus, G. F., & Fisher, S. E. (2003). FOXP2 in focus: What can genes tell us about speech and language? *Trends in Cognitive Sciences, 7* (6), 257–262.

Marcusson, J. O., Morgan, D. G., Winblad, B., & Finch, C. E. (1984). Serotonin-2 binding sites in human frontal cortex and hippocampus: Selective loss of S-2 A sites with age. *Brain Research, 311,* 51–56.

Mareschal, D., & Johnson, M. H. (2003). The "what" and "where" of infant object representations. *Cognition, 88,* 259–276.

Mareschal, D., Johnson, M. H., Sirois, S., Spratling, M., Thomas, M., & Westermann, G. (2007). *Neuroconstructivism: How the brain constructs cognition.* Oxford: Oxford University Press.

Mareschal, D., Plunkett, K., & Harris, P. (1999). A computational and neuropsychological account of object-oriented behaviours in infancy. *Developmental Science, 2,* 306–317.

Mareschal, D., & Thomas, M. S. C. (2007). Computational modelling in developmental psychology. *IEEE Transactions on Evolutionary Computation (Special Issue on Autonomous Mental Development), 11,* 137–150.

Marin-Padilla, M. (1990). The pyramidal cell and its local-circuit interneurons: A hypothetical unit of the mammalian cerebral cortex. *Journal of Cognitive Neuroscience, 2,* 180–194.

Markham, J., & Greenough, W. T. (2004). Experience-driven brain plasticity: Beyond the synapse. *Neuron Glia Biology, 1,* 351–364.

Marler, P. (2002). The instinct to learn. In M. H. Johnson, Y. Munakata, & R. Gilmore (Eds.), *Brain development and cognition: A reader* (2nd ed., pp. 305–330). Oxford: Blackwell.

Marr, D. (1982). *Vision.* San Francisco: W.H. Freeman.

Matsuzawa, J. (1985). Colour naming and classification in a chimpanzee (Pan troglodytes). *Journal of Human Evolution, 14,* 283–291.

Matsuzawa, T. (1991). Nesting cups and metatools in chimpanzees. *Behavioral and Brain Sciences, 14,* 570–571.

Matsuzawa, T. (2007). Comparative cognitive development. *Development Science, 10,* 97–103.

Maurer, D. (1985). Infants' perception of facedness. In T. N. Field & N. Fox (Eds.), *Social perception in infants* (pp. 73–100). Hillsdale, NJ: Ablex.

Maurer, D. (1993). Neonatal synesthesia: Implications for the processing of speech and faces. In B. de Boysson-Bardies, S. de Schonen, P. Jusczyk, P. McNeilage, & J. Morton (Eds.), *Developmental neurocognition: Speech and face processing in the first year of life* (pp. 109–124). Dordrecht: Kluwer.

Maurer, D., & Barrera, M. (1981). Infants' perception of natural and distorted arrangements of a schematic face. *Child Development, 47,* 523–527.

Maurer, D., Lewis, T. L., & Mondloch, C. J. (2008). Plasticity of the visual system. In C. A. Nelson and M. Luciana (Eds.), *Handbook of developmental cognitive neuroscience* (2nd ed., pp. 415–438). Cambridge, MA: MIT Press.

Maurer, U., Brem, S., Bucher, K., & Brandeis, D. (2005). Emerging neurophysiological specialization for letter strings. *Journal of Cognitive Neuroscience, 17,* 1532–1552.

Maurer, U., Brem, S., Bucher, K., Kranz, F., Benz, R., Halder, P., Steinhausen, H.-C., & Brandeis, D. (2007). Impaired tuning of a fast occipito-temporal response to print in dyslexic children learning to read. *Brain, 130,* 3200–3210.

Maurer, U., Brem, S., Kranz, F., Bucher, K., Benz, R., Halder, P., Steinhausen, H.-C., & Brandels, D. (2006). Coarse neural tuning for print peaks when children learn to read. *NeuroImage, 33,* 749–758.

Maylor, E. A. (1985). Facilitory and inhibitory components of orienting in visual space. In M. I. Posner & O. M. Marin (Eds.), *Attention and performance XI* (pp. 189–204). Hillsdale, NJ: Erlbaum.

McCabe, B. J., Cipolla-Neto, J., Horn, G., & Bateson, P. P. G. (1982). Amnesic effects of bilateral lesions placed in the hyperstriatum ventrale of the chick after imprinting. *Experimental Brain Research*, *48*, 13–21.

McDonough, L., Mandler, J. M., McKee, R. D., & Squire, L. R. (1995). The deferred imitation task as a nonverbal measure of declarative memory. *Proceedings of the National Academy of Sciences, USA*, *92*, 7580–7584.

McManus, I. C., & Bryden, M. P. (1991). Geschwind's theory of cerebral lateralization: Developing a formal causal model. *Psychological Bulletin*, *110*, 237–253.

McManus, I. C., & Bryden, M. P. (1993). The neurobiology of handedness, language and cerebral dominance: A model for the molecular genetics of behavior. In M. H. Johnson (Ed.) *Brain development and cognition: A reader*. Oxford: Blackwell.

Meaburn, E., Dale, P. S., Craig, I. W., & Plomin, R. (2002). Language-impaired children: No sign of the FOXP2 mutation. *Neuroreport*, *13*, 1075–1077.

Meek, J. H. (2002). Basic principles of optical imaging and application to the study of infant development. *Developmental Science*, *5* (3), 371–380.

Meek, J. H., Firbank, M., Elwell, C. E., Atkinson, J., Braddick, O., & Wyatt, J. S. (1998). Regional hemodynamic responses to visual stimulation in awake infants. *Paediatric Research*, *43*, 840–843.

Mehler, J., Nespor, M., Gervain, J., Endress, A., & Shukla, M. (2008). Mechanisms of language acquisition: Imaging and behavioural evidence. In C. A. Nelson & M. Luciana (Eds.), *Handbook of developmental cognitive neuroscience* (2nd ed. pp. 325–336). Cambridge, MA: MIT Press.

Meltzoff, A. N., & Borton, R. W. (1979). Intermodal matching by human neonates. *Nature*, *282*, 403–404.

Meltzoff, A. N., & Moore, M. K. (1977). Imitation of facial and manual gestures by human neonates. *Science*, *198*, 74–78.

Menon, V., Boyett-Anderson, J. M., & Reiss, A. L. (2005). Maturation of medial temporal lobe response and connectivity during memory encoding. *Brain Research Cognitive Brain Research*, *25*, 379–385.

Mercure, E., Ashwin, E., Dick, F., Halit, H., Auyeung, B., Baron-Cohen, S. et al. (2009). IQ, fetal testosterone and individual variability in children's functional lateralization. *Neuropsychologia*, *47*, 2537–2543.

Mercure, E., Dick, F., Halit, H., Kaufman, J., & Johnson, M. H. (2008). Differential lateralization for words and faces: category or psychophysics? *Journal of Cognitive Neuroscience*, *20*, 2070–2087.

Merigan, W., & Maunsell, J. (1993). How parallel are the primate visual pathways? *Annual Review of Neuroscience*, *16*, 369–402.

Merzenich, M. M., Wright, B. A., Jaenkins, W., Xerri, C., Byl, N., Miller, S. L., et al. (2002). Cortical plasticity underlying perceptual, motor, and cognitive skill development: Implications for neurorehabilitation. In M. H. Johnson, Y. Munakata, & R. Gilmore (Eds.), *Brain development and cognition: A reader* (2nd ed. pp. 292–304). Oxford: Blackwell.

Meulemans, T., Van der Linden, M., & Perruchet, P. (1998). Implicit sequence learning in children. *Journal of Experimental Child Psychology*, *69*, 199–221.

Michel, G. F. (1981). Right-handedness: A consequence of infant supine head orientation preference? *Science*, *212*, 685–687.

Mills, D. L., Coffey-Corina, S. A., & Neville, H. J. (1993). Language acquisition and cerebral specialization in 20-month-old infants. *Journal of Cognitive Neuroscience*, *5*, 317–334.

Mills, D. L., & Conboy, B. T. (2009). Early communicative development and the social brain. In M. de Haan & M. R. Gunnar (Eds.), *Handbook of developmental social neuroscience.* New York: Guilford Press.

Milner, A. D., & Goodale, M. A. (1995). *The visual brain in action.* Oxford: Oxford University Press.

Milner, B. (1982). Some cognitive effects of frontal-lobe lesions in man. *Philosophical Transactions of the Royal Society of London, Series B, Biological Sciences, 298,* 211–226.

Minshew, N. J., & Williams, D. L. (2007). The new neurobiology of autism: Cortex, connectivity, and neuronal organization. *Archives of Neurology, 64,* 945–950.

Mishkin, M., Suzuki, W. A., Gadian, D. G., & Vargha-Khadem, F. (1997). Hierarchical organization of cognitive memory. *Philosophical Transactions of the Royal Society, London B Biological Sciences, 352,* 1461–1467.

Miyashita-Lin, E. M., Hevner, R., Wassarman, K. M., Martinez, S., & Rubenstein, J. L. (1999). Early neocortial regionalization in the absence of thalamic innervation. *Science, 285,* 906–909.

Molnar, Z., & Blakemore, C. (1991). Lack of regional specificity for connections formed between thalamus and cortex in coculture. *Nature, 351,* 475–477.

Moore, R. J., Vadeyar, S. H., Fulford, J., Tyler, D. J., Gribben, C., Baker, P. N., et al. (2001). Antenatal determination of fetal brain activity in response to an acoustic stimulus using functional magnetic resonance imaging. *Human Brain Mapping, 12,* 94–99.

Morton, J., Mehler, J., & Jusczyk, P. W. (1984). On reducing language to biology. *Cognitive Neuropsychology, 1,* 83–116.

Mosconi, M. W., Mack, P. B., McCarthy, G., & Pelphrey, K. A. (2005). Taking an intentional stance on eye gaze shifts: A functional neuroimaging study of social perception in children. *Neuroimage, 27,* 247–252.

Munakata, Y., McClelland, J. L., Johnson, M. H., & Siegler, R. S. (1997) Rethinking infant knowledge: Toward an adaptive process account of successes and failures in object permanence tasks. *Psychological Review, 104,* 686–713.

Munakata, Y., Stedron, J. M., Chatham, C. H., & Kharitonova, M. (2008). Neural network models of cognitive development. In C. A. Nelson & M. Luciana (Eds.), *Handbook of developmental cognitive neuroscience* (2nd ed., pp. 367–382). Cambridge, MA: MIT Press.

Nagy, Z., Westerberg, H., & Klingberg, T. (2004). Maturation of white matter is associated with the development of cognitive functions during childhood. *Journal of Cognitive Neuroscience, 16,* 1227–1233.

Nelson, C. (1994). Neural correlates of recognition memory in the first postnatal year. In G. Dawson & K. Fischer (Eds.), *Human behavior and the developing brain* (pp. 269–313). New York: Guilford Press.

Nelson, C. A. (1995). The ontogeny of human memory: A cognitive neuroscience perspective. *Developmental Psychology, 31,* 723–738.

Nelson, C. A. (2003). The development of face recognition reflects an experience-expectant and activity-dependent process. In O. Pascalis & A. Slater (Eds.), *The development of face processing in infancy and early childhood: Current perspectives* (pp. 79–98). New York: Nova Science Publishers.

Nelson, C. A., de Haan, M., & Thomas, K. M. (2006). *Neuroscience and cognitive development: The role of experience and the developing brain.* New York: John Wiley & Sons.

Nelson, C. A., & Luciana, M. (Eds.) (2008). *Handbook of developmental cognitive neuroscience* (2nd ed.). Cambridge, MA: MIT Press.

Nelson, C. A., & Ludemann, P. M. (1989). Past, current and future trends in infant face perception research. *Canadian Journal of Psychology, 43*, 183–198.

Nelson, C. A., & Webb, S. J. (2003). A cognitive neuroscience perspective on early memory development. In M. de Haan & M. H. Johnson (Eds.), *The cognitive neuroscience of development* (pp. 99–126). Hove: Psychology Press.

Nelson, E. E., Leibenluft, E., McClure, E. B., & Pine, D. S. (2005). The social re-orientation of adolescence: a neuroscience perspective on the process and its relation to psychopathology. *Psychological Medicine, 35*, 163–174.

Neville, H. J., & Bavelier, D. (2002). Specificity and plasticity in neurocognitive development in humans. In M. H. Johnson, Y. Munakata, & R. Gilmore (Eds.), *Brain development and cognition: A reader* (2nd ed., pp. 251–270). Oxford: Blackwell.

Neville, H. J., Bavelier, D., Corina, D., Rauschecker, J. P., Karni, A., Lalwani, A., et al. (1998). Cerebral organization for language in deaf and hearing subjects: Biological constrains and effects of experience. *Proceedings of the National Academy of Sciences of the United States of America, 95*, 922–929.

Newsome, W. T., Wurtz, R. H., & Komatsu, H. (1988). Relation of cortical areas MT and MST to pursuit eye movements. II. Differentiation of retinal from extraretinal inputs. *Journal of Neurophysiology, 60* (2), 604–620.

Nowakowski, R. S. (1987). Basic concepts of CNS development. *Child Development, 58*, 568–595.

Nowakowski, R. S., & Hayes, N.L. (2002). General principles of CNS development. In M. H. Johnson Y. Munakata, & R. Gilmore (Eds.), *Brain development and cognition: A reader* (2nd ed., pp. 57–82). Oxford: Blackwell.

O'Hare, E. D., & Sowell, E. R. (2008). Imaging human developmental changes in the grey and white matter of the human brain. In C. A. Nelson & M. Luciana (Eds.), *Handbook of developmental cognitive neuroscience* (2nd ed., 23–38). Cambridge, MA: MIT Press.

O'Leary, D. D. M. (2002). Do cortical areas emerge from a protocortex? In M. H. Johnson, Y. Munakata, & R. O. Gilmore (Eds.), *Brain development and cognition: A reader* (pp. 217–230). Oxford: Blackwell.

O'Leary, D. D. M., & Nakagawa, Y. (2002). Patterning centers, regulatory genes and extrinsic mechanisms controlling arealization of the neocortex. *Current Opinion in Neurobiology, 12*, 14–25.

O'Leary, D. D. M., & Stanfield, B. B. (1985). Occipital cortical neurons with transient pyramidal tract axons extend and maintain collaterals to subcortical but not intracortical targets. *Brain Research, 336*, 326–333.

O'Leary, D. D. M., & Stanfield, B. B. (1989). Selective elimination of axons extended by developing cortical neurons is dependent on regional locale: Experiments utilizing fetal cortical transplants. *Journal of Neuroscience, 9*, 2230–2246.

O'Reilly, R. C. (1998). Six principles for biologically-based computational models of cortical cognition. *Trends in Cognitive Sciences, 2*, 455–462.

O'Reilly, R. C. (2006). Biologically based computational models of high-level cognition. *Science, 314*, 91–94.

O'Reilly, R., & Johnson, M. H. (1994). Object recognition and sensitive periods: A computational analysis of visual imprinting. *Neural Computation, 6*, 357–390.

O'Reilly, R., & Johnson, M. H. (2002). Object recognition and sensitive periods: A computational analysis of visual imprinting. In M. H. Johnson, Y. Munakata, & R. Gilmore (Eds.), *Brain development and cognition: A reader* (2nd ed., pp. 392–414). Oxford: Blackwell.

Ofen, N., Kao, Y. K., Sokol-Hessner, P., Kim, H., Whitfield-Gabrieli, S., & Gabrieli, J. (2007). Development of the declarative memory system in the human brain. *Nature Neuroscience, 10*, 1198–1205.

Ohnishi, T., Moriguchi, Y., Matsuda, H., Mori, T., Hirakata, M., Imabayashi, E., et al. (2004). The neural network for the mirror system and mentalizing in normally developed children: An fMRI study. *Neuroreport, 15*, 1483–1487.

Olesen, P. J., Nagy, Z., Westerberg, H., & Klingberg, T. (2003). Combined analysis of DTI and fMRI data reveals a joint maturation of white and grey matter in a fronto-parietal network. *Cognitive Brain Research, 18*, 48–57.

Olesen, P. J., Westerberg, H., & Klingberg, T. (2004). Increased prefrontal and parietal activity after training of working memory. *Nature Neuroscience, 7*, 75–79.

Oliver, A., Johnson, M. H., Karmiloff-Smith, A., & Pennington, B. (2000). Deviations in the emergence of representations: A neuroconstructivist framework for analysing developmental disorders. *Developmental Science, 3*, 1–23.

Oliver, A., Johnson, M. H., & Shrager, J. (1996). The emergence of hierarchical clustered representations in a Hebbian neural network model that simulates aspects of development in the neocortex. *Network: Computation in Neural Systems, 7*, 291–299.

Olson, E. A., & Luciana, M. (2008). The development of prefrontal cortex functions in adolescence: Theoretical models and a possible dissociation of dorsal versus ventral subregions. In C. A. Nelson & M. Luciana (Eds.), *Handbook of developmental cognitive neuroscience* (2nd ed., pp. 575–590). Cambridge, MA: MIT Press.

Overman, W., Bachevalier, J., Turner, M., & Peuster, A. (1992). Object recognition versus object discrimination: Comparison between human infants and infant. *Behavioral Neuroscience, 106*, 15–29.

Owen, A. M. (1997). Tuning into the temporal dynamics of brain activation using functional magnetic resonance imaging (fMRI). *Trends in Cognitive Sciences, 1* (4), 123–125.

Oyama, S. (2000). *The ontogeny of information: developmental systems and evolution* (2nd rev. ed.). Durham, NC: Duke University Press.

Ozonoff, S., Pennington, B. F., & Rogers, S. J. (1991). Executive function deficits in high-functioning autistic individuals: Relationship to theory of mind. *Journal of Child Psychology and Psychiatry, 32*, 1081–1105.

Pallas, S. L. (2001). Intrinsic and extrinsic factors shaping cortical identity. *Neurosciences, 24*, 417–423.

Pandya, D. N., & Yeterian, E. H. (1990). Architecture and connections of cerebral cortex: Implications for brain evolution and function. In A. B. Scheibel & A. F. Weschsler (Eds.), *Neurobiology of higher cognitive function* (pp. 53–84). New York: Guilford Press.

Parmelee, A. H., & Sigman, M. D. (1983). Perinatal brain development and behavior. In M. M. Haith & J. Campos (Eds.), *Infancy and biological development: Volume II of Mussen's Manual of Child Psychology* (pp. 95–155). New York: Wiley.

Pascalis, O., de Haan, M., & Nelson, C. A. (2002). Is face processing species-specific during the first year of life? *Science, 14*, 199–209.

Pascalis, O., de Haan, M., Nelson, C. A., & de Schonen, S. (1998). Long-term recognition memory for faces assessed by visual paired comparison in 3- and 6-month-old infants *Journal of Experimental Psychology: Learning, Memory and Cognition, 24*, 249–260.

Pascalis, O., & de Schonen, S. (1994). Recognition memory in 3- to 4-day-old human neonates. *Neuroreport*, *5*, 1721–1724.

Pascalis, O., de Schonen, S., Morton, J., Deruelle, C., & Fabre-Grenet, M. (1995). Mother's face recognition by neonates: A replication and an extension. *Infant Behavior and Development*, *18*, 79–85.

Passarotti, A. M., Paul, B. M., Bussiere, J. R., Buxton, R. B., Wong, E. C., & Stiles, J. (2003). The development of face and location processing: An fMRI study. *Developmental Science*, *6* (1), 100–117.

Passarotti, A. M., Smith, J., DeLano, M., & Huang, J. (2007). Developmental differences in the neural bases of the face inversion effect show progressive tuning of face-selective regions to the upright orientation. *NeuroImage*, *34*, 1708–1722.

Paulesu, E., Frith, U., Snowling, M., Gallagher, A., Morton, J., Frackowiak, R. S. J., et al. (1996). Is developmental dyslexia a disconnection syndrome? Evidence from PET scanning. *Brain*, *119*, 143–157.

Pearson, D. A., & Lane, D. M. (1990). Visual attention movements: A developmental study. *Child Development*, *61*, 1779–1795.

Peña, M., Maki, A., Kovacic, D., Dehaene-Lambertz, G., Koizumi, H., Bouquet, F., & Mehler, J. (2003). Sounds and silence: An optical topography study of language recognition at birth. *Proceedings of the National Academy of Sciences of the United States of America*, *100*, 11702–11705.

Pennington, B. (2001). Genetic methods. In C. A. Nelson & M. Luciana (Eds.), *Handbook of developmental cognitive neuroscience* (pp. 149–158). Cambridge, MA: MIT Press.

Pennington, B. (2002). Genes and brain: Individual differences and human universals. In M. H. Johnson, Y. Munakata, & R. Gilmore (Eds.), *Brain development and cognition: A reader* (2nd ed., pp. 494–508). Oxford: Blackwell.

Pennington, B., & Welsh, M. (1995). Neuropsychology and developmental psychopathology. In D. Cicchetti & D. J. Cohen (Eds.), *Developmental psychopathology, Vol. 1: Theory and methods* (pp. 254–290). New York: Wiley.

Pepperberg, I. M. (1987). Acquisition of the same–different concept by an African gray parrot (*Psittacus Erthacus*): Learning with respect to categories of colour, shape and material. *Animal Learning and Behaviour*, *15*, 423–432.

Perisco, A. M., & Bourgeron, T. (2006). Searching for ways out of the autism: genetic, epigenetic and environmental clues. *Trends in Neuroscience*, *29*, 349–358.

Pfeifer, J. H., Lieberman, M. D., & Dapretto, M. (2007). "I know you are but what am I?!": Neural bases of self- and social knowledge retrieval in children and adults. *Journal of Cognitive Neuroscience, 19*, 1323–1337.

Phillips, M. L., Drevets, W. C., Rauch, S. L., & Lane, R. (2003). Neurobiology of emotion perception: The neural basis of emotion perception. *Biological Psychiatry*, *54*, 504–514.

Piaget, J. (1954). *The construction of reality in the child* (M. Cook, Trans.). New York: Basic Books.

Piaget, J. (2002). The epigenetic system and the development of cognitive functions. In M. H. Johnson, Y. Munakata, & R. Gilmore (Eds.), *Brain development and cognition: A reader* (2nd ed., pp. 29–35). Oxford: Blackwell.

Piven, J., Berthier, M. L., Starkstein, S. E., Nehme, E., Pearlson, G., & Folstein, S. (1990). Magnetic resonance imaging evidence for a deficit of cerebral cortical development in autism. *American Journal of Psychiatry*, *147*, 734–739.

Plomin, R., DeFries, J. C., McClearn, G. E., & McGuffin, P. (2008). *Behavioural genetics* (5th ed.). New York: Worth Publishers.

Posner, M. I. (1988). Structures and functions of selective attention. In T. Boll & B. Bryant (Eds.), *Clinical neuropsychology and brain function: Research, measurement, and practice* (pp. 171–202). Washington, DC: American Psychological Association.

Posner, M. I., & Cohen, Y. (1980). Attention and the control of movements. In G. E. Stelmach & J. Roguiro (Eds.), *Tutorials in motor behavior* (pp. 243–258). Amsterdam: North Holland.

Posner, M. I., & Cohen, Y. (1984). Components of visual orienting. In H. Bouma & D. G. Bouwhis (Eds.), *Attention and performance* (pp. 531–556). Hillsdale, NJ: Lawrence Erlbaum.

Posner, M. I., & Petersen, S. E. (1990). The attention system of the human brain. *Annual Review of Neuroscience, 13*, 25–42.

Posner, M. I., Rafal, R. D., Choate, L., & Vaughan, J. (1985). Inhibition of return: Neural basis and function. *Cognitive Neuropsychology, 2*, 211–228.

Posner, M. I., & Rothbart, M. K. (1981). The development of attentional mechanisms. In J. H. Flower (Ed.), *Nebraska symposium on motivation* (pp. 1–51). Lincoln, NE: University of Nebraska Press.

Previc, F. H. (1994). Assessing the GBG model. *Brain & Cognition, 26*, 174–180.

Puce, A., Allison, T., Bentin, S., Gore, J. C., & McCarthy, G. (1998). Temporal cortex activation in human viewing eye and mouth movements. *Journal of Neuroscience, 18*, 2188–2199.

Puce, A., Allison, T., & McCarthy, G. (1999). Electrophysiological studies of human face perception. III: Effects of top-down processing on face-specific potentials. *Cerebral Cortex, 9*, 445–458.

Purpura, D. P. (1975). Normal and aberrant neuronal development in the cerebral cortex of human fetus and young infant. In N. A. Buchwald & M. A. B. Brazier (Eds.), *Brain mechanisms of mental retardation* (pp. 141–169). New York: Academic Press.

Pylyshyn, Z. W., & Storm, R. W. (1988). Tracking multiple independent targets: Evidence for a parallel tracking mechanism. *Spatial Vision, 3*, 179–197.

Quartz, S. R., & Sejnowski, T. J. (1997). The neural basis of cognitive development: A constructivist manifesto. *Behavioral and Brain Sciences, 20*, 537–556.

Rabinowicz, T. (1979). The differential maturation of the human cerebral cortex. In F. Falkner & J. M. Tanner (Eds.), *Human growth, Vol. 3: Neurobiology and nutrition* (pp. 141–169). New York: Plenum Press.

Rafal, R., Smith, J., Krantz, J., Cohen, A., & Brennan, C. (1990). Extrageniculate vision in hemianopic humans: Saccade inhibition by signals in the blind field. *Science, 250*, 1507–1518.

Ragsdale, C. W., & Grove, E. A. (2001). Patterning in the mammalian cerebral cortex. *Current Opinions in Neurobiology, 11*, 50–58.

Rakic, P. (1987). Intrinsic and extrinsic determinants of neocritical parcellation: A radial unit model. In P. Rakic and W. Singer (Eds.), *Neurobiology of neocortex.* Report of the Dahlem workshop on neurobiology of neocortex, Berlin: 17–22 May, John Wiley & Sons.

Rakic, P. (1988). Specification of cerebral cortical areas. *Science, 241*, 170–176.

Rakic, P. (1995). Corticogenesis in human and nonhuman primates. In M. S. Gazzaniga (Ed.), *The cognitive neurosciences* (pp. 127–145). Cambridge, MA: MIT Press.

Rakic, P. (2002). Intrinsic and extrinsic determinants of neocortical parcellation: A radial unit model. In M. H. Johnson, Y. Munakata, & R. Gilmore (Eds.), *Brain development and cognition: A reader* (2nd ed., pp. 57–82). Oxford: Blackwell.

Rakic, P., Bourgeois, J.-P., Eckenhoff, M. F., Zecevic, N., & Goldman-Rakic, P. S. (1986). Concurrent overproduction of synapses in diverse regions of primate cerebral cortex. *Science, 232,* 153–157.

Rauschecker, J. P., & Singer, W. (1981). The effects of early visual experience on the cat's visual cortex and their possible explanation by Hebb synapses. *Journal of Psychology (London), 310,* 215–239.

Ravikumar, B. V., & Sastary, P. I. (1985). Muscarinic cholinergic receptors in human foetal brain: Characterization and ontogeny of [3H] quinuclidinyl benzilate bind sites in frontal cortex. *Journal of Neurochemistry, 44,* 240–246.

Reilly, J., Bates, E., & Marchman, V. (1998). Narrative discourse in children with early focal brain injury. *Brain and Language, 61,* 335–375.

Reiss, A. L., Eliez, J., Schmitt, E., Straus, E., Lai, Z., Jones, W., et al. (2000). Neuratomy of Williams syndrome: A high resolution MRI study. *Journal of Cognitive Neuroscience, 12,* (Supplement) 65–73.

Reynolds, G. D., & Richards, J. E. (2005). Familiarization, attention and recognition memory in infancy: An event-related potential and cortical source localization study. *Developmental Psychology, 41,* 598–615.

Richards, J. E. (1991). Infant eye movements during peripheral visual stimulus localization as a function of central stimulus attention status. *Psychophysiology, 28,* S4.

Richards, J. E. (2001). Attention in young infants: A developmental psychophysiological perspective. In C. A. Nelson & M. Luciana (Eds.), *Handbook of developmental cognitive neuroscience* (pp. 321–338). Cambridge, MA: MIT Press.

Richards, J. E. (2003). The development of visual attention and the brain. In M. de Haan & M. H. Johnson (Eds.), *The cognitive neuroscience of development* (pp. 73–93). Hove: Psychology Press.

Richards, J. E. (2008). Attention in young infants: A developmental psychophysiological perspective. In C. A. Nelson & M. Luciana (Eds.), *Handbook of developmental cognitive neuroscience* (2nd ed., pp. 479–498). Cambridge, MA: MIT Press.

Rivera-Gaxiola, M., Silva-Pereyra, J., & Kuhl, P. K. (2005). Brain potentials to native and non-native speech contrasts in 7- and 11-month-old American infants. *Developmental Science, 8,* 162–172.

Rizzolatti, G., & Craighero, J. (2004). The mirror-neuron system. *Annual Review of Neuroscience, 27,* 169–192.

Rodman, H. R., Skelly, J. P., & Bross, C. G. (1991). Stimulus selectivity and state dependence of activity in inferior temporal cortex in infant monkeys. *Proceedings of the National Academy of Sciences of the United States of America, 88,* 7572–7575.

Roe, A. W., Pallas, S. L., Hahm, J. O., & Sur, M. (1990). A map of visual space induced in primary auditory cortex. *Science, 250,* 818–820.

Rogers, S. J., & Pennington, B. F. (1991). A theoretical approach to deficits in infantile autism. *Development and Psychopathology, 3,* 137–162.

Rovee-Collier, C. (1997). Dissociations in infant memory: Rethinking the development of implicit and explicit memory. *Psychology Review, 104,* 467–498.

Rovee-Collier, C., & Cuevas, K. (2009). Multiple memory systems are unnecessary to account for infant memory development: An ecological model. *Developmental Psychology, 45,* 160–174.

Rumsey, J. M., & Ernst, M. (2000). Functional neuroimaging of autistic disorders. *Mental Retardation and Developmental Disabilities Research Reviews, 6,* 171–179.

Rutter, M. (1998). Developmental catch-up, and deficit, following adoption after severe global early privation. *Journal of Child Psychology and Psychiatry and Allies Disciplines, 39,* 465–476.

Rutter, M., Andersen-Wood, L., Beckett, C., Bredenkamp, D., Castle, J., Groothues, C. et al. (1999). Quasi-autistic patterns following severe early global privation. *Journal of Child Psychology and Psychiatry and Allied Disciplines, 40* (4), 537–549.

Saffran, J. R., Johnson, E. K., Aslin, R. N., & Newport, E. L. (1999). Statistical learning of tone sequences by adults and infants. *Cognition, 70,* 27–52.

Sampaio, R.C., & Truwit, C.L. (2001). Myelination in the developing human brain. In C.A. Nelson & M. Luciana (Eds.), *Handbook of developmental cognitive neuroscience* (2nd ed., pp. 35–45) Cambridge, MA: MIT Press.

Sanes, D.H., Reh, T.A., & Harris, W.A. (2006). *The development of the nervous system* (2nd ed.). Burlington, MA: Elsevier Academic Press.

Schacter, D., & Moscovitch, M. (1984). Infants' amnesia and dissociable memory systems. In M. Moscovitch (Ed.), *Infant memory* (pp. 173–216). New York: Plenum Press.

Schatz, J., Craft, S., Koby, M., & DeBaun, M. (2000). A lesion analysis of visual orienting performance in children with cerebral vascular injury. *Developmental Neuropsychology, 17,* 49–61.

Schatz, J., Craft, S., White, D., Park, T. S., & Figiel, G. (2001). Inhibition of return in children with perinatal brain injury. *Journal of the International Neuropsychological Society, 7,* 275–284.

Scherf, K. S., Behrmann, M., Humphreys, K., & Luna, B. (2007). Visual category-selectivity for faces, places and objects emerges along different developmental trajectories. *Developmental Science, 10,* F15–F30.

Schilbach, L., Wohlschläger, A. M., Krämer, N. C., Newen, A., Shah, N. J., Fink, G. R., & Vogeley, K. (2006). Being with virtual others: Neural correlates of social interaction. *Neuropsychologia, 44,* 718–730.

Schiller, P.H. (1985). A model for the generation of visually guided saccadic eye movements. In D. Rose & V.G. Dobson (Eds.), *Models of the visual cortex* (pp. 62–70). Chichester: Wiley.

Schlaggar, B. L., Brown, T. T., Lugar, H. M., Visscher, K. M., Miezin, F. M., & Petersen, S. E. (2002). Functional neuroanatomical differences between adults and school-age in the processing of single words. *Science, 296,* 1476–1479.

Schlaggar, B. L., & O'Leary, D. D. M. (1991). Potential of visual cortex to develop an array of functional units unique to somatosensory cortex. *Science, 252,* 1556–1560.

Schlaggar, B. L., & O'Leary, D. D. M. (1993). Patterning of the barrel field in somatosensory cortex with implications for the specification of neocortical areas. *Perspectives on Developmental Neurobiology, 1* (2), 81–91.

Schlaggar, B. L., & McCandliss, B. D. (2007). Development of neural systems for reading. *Annual Review of Neuroscience, 30,* 475–503.

Schliebs, R., Kullman, E., & Bigl, V. (1986). Development of glutamate binding sites in the visual structures of the rat brain: Effect of visual pattern deprivation. *Biomedica Biochemica Acta, 45,* 495–506.

Schneider, W., Noll, D., & Cohen, J. D. (1993). Functional topographic mapping of the cortical ribbon in human vision with conventional MRI scanners. *Nature, 365,* 150–153.

Senju, A., & Johnson, M. H. (2009). The eye contact effect: Mechanisms and development. *Trends in Cognitive Sciences, 13*, 127–134.

Seress, L. (2001). Morphological changes of the human hippocampal formation from mid-gestation to early childhood. In C.A. Nelson & M. Luciana (Eds.), *Handbook of developmental cognitive neuroscience* (pp. 45–58). Cambridge, MA: MIT Press.

Seress, L., & Ábrahám, H. (2008). Pre- and postnatal morphological development of the human hippocampal formation. In C.A. Nelson & M. Luciana (Eds.), *Handbook of developmental cognitive neuroscience* (2nd ed., pp. 187–212). Cambridge, MA: MIT Press.

Shackman, J.E., Wismer Fries, A.B., & Pollak, S.D. (2008). Environmental influences on brain-behavioral development: evidence from child abuse and neglect. In C.A. Nelson & M. Luciana (Eds.), *Handbook of developmental cognitive neuroscience* (2nd ed., pp. 869–882). Cambridge, MA: MIT Press.

Shankle, W. R., Kimball, R. A., Landing, B. H., & Hara, J. (1998). Developmental patterns in the cytoarchitecture of the human cerebral cortex from birth to 6 years examined by correspondence analysis. *Proceedings of the National Academy of Sciences of the United States of America, 95*, 4023–4028.

Shatz, C.J. (2002). Emergence of order in visual system development. In M.H. Johnson Y. Munakata & R. Gilmore (Eds.), *Brain development and cognition: A reader* (2nd ed., pp. 231–244). Oxford: Blackwell.

Shaw, P., Greenstein, D., Lerch, J., Clasen, L., Lenroot, R., Gogtay, N. et al. (2006). Intellectual ability and cortical development in children and adolescents. *Nature, 440*, 676–679.

Shaw, P., Kabani, N. J., Lerch, J. P., Eckstrand, K., Lenroot, R., Gogtay, N. et al. (2008). Neurodevelopmental trajectories of the human cerebral cortex. *The Journal of Neuroscience, 28*, 3586–3594.

Shepherd, G. M. (1972). The neuron doctrine: A revision of functional concepts. *Yale Journal of Biology and Medicine, 45*, 584–599.

Shimojo, S., Birch, E., & Held, R. (1983). Development of vernier acuity assessed by preferential looking. *Supplement: Investigative Ophthalmology & Visual Science, 24*, 93.

Shrager, J., & Johnson, M.H. (1995). Waves of growth in the development of cortical function: A computational model. In I. Kovacs & B. Julesz (Eds.), *Maturational windows and adult cortical plasticity.* (pp. 31–44). Reading, MA: Addison-Wesley.

Shultz, T. R. (2003). *Computational developmental psychology*, Cambridge, MA: MIT Press.

Shultz, T. R., & Rivest, F. (2001). Knowledge-based cascade-correlation: Using knowledge to speed learning. *Connection Science, 13*, 43–72.

Shultz, T. R., Rivest, F., Egri, L., Thivierge, J.-P., & Dandurand, F. (2007). Could knowledge-based neural learning be useful in developmental robotics? The case of KBCC. *International Journal of Humanoid Robotics, 4*, 245–279.

Siegel, M., Körding, K. P., & König, P. (2000). Integrating top-down and bottom-up sensory processing by somato-dendritic interactions. *Journal of Computational Neuroscience, 8*, 161–173.

Sigman, M., Pan, H., Yang, Y., Stern, E., Silbersweig, D., & Gilbert, C. D. (2005). Top-down reorganization of activity in the visual pathway after learning a shape identification task. *Neuron, 46*, 823–835.

Silva, A. J., Paylor, R., Wehner, J. M., & Tonegawa, S. (1992). Impaired spatial learning in alpha-calcium-calmodulin kinase II mutant mice. *Science, 257*, 206–211.

Silva, A. J., Stevens, C. F., Tonegawa, S., & Wang, Y. (1992). Deficient hippocampal long-term potentiation in a-calcium-calmodulin kinase II mutant mice. *Science, 257*, 201–206.

Simion, F., Macchi Cassia, V., Turati, C., & Valenza, E. (2003). Non-specific perceptual biases at the origins of face processing. In O. Pascalis & A. Slater (Eds.), *The development of face processing in infancy and early childhood: Current perspectives.* (pp. 13–26). New York: Nova Science Publishers.

Simion, F., Valenza, E., Umilta, C., & Dalla Barba, B. (1995). Inhibition of return in newborns is temporo-nasal asymmetrical. *Infant Behavior and Development, 18*, 189–194.

Simion, F., Valenza, E., Umilta, C., & Dalla Barba, B. (1998). Preferential orienting to faces in newborns: A temporal-nasal asymmetry. *Journal of Experimental Psychology – Human Perception and Performance, 24* (5), 1399–1405.

Singer, W., & Gray, C. M. (1995). Visual feature integration and the temporal correlation hypothesis. *Annual Review of Neuroscience, 18*, 555–586.

Slater, A. M., Mattock, A., & Brown, E. (1990). Size constancy at birth: Newborn infants' responses to retinal and real size. *Journal of Experimental Child Psychology, 49*, 314–322.

Slater, A. M., Morison, V., & Rose, D. (1982). Perception of shape by the new-born baby. *British Journal of Developmental Psychology, 1*, 135–142.

Sluzenski, J., Newcombe, M., & Ottinger, W. (2004). Changes in reality monitoring and episodic memory in early childhood. *Developmental Science, 7*, 225–245.

South, M., Ozonoff, S., & Schultz, R.T. (2008). Neurocognitive development in autism. In C. A. Nelson & M. Luciana (Eds.), *Handbook of developmental cognitive neuroscience.* (2nd ed., pp. 701–715). Cambridge, MA: MIT Press.

Southgate, V., Johnson, M. H., Osborne, T., & Csibra, G. (2009). Predictive motor activation during action observation in human infants. *Biology Letters 5*, 769–772.

Sowell, E. R., Peterson, B. S., Thompson, P. M., Welcome, S. E., Henkenius, A. L., & Toga, A. W. (2003). Mapping cortical change across the human life span. *Nature Neuroscience, 6*, 309–315.

Sowell, E. R., Thompson, P. M., Leonard, C. M., Welcome, S. E., Kan, E., & Toga, A. W. (2004). Longitudinal mapping of cortical thickness and brain growth in normal children. *Journal of Neuroscience, 24*, 8223–8231.

Spelke, E. S., Breinlinger, K., Macomber, J., & Jacobsen, K. (1992). Origins of knowledge. *Psychological Review, 99* (4), 605–632.

Spencer, J. P., Thomas, M. S. C., & McClelland, J. L. (2009). *Toward a unified theory of development: Connectionism and dynamic systems*, Oxford: Oxford University Press.

Spiridon, M., & Kanwisher, N. (2002). How distributed is visual category information in human occipital-temporal cortex? An fMRI study. *Neuron, 35* (6), 1157–1165.

Spratling, M., & Johnson, M. H. (2004). A feedback model of visual attention. *Journal of Cognitive Neuroscience, 16*, 219–237.

Spratling, M., & Johnson, M. H. (2006). A feedback model of perceptual learning and categorization. *Visual Cognition, 13*, 129–165.

Spreen, O., Risser, A. T., & Edgell, D. (1995). *Developmental neuropsychology*, New York: Oxford University Press.

Squire, L. R., Stark, C. E., & Clark, R. F. (2004). The medial temporal lobe. *Annual Review of Neuroscience, 27*, 279–306.

Stanwood, G.D., & Levitt, P. (2008). The effects of monoamines on the developing nervous system. In C.A. Nelson & M. Luciana (Eds.), *Handbook of developmental cognitive neuroscience* (2nd ed. pp. 83–94). Cambridge, MA: MIT Press.

Starkey, P., & Cooper, R. G. (1980). Perception of number by human infants. *Science, 200,* 1033–1035.

Starkey, P., Spelke, E. S., & Gelman, R. (1983). Detection of intermodal correspondences by human infants. *Science, 222,* 179–181.

Starkey, P., Spelke, E. S., & Gelman, R. (1990). Numerical abstraction by human infants. *Cognition, 36,* 97–127.

Stechler, G., & Latz, E. (1966). Some observations on attention and arousal in the human infant. *Journal of the American Academy of Child and Adolescent Psychiatry, 5,* 517–525.

Stein, B.E. (1984). Multimodal representation in the superior colliculus and optic tectum. In H. Vanegas (Ed.), *Comparative neurology of the optic tectum.* (pp. 819–841). New York: Plenum.

Stern, J. A. (1977). *The first relationship: Infant and mother,* Cambridge, MA: Harvard University Press.

Stiles, J. (2008). *The fundamentals of brain development: Integrating nature and nurture.* Cambridge, MA: Harvard University Press.

Stiles, J., Bates, E., Thal, D., Trauner, D., & Reilly, J. (2002). Linguistic and spatial cognitive development in children with pre- and perinatal focal brain injury: A ten-year overview from the San Diego Longitudinal Project. In M.H. Johnson Y. Munakata & R. Gilmore (Eds.), *Brain development and cognition: A reader* (2nd ed. pp. 272–291). Oxford: Blackwell.

Stiles, J., & Thal, D. (1993). Linguistic and spatial cognitive development following early focal brain injury: Patterns of deficit and recovery. In M.H. Johnson (Ed.), *Brain development and cognition: A reader* (pp. 643–664). Oxford: Blackwell.

Streit, P. (1984). Glutamate and aspartate as transmitter candidates for systems of the cerebral cortex. In E.G. Jones & A. Peters (Eds.), *Cerebral cortex: Functional properties of cortical cells* (Vol. 2, pp. 119–143). New York: Plenum Press.

Streri, A. (1987). Tactile discrimination of shape and intermodal transfer in 2- to 3-month old infants. *British Journal of Developmental Psychology, 5,* 213–220.

Streri, A., & Pecheux, M.-G. (1986). Vision-to-touch and touch-to-vision transfer of form in 5-month-old infants. *British Journal of Developmental Psychology, 4,* 161–167.

Stryker, M. P., & Harris, W. (1986). Binocular impulse blockade prevents the formation of ocular dominance columns in cat visual cortex. *Journal of Neuroscience, 6,* 2117–2133.

Stuss, D. T. (1992). Biological and psychological development of executive functions. *Brain and Cognition, 20,* 8–23.

Supekar, K., Musen, M., & Menon, V. (2009). Development of large-scale functional brain networks in children. *PLoS Biology, 7,* e1000157.

Sur, M., Garraghty, P. E., & Roe, A. W. (1988). Experimentally induced visual projections into auditory thalamus and cortex. *Science, 242,* 1437–1441.

Sur, M., Pallas, S. L., & Roe, A. W. (1990). Cross-modal plasticity in cortical development: Differentiation and specification of sensory neocortex. *Trends in Neuroscience, 13,* 227–233.

Symons, L. A., Hains, S. M. J., & Muir, D. W. (1998). Look at me: Five-months-old infants' sensitivity to very small deviations in eye-gaze during social interactions. *Infant Behavior and Development, 21,* 531–536.

Taga, G., Asakawa, K., Maki, A., Konishi, Y., & Koizumi, H. (2003). Brain imaging in awake infants by near-infrared optical topography. *Proceedings of the Natonal Academy of Sciences of the United States of America, 100,* 10722–10727.

Tager-Flusberg, H. (2003). Developmental disorders of genetic origin. In M. de Haan & M.H. Johnson (Eds.), *The cognitive neuroscience of development.* (pp. 237–261). Hove: Psychology Press.

Tallal, P., Miller, S. L., Bedi, G., Byma, G., Wang, X., Nagarajan, S. J. et al. (1996). Language comprehension in language-learning impaired children improved with acoustically modified speech. *Science, 271,* 81–84.

Tallal, P., & Stark, R.E. (1980). Speech perception of language-delayed children. In G.H. Yeni-Komshian J.F. Kavanagh & C.A. Ferguson (Eds.), *Child phonology: Perception* (Vol. 2, pp. 155–171). New York: Academic Press.

Tallal, P., Stark, R. E., Clayton, K., & Mellits, D. (1980). Developmental dysphasia: Relation between acoustic processing deficits and verbal processing. *Neuropsychologia, 18* (3), 273–284.

Tallon-Baudry, C., Bertrand, O., Peronnet, F., & Pernier, J. (1998). Induced-band activity during the delay of a visual short-term memory task in humans. *Journal of Neuroscience, 18,* 4244–4254.

Teszner, D., Tzavaras, A., Gruner, J., & Hecaen, H. (1972). L'asymetrie droite–gauche du planum temporale: A propos de l'étude anatomique de 100 cerveaux. *Revue Neurologique, 126,* 444.

Thatcher, R. W. (1992). Cyclic cortical reorganization during early childhood. Special Issue: The role of frontal lobe maturation in cognitive and social development. *Brain and Cognition, 20,* 24–50.

Thatcher, R. W., Walker, R. A., & Giudice, S. (1987). Human cerebral hemispheres develop at different rates and ages. *Science, 236,* 1110–1113.

Thelen, E., & Smith, L. B. (1994). *A dynamic systems approach to the development of cognition and action,* Cambridge, MA: MIT Press.

Thivierge, J.-P., Totine, D., & Shultz, T.R. (2005). Simulating frontotemporal pathways involved in lexical ambiguity resolution. In *Proceedings of the Twenty-seventh Annual Conference of the Cognitive Science Society* (pp. 2178–2183). Mahwah, NJ: Erlbaum.

Thomas, K. M., Drevets, W. C., Dahl, R. E., Ryan, N. D., Birmaher, B., Eccard, C. H. et al. (2001). Amygdala response to fearful faces in anxious and depressed children. *Archives of General Psychiatry, 58,* 1057–1063.

Thomas, K. M., Hunt, R. H., Vizueta, N., Sommer, T., Durston, S., Yang, Y. et al. (2004). Evidence of developmental differences in implicit sequence learning: An fMRI study of children and adults. *Journal of Cognitive Neuroscience, 16,* 1339–1351.

Thomas, M. S. C., & Johnson, M. H. (2006). The computational modelling of sensitive periods. *Developmental Psychobiology, 48,* 337–344.

Thomas, M., & Johnson, M. H. (2008). New advances in understanding sensitive periods in brain development. *Current Directions in Psychological Science, 17,* 1–5.

Thomas, M., & Karmiloff-Smith, A. (2003). Modeling language acquisition in atypical phenotypes. *Psychological Review, 110,* 647–682.

Thomas, K. M., & Nelson, C. A. (2001). Serial reaction time learning in preschool- and school-age children. *Journal of Experimental Child Psychology, 79,* 364–387.

Thomas, K.M., & Tseng, A. (2008). Functional MRI methods in developmental cognitive neuroscience. In C.A. Nelson & M. Luciana (Eds.), *Handbook of developmental cognitive neuroscience* (2nd ed. pp. 311–324). Cambridge, MA: MIT Press.

Thompson, D. W. (1917). *On growth and form.* Cambridge: Cambridge University Press.

Tillema, J. M., Byars, A. W., Jacla, L. M., Schapiro, M. B., Schmithorst, V. J., Szaflarski, J. P., & Holland, S. K. (2008). Cortical reorganization of language functioning following perinatal left MCA stroke. *Brain and Language, 105*, 99–111.

Tinbergen, N. (1951). *The study of instinct*, New York: Oxford University Press.

Tipper, S. P., Bourque, T. A., Anderson, S. H., & Brehaut, J. C. (1989). Mechanisms of attention: A developmental study. *Journal of Experimental Child Psychology, 48*, 353–378.

Toga, A. W., Thompson, P. M., & Sowell, E. R. (2006). Mapping brain maturation. *Trends in Neuroscience, 29*, 148–158.

Tole, S., Goudreau, G., Assimacopoulos, S., & Grove, E. A. (2000). Emx2 Is required for growth of the hippocampus but not for hippocampal field specification. *The Journal of Neuroscience, 20* (7), 2618–2625.

Townsend, J., & Courchesne, E. (1994). Parietal damage and narrow "spotlight" spatial attention. *Journal of Cognitive Neuroscience, 6* (3), 220–232.

Tramo, M. J., Loftus, W. C., Thomas, C. E., Green, R. L., Mott, L. A., & Gazzaniga, M. S. (1996). The surface area of human cerebral cortex and its gross morphological sub-divisions. *Journal of Cognitive Neuroscience, 7*, 292–302.

Tranel, D., & Damasio, A. R. (1985). Knowledge without awareness: An autonomic index of facial recognition by prosopagnosics. *Science, 228*, 1453–1454.

Trick, L. M., & Pylyshyn, Z. W. (1994). Why are small and large numbers enumerated differently? A limited-capacity preattentive stage in vision. *Psychological Review, 101*, 80–102.

Turkewitz, G., & Kenny, P. A. (1982). Limitations on input as a basis for neural organization and perceptual development: A preliminary theoretical statement. *Developmental Psychobiology, 15*, 357–368.

Tzourio-Mazoyer, N., de Schonen, S., Crivello, F., Reutter, B., Aujard, Y., & Mazoyer, B. (2002). Neural correlates of woman face processing by 2-month-old infants. *Neuro-image, 15*, 454–461.

Udwin, O., & Yule, W. (1991). A cognitive and behavioural phenotype in Williams syndrome. *Journal of Clinical and Experimental Neuropsychology, 13*, 232–244.

Van der Mark, S., Bucher, K., Maurer, U., Schiulz, E., Brem, S., Buckelmuller, J. et al. (2009). Children with dyslexia lack multiple specializations along the visual word-form (VWF) system. *NeuroImage, 47*, 1940–1949.

Van Elk, M., van Schie, H. T., Hunnius, S., Vesper, C., & Bekkering, H. (2008). You'll never crawl alone: Neurophysiological evidence for experience-dependent motor resonance in infancy. *NeuroImage, 43*, 808–814.

Van Essen, D. C., Anderson, C. H., & Fellman, D. J. (1992). Information processing in the primate visual system: An integrated systems perspective. *Science, 255*, 419–423.

Vargha-Khadem, F., Gadian, D. G., Watkins, K. E., Connelly, A., van Paesschen, W., & Mishkin, M. (1997). Differential effects of early hippocampal pathology on episodic and semantic memory. *Science, 277*, 376–380.

Vargha-Khadem, F., Issacs, E., & Muter, V. (1994). A review of cognitive outcome after unilateral lesions sustained during childhood. *Child Neurology, 9* (supplement), 2S67–2S73.

Vargha-Khadem, F., Watkins, K., Alcock, K. J., Fletcher, P., & Passingham, R. E. (1995). Praxic and nonverbal cognitive deficits in a large family with a genetically transmitted speech and language disorder. *Proceedings of the National Academy of Sciences of the United States of America, 92*, 930–933.

Vaughan, H.G., & Kurtzberg, D. (1989). Electrophysiological indices of normal and aberrant cortical maturation. In P. Kellaway & J. Noebels (Eds.), *Problems and concepts of developmental neurophysiology.* (pp. 263–287). Baltimore, MD: The Johns Hopkins University Press.

Vecera, S. P., & Johnson, M. H. (1995). Eye gaze detection and the cortical processing of faces: Evidence from infants and adults. *Visual Cognition, 2,* 101–129.

Ververs, I. A. P., de Vries, J. I. P., van Geijn, H. P., & Hopkins, B. (1994). Prenatal head position from 12–38 weeks. I. Developmental aspects. *Early Human Development, 39,* 83–91.

Volpe, J. J. (1987). *Neurology of the newborn,* (2nd ed.), Philadelphia: Saunders.

Von Melchner, L., Pallas, S. L., & Sur, M. (2000). Visual behaviour mediated by retinal projections directed to the auditory pathway. *Nature, 404,* 871–876.

Wada, J. A., Clark, R., & Hamm, A. (1975). Cerebral hemispheric asymmetry in humans. *Archives of Neurology, 32,* 239.

Waddington, C. H. (1975). *The evolution of an evolutionist,* New York: Cornell University Press.

Wainwright, A., & Bryson, S. E. (2002). The development of exogenous orienting: Mechanisms of control. *Journal of Experimental Child Psychology, 82,* 141–155.

Wallace, R. B., Kaplan, R., & Werboff, J. (1977). Hippocampus and behavioral maturation. *International Journal of Neuroscience, 7,* 185.

Wang, A. T., Lee, S. S., Sigman, M., & Dapretto, M. (2006). Neural basis of irony comprehension in children with autism: The role of prosody and context. *Brain, 129,* 932–943.

Wattam-Bell, J. (1990). The development of maximum velocity limits for direction discrimination in infancy. *Perception, 19,* 369.

Wattam-Bell, J. (1991). Development of motion-specific cortical responses in infants. *Vision Research, 31,* 287–297.

Weaver, I. C. G., Cervoni, N., Champagne, F. A., Alessio, A. C. D., Sharma, S., Seckl, J. R. et al. (2004). Epigenetic programming by maternal behavior. *Nature Neuroscience, 7,* 847–854.

Webb, S. J., & Nelson, C. A. (2001). Perceptual priming for upright and inverted faces in infants and adults. *Journal of Experimental Child Psychology, 79* (1), 1–22.

Webster, M. J., Bachevalier, J., & Ungeleider, L. G. (1995). Transient subcortical connections of inferior temporal areas TE and TEO in infant macaque monkeys. *Journal of Comparative Neurology, 352,* 213–226.

Welsh, M., DeRoche, K., & Gilliam, D. (2008). Neurocognitive models of early treated phenylketonuria: Insights from meta-analysis and new molecular genetic findings. In C. A. Nelson & M. Luciana (Eds.), *Handbook of developmental cognitive neuroscience* (2nd ed. pp. 677–690). Cambridge, MA: MIT Press.

Werker, J. F., & Polka, L. (1993). Developmental changes in speech perception: New challenges and new directions. *Journal of Phonetics, 21,* 83–101.

Werker, J. F., & Tees, R. C. (1999). Influences of infant speech processing: Toward a new synthesis. *Annual Review of Psychology, 50,* 509–535.

Werker, J.F., & Vouloumanos, A. (2001). Speech and language processing in infancy: A neurocognitive approach. In C.A. Nelson & M. Luciana (Eds.), *Handbook of developmental cognitive neuroscience* (pp. 269–280). Cambridge, MA. MIT Press:

Whalen, J., Gallistel, C. R., & Gelman, R. (1999). Nonverbal counting in humans: The psychophysics of number representation. *Psychological Science, 10,* 130–137.

White, T., & Hilgetag, C.C. (2008). Gyrification and development of the human brain. In C.A. Nelson & M. Luciana (Eds.), *Handbook of developmental cognitive neuroscience* (2nd ed. pp. 39–50). Cambridge, MA: MIT Press.

Wimmer, H., & Perner, J. (1983). Beliefs about beliefs: Representation and constraining function of wrong beliefs in young children's understanding of deception. *Cognition, 13,* 103–128.

Witelson, S. F. (1987). Neurobiological aspects of language in children. *Child Development, 58* (3), 653–688.

Witelson, S. F., & Pallie, W. (1973). Left hemisphere specialization for language in the newborn: Neuroanatomical evidence of asymmetry. *Brain, 94,* 641.

Wolff, P. H., Matsumiya, Y., Abroms, I. F., Van Velzar, C., & Lombroso, C. T. (1974). The effect of white noise on the somatosensory evoked response in sleeping newborn infants. *Electroencephalography and Clinical Neurophysiology, 37,* 269–274.

Wood, F., Flowers, L., Buchsbaum, M., & Tallal, P. (1991). Investigation of abnormal left temporal functioning in dyslexia through rCBF, auditory evoked potentials, and positron emission tomography. *Reading and Writing: An Interdisciplinary Journal, 3,* 379–393.

Wozniak, J.R., Mueller, B.A., & Lim, K.O. (2008). Diffusion tensor imaging. In C.A. Nelson & M. Luciana (Eds.), *Handbook of developmental cognitive neuroscience* (2nd ed. pp. 301–310). Cambridge, MA: MIT Press.

Wynn, K. (1992). Addition and subtraction by human infants. *Nature, 358,* 749–750.

Wynn, K. (1998). Psychological foundations of number: Numerical competence in human infants. *Trends in Cognitive Sciences, 2,* 296–303.

Xu, F., & Spelke, S. (2000). Large number discrimination in 6-month-old infants. *Cognition, 74,* B1–B11.

Yakovlev, P.I., & Lecours, A. (1967). The myelogenetic cycles of regional maturation of the brain. In A. Minokowski (Ed.), *Regional development of the brain in early life* (pp. 3–70). Philadelphia: Davis.

Yamada, H., Sadato, N., Konishi, Y., Kimura, K., Tanaka, M., Yonekura, Y. et al. (1997). A rapid brain metabolic change in infants detected by fMRI. *Neuroreport, 8,* 3775–3778.

Yamada, H., Sadato, N., Konishi, M., Muramoto, S., Kimura, K., Tanaka, M. et al. (2000). A milestone for normal development of the infantile brain detected by functional MRI. *Neurology, 55,* 218–223.

Yovel, G., & Duchaine, B. (2006). Specialized face perception mechanisms extract both part and space information: evidence from developmental prosopagnosia. *Journal of Cognitive Neuroscience, 18,* 580–593.

Zhang, T. Y., & Meaney, M. J. (2010). Epigenetics and the environmental regulation of the genome and its function. *Annual Review of Psychology, 61,* 439–66.

Zipser, D., & Andersen, R. A. (1988). A back-propagation programmed network that simulates response properties of a subset of posterior parietal neurons. *Nature, 331,* 679–684.

Zwaigenbaum, L., Bryson, S., Roberts, W., Rogers, T., Brian, J., & Szatmari, P. (2005). Behavioral markers of autism in the first year of life. *International Journal of Developmental Neurosciences, 23,* 143–152.

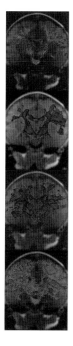

Index

Note: page numbers in **bold** refer to figures; locators in the form x.x(cp) (e.g. 2.1(cp)) refer to color plates; page numbers in *italics* refer to tables.

Developmental Cognitive Neuroscience (Third Edition) Mark H. Johnson with Michelle de Haan
© 2011 Mark H. Johnson